Divine Providence
in the
England
of
Shakespeare's
Histories

Divine Providence
in the
England
of
Shakespeare's
Histories

Henry Ansgar Kelly

Harvard University Press

Cambridge, Massachusetts

1970

PR 409
.P7K4

Library of Congress Catalog Card Number 75-111485

SBN 674-21292-4

Publication of this book has been aided by a grant from the
Hyder Edward Rollins Fund

Printed in the United States of America

For my mother

Historiographers of earlier times made an abundant use of supernatural elements in their accounts of the events of past and present, and this practice is in many ways so foreign to modern usage that it is often difficult to understand or sympathize with it. Perhaps it will not be out of place therefore to single out this aspect of the older histories for separate study, in an effort to define its basic structures.

It is our purpose here to study the processes involved in the supernatural references that appear in the historical treatments of an important segment of English history, the period covered by Shakespeare's double tetralogy (A.D. 1398–1485); and a primary aim of our discussion will be to analyze and evaluate the use that Shakespeare himself made of this aspect of the historical writings of his day. It is not by mere sufferance that Shakespeare and other poets are admitted to ranks of the historiographers, since dramatic and poetic portrayals were considered by many in their time to be a legitimate and even superior medium for the recording and interpreting of the past. From this point of view, Shakespeare is the greatest of the Renaissance historiographers.

Since the primary materials for this subject are virtually limitless, it will be necessary to impose some restrictions on our treatment at the outset. The lead of the chronicles themselves will be followed in centering interest upon the political and military vicissitudes of England during the fifteenth century, as reflected chiefly in the persons and affairs of kings and kings-to-be. The supernatural is manifested primarily in interpretations of the workings of divine providence in the lives and destinies of these kings, and it is toward this feature that our attention will be particularly directed. The various aspects of the providential and the supernatural — prodigies, prophecies, miracles, the questions of fate and fortune, predestination and free will, natural and special providence, grace, the intercession of saints, the workings of good and evil spirits, reward and punishment after death, and other theological problems — will be attended to only as they touch upon our central interests. However, since providential interpretations are always based upon moral evaluations of the men involved in the events, it will often be necessary to discuss an author's judgments on the morality of the human actions he records, even where there is no explicit allegation of divine favor or disfavor. God is always assumed to support the cause of justice, and it is therefore necessary to know what causes the author considers just before we can properly deal with his attitudes toward the supernatural impetus behind the visible course of events.

The materials used will be largely the formal chronicles and literary works devoted to the history of these times, especially those known and made use of by later generations. Other writings, including letters and public documents, will be drawn on for the most part only as they appear in the chronicles.

In this discussion we are interested above all not in facts but in opinions, not in events but in interpretations of events and of the supernatural causes behind them. In other words, we will be dealing with those aspects commonly neglected in the ordinary historical study of the works under investigation here. It is hoped that this approach will make some contribution to our knowledge of the philosophy of history implicit in the minds of the authors and of the metahistorical tendencies of their interpretations. Literary considerations will also be a main concern, and we shall follow the line of inquiry auspiciously initiated by E. M. W. Tillyard in *Shakespeare's History Plays*. Our approach will differ from Professor Tillyard's, however, in that we shall concentrate on only one aspect of the themes he deals with, namely, the providential. In this way it is hoped that we may not only supplement his data but effect some serious modifications in his conclusions as well.

H.A.K.

Rome
August 1969

Contents

Divine Providence
in the
England
of
Shakespeare's
Histories

Introduction

The authors with whom we will be dealing, the medieval and Renaissance compilers of English history, were of course heir to the common traditions of Christianity. We must say "traditions," for Christianity contains many disparate elements which have often been welded together in a theological reconciliation, but which just as often have been viewed in abstraction from supplementary or contradictory doctrines.

The subject of divine providence provides a good illustration of this phenomenon. The Bible contains an assortment of notions about God's government of the world, particularly in terms of reward and punishment visited upon mankind, which belong to different stages of cultural and moral development. In the Book of Deuteronomy, for instance, the second commandment of the decalogue contains this statement of divine justice: "For I, Yahweh your God, am a jealous God and I punish the fathers' fault in the sons, the grandsons, and the great-grandsons of those who hate me; but I show kindness to thousands, to those who love me and keep my commandments." [1] We see in this pronouncement a reflection of a very early concept of justice among the Hebrew people, one that is satisfied with a kind of collective justice operative in terms of families or nations. It is a notion that seems hardly fair; we may not be inclined to quarrel with the clause that implies inherited blessings, but the punishment of children for the sins of the fathers seems a manifest injustice. And in fact this harsh law is toned down two chapters further

Note: See Bibliography for explanations of shortened references in footnote citations.

[1] Deut. 5.9–10; cf. Exod. 34.6–7; Num. 14.18. All translations of Scripture in the Introduction are taken from the *Jerusalem Bible*, ed. Alexander Jones (London 1966).

on in Deuteronomy: "Know then that Yahweh your God is God indeed, the faithful God who is true to his covenant and his graciousness for a thousand generations towards those who love him and keep his commandments, but who punishes in their own persons those that hate him."[2] We find this picture of God far more acceptable, for now he punishes men only for their own guilt; and we conclude that it represents a more sophisticated level of morality among the Hebrews.

In the Middle Ages, however, the Bible was not interpreted in this historical fashion. Both statements from Deuteronomy are equally the word of God. And while the second was no doubt the more acceptable view to Christians in general, the first was the better known, occurring as it does among the ten commandments. Furthermore, a doctrine very much akin to it received great prominence in the Christian Church; the notion of original sin, especially as elaborated by Augustine, involved not only the first four or thousand generations, but all generations until the end of time, in the guilt and punishment of Adam's sin. The concept of inherited divine retribution was therefore readily available to any historiographer whom personal inclinations or the force of events inclined to such a primitive and rigorous view.

The idea of a just God easily suggests that suffering is often a punishment for sin. We find this idea verified several times in the Gospels. However, many simple minds tend to see all suffering as a punishment for sin. This view is reflected in the question of the disciples of Jesus: "Rabbi, who sinned, this man or his parents, for him to have been born blind?" Jesus answers that his affliction was not the result of sin; rather its purpose was to make manifest the works of God in him.[3]

The Book of Job also opposes the simplistic notion that all suffering is the result of one's sins, and stresses that it can be intended as a trial and a discipline. The point is also made that the ways of God are unsearchable, and that therefore it may be beyond the power of human reason to account for specific instances of suffering. Furthermore, the Vulgate version of Job hints at the Christian notion of reward and punishment after death, when all the inequalities of this life will be adjusted. In this way God's justice was finally reconciled with the events of everyday reality, and at the same time it remained impossible

[2] Deut. 7.9–10.
[3] John 9.1–3.

to state with any certainty the ultimate divine reason for any specific disaster.

However, the temptation to interpret God's providence was always present, and it received great encouragement especially from the historical books of the Old Testament, primarily the Books of Samuel, Kings, and Chronicles. Here Christian chroniclers could see concrete examples of God's dealings with kings, where reward and punishment are largely visualized in terms of temporal blessings and visible catastrophes, with no otherworldly overtones whatever. And perhaps even more important were the relevant expressions found in the Psalms, whose weekly repetition in the divine office, which was participated in by most of the early chroniclers, would make their application almost automatic.

As for postbiblical thought on this question, perhaps the treatment best known to subsequent generations was that developed in Augustine's *City of God,* and his formulation was accepted after as well as before the Reformation. Augustine states that "to the divine providence it has seemed good to prepare in the world to come for the righteous good things, which the unrighteous shall not enjoy, and for the wicked evil things, by which the good shall not be tormented. But as for the good things of this life and its ills, God has willed that these should be common to both, that we might not too eagerly covet the things which wicked men are seen equally to enjoy, nor shrink with an unseemly fear from the ills which even good men often suffer." [4] But Augustine goes on in this same chapter to say: "Often, even in the present distribution of temporal things, does God plainly evince his own interference. For if every sin were now visited with manifest punishment, nothing would seem to be reserved for the final judgment; on the other hand, if no sin received now a plainly divine punishment, it would be concluded that there is no divine providence at all." He draws the conclusion that when manifestly wicked persons suffer great afflictions, they are being punished by God; but when virtuous men suffer similarly, they are being benefited by God. "For even in the likeness of the sufferings, there remains an unlikeness in the sufferers; and though exposed to the same anguish, virtue and vice are not the same thing. For as the same fire causes gold to glow brightly, and chaff to smoke; and under the same flail the straw is beaten small, while the grain is cleansed; and as the

---

[4] *The City of God* 1.8, trans. Marcus Dods (New York 1950) 10–11.

lees are not mixed with the oil, though squeezed out of the vat by the same pressure, so the same violence of affliction proves, purges, clarifies the good, but damns, ruins, exterminates the wicked."

It will easily be seen that in spite of Augustine's "rules" for interpreting the operation of divine providence, their application to actual events must remain largely a matter of conjecture and personal opinion. It was admitted by all concerned that absolutely everything that happened, happened through the causation and concurrence of Providence, and furthermore it was agreed that God's ways were mysterious and unsearchable, in spite of (and because of) the general principle that they were in accord with wisdom and justice and mercy.

Particular interpretations of the reasons for God's disposal of events would therefore always depend upon each author's individual criteria of wisdom, justice, and mercy when applied to God. And when the subject matter of these interpretations was political, it was understandable that political bias could play a very large role in their formulation.

An important factor that contributed to the proliferation of providential judgments in the pages of medieval and Renaissance chroniclers was the prevailing conception of the primary function of history as an exemplary discipline. Events of the past were recounted in order to provide lessons for the present. And lessons of divine sanctions on good and evil actions formed no small part of this pedagogic; in fact, the whole of history could be and often was reduced (or exalted) to this level.

In her study of Shakespeare's Histories, Lily Campbell confines herself to discussing the kind of lessons drawn from history by Renaissance and Reformation historiographers.[5] But it is not clear that these writers added anything to lessons pointed out by their medieval predecessors. However, it is true that an author would be inclined to place more stress upon the exemplary aspects than upon partisan concerns when dealing with events no longer bearing upon present politics. It will be no surprise, therefore, to discover that the sixteenth-century historians of fifteenth-century history can often bring to their subject a more measured concentration upon eternal verities than was usually managed by the contemporary chroniclers before them, even to the point of endorsing contradictory views of persons and events for the sake of the different lessons they suggest.

[5] Lily B. Campbell, *Shakespeare's "Histories"; Mirrors of Elizabethan Policy* (San Marino 1947) Pt. I: "History, Historiography, and Politics."

It is always possible, however, that the later writers would be tempted to slant their interpretation of the past in order to emphasize a parallel or draw a moral for situations that existed in their own day. One of the purposes of the present investigation is to ascertain how many of the judgments and opinions of the later writers are original with them, and how many are simply taken over from their sources. It is only in this way that we will be able to discover their personal views upon the subjects that they treat.

One

Contemporary
Accounts
of
Fifteenth-Century
England

The Divided Royal Family in the Fifteenth Century

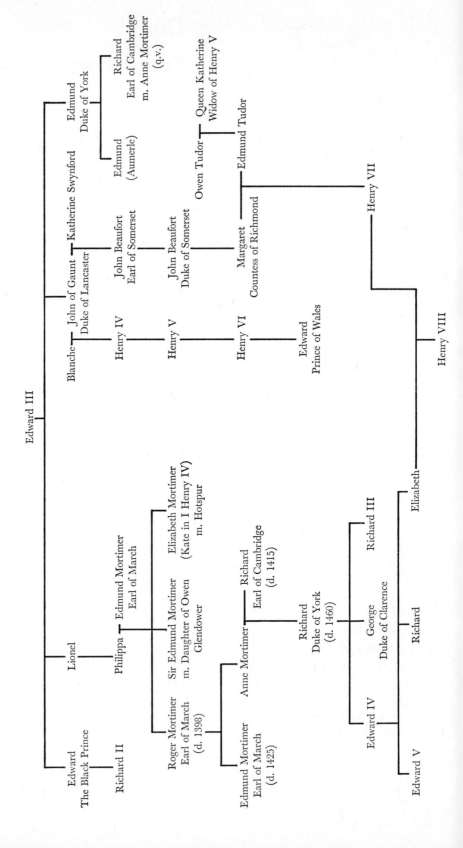

I

The
Lancaster
Myth

The period of English history which we are studying from a providential viewpoint divides easily into two sections; the first extends from the downfall of Richard II to the death of Henry V (1399–1422), and the second from the reign of Henry VI to the accession of Henry VII, with special emphasis on the years 1450–1485. Shakespeare has conveniently allotted a tetralogy to each period, though, less conveniently, he treated the second period first.

From the political point of view, the contemporary historiographers can be divided roughly into four camps, the supporters of Richard II, and the supporters of each of the three dynasties that followed his reign. But since the histories that we will study were chiefly written within the periods of these dynasties, we can treat their providential and moral judgments under the categories of the "myths" of Lancaster, York, and Tudor.

"Myth" is perhaps not the best word to express the concepts it will do service for ("mystique" or "bias" might have been better), but it has become familiar through Professor Tillyard's usage, and for this reason it will be retained here. Tillyard's formulation of the Tudor myth will be in view implicitly throughout our study.

According to Tillyard, and numerous others since who have accepted his thesis, the chief historiographers of the Tudor period justified the Tudor dynasty's claim to the throne by an elaborate defense, to which he gives the general name "Tudor myth." It begins with Polydore Vergil, who, according to Tillyard, sees the stretch of history from Richard II to Henry VII in a solemn moral light, showing "the justice of God punishing and working out the effects of a crime, till prosperity is re-established in the Tudor monarchy," which providentially united the Celtic line as well as the York and Lancaster lines. Edward Hall states the theme much more strongly, and is followed closely by Shakespeare. For Henry IV's crime, first of usurping the throne and then of allowing Richard to be killed against his oath, "God punished Henry by making his reign unquiet but postponed full vengeance till a later generation, for Henry (like Ahab) humbled himself . . . The curse reaches its full issue in the Wars of the Roses," in which the Yorkists as well as the Lancastrians are incriminated. Meanwhile, Providence is protecting Henry Tudor, and finally the Holy Ghost inspires the Duke of Buckingham to put Henry on the throne and marry him to the York heiress.[1] The Tudor myth that we shall discover in the pages to follow, however, will differ drastically from Tillyard's.

The category of "Lancaster myth" applies strictly speaking only to the versions of history supporting the regimes of the three Lancastrian kings, Henry IV, Henry V, and Henry VI. The opposition that arose to Henry VI constitutes an integral part of the York myth. But, as was pointed out above, there was also historiographical opposition to Henry IV, which we might perhaps have designated as a "Ricardian myth." But since the opposition extends beyond the time of Richard's death, we can deal with it more accurately under the designation of "anti-Lancastrian." Some of the early anti-Lancastrian sentiments will later be utilized by the proponents of the York myth.

The Justification of Richard's Overthrow

We begin our historiographical survey with the views of contemporary chroniclers concerning the deposition of Richard II. According to the official view of the Rolls of Parliament, which was adopted by many of the chronicles, Richard II recognized his faults and cheerfully resigned in favor of Henry Bolingbroke;

---

[1] E. M. W. Tillyard, *Shakespeare's History Plays* (London 1944 ——) 36–37, 59–61. Tillyard is in some doubt as to what crime started the century-long curse. In the account of Vergil cited above, he is clearly speaking of Henry IV's usurpation, but just before this he notes that according to Vergil it was Richard's crime of killing his uncle, the Duke of Gloucester (Thomas of Woodstock), that first caused Richard to lose the support of his other uncles, Gaunt and York, and that this was the chief cause of his overthrow. He admits that Hall makes little of Richard's crime; but when he comes to restate the Tudor myth in general terms, Tillyard describes the curse as one "incurred through the murder of Woodstock, one of Edward III's seven sons, and not merely passed on but greatly intensified by the murder of Richard" (p. 291).

no mention, of course, is made of the closer claim of the eight-year-old Edmund Mortimer, Earl of March. The whole proceeding therefore was perfectly legal and of great benefit to the realm.

Perhaps the foremost exponent of this version of the transfer of the royal authority was Thomas Walsingham, the last of the chroniclers of the Benedictine monastery of St. Albans near London. Walsingham's work extends over a period of almost fifty years (1376–1422), and the changes that are observable in his attitude toward the house of Lancaster are striking. The scathing attacks against John of Gaunt in the earlier history are later suppressed, perhaps out of conviction as well as out of fear or political expediency.[2] V. H. Galbraith believes that revisions were made several times after 1399, but it seems likely that the most important of them were made when the various chronicles of the kingdom were called in by the government for inspection when Henry was holding Richard captive in the Tower before his deposition.[3]

After his "conversion," Walsingham favored John of Gaunt with several providential benefits;[4] and he was to be even more generous to his son Henry. But as far as King Richard was concerned, Walsingham lost early in his reign any regard he had had for the youthful king, and maintained a fairly consistent hostility toward him for the rest of his life. Although he was grateful for Richard's suppression of the Lollards, and considered his return from Ireland in 1394 for this purpose inspired by God,[5] Walsingham alone among the chroniclers suggests homosexual offenses in Richard (in his *Historia anglicana* account of 1386).[6]

[2] The various parts and versions of Walsingham's history have been issued in five different publications, which are listed in the Bibliography, along with the abbreviations used to designate these and other chronicles referred to in the course of our investigation. V. H. Galbraith untangles the bibliographical problems of Walsingham's works in *The St. Albans Chronicle, 1406–20* (Oxford 1937): 2Wals ix–lxxi. For an account of the tactical change in the early history, see Galbraith, 2Wals l–li, and Sir Edmund Maunde Thompson's edition of the voluntarily suppressed *Chronicon Angliae* (oWals xvii–xxiv).

[3] 1Wals (*Annales Ricardi secundi et Henrici quarti*) 252 (cf. Otterbourne 209–210, based on 1Wals); see also the chronicle of Adam of Usk (Usk 182–184).

[4] 3Wals (*Historia anglicana*) 2.41, 43 (= oWals 327, 328); 3Wals 2.194. For an instance of his earlier views, see oWals 204, revised in 3Wals 1.373, where, among other ingenious changes, "Dei gratia" is substituted for a sarcastic "dux bonus."

[5] 1Wals 173; 3Wals 2.216.

[6] 3Wals 2.148. This charge is not repeated except possibly in *Richard II* (3.1.11–15), where Bolingbroke says to Bushy and Green:

> You have in manner with your sinful hours
> Made a divorce betwixt his queen and him,
> Broke the possession of a royal bed

Richard's providential decline began in 1397 after the murder of Thomas of Woodstock and the execution of the Earl of Arundel, when Richard ordered the end of prayers for them and for himself, as if desirous of preventing God from converting him from his evil ways.[7] Two years later there occurred prodigies which were thought to foretell the triumph of the lords over Richard after their eclipse, and the falling away of the people from him.[8] But Richard failed to observe these signs of coming disaster, for his fates urged him on to his ruin, which they had irrevocably set for that year.[9] He refused to listen to a prophet who preached to him the alternatives of reform or destruction;[10] nevertheless, Richard is said to have paid the most scrupulous attention to such prophecies, and he finally got the message: a verse going the rounds warned that "the pomp of John" would scarcely last for two years, and because the king was first baptized John he feared that it applied to him. He realized the danger he was in, as he was preparing to go on his Irish campaign, and he was afraid that matters would worsen.[11]

While Richard was in Ireland, God decreed a humiliation of his pride, and, in order to aid the English people, who had no other resource but in him, he inspired Henry Bolingbroke to return to claim his hereditary rights. The people accordingly received him as a savior sent by God to release them from their slavery.[12] Furthermore, God caused Richard to delay his departure from Ireland for a week, thereby enabling Henry to secure his forces in England.[13]

And stained the beauty of a fair queen's cheeks
With tears drawn from her eyes by your foul wrongs.

But it is more probable that Henry is speaking of dissipation in general; and we should note too that Henry's characterization of the queen's sentiments is belied by the scene in which she appears with Bushy, Green, and Bagot (2.2).

[7] 1Wals 207.

[8] The laurels withered and revived, and a part of the river near Bedford dried up (1Wals 229; cf. 3Wals 2.229; *Ypodigma Neustriae*: 4Wals 380–381). Holinshed offers a possible explanation for the latter phenomenon, namely, that the river went underground at that point (1–2Hol. 2.848).

[9] "Sed urgebant eum fata sua, quae irrevertibiliter texuerant ejus ruinam hoc anno futuram" (1Wals 230). This obviously poetic expression may involve the idea of divine punishment or on the other hand carry no supernatural weight at all.

[10] 1Wals 231–232. This prophet, the hermit William Norham, whom Richard imprisoned for his efforts, seems to be the same northern hermit who later has unpleasant information for Henry IV as well, and is rewarded this time with decapitation. See the continuation of the *Eulogium historiarum* (Eul 380, 397), and cf. 1Wals 372.

[11] 1Wals 237–238.

[12] 1Wals 240–242.

[13] 1Wals 248. Most of these providential interpretations do not appear in the

According to the official charges against Richard, which Walsingham and other chroniclers after him copy out, Richard would have impoverished the realm if God had not provided against it. In his formal challenge for the crown, Henry stated that God had helped him vindicate his right to it.[14] Walsingham adds to all this in an extraordinarily ingenuous (or disingenuous) fashion by seeing an evident miracle of God in the fact that Henry was crowned king on the anniversary of the day that he was exiled from the realm.[15] Moreover, as an auspice of more abundant grace, Henry was the first to be crowned with the miraculous oil that the Blessed Virgin had revealed to Thomas à Becket, which had been providentially kept from Richard's use, and, as was thought, providentially bestowed on Henry.[16]

By a just judgment of God, Archbishop Walden, whose appointment had been secured by Richard, was removed from the see of Canterbury,[17] and Henry's fellow exile, Archbishop Arundel, recovered his old position. In his official capacity, Arundel delivered a sermon upon Henry's accession, which was recorded in the London Chronicles. He took for his text, "Vir dominabitur in populo," the implication of which was, as Froissart puts it, that God had given them a man for their sovereign, in contrast to the childish rulers who had preceded him.[18]

Furthermore, after Henry's installation as king, it was the divine virtue that miraculously alerted him to the plot of the earls against him, and Kent, Salisbury, and Huntington felt the vengeance and wrath of God light upon them. When Henry heard the outcome (namely, that the earls had been disposed of not by his but by God's wisdom), he thanked God effusively for this miracle.[19] Richard on the other hand was reported to have

abridged versions (3–4Wals), but this is probably due not to any designed withdrawal of grace from Henry in the mind of Walsingham but simply to the process of pruning away the embellishments, since a number of providences in Henry's behalf do occur later in the shorter histories. According to Galbraith (2Wals liv–lxvi), both 1Wals and 3Wals apparently were written at intervals close to the events they record. It would seem that 4Wals was compiled at a later date, but as Galbraith points out, it is identical with 3Wals from 1403 to its end in 1419.

[14] 1Wals 270, 281. Henry confirms this opinion of his in a letter to the Duke of Juliers, in which he says that divine providence delivered the rule of England to him. See *Royal and Historical Letters during the Reign of Henry the Fourth,* ed. F. C. Hingeston, Rolls Series 18 (London 1860) 3.

[15] 1Wals 296–297; cf. 3Wals 239 and 4Wals 388, where the miracle is made a matter of opinion. Presumably, of course, the date was set by Henry himself.

[16] 1Wals 297–300; cf. 3Wals 239–240; 4Wals 388. See below at nn. 80 and 91.

[17] 1Wals 213.

[18] CLgreat 69–71; CLk 44–46; Frois 699.

[19] 1Wals 323–330; cf. 3Wals 243 and 4Wals 389.

become so despondent on hearing this news that he wished to starve himself to death, and he could not recover when he changed his mind.[20]

Walsingham's favorable view of Henry IV's ascent to the throne was supplemented with providential judgments by other chroniclers, such as Adam of Usk, the monk of Evesham, Thomas Otterbourne (who copied from Walsingham), and the authors of the Kirkstall Chronicle and the continuation of the *Eulogium historiarum*. But the best known of the Henricians is the poet John Gower, whose *Chronica tripertita* is devoted exclusively to this subject. This chronicle is an appendix to the *Vox clamantis*, which in its early form had excused Richard from blame for the evils then regnant in England, but which now concluded with an indictment against him as the chief cause of the sufferings an angry God had sent them. Gower's change of support from Richard to Henry occurred long before there was any likelihood of Henry's becoming king, as is evident from his revision of the *Confessio amantis* early in the 1390's. In the *Chronica*, he regards the insurrection of Woodstock and his fellow nobles against Richard in 1387 as a providential warning. But since Richard ignored it and continued to do the work of hell (one result of which was the martyrdom of Woodstock and the sending of Arundel's soul to heaven), God determined to cast down this odious tyrant and exalt the pious and beloved Henry.[21]

The author of *Richard the Redeless* agrees in seeing Bolingbroke's insurrection as the work of God, who summoned his servants to put an end to the abuses that had prospered unchecked by Richard. Richard is addressed during the time of his internment in the Tower before he was deposed, and the writer does not yet know whether God will give him grace to amend and be king again or whether he will give the rule to another.[22] But this poet's attitude of pity and concern for Richard is in great contrast to Gower's scathing remarks against his former patron. In making Richard II a completely evil tyrant and Henry IV a saint, Gower is anticipating the treatment that will be accorded to Richard III and Henry VII in very similar circumstances. It is interesting to note that, according to Gower,

[20] 1Wals 330–331; cf. 3Wals 245; 4Wals 390–391.
[21] Gower 305–324.
[22] *Richard the Redeless* in *Mum and the Sothsegger* (EETS) 1–2, 22–23. The reasons given by the editors for considering *Richard the Redeless* as written by the author of *Mum*, even if convincing, seem to be no justification for considering the two works as one poem, since their formats differ (*Mum* is a dialogue).

Henry IV's accession was fated, predicted by saints, and fulfilled by God.[23] The same would be said of Henry VII.

The details of Bolingbroke's conquest resemble those elaborated by Walsingham. The people called upon Christ for vengeance,[24] for God turns to those who turn to him.[25] And God did not allow such abominations to go unpunished, but inspired Bolingbroke and providentially arranged for his return to England. And when he arrived, he first knelt down and prayed to God for victory.[26]

When Richard returned from Ireland, Fortune turned her wheel, and he cursed his fates; nevertheless, the fear of Christ was not yet upon him. The outcome, however, proved that men will not serve a ruler who is not sustained by the Lord.[27] The English people unanimously deposed Richard, and in so doing gave praise to Christ, who had led them out from captivity under the Herod-like Richard and brought them to a glorious kingdom.[28]

And it was God, who disposes all things and sets the times for them, who fixed the day on which Henry was to be blessed by him; accordingly, he was declared king on the feast of Edward the Confessor. God had predestined him for this title so that he might bring justice to the realm. Henry had a threefold right to the crown, for not only was he the heir to the throne, but he was also elected by the people; and furthermore his conquest of the realm proved his right to it. The people accordingly rejoiced when Henry was crowned, since Christ wished him to be venerated, and they worshiped Christ for raising up such a king; the whole earth in fact joined them in praising God.[29]

However, the devil instigated the earls to rebel against this pious king in an effort to destroy him and his race; but God uncovered their plot and vengeance fell on them, for his wrath miraculously effected their ruin at the hands of the common people. Richard, on hearing of it, railed against Fortune and wept over their destruction; he was so grief-stricken over their deaths that he ceased to eat and so died. The people rejoiced,

---

[23] Gower 339:

> Istud fatatum fuit, a sanctisque relatum;
> Quod tunc complevit Deus, ex quo terra quievit.

[24] Gower 331.

[25] Gower 311.

[26] Gower 329, 333–334.

[27] Gower 335.

[28] Gower 330.

[29] Gower 338.

for Christ had destroyed the one person they feared the most. God hates evil-living rulers, and does not allow sinners to continue in authority, as Richard's end demonstrates.[30] Gower notes that the upright King Henry had Richard buried with the rites of the Church. We shall hear much more about the burial of Richard later.

The Minority Report of the French Chroniclers

Richard had his friends among the chroniclers, especially those who came from the Continent. The most celebrated of these is John Froissart, who was greatly indebted to Richard and lamented his tragic end. Froissart and the other French authors had no reason to write in fear or flattery of Henry (Froissart did in fact admire him), and yet their providential interpretations often correspond with, rather than contradict, those of the Lancastrian annalists. The reasoning behind their judgments however is usually quite different. They also occasionally report the providential sentiments of the people in Henry's favor, but hardly with approval on their own part.

Froissart is aware of Richard's faults, but he also places great stress upon the crimes and provocations of Woodstock and his associates against him.[31] He says it was the devil who caused Mowbray to denounce Bolingbroke to Richard for some well-meant words he had spoken,[32] thereby starting Richard himself on the road to ruin a result of the measures he took against Bolingbroke. The wise John of Gaunt was afraid that Richard would destroy himself by heeding the advice of his evil counselors. He pointed to the troubles caused by domestic quarrels

---

[30] Gower 340–342.

[31] Frois 635–644, 655–659. Cf. the chronicle of the English Cistercian house of Dieulacres, which records the opinion that God inspired Richard to punish these rebels, thereby fulfilling, in a sense favorable to Richard, a prophecy that Walsingham and Gower make much of in a reading favorable to Woodstock and his companions (Dieulacres 168–169; 1Wals 206; Gower 313).

The pro-Ricardian "Author A" of Dieulacres goes on to cite two prophecies of Bridlington in Richard's favor (pp. 169, 170). Adam of Usk, the Welshman, on the other hand, is especially sedulous in observing the prophecies of Bridlington, Merlin, and others as well as natural prophecies (i.e., portents), in a sense prejudicial to Richard, and once at least (p. 171) the fulfillment is attributed directly to God's righteous judgment. Cf. also Brut 590. On the question of political prophecies at this time, see John Webb (Créton 250–271) and John Taylor (Kirkstall 22–23, 29–30, 40–42). See also Morton W. Bloomfield, *Piers Plowman as a Fourteenth-Century Apocalypse* (New Brunswick, N.J. [1961]) 91–94.

[32] Frois 661.

abroad, and was afraid that the same would occur in England unless God prevented it in some way.[33]

While Henry was in exile, his knights told him that the affection of the English people would soon deliver him from all danger, if it pleased God.[34] When he received an invitation from the Londoners through Archbishop Arundel to take over the country, his advisers assured him that it was an opportunity sent by God, who had taken compassion on him, but that the opportunity would not be renewed if he refused to accept it then.[35]

At the interview between Richard and Henry, Richard prognosticated his downfall from the fact that his greyhound abandoned him and started to fawn upon Henry, as if it knew instinctively that he would be the ruler from then on.[36]

On the day of his coronation Henry went to confession, "as he had good need to do," and then, according to his custom, he heard three masses.[37] We have already seen Froissart's report of the providential intent of the Archbishop of Canterbury's sermon, which was given at the coronation. On the subject of the earls' plot, Froissart rather surprisingly says that God was very kind to the king (Henry), for he had news of the affair in time to take action against it.[38]

As for Richard's end, Froissart heard the report of his death, but could not learn the cause of it. And instead of making a specific providential application, he simply takes it as a sad instance of the mutability of the fortunes of the world. Froissart himself benefited greatly from Richard's liberality, he says, and is therefore bound to pray to God for his soul; it pains him to

[33] Frois 663–664.
[34] Frois 680. "If it please God" is, of course, a rather perfunctory conversational tag in Froissart and cannot bear much weight.
[35] Frois 684–685.
[36] Frois 692–693. Usk 196 tells the story of the greyhound also, saying that it left Richard when it sensed his fall and came to Bolingbroke, who welcomed it as a prophecy of his good fortune.
The whole subject of prognostication is a complex one, and it is difficult to give a general philosophy that could definitely apply to all authors. Often one receives the impression that the authors themselves are rather vague about the whole process, and they simply record strange phenomena for the benefit of others who might be able to intepret ulterior meanings in them. For instance, when speaking of a prodigy that occurred in 1338 (willows in January bore blossoms like roses), Walsingham says: "Interpretetur qui poterit signi prodigium, cujus relator esse delegi potius quam expositor" (oWals 8).
[37] Frois 699. Lord Berners in his translation of Froissart omits the quoted phrase (Berners 380).
[38] Frois 705. Berners 392 simply says that "God did aid King Henry."

have to write of his death, and he does so only because it is an event that belongs in his chronicles.[39]

Earlier, Froissart characterized Richard's downfall in terms of destiny, implying perhaps the familiar notion of the incomprehensibility of God's judgments. He says that whatever misfortunes fate has decreed cannot be prevented but must follow their course, and those that happened to Richard "are wonderful indeed to think on" (or as Berners says, "so marvelous that it is hard to think thereon"). He might well have avoided them, but what must be, will be.[40] And he remembers that knights of his acquaintance had foretold the reigns of both Richard and Henry long before either came to pass.[41]

It will be well to look at two more contemporary French accounts of Richard's overthrow, both of which will be of importance in later chronicles. One is a poem by Jean Créton, who accompanied Richard to Ireland and who was present at his arrest by Bolingbroke. His work is marginally referred to by Holinshed as a French pamphlet belonging to Master John Dee.[42]

In Créton's mind, the Lord must have been angry with Richard for some reason, since a great tempest on the sea prevented passage between England and Ireland for a long time, during which Bolingbroke seized the greater part of the realm by the most abominable kind of treachery. For instance, he had Archbishop Arundel preach to the people in London, showing them papal pardons and promising them that by aiding Bolingbroke against Richard they would assure themselves of a place in heaven after death.[43]

After arriving in Wales and hearing of the dispersal of his army, Richard cried out to Christ crucified, beseeching mercy if he had done anything wrong, and protesting that to the best of his ability he never consented to bring evil upon anyone not deserving of it. He added that unless God quickly sent him aid, he would be lost.[44]

The Welsh pitied Richard and protested against the outrageous way in which the English had treated their king, and

---

[39] Frois 708–709.

[40] Frois 678; Berners 340. Cf. Froissart's remark on Mowbray's determination to denounce Bolingbroke: "for the devil entered his brain, and what has been ordained to happen must come to pass" (661).

[41] Frois 678, 709. One of the knights was drawing on the prophecies of Merlin contained in "a book called Brut."

[42] 1–2Hol 2.850.

[43] Créton 45–53.

[44] Créton 97–98.

Créton warns that God will eventually punish them for it, "for he who willingly doth evil or injury to another is often to be greatly punished of God, who is powerful above the present race of men as well as the past." Créton then indulges in a stereotyped tirade against Fortune; and Richard himself, in his prayer to the Blessed Virgin, complains that Fortune is treating him badly.[45] He complains too that his people have failed in their duty to him, and warns that God will punish them eternally on the last day. He laments over his queen, taken away from him by the violence of Fortune. But in spite of all his sufferings, he is sufficiently resigned to praise God in heaven; and this prayer is no doubt intended as a recognition that whatever God wills is for the best.[46]

When Northumberland came to parley with Richard about going to Flint and swore upon the Blessed Sacrament that no treachery was involved, his blood must have turned at it, Créton says, because he knew it was a lie. In fact, both Richard and Northumberland had bad intentions in making this agreement, but Richard's guilt was not so great, since he was forced to it. As for Northumberland, a shameful death was in store for him unless he appeased God by repentance. Richard's deceit lay in his plan to gather forces against Henry as soon as the opportunity offered. In expounding this strategy, he expressed his conviction that if he and his supporters trusted in God, he would aid them. But when he was betrayed and taken prisoner, he told the perjured Northumberland that he ought to fear divine punishment for his deed, and prayed God to reward him as he deserved.[47]

An old knight of Bolingbroke's told Créton at this time that the arrest of Richard fulfilled the prophecies of Bede and Merlin, which he proceeded to cite and interpret. "Thus," says Créton, "the knight held this prophecy to be true, and attached thereunto great faith and credit; for such is the nature of them in their country that they very thoroughly believe in prophecies, phantoms, and witchcraft, and employ . . . them right willingly. Yet in my opinion this is not right, but is a great want of faith." [48]

[45] Créton 105, 110–113. Again later on, when he prays to Christ crucified, Richard alludes to Lady Fortune's ineluctable ways: "Glorious God! who didst die for us, suspended on the cross, look mercifully upon me. None other than thou can aid my present need; and if I must lose my land and my life, should Fortune will it, I must take it all in good part; for her authority must be obeyed" (115–116).
[46] Créton 114–119.
[47] Créton 140–156.
[48] Créton 168–170; Adam of Usk also says that one of Merlin's prophecies was fulfilled at Flint by Richard (Usk 179).

On the way to London, Richard attempted to escape, but, Créton says, it must not have been the Lord's will that he do so, for he was caught and viciously thrust back into the tower where he was being held. The journey was resumed, and, upon arrival at London, the people welcomed Bolingbroke and devoutly thanked God, saying that he had shown them a miracle in sending Bolingbroke to them, and that obviously it must have been the will of God that he take over since he could not otherwise have conquered all England in less than a month. Henry's asking the citizens what he should do with Richard reminded Créton of Pilate who, also attempting to escape guilt, asked the crowd what was to be done with their king, and then turned him over to them to be killed.[49]

Créton and his companions asked and received permission from Bolingbroke to return to France; on his arrival, Créton addressed a ballade to Henry on the subject of his treachery. In the refrain of this poem he predicts Henry's damnation: "Tu en perdras en la fin corps et ame."[50] Créton believes that it would help any man to achieve eternal salvation if he were to attack and destroy Bolingbroke and his fellow traitors.[51]

He hears later of the deposition Parliament, and wonders that God could have endured the evil that all these people had in their hearts, and he believes they will pay dearly for it, because even if they are not punished in this life, the just Judge who knows their deeds will punish them hereafter. The Archbishop of Canterbury preached on the biblical episode of Jacob receiving the blessing of Isaac rather than his older brother Esau. "This he set forth as true," Créton says. "Alas, what a text for a sermon!" The people agreed to have Bolingbroke as their king and gave praise to Christ as they did so. Bolingbroke accordingly accepted their call and ascended the throne, since it had been ordained by God. "There, alas! was King Richard deprived of it for the whole of his life: such was the grudge they had against him. But, if it please God, they will deal the same by him whom they have placed thereon."[52]

When he tells of the failure of the plot of the earls, Créton prays that they may go to heaven, for they died like martyrs. Richard was overcome by these sad tidings, and called upon Death to come take him, and asked God to have mercy on him,

[49] Créton 175–179.
[50] Créton 182–187; 379–380.
[51] Créton 189–190.
[52] Créton 191–203.

for he could no longer live in such misery. It is said then that Richard refused to eat and so died, but Créton does not believe it, for others say he is still in prison. However, Henry and others of his blood paraded a dead body through London, alleging it to be the body of Richard, and making a great show of mourning after it, without regard for the evils they inflicted upon him. And this will be a great burden to them on the last day, the poet continues, when God will sentence the wicked to the everlasting flames of hell. But if the body were really that of Richard, Créton prays that he may be taken to heaven, for in his opinion he hated every kind of wrongdoing, and he saw nothing in him "save catholic faith and justice." Créton himself served him for seven months in an effort to merit in some way the benefits he had promised him.[53]

In concluding, Créton says: "Let us now beseech God, who humbly suffered his naked body to be suspended upon the cross for the redemption and restoration of sinners from the false foes of hell, that he will speedily avenge the great evils and ingratitude, the outrage and injustice which the wicked English have committed against their king and queen." He greatly desires to see this happen, he says, "for I solemnly declare that, according to my ability, I have uttered no evil or slander of them whereof they have not been guilty." [54]

Our third French source is the *Chronicque de la traïson et mort de Richart deux roy Dengleterre*, referred to by Holinshed as an old French pamphlet belonging to John Stow.[55] The author of this work expresses no providential opinions of his own but simply reports the comments of the people involved. His account of Richard and Northumberland at Flint resembles Créton's very closely, and suggests interdependence between the two works. While at Flint, Richard's servants told him they would throw in their lot with him, whatever happened, since it was the will of God; and Richard in his lament addressed God and the saints. Furthermore, he bade his friends remember how their Savior was undeservedly betrayed into the hands of his enemies.[56] But according to *Traïson*, it was the Londoners, not the old knight, who alluded to Merlin's prophecy and its fulfillment in Bolingbroke, when they greeted him on his entrance to the city.[57] They

---

[53] Créton 216–221.
[54] Créton 237–239.
[55] 1–2Hol 2.836.
[56] Traïson 199–201.
[57] Traïson 213. Benjamin Williams in his edition of the *Traïson* cites another

also thanked God and prayed for Henry when the revolt of the earls fell through.[58]

According to Froissart, Henry refused to have Richard put to death. But the *Traïson* asserts that on the day that Henry took to the field against the earls, he sent for Peter Exton to despatch Richard, alleging a sentence of execution passed by Parliament.[59] Richard defended himself valiantly, but was finally struck down by Exton himself, and he died, praying God for mercy. The author laments that the king died without being able to go to confession, and ends his account with a prayer of his own for God's mercy upon Richard's soul. In one manuscript, however, there follows an account of the story that his death was caused by voluntary starvation. The author concludes: "In this manner died King Richard, as they say; howbeit, many maintain with more reason that he died in the manner described in the last chapter; to whose soul God grant true pardon!" [60]

In these accounts sympathetic to Richard there is surprisingly little use made of the providential theme of the disciplining of God's servants through suffering. It is explicitly stressed only in the Dieulacres Chronicle, which denounces the interpretation of Richard's downfall as God's punishment for his sins; for the true interpretation, it says, is that God chastises those whom he loves, and this explains Richard's catastrophe.[61]

The Further Dealings of Divine Providence with Henry IV

In our review of the accounts of Richard's character and the explanations of his downfall, we have met with diametrically opposed interpretations. These divergent views were imperfectly assimilated in later accounts and resulted in paradoxes and contradictions in the pictures they gave of Richard.[62] The same, of

French source which draws on Merlin, the *Ballade de Eustace Deschamps, dit Morel, de la mort du roy Richart Dangleterre.* Deschamps accuses Henry IV and England of killing Richard, and goes on to say that they will be destroyed for their sins, which will fulfill the prophecy of Merlin (Traïson lxxiv–lxxv n. 3).

[58] Traïson 247, 258.

[59] The only sentence mentioned before was that Richard was to be kept in prison and well fed. "Thus," the author adds, "was he falsely sentenced by the said Parliament" (Traïson 223).

[60] Traïson 248–251, 262. These prayers of the author are examples of the conventional aspirations for those whose deaths are recorded in the chronicles, but here perhaps they may take on an added significance because it is mentioned that Richard was deprived of the sacraments.

[61] Dieulacres 169.

[62] See Ernest W. Talbert, *The Problem of Order* (Chapel Hill 1962) 159, 232–

course, holds true automatically for Henry. But as Henry's reign progressed, there was a change noticeable even in some of the chroniclers who supported him earlier. The chief turning point seems to have been the execution of Richard Scrope, Archbishop of York.

Let us return to Walsingham's account. Just as Gower had stated that Christ's influence remained with Henry in order to preserve the great benefits that had accrued to the realm through his coming,[63] Walsingham continued to see the action of God working in Henry's behalf. Accordingly, it was through God's will and protection that Henry was saved from an iron deathtrap that his enemies had placed in his bed.[64] Similarly, or conversely, when Henry encountered continual bad weather in his campaigns in Wales, Walsingham says it was thought that Glendower attempted, and nearly succeeded in the attempt, to destroy Henry by raising the elements against him through the means of diabolical sorcery, an odious practice whose punishment is eternal damnation.[65]

The troubles in Wales and the north of England were thought to have been foreshadowed by the comet that appeared early in Henry's reign,[66] and when Hotspur came to Shrewsbury, he realized that he would be killed there, in fulfillment of a prophecy.[67] Henry had told Hotspur that by the grace of God he could

233. Attempts were frequently made to reconcile the opinions of the divergent accounts by judging Richard guilty of certain mistakes or crimes, but as not deserving of the extreme punishment he received. And this is in fact basically the attitude of the author of *Richard the Redeless* and, to a lesser extent, of Froissart.

[63] Gower 336–337.

[64] 1Wals 337–338: 3Wals 248; 4Wals 392. This incident occurred ca. 1401. It is interesting to notice that just before this, Walsingham records that the people began to murmur against Henry because he was not paying for the foodstuffs which he bought on credit (1Wals 337).

[65] 1Wals 343–344; 3Wals 250–251; cf. 4Wals 395. Cf. also 0Wals 98, where he recounts the parliamentary charges of magic against the Dominican friar who enabled Alice Perrers to maintain her hold over Edward III; see also 1Wals 301 and 309, where Richard's dealings in magic are indicated, and it is charged that his followers demented him through magic. The pro-Henrician continuator of the Dieulacres Chronicle ("Author B") has an interesting comment on the Welsh episode. He says that while it is true that such storms could easily be caused by the devils Glendower is thought to use in his magic, still the true answer, in the opinion of the discreet, is that the English failed in their venture because they have no right to Wales (p. 176). Cf. 2Hard 360, who says that everyone thought witches were to blame.

[66] 1Wals 338; cf. 3Wals 248; 4Wals 392–393; also Dieulacres 175; Brut 363; Eul 398; CLgreat 85.

[67] 1Wals 365; cf. 378, where he records the vision and prophecy of a Continental hermit, who saw the angels of vengeance over England striking sinners with his sword; but peace would be restored, he said, "quia non in perpetuum irascetur

overcome any enemy that would rise against him. And although Henry's victory is not explicitly described as providential, it may perhaps be implied by Walsingham's whole treatment, especially since he attacks Hotspur for his pride and rashness in spurning Henry's lenient offers.[68]

In the following year (1404) there occurred a victory of the common people of Plymouth over a French raiding party, which Walsingham attributes to God. It is further described at length by Henry himself in a speech (or sermon) that he gave at a victory celebration in Westminster Abbey. Henry tells the people how much has been done for their land by God, who humbles or exalts whom he pleases, according to their merits.[69] This is the first example so far of a theme that plays a very large role in earlier and later events described by Walsingham and other chroniclers—God's providential care for his English people and his destruction of their sinful enemies. It is interesting to note that before this decisive victory of the Plymouthites over the Sieur de Castellis, when the English were suffering occasional defeats as well as winning occasional victories, the whole affair is given a literary analysis and visualized as directed not by God but by the goddess Fortuna.

When Walsingham comes to treat of Henry's measures against the insurrection of the Archbishop of York in 1405, his tone is definitely altered. The treacherous way in which the archbishop was seized, he says, seems to fulfill a prophecy of the saintly John of Bridlington.[70] And he reports that the Archbishop of Canterbury warned Henry that any proceeding against York would in all probability be avenged not only by human law but by God himself.[71] Henry pretended to sympathize with his point of view; meanwhile York was condemned and quickly executed. Walsingham expands upon the archbishop's pious and resigned death, which was a worthy martyrdom, "juxta quorundam opiniones."

Deus," etc. And Walsingham notes that the battle of Shrewsbury followed shortly after. Usk 253 also sees Hotspur's death as fulfilling a prophecy.

[68] 1Wals 361–371; 3Wals 255–258; 4Wals 398–402 (only 1Wals has Henry's claim to divine grace). King Henry explicitly wins by God's aid in Usk 256; Dieulacres 180; Giles 33–34; cf. Brut 549.

[69] 1Wals 382–386.

[70] 1Wals 407; cf. 3Wals 269 and 4Wals 414, where this judgment is categorically stated. The prophecies ascribed to Bridlington, which, as we have seen, were also applied extensively to Richard II, were written by an Austin friar named John Erghome (see Taylor, Kirkstall 23). In the previous year (1404), Walsingham noted the innumerable miracles worked by God around the body of Bridlington, "ad gloriam sancti sui" (1Wals 388; 3Wals 262; 4Wals 405–406).

[71] 1Wals 408.

He recounts a miracle that many said was performed at the prayer of the archbishop, and tells of the other numerous miracles which the people said were performed at his tomb. And when Henry forbade them access to it, and the ministering attendants were put to the torture, the miracles were proclaimed all the more.[72]

Walsingham does mention that the pope excommunicated all the slayers of the archbishop,[73] but he is careful not to say anything directly against the king. This silence is no doubt largely prudential, and a peculiarity of the continuation of his long chronicle would seem to confirm this view. Under the events of some years later (1409), we find a blank space of about thirty lines, in which the rubricator placed the headings, "De regis infirmitate" and "Continuantur miracula apud Ebor." [74] The juxtaposition of these topics is possibly explained by other contemporary chronicles, which record that God not only showed his favor for the archbishop by working miracles through his intercession, but also his disfavor for Henry by smiting him with an incurable leprosy that worsened as time went on and finally put an end to his life.[75] It may well be, therefore, that Walsingham left this space blank to be filled in at a later and safer time.[76]

After 1405, Walsingham is very reticent on the subject of

[72] 1Wals 407–411; cf. 3Wals 269–271; 4Wals 413–415. The archbishop's miracles are also reported in Usk 275; Brut 367; Brut k 314; South 277; North 282; Eul 405, 421; and many of the later chronicles. Only the London Chronicles give an unfavorable report of the archbishop; there it is said that he was beheaded for the untrue cause he espoused (CLgreat 86; CLf 100).

[73] 1Wals 417–418; cf. Eul 408; Giles 48.

[74] 2Wals 46. There is also a third heading: "De fulmine horribili cadente London. in Southwerk xxiii die mensis Maji."

[75] Eul 405, 408, 421; North 282–284; cf. Giles 46–49, and the later chronicles. In Eul 421, immediately after the account of Henry's death from the leprosy he contracted when Scrope was executed, there follows an account of a miracle worked through the intercession of St. Richard Scrope (i.e., the Archbishop of York martyred by Henry) later in the same year (1413). These are the last entries in the history.

[76] This hypothesis is perhaps weakened by the fact that not long before we read that Henry fell ill (in 1408), but recovered and thanked God (2Wals 29), and this illness might be the one referred to by the rubricator at the blank section. Cf. also the report of the pro-Henrician Adam of Usk, who speaks of Scrope's miracles but not of Henry's leprosy (p. 275); he does say, however, that Henry was poisoned in 1408 and rotted away ever after, an eventuality that was augured by a portent at his coronation (p. 298; similarly, Richard's future misfortunes were portended by three untoward events at Richard's coronation, p. 200–202).

However, John Capgrave in his English chronicle reports the common opinion that Henry was a leper from the time of Scrope's execution until his death (2Capgrave 291), and although this chronicle is written with a Yorkist bias, it draws extensively on Walsingham's long chronicle, and Capgrave may have been using a MS of it that contained this report.

Henry's dealings with God and vice versa. We might mention that Walsingham gives a prophecy that was said to be fulfilled in Northumberland's defeat and death in 1408, and in 1412 there is a providential victory over the French at St. Cloud, for which the king and his nobles praised and thanked God.[77] Henry saw an opportunity here to recover France and told the Archbishop of Canterbury that they should take advantage of the munificence of God and regain their rights in France. And Walsingham conjectures that he would have been able to do it if his health had supported him, but he was weighed down with an incurable disease.[78] And at the beginning of 1413, he fell very ill, and then, God willing, recovered for a bit, but finally died, after reigning gloriously for thirteen years.[79]

It would perhaps be a logical conclusion from Walsingham's account to say that divine providence prevented Henry from attaining to the glory of winning France, and if he considered the king's sickness to have been a result of Archbishop Scrope's execution, this providential disposition would take on an aspect of retribution. But chroniclers are not always logical or consistent, and it would be rash to ascribe such sentiments to Walsingham when writing about Henry's death in 1413, even if it were admitted that he leaned in this direction some years earlier. And though his latter-day feelings about Henry could not be called effusive, they seem at least rather benign.

We may note that Walsingham has nothing to say of the familiar story of Henry IV's intended crusade and the prophecy of his dying in Jerusalem. This may be significant, if it is remembered that when Henry was crowned, Walsingham applied to him *in globo* the prophecy made by the Blessed Virgin when she gave the cruet of sacred oil to Thomas à Becket. She declared that after some evil kings of England had suffered great losses, good kings would be anointed by this chrism, and the first would peacefully ("sine vi") regain Normandy and Aquitaine, and would build many churches in the Holy Land.[80] It has been suggested that this was the prophecy that set Henry thinking about a crusade and that he believed was fulfilled by his dying in the Jerusalem chamber.[81] But according to Adam of Usk, it was Henry's horoscope that said he was to die in Jerusalem.[82]

[77] 2Wals 28, 61; 3Wals 278, 286; 4Wals 423–424, 434.
[78] 2Wals 64.
[79] 2Wals 68–69; cf. 3Wals 289 and 4Wals 437, where he is cut off by fate.
[80] 1Wals 298.
[81] So John Webb, Créton 264–266.
[82] Usk 298.

Thomas of Elmham, in a poem written about 1420, says that a false prophecy had foretold that Henry would win the Holy Land in a crusade; but an unforeseen Holy Land was provided for him without his knowledge in the Bethlehem room at Westminster. The continuation of the *Eulogium* has him die in the Jerusalem room, without referring to a prophecy.[83]

According to the *Brut* (in the manuscript covering the events of 1377–1419), Henry actually prepared galleys of war for the voyage to Jerusalem, where he hoped to die. But when he was stricken and brought to the Jerusalem chamber, he said that his prophecy foretold that he would die in Jerusalem.[84] This account was taken over by Caxton and Fabyan.

It is worthy of notice that a similar desire to go on crusade is attributed by the *Brut* and other chronicles to the dying Henry V, who said he had intended to conquer Jerusalem after pacifying France.[85] And John Audelay in 1429 says of the young Henry VI:

> On him shall fall the prophecy
> That hath been said of King Harry,
> The holy cross win ere he die
> That Christ hallowed on Good Friday.[86]

It is remarkable that even the chronicles which interpret Henry IV's death as the result of the leprosy inflicted upon him for the execution of Archbishop Scrope[87] have nothing to say of his usurpation of the throne from the closer heirs in the Mortimer family. It is simply assumed by all that he is the true king, and Prince Henry the rightful successor to the crown. Even the continuation of the *Eulogium,* with its strong Franciscan flavor, does not treat the problem directly, although it does detail at great length the efforts of the Friars Minor to further the cause of King Richard and to counteract the reports of his death. It gives the position of the Franciscan master of theology whom Henry IV interviewed before his execution: he held that if Richard were alive he was still king, because his resignation was forced; and

---

[83] 2Elmham 122; Eul 421.

[84] Brut 372.

[85] Brut 493; Waurin 2.388; Mons 1.483; oHard 216v (1Hard 744); 2Hard 388; 1–2Caxton 555; Trans 182. John Capgrave in his *Liber de illustribus Henricis* describes Henry Bolingbroke's crusading in the 1390's, and his visit to Jerusalem at that time (1Capgrave 98–101).

[86] Audelay 110.

[87] This is specifically the judgment of the Whalley-Stanlow chronicle (North 282–284), and it is strongly suggested in Eul 405, 408, 421. Giles's Chronicle lacks an account of Henry's death.

if he were dead, Henry had lost all right to the kingship because he had procured his death. One of them admitted later that he and his fellow friars were plotting against Henry, not to kill him, but to reduce him from king to Duke of Lancaster.[88]

The *Eulogium* continuation also treats of the attempted abduction of the Mortimer children and mentions the opinion of those who said they were the true heirs to the throne.[89] But these passages do not allow us to conclude that the author sympathized with these views or plots entirely or even partially. He does, however, seem to concur in the opinion that the friars were unjustly convicted; at least he recounts without comment that the members of the jury who convicted them came to them weeping, before their execution, and asked their forgiveness, saying that they had been threatened with death if they failed to bring in a verdict of guilty.[90] But in his own name the author had previously described Richard's fall as brought about by divine providence ("vigili jubente caelesti"), and said that he died of voluntary starvation; Henry claimed the throne as the nearest male heir, and was the first to be anointed with the oil which was captured from Richard, along with the writing which said it was given by the Blessed Virgin, and which gave her prophecy concerning it. And when he speaks of the challenge that the Duke of Orleans sent to Henry IV, in which he refused to recognize him as king and accused him of the murder of his kinsman

[88] Eul 390–394.

[89] Eul 402; a similar account is to be found in CLn 89–90. When the Earl of March, Roger Mortimer, was killed in Ireland in 1398, his title passed to his son, Edmund (b. 1391), who was confused in the sixteenth century with his uncle, Sir Edmund Mortimer, brother-in-law of Hotspur and son-in-law of Glendower.

In the entry for 1385, the *Eulogium* continuation says that Richard II declared the Earl of March heir to the throne (p. 361). And in 1394, it recounts that John of Gaunt attempted to get his son Henry declared heir. He was opposed by March, who said he was descended from Prince Lionel. Gaunt alleged the story of Edward Crouchback, but March denied its authenticity by appealing to the chronicles. Richard then imposed silence on both parties (pp. 369–370; cf. 2Hard 353–354n.). However, M. V. Clarke believes that this report of the recognition of March as heir was interpolated into the *Eulogium* by Yorkists in the time of Henry VI. See her *Fourteenth Century Studies*, ed. L. S. Sutherland and M. McKisack (Oxford 1937) 107 n. 5. See also Gaillard T. Lapsley, *Crown, Community and Parliament* (Oxford 1951) 325 n. 5.

According to Walsingham's early anti-Lancastrian chronicle, John of Gaunt, after the death of the Black Prince in 1376, requested Parliament to consider the succession to the throne in the event of Prince Richard's death. He desired them to follow the French example and ignore claims derived through the female, so that he himself would succeed to the throne. He feared the Earl of March (Roger's father, Edmund), knowing him to be a good and just man; March had married the daughter of Gaunt's elder brother, Lionel. But the Commons refused to discuss the matter (oWals 92–93).

[90] Eul 391–394. Two juries before them refused to convict the friars.

Richard II, he calls Orleans an extremely proud and evil man.[91]

The Burgundian chroniclers Waurin and Monstrelet give in full the letters exchanged between Henry IV and Orleans, in which Henry vehemently denies complicity in the death of Richard, and maintains at length that divine providence placed him on the throne, for it could never have been done without the special grace of God, and sorcerers and devils would have been powerless to effect it. Perhaps Henry added this last clause because of Orleans' stipulations that no charms or incantations were to be used in the tourney, because they were forbidden by the Church.[92]

In this exchange, Orleans indicated that God had no doubt hidden his meaning, and that he would eventually bring Henry to confusion. The chroniclers then report the communication sent to Henry by Count Waleran de St. Pol denouncing him for his part in the murder of Richard; the count feels obliged to take action against Henry in an attempt to avenge it, for if he failed to do so, it would provoke against himself the indignation of God and of all honorable men.[93] And according to Waurin, it would seem, God did not wait to punish Henry, for as soon as he usurped the crown, he says, he fell ill of leprosy, which afflicted him to such an extent that it brought him at last to his deathbed.[94]

It is Waurin and Monstrelet also who give us the "crown scene" at the end of Henry's life. When called to account for his action in removing the crown, the prince told his father that he thought he was dead, and that therefore he took the crown because he had the next right to it. The king said: "And how, fair son, have you a right to it, for I never had any, that you know well." And the prince replied: "My Lord, as you have held and guarded it with the sword, so it is my intention to hold, guard, and defend it all my life." And Henry answered: "Fair son, do now with it as shall seem good to you. I leave the rest to God and to you, to whom I pray that he will have pity and mercy on my soul."[95]

[91] Eul 383–387, 395.
[92] Waurin 2.64–85; Mons 1.16–23.
[93] Waurin 2.85–86; cf. Mons 1.23.
[94] Waurin 2.166.
[95] Waurin 2.166–167; Mons 1.240. Just before this Monstrelet notes that history ranks Henry IV as a valiant knight, but it also records the shameful way in which he obtained the crown, by dethroning Richard II after he had reigned peacefully for twenty-two years. And he also says that before Henry's death, he was much oppressed by leprosy, which finally put a pitiful end to his life

However, it would be a long time before these unfavorable reports about Henry would prevail, and favorable views of his death were more in keeping with the histories of Henry V that followed. The accounts of Henry's crusade and his death in the Jerusalem chamber have already been referred to. The Earl of Ormond's story of the pious instructions that Henry gave to his son on his deathbed, as recorded by the Translator of Livius in the next century,[96] seems typical of the dominant contemporary attitude toward the Henrys.[97]

Henry V, Soldier of God

If the contemporary English chroniclers were reticent on the subject of Henry IV's right or lack of right to the throne, it is even more true of their accounts of Henry V, and the opinion that he was not the true heir is not mentioned even to be condemned.

In our treatment of Henry V, we will start with the so-called "Chaplain's Account" of the first few years of his reign (*Henrici quinti Angliae regis gesta*).[98] This history is an intimate record

---

(p. 239). There is one English chronicle that says Henry was stricken with leprosy at the end of his life (South 277), and Brut k 315 simply says he was seized by an incurable infirmity. The later version of the *Brut* (compiled in Yorkist times) records the report that God touched Henry, and he was a leper before he died, for not performing the penances assigned by the pope for his guilt in Richard's death (Brut 494–495).

[96] Trans 13–16. Henry told the prince not to defer justice till tomorrow lest God do justice upon him today and take his authority away from him. He should fear God and worship him above all, and never attribute anything to himself but rather believe that everything comes from God. The prince followed these and other sound doctrines that his father gave him, "whereby he obtained grace of our Lord to obtain to great victories, and to many glorious and incredible conquests through the help and succor of our Lord, whereof he was never destitute."

[97] Cf. 2Elmham 122, which says that Henry went to a deserved reward, and was taken by the King of Heaven, who is merciful to the fervent. The account of the Pseudo-Elmham, written at mid-century, pictures Henry as making a conventional confession of sins on his deathbed and confiding in God's mercy (PsElmham 14–15).

[98] This chronicle is by one of the chaplains who accompanied Henry on his first expedition to Normandy in 1415. His modern editor, Benjamin Willams, thought that John de Bordin was the most likely candidate among them, but it was later believed that Thomas of Elmham was the author. However, V. H. Galbraith has called this latter identification into question since there is no evidence that Elmham was ever in France, and the portions of his *Liber metricus* (1Elmham) that are not dependent on the *Gesta* can be dismissed as secondhand (2Wals xxiii n. 2). In this discussion the author will be referred to as the Chaplain, and his work as the *Gesta*. It is not to be confused with the *Vita et gesta Henrici quinti*, edited by Thomas Hearne in 1737 and erroneously attributed to Elmham, but after Kingsford known as the Pseudo-Elmham.

of the king by a man apparently close to him, and it will enable us better to understand the remarkable power that the character of Henry V exercised over all subsequent chroniclers of his life. It seems clear from this account that the prevailing characterization of Henry as specially guided and aided by divine providence is only a reflection of his own intense personal conviction to the same effect.

The Chaplain begins with Henry V's coronation and says that even though all of the new king's efforts were for the glory of God, God determined to test his servant by fire and to send him various tribulations. He is referring to the insurrection of the Lollard Oldcastle, one of Henry's most valued servants. Oldcastle, of course, was working under the guidance of Satan, and the king, with God's assistance, naturally won out against him. The Chaplain draws the providential moral with a rhetorical flourish. God scourged both Henry and Oldcastle by means of each other, but for the destruction of the one and the perfection of the other ("istum ut consumeret, alterum ut consummaret").[99]

Another trial for Henry, similarly arranged by both God and the devil, was the plot against him by the Earl of Cambridge and his companions. God's instrument in exposing the plot was the young Earl of March.[100] The Chaplain does not mention, as Monstrelet does, the reason for March's involvement, namely, that he was held to be the true heir and Cambridge offered to make him king.[101]

Henry considered God to be entirely on his side in his war against the French. At Harfleur he invoked against the city the ultimatum that God dictated to the Israelites for their use against enemy cities (in a city that refuses to surrender peacefully, they are to put all the male adults to the sword).[102] As usual, misfortune on Henry's side is ascribed to God's desire to test the patience of his anointed one. After the town capitulated, Henry sent the poor people and all the women and children of the town into the interior of France with an armed escort, and thus by a just judgment of God it was proved that they had been merely guests where they had regarded themselves as the true residents.[103]

[99] Gesta 1–7.
[100] Gesta 10–11.
[101] Mons 1.332; Waurin 2.182–83.
[102] Deut. 20.10–14. According to the French chronicles (C de Norm 11–13; Mons 1.321), Henry used this scriptural threat in a letter he sent to the French king.
[103] Gesta 10, 21, 26–33.

After many other providential aids and disciplinary afflictions (the Chaplain also records the incident of the soldier who stole a pyx from a church and was hanged for it at Henry's orders),[104] the English arrived at Agincourt. Henry piously considered that victory did not depend upon the number of soldiers but on the gift of God; he had begun his march in spite of the fact that sickness had decimated his forces, and it is believed that God was his guide.[105] On the evening before the battle, the king's soldiers went to confession and took up the weapons of penitence, and they were only lacking in sufficient priests to minister to them. And when Sir Walter Hungerford expressed the wish for the thousand extra archers he had left behind, Henry replied that he spoke foolishly, for by the God in heaven in whose grace he trusted, he would not wish to have one extra man added to his forces. "For these people that I have are the people of God, whom he has deigned to give me at this time. Or do you not believe that the Almighty is able with these few lowly soldiers of his to overcome the pride of the French opposed to us, who glory in their numbers and their own powers?" And the Chaplain adds his own opinion that by the very justice of God nothing untoward could happen to a child of his with such great confidence in him, just as nothing went wrong for Judas Maccabaeus until he began to lack confidence, whereupon he fell into merited ruin.[106]

The Chaplain goes on to describe at great length the action of God on behalf of the English and against the French during the battle, following the same pattern of providential victory after providential suffering, with the divine vengeance falling at last on the pride of the enemy. He adds that he and his fellow chaplains were constantly praying to God during the fighting and uniting their prayers with those of all the people of England.[107]

The victory, of course, is considered a miracle, since the English were outnumbered 60,000 to 6000 and only 13 or 14 Englishmen were killed, as opposed to nearly 5000 of the French.[108] And in the imagery of the holy wars of the Old Testament, the Chaplain ascribes all the glory to God and urges reform of life and greater fervor of worship in England out of gratitude to him: "Quia

[104] Gesta 41; repeated in 1Elmham 116; TLTrans 44–45; PsElmham 53.
[105] Gesta 36–47.
[106] Gesta 47.
[107] Gesta 49–56.
[108] Gesta 58. This is the lowest of the incredibly low figures the English chronicles give for the English casualties at Agincourt.

mirabilia fecit in Israel et dedit victoriam christo suo." [109] The Psalms are also invoked over the sad sight of the slaughtered French — it is pitiable indeed, but unless they repent, their state will become even worse, and the sword of God's anger will cut them off if they are not converted.[110]

When the English forces returned home, they were greeted with jubilation because of the victory that God had mercifully granted them against a rebellious and savage people. And it could be gathered from Henry's appearance that in his silent meditation he referred all the glory to God alone.[111]

The pattern of God's cooperation with Henry V observable in the Chaplain's history is to be found also in the other manifold accounts of his life, beginning with or even preceding his accession to the throne and ending only with his death.[112] Agincourt is especially emphasized, and if there is any difference in tone from that of the Chaplain's version, it is only that the theme of the providential chastisement of Henry is muted or omitted entirely. His piety and trust in God are enhanced by many devotional practices and speeches before and after the battle. For example, in a London Chronicle, he is pictured as exhorting his men to help maintain England's right for the love of "sweet Jesu." He says he wants no blood spilled here but that of those who are to blame for this trespass (that is, the French); and he prays to God: "When thou sittest in judgment, there hold me excused tofore thy face, as thou art God omnipotent." [113] It was even said that St. George was seen fighting on the side of the English.[114] This story is no doubt a hagiographical expansion of the affirmation that God and St. George fought for the English and gave them the victory.[115]

We are told also that after the battle, when Henry was thanking God for the victory, because it seemed that it was given through the suffrages of Saints Crispin and Crispinian, he ordered that their commemoration be said every day in the masses he heard.[116] It seems indubitable that this kind of piety was an

[109] Gesta 59.

[110] Gesta 56–57.

[111] Gesta 61–68.

[112] For example, 2–4Wals, Otterbourne, Usk, VersH5, 1Elmham, 1–2Agincourt, Strecche, Page, South, North, 1Capgrave, TLTrans, PsElmham, and the various versions of the *Brut* and the Chronicles of London.

[113] CLk 119–120 (the words quoted are obviously taken from a poem, some of which is cited in stanza form further on).

[114] 1Elmham 123; 1Capgrave 117; Brut 557; 2Agincourt 106.

[115] Strecche 153; Brut 379, 597; Davies 41.

[116] Brut k 326; TLTrans 61.

authentic element in Henry's character, and not just an embellishment of the chroniclers. As an indication of this, we may mention the long additions Henry made to the divine office when hearing of his brother's naval victory on the Vigil of the Assumption in the following year (1416); the Chaplain describes these additions in full for every day of the week. He says that Henry was inspired by the biblical accounts of the people of God who sang canticles of praise and blessing to God when they were victorious over their enemies.[117]

The Chaplain goes on to describe Henry's devotion in attending the recitation of the office; and previously he mentioned that on the morning of Agincourt, Henry did not prepare for battle until after the office and masses were heard.[118]

It seems evident then that Henry V regarded himself directed by divine grace in his French campaigns, and furthermore that he believed himself to be the divinely appointed instrument of chastisement against his enemies, who were also the enemies of God. After Agincourt, Henry tells the French: "It is not we who have made this great slaughter, but the omnipotent God, and, as we believe, for a punishment of the sins of the French." [119] And the Earl of Ormond tells of the visit of the Spanish fanatic Vincent Ferrer to the English camp, where he denounced Henry for inflicting these sufferings on the people. Henry answered: "I am the scourge of God, sent to punish the people of God for their sins." The two men consulted in private for a while, and Vincent emerged a confirmed Henrician, and told the king's soldiers to serve him well, for in so doing they would be most pleasing to God. Vincent was now convinced that Henry was a true Christian, and that God would aid him in all these wars.[120]

[117] Gesta 89–92.
[118] Gesta 49, 92; cf. Waurin, who says that Henry heard his usual three masses on this morning (2.201). Waurin was present at the battle of Agincourt on the French side, and he reports that all the English were engaged in devotional exercises on the day before the battle, praying to God to help them; and they remained thus occupied until sunset. That night the French made much racket on their side, which was said to have been audible on the English side; but they themselves could not hear anything of the like from the English, for all who could find priests went to confession, and everyone attended to his own business.
[119] Mons 343. Henry is here addressing Montjoy, the French herald. Cf. Waurin 216–217, where Henry is portrayed making a similar but more detailed statement to the Duke of Orleans. And Waurin says later in his own name that if France had been united, Henry could not have advanced as far as he did with such ease: "But for the sins of the French, it pleased our Lord that they should be punished" (p. 231).
[120] Trans 130–132. In the introduction, Kingsford says that this story has the signs of authenticity about it, even though it could not have taken place at Rouen (xxxiv–xxxvi).

The Chaplain's history is also of importance in that it gives us an account of the address made to Parliament in March 1416 by the chancellor, Henry Beaufort, Bishop of Winchester, who formulated a providential code of international justice, according to which nations or autonomous states, since they have no human judges over them, must lay their disputes before God, the supreme judge, and this is done by going to war and discovering in the outcome which side is declared in the right by the divine verdict.[121] And as in human courts three verdicts are decisive, so in the history of the conflict between England and France, England was declared in the right by God in three monumental victories, Sluys, Poitiers, and finally the recent triumph of Agincourt. And because the French refused to obey these divine sentences of vengeance against them, the Lord, as a just judge, deprived them of their three greatest weapons against the English, namely, their ports of Calais and Harfleur, their boldness in war, and their manpower.[122]

In the following October another Parliament was held, and the chancellor requested financial aid; since a peace could not be made with France, there was nothing left but to take up the sword and appeal to the divine judgment once more.[123]

As in the previous two reigns, Walsingham's account of the reign of Henry V provides a good example of the prevailing sentiments of his contemporaries. In speaking of the snowstorm on the day of his coronation (9 April 1413), he says that many interpreted it to mean that the forces of fate had affected the weather in this way to signify that the new king's reign would be frigid and severe. But others, wiser men, certainly (according to Walsingham), took the inclemency of the weather as a good sign, indicating that the king would make the snows of vice fall and the severe fruits of virtue emerge in the realm; and in fact, as soon as he had been installed by the sacred rites of kingship, he was suddenly converted into a new man, and cultivated uprightness, moderation, modesty, and gravity, letting no form of virtue pass him by which he did not wish to implant in himself.[124]

[121] We might note that a similar concept underlies the medieval trials by ordeal and combat.

[122] Gesta 73–75. Cf. 1Elmham 131–132; 1Capgrave 117–118.

[123] Gesta 105–106. The Chaplain's account ends with a prayer for Henry's continual success (107–108). There is a continuation to the time of Henry's death in 1422; but it is obviously not by the same author; for one thing, there is not a providential judgment in the whole of it. It seems rather to be based on the PsElmham account, which in turn is based on Tito Livio.

[124] "Qui revere mox ut initiatus est regni infulis repente mutatus est in virum alterum, honestati, modestiae et gravitati studiens, nullum virtutum genus per-

Walsingham includes the report that Henry transferred the body of Richard II to Westminster and had him reburied with great honor, for the king said that he owed as much veneration to Richard as to his own father;[125] but Walsingham does not mention, as later chroniclers do, that he performed this service for Richard to make reparation for his father's part in his death.

Walsingham, like the Chaplain and many other contemporary annalists, sees Henry's suppression of the Lollard plot as providentially inspired and aided, and moreover as the fulfillment of a prophecy.[126] He also follows suit in tracing the divine guidance in all of Henry's military campaigns, as well as in the discovery of the Cambridge plot to make the Earl of March king. Again there is no word of any supposed right that March had to the kingship, or of anyone's doubt concerning Henry's right.[127] Walsingham himself never had any doubts on this score, it would seem, and Henry's efforts on behalf of the Church and England would be more than sufficient to win him providential approval in this Benedictine's world-view.

We may sum up the Lancaster myth as follows: The corrupt reign of Richard II was providentially overthrown by Henry Bolingbroke, his cousin, who was next in line for the crown. God continued to bestow his beneficence upon the new king until the end of his life, and showed his favor even more to his pious son, Henry V, and aided him in maintaining his sovereignty both in England and in France.

Even the chroniclers who disputed Henry IV's right to the throne at first did not suggest that any actual providential calamity befell him for his usurpation, though they had no doubt that he deserved punishment. Only the late Burgundian chronicler Waurin, no doubt writing with Yorkist retrospect, reports

---

transiens quod non cuperet in se transferri" (2Wals 69; cf. 3Wals 290; 4Wals 437–438). The implication seems to be that Henry had been addicted to vices before he began his reign, and this is certainly the interpretation given by later chroniclers. The version of the *Brut* used by Caxton, which was compiled after 1361, says he had been wild before, but now was changed suddenly into a new man (Brut 494). It is thought by some that Walsingham is referring to Henry's friendship with Oldcastle; but by Walsingham's own account, Henry showed himself opposed to Lollardry as early as March 1410, when he made strenuous efforts to persuade the convicted heretic John Badby to recant (2Wals 51–52; 3Wals 282; 4Wals 428–429).

[125] 2Wals 77; 3Wals 297; 4Wals 446.

[126] 2Wals 77–80; 3Wals 297–299; 4Wals 447–449.

[127] 2Wals 87–88. As in the *Gesta*, Mortimer informed Henry of the plot. This aspect of the episode was not picked up by later chroniclers. In fact, there is no mention at all of Mortimer in Walsingham's shorter chronicles (3Wals 306; 4Wals 457).

that he was stricken with leprosy for the deed. Other chroniclers speak of a providential visitation of leprosy upon him as a result of his role in the execution of Archbishop Scrope, but without any reflection upon the legitimacy of his kingship. And if some shadows of divine retribution were seen by some over the person of Henry IV, the career of his son was completely unclouded by the least hint of divine disfavor.

At the end of Walsingham's *Historia anglicana,* he speaks of
the effect that Henry V's death had upon the people; he says
that there were many who were frightened at this sudden and
terrible "mutatio dextrae Excelsi," [1] and who feared that the
words of Solomon, "Woe to the land whose king is a child," [2]
would apply to England and its child-king, unless God, "who
works the same kind of marvels in small things as in great, whose
hand is not shortened in doing good, provided that in his and
our eyes we become like our king, humble children, and un-
divided in our actions and good counsels," assisted them. [3]

This was not to be the last time that the *Vae terrae* of "Solomon" was to be applied to Henry VI, but its force was to be
felt most bitingly after he attained his majority. The Austin
friar John Capgrave, in speaking of young Henry's coronation
in Paris in 1431, refutes the application of the saying to Henry,
since, as he maintains, it refers not to youth in years, but to
immaturity of morals; and he goes on to stress the great piety
of the young king. [4]

Henry does seem to have equalled or even exceeded his
father's religious fervor, but he was lacking in his political and
military sagacity, and it inevitably began to appear, to some,
at least, that God had forsaken him in this respect. The French,
of course, believed that the English were driven out of France
with the help of divine grace because they had no right to be

[1] Citing Ps. 76.11.
[2] Eccles. 10.16.
[3] 3Wals 344 (cf. Isa. 59.1; Matt. 18.4).
[4] 1Capgrave 128–133. A man was judged guilty of death for applying the saying
to Henry VI in 1444 (CLf 118). See also Waurin 4.350–351; 5.342; *A Political
Retrospect* 268; cf. Mirror 391; 1H6 4.1.192.

there.[5] But since English fortunes began to decline from the time of the marriage of Henry VI to Margaret of Anjou in 1445,[6] which had at first seemed greatly pleasing to God and all the kingdom,[7] there were many people who came to believe, at least after Henry's expulsion in 1461, that his and England's misfortunes were due to the failure to keep his promises to marry the sister of the Earl of Armagnac.[8]

Yorkist Reviews of the Lancastrian Regimes

But the partisans of the Duke of York came to see a deeper reason for Henry's troubles, one that related directly to York's claim to the crown — namely, the providential punishment of the house of Lancaster for its unjust possession of the realm.

One of the most interesting and important sources of this view is John Hardyng, who had served the Percys against Henry IV, and fought under Henry V at Agincourt. He spent much time peddling forged documents concerning England's dominion over Scotland, first to Henry V and later to Henry VI. It is probable that Hardyng did the forging himself, and he wrote his versified chronicle with a main view to justifying the accuracy of the documents.

The first version of his history was written around 1446–1457, and presented to Henry VI apparently in 1457. However, as C. L. Kingsford says, Hardyng's reward did not seem to fit his estimate of his merits, and so he began almost at once to prepare a fresh version of the history for Richard, Duke of York, his new patron.[9] He could not have finished it before 1465, when he was at least eighty-seven years old.[10] But the earlier version was imperfectly assimilated to his new viewpoint, and the resulting second version

---

[5] CdeNorm 164; Waurin 5.166; "Mons" 2.155, 170, 189, 198–199; Gaguin 138v.

[6] CLgreat 175.

[7] 1Capgrave 135.

[8] Brut 511–512 (followed by Caxton and Fabyan; the latter says explicitly that it would appear that God was not pleased with this marriage, p. 618). This version of the *Brut*, which extends to 1461, does not picture Henry VI, much less Henry V, as providentially punished for reigning without right, although Edward IV is said to win by the help of God at Towton (p. 533). This *Brut* is remarkable for giving the fullest description of the penance imposed by the pope upon Henry IV for the death of Richard II, as will be discussed below.

[9] C. L. Kingsford, 1Hard 466. The MS of this first version, Lansdowne 204 (= oHard), remains unedited, except for the portions printed by Kingsford (1Hard). In his analysis, Kingsford aimed at pointing out the most substantial differences between the two versions. Cf. also Kingsford's *English Historical Literature in the Fifteenth Century* (Oxford 1913) 140–149. More excerpts are given in Appendix A below.

[10] See Sir Henry Ellis, 2Hard xiii.

is a hodgepodge of conflicting interests, which will be observable in the later histories that made use of Hardyng and similar accounts.

In the preface to his reworked chronicle, the old man addresses the Duke of York, who was to die during the course of his rewriting of the history, so that at the end he is addressing Edward IV, and even Edward's queen, whom the king publicly acknowledged in September 1464. It is possible to trace Hardyng's change of allegiance quite easily in the sections dealing with the three Lancastrian kings, since for the most part the rough stanzas of rime royal (which he calls "balade") represent or reflect his original encomiastic strain, and the prose headings the Yorkist correctives to this feature.

Hardyng begins the preface addressed to York with the disarming admission that he was not equipped to write such a work, but that he wanted something to occupy his mind and keep him from sin and insolence. He then outlines York's right to the throne as heir to Edward III through the female line, and says that God gave to Moses in the Book of Numbers the law that a daughter is able to inherit, and that since Christ himself claimed the right to kingship through his mother's descent, there is no reason why York should not be the true king.[11]

Next he recounts the story of the Lancastrian dynasty. Henry IV became king by wrongfully deposing Richard II. His son, Henry V, ruled after him; and Hardyng does nothing at this point but describe his martial ability, which exceeded that of any other king or emperor, and by which he won Normandy and a great part of France. But his heir, Henry VI, he says, was by God's will endowed with small discretion and great simple-mindedness. For when Henry IV was crowned, there were many wise men who said that the third heir would be uncrowned in sorrow, and their reason was the common adage that "of evil gotten good the third should not enjoice." [12] This proverb was to be used frequently in the historiography of the fifteenth century. Waurin, for instance, says: "And here end the grand conquests of the noble King Henry of England, the fifth of this name, which he made after the death of King Henry his father, the usurper of the crown of the glorious King Richard, and the author of his sad death in the manner set forth in the last book of our fourth volume [Waurin follows the *Traïson* account].

[11] 2Hard 15-17.
[12] 2Hard 18.

Which death was avenged in the way you shall afterwards hear in the sixth and last volume, according to the authority which says: *de male acquisitis non gaudebit tertius heres*." [13] This passage was no doubt inserted after Henry VI's death (from "displeasure") in 1471, which Waurin relates in his last volume.[14] He applies this adage again to Henry VI as well as the *Vae terrae* when speaking of Edward IV's assumption of the crown in 1461; he finds the former saying well verified in Henry, "lequel pour la cause que le roy Henry le quart, son tayon, uza de tel trahison envers le roy Richard son seigneur souverain devoit il perdre tout succession dheritage pour lui et sa posterite." [15]

Another instance can be found in the register of the Abbey of St. Albans, in the author's verses on Edward IV's right to the crown:

> Sic vetus id dictum fuerat bene verificatum,
> "De male quaesitis vix gaudet tertius heres";
> Stare diuque nequit, mala quicquid vis stabilivit.[16]

A Political Retrospect attributes this saying to Scripture in relating it to Henry VI.[17] We shall find echoes of the same proverb (sometimes in its alternate form, that evil-gotten goods do not long endure) applied to Henry in Vergil, Hall, and Shakespeare, and to Richard III in André, More-Hall-Holinshed, and the *Mirror for Magistrates*.[18]

Perhaps Hardyng is also implying the corollary proverb, namely, that he who is in the right shall rejoice, that is, have his right restored to him; he does at any rate go on to say that York in contrast to Henry VI is by God's grace provided with the means of ruling well:

> O my lord of York, God hath provide
> In this for you, as men sayen commonly,
> So that no sloth you from his grace divide,

[13] Waurin 2.393–394.
[14] Waurin 5.675.
[15] Waurin 5.342–343.
[16] Whet 414.
[17] Below at n. 45.
[18] Warkworth 26 seems to apply a similar sentiment ("such goods as were gathered with sin were lost with sorrow") to George Neville, Archbishop of York (Warwick's brother), not only for his covetousness but also for his treachery to Henry VI. Cf. also Usk 76/245, who applies the adage to the Duke of Milan ("In male quaesitis vix gaudebit tertius"). The proverb is a rather common one and appears in English as early as the *Handlyng Synne* of Robert Mannyng (ca. 1317).

> But take it as he hath it sent manly,
> And rule well now ye have the remedy.[19]

He recommends that he treat the Percys well, and, since they too have descended from the line of March, that he enlist their aid and make them content, and remind them that by process of time and destiny his right might become theirs, and that through God's power they might eventually become his successors.[20]

But when Hardyng comes to discuss York's right to Scotland, he gives a providential justification of Richard II's overthrow. In speaking of Thomas of Woodstock, a man greatly feared by the Scots, Hardyng says he was murdered by King Richard, and the latter in turn was served his just deserts by Henry IV, who put him to a death preordained by God's judgment; for he has passed the sentence that whoever slays shall be slain, and murder always cries out for vengeance.[21] This stanza is not a holdover from the original version but corresponds to his original view; at the place where he recorded Richard's death in the early manuscript he copied in the margin a version of the concluding lines from Gower's *Tripartite Chronicle,* with his judgment that "God hates rulers in the world who live evil lives; a sinner cannot be a ruler — Richard bears witness, his end proves it clearly." [22]

In the body of his history, Hardyng tells the story of Bolingbroke's return to England; when he landed, he swore upon the sacrament that he claimed nothing but his heritage, and swore also to set up a good government for Richard. When he had control of the country, Henry dismissed the Percys, and they returned to the North on the assumption that he would keep his oath. Richard then resigned his crown to Henry, an action that no one objected to at the time. And when Parliament deposed him for his misgoverning, even though they knew that the Earl of March was next in line to the throne, they were intimidated by Henry into giving the kingship to him.[23] He abridges the account of his coronation, omitting his earlier

[19] As we shall see, Shakespeare has York make similar points concerning his own heaven-sent gifts and Henry's lack of them (2H6).

[20] 2Hard 18–19.

[21] 2Hard 19. There is a marginal reference to "Mat. xxvii." Perhaps Matt. 7.2 is meant: "For with what judgment ye judge, ye shall be judged."

[22] oHard 204 (see Appendix A). In 2Hard 357 it says he was "buried at Langley, for men should have no remembrance of him." But a similar statement appears in oHard 210 (also in Appendix A).

[23] 2Hard 350–351.

statement that Archbishop Arundel fully anointed him "with holy creme that no wyght myght expell." [24]

In the portion dealing with Henry IV's reign, Hardyng did not take great pains to incorporate his new viewpoint into the text itself. For instance, he says simply that the Archbishop of York was beheaded for treason,[25] without entering into a defense of him, or of the Percys. He adds a long note, however, in which he says he speaks from personal knowledge with regard to the Percys, for he himself had been a member of their household during this time. "Their quarrel," he says, "was so sweet, devout, and by good advice and counsel of Master Richard Scrope, Archbishop of York, for whom God almighty hath showed many miracles sith that time hitherward." He gives a letter (perhaps another of his forgeries), which the Percys allegedly sent to Henry IV, accusing him of perjury because he had forced Richard to resign, in violation of an oath he had taken to the contrary, and then starved him to death, meanwhile usurping the throne from Richard and his heir, the Earl of March; and they intended to prove Henry a traitor in combat, with the aid of almighty God.[26]

When he speaks of Henry's last sickness, Hardyng adds a new rubric: "The words that the king said at his death of high complaint, but nought of repentance of usurpment of the realm, ne of the restorement of right heirs to the crown." But in the verses he does not deviate from the sentiments he expressed in the first version. With contrite heart and humble aspect, he prays God for his mercy:

"O Lord," he said, "O God omnipotent,
Now see I well thy godhead loveth me,
That suffered never my foes to have their intent
Of mine person in mine sickness, ne in mine infirmity;
But ay hast kept it fro their malevolence,
And chastised me by thy benevolence."

Henry's prayer continues in this vein — he thanks God for visiting him with sickness as he does now, and refers to the

---

[24] oHard 203.

[25] 2Hard 362–363; cf. oHard 207, which does not add "for treason."

[26] 2Hard 351n; cf. J. M. W. Bean, "Henry IV and the Percies," *History* 44: 216–217 (1959). Hardyng mentions the archbishop's miracles in the first version when speaking of Henry V (oHard 210; see Appendix A).

leprous aspect of his face, and seems to welcome it as a penance for the excessive pride that he had taken in his handsome appearance in the past; and finally, with all his heart he commends his soul into God's hands forever.

And so he died, Hardyng tells us, in faith and "whole creance," and was buried at Canterbury with great reverence and with all the ceremony that befitted a king and that was in keeping with his "high magnificence." He then proceeds to pity him for the great trials that he had during his life — poison was placed in his clothing and food, sharpened and poisoned irons laid in his bed, enchantments used to waste him away and destroy him:

> And some gave him battle full felonment
> In fields within his realm him for to noy;
> And on themselves the hurt and all the annoy
> Ay fell at end, that hanged were and headed
> As traitors ought to been in every stead.

Finally Hardyng does add a stanza derogating from Henry's reputation, in which he says that England rejoiced in him at first, but very little at the end.[27]

In his account of Henry V, Hardyng omits his statement that the realm was "glad of him" and obedient to all his decrees; he substitutes a remark about the storms that occurred on the day of his coronation, and adds a stanza saying that in the hour in which he was crowned he became a new man and "then set upon all right and conscience." As in the first version, he recounts how Henry allowed the people to venerate Archbishop Scrope as a saint and arranged for the reburial of Richard II at Westminster.[28] He repeats too his account of Henry's restoration of the Percy lands;[29] but in retelling the failure of the Cambridge conspiracy he no longer speaks of the conspirators' attempt to kill the king "for their avail," but says that they "purposed th' Earl of March to crown King of England by their provision." He abbreviates his original account of the battle of Agincourt and omits his sentiment that the English victory against such great odds was "but grace of God's omnipotence." [30]

When he introduces the stanzas dealing with the death of

[27] 2Hard 369–371. See oHard 209rv for the corresponding passage in the first version (Appendix A).

[28] 2Hard 371–372; cf. oHard 209v–210 (text in Appendix A).

[29] oHard 210; 2Hard 372.

[30] oHard 210v–211 (in Appendix A); 2Hard 374–376; in a Latin prose account he says that Henry had praise given to God alone for the victory (2Hard 391n).

Henry V, Hardyng notes a serious exception to the king's conscientiousness; he says: "For all his righteousness and justice that he did he had no conscience of usurpment of the crown." [31] He omits his poetic attempt at describing the role of the Fates in Henry's death and speaking of the everlasting sojourn of the soul with God, as well as his account of Henry's reception of the sacraments "in all whole faith and Christian whole creance," and his conviction that the king's soul has gone to heaven,

> As by his works it doth right well appear,
> That loved ever in Christian faith and law,
> Keeping the peace in all his lands through awe.[32]

But the remaining stanzas are in high praise of the king. He asks God, since he is omnipotent, why he did not prevent this king's death, just when he had leagued with the emperor to conquer the Holy Land and settle it with Christians — why did he thus favor the infidels more than Henry's benevolence? Hardyng's greatest praise for him is that he kept the peace throughout England, and all wrongs were corrected under his impartial rule, which enabled him to make all his great conquests abroad. And for this he well deserved the love of God and of his people, who might otherwise have slain or overthrown him; but as it was he stood surely in "rightful governance" for the good of the commonweal and the pleasure of God.[33]

Whereas Hardyng concluded the first version of his chronicle by telling Henry VI that God preserved him and his kingdoms while he was "innocent" and that he must himself maintain peace and law if he is to continue prosperously,[34] he ends the second version, as we shall see, by telling Edward IV that by Henry's very innocence God has restored his family to the rule.[35]

John Capgrave offers another example of a chronicler who turned his back on the Lancastrians when the Yorkists came to

---

[31] 2Hard 387.

[32] oHard 215v–216 (see Appendix A).

[33] 2Hard 387–389. This praise of Henry V has been somewhat shortened from the original version (1Hard 744–746), where, in asking God why he did not let him live longer, Hardyng not only refers to his intended crusade, but adds that he could have reconquered all his heritage in France. He goes on to ask in what way England has offended him, to make him punish them by taking this king away from them forever. "O Lord," he says, "who shall England now defend?" Then follows his thesis that it was Henry's policy of pacification and control in his own country that made possible his successes abroad, and he appeals to Henry VI to put down the mischief in the land.

[34] oHard 222v (1Hard 750).

[35] 2Hard 410.

power. He previously wrote accounts highly favorably to all three Henrys, in his *Liber de illustribus Henricis;* but in his *Chronicle of England,* addressed after 1461 to the providentially restored and reigning Yorkist king, Edward IV, he treats Henry IV as a usurper, both in the dedication and in his account of Henry's death. But he makes heavy use of Walsingham's fuller chronicle and neglects to modify the emphasis found in the account of Richard's deposition and Henry's election, which is unfavorable to Richard and favorable to Henry. He mentions, for instance, that Henry was crowned with the sacred oil that was found by revelation in France, and he repeats the view that Henry escaped the lethal trap in his bed by the will of God.[36] Unlike the cautious Walsingham, Capgrave records the common opinion that Henry was a leper from the time he beheaded Archbishop Scrope;[37] but the whole affair of the rising and its aftermath is in no way connected with Henry's usurpation, which is not even mentioned.[38]

However, in his account of Henry's dying moments, Capgrave departs from the usual sources and gives us a scene which, though resembling that of Monstrelet and Waurin (and Hall and Shakespeare), may well be authentic. He says it is reported that certain members of the nobility directed the king's confessor, Friar John Tille, to encourage repentance in Henry for three particular sins: the death of Richard II, the death of Archbishop Scrope, and "the wrong title of the crown." Henry answered, when these matters were put to him: "For the two first points, I wrote unto the pope the very truth of my conscience; and he sent me a bull, with absolution and penance assigned, which I have fulfilled. And as for the third point, it is hard to set remedy; for my children will not suffer that the regalie go out of our lineage." [39]

The continuation of the *Brut* from 1419 to 1461 (which was used by Caxton) has an appendix to the life of Henry V which

---

[36] 2Capgrave 273–274, 278.

[37] Or, as was conjectured in the last chapter, perhaps Capgrave was using a copy of Walsingham that contained this account.

[38] 2Capgrave 289–293.

[39] 2Capgrave 302. This chronicle of Capgrave's, which continues only to 1417, gives a favorable picture of Henry V. As in 2Hard, the significance of the Cambridge plot is not stated, and the execution of the conspirators is simply recorded without further comment (309). Capgrave's account of Henry's speech before the battle of Agincourt ("The King comforted greatly his men, that they should trust in God, for their cause was rightful," 312) seems most closely related to Tito Livio (TLTrans 54–55). Both Livio and Capgrave had Humphrey of Gloucester as their patron.

confirms Capgrave's report of Henry IV's petition for absolution from the Pope; but there is a conflict in the account that follows, since according to Capgrave, Henry said that he fulfilled the penance imposed by the bull, whereas the *Brut,* in speaking at great length of the papal requirements for Richard's burial and the prayers and good works to be offered for the repose of his soul, says that they were all performed by his son, since Henry himself left them unperformed, and, as we have seen, was considered to have been smitten by God with leprosy for his inaction.[40] But perhaps Henry in Capgrave's account was referring to further works of penance of a more personal nature, which would no doubt be included in such an absolution, apart from those dealing with the reinterment of Richard's body. Hardyng gave a probable reason for Richard's burial at Langley in the first place, namely, to prevent the people from being reminded of him, and the same reason would also serve as an explanation of why he was left there.

As we have seen, Hardyng included the reburial of Richard in the list of measures that Henry V effected upon acceding to the throne, all of which seemed to reverse the policy of his father against the partisans of Richard. This view of Henry is confirmed by other chronicles written about this time. In Davies' Chronicle, another continuation of the *Brut* (used later by Stow and possibly by Hall), it is said that Henry was motivated by his great love for Richard in reburying him.[41] And in the second continuation of the Croyland Chronicle, it is said that Henry V was far from approving of Richard's dethronement and imprisonment, and that he considered the promoters of his death guilty of treason. By way of some atonement for his father's offense, he had Richard's body transferred from Langley to Westminster.[42]

In all these accounts, therefore, Henry V is left untouched both

[40] See above, Chap. I, n. 95. Fabyan (p. 589) in turn used this account, but confused the religious foundations begun under Henry V with the penance to be performed for Richard. And Shakespeare in turn drew on Fabyan's account for Henry's prayer before the battle of Agincourt.
[41] Davies 39. In its history of Richard II and Henry IV, this chronicle makes use of the *Eulogium* continuation. It gives a completely favorable account of Henry V.
[42] Croy 364. Cf. Waurin 2.172: "King Henry, who was the most virtuous and prudent of all the Christian princes reigning in his time, in order to clear and release the soul of his late father," had Richard reinterred at Westminster. In Thomas of Elmham's poem on the death of Henry IV, written after 1420, the king asks the prince to pay his debts; perhaps this is an occult reference to his reburial of Richard (2Elmham 121).

by God and man for his father's offense, and the fact that he kept the realm from its true heirs is not allowed to diminish his heroic stature or the intensity of his piety. Hardyng explained the situation by referring to the piece of folk-wisdom that designated the third generation as the time for the restitution, or at least the loss, of ill-gotten goods.

The theme of these Yorkist histories, which is often obscured or contradicted by earlier material of a contrary tendency, is put into somewhat more coherent form in the speech given to Edward by the author of Whethamstede Register, when he is explaining his claims at Westminster to the citizens of London in March 1461. He says that after Henry IV usurped the crown he reigned fourteen years, but not always prosperously or peacefully. Then Henry V reigned, who, though prosperous, had no just title to the crown. Then came Henry VI, and though he was a simple, just, and God-fearing man, he nevertheless sustained many misfortunes and lost all his overseas holdings. And now that he has fled and the throne is empty, is not Edward himself the one who should rightfully rule, under the direction of God? [43] Although the troubles of Henry IV and Henry VI are not explicitly said to be the result of divine justice, this may be his meaning, and God's direction in the final phrase may be intended to cover all that went before.

We may also cite the petition presented by the Commons to Edward's first Parliament in November 1461. After recalling Edward's victories, which were granted to him by the pleasure of Almighty God, they established the hereditary basis of his claim to the throne. Starting with Henry III, they come down to the time of Richard II:

Of the which crown, royal power, estate, dignity, preeminence, governance, and lordship the said King Richard II was lawfully, rightfully, and justly seized and possessed, and same joyed in rest and quiet, without interruption or molestation, unto the time that Henry, late Earl of Derby, son of the said John of Gaunt, the fourth gotten son of the said King Edward III and younger brother of the said Lionel, temerously against righteousness and justice, by force and arms, against his faith and legiance, reared war at Flint in Wales against the said King Richard, him took and imprisoned in the Tower of London of great violence; and, the same King Richard so being in prison and

[43] "Nunquid jure regimus, nunquid lege ducimus, nunquid recto agimus titulo, et, dirigente Domino, juridice gubernamus?" (Whet 406–407).

living, [Henry] usurped and intruded upon the royal power, estate, dignity, preeminence, possessions, and lordship aforesaid, taking upon him usurpously the crown and name of king and lord of the same realm and lordship; and not therewith satisfied or content, but more grievous thing attempting, [he] wickedly, of unnatural, unmanly, and cruel tyranny, the same King Richard, king anointed, crowned, and consecrate, and his liege and most high lord in the earth, against God's law, man's legiance and oath of fidelity, with uttermost punition attorment-ing, murdered and destroyed, with most vile, heinous, and lamentable death; whereof the heavy exclamation in the doom of every Christian man soundeth into God's hearing in heaven, not forgotten in the earth, specially in this realm of England, which therefore hath suffered the charge of intolerable persecu-tion, punition, and tribulation, whereof the like hath not been seen or heard in any other Christian realm, by any memory or record.

That is to say, because of Henry's usurpation and murder of Richard, which every Christian condemns in God's hearing, England has suffered untold hardships; but whether these hard-ships are a result of God's punishment or of the "inward wars moved and grounded by occasion of the said usurpation" (which are described below) is not clear. At all events, the crown should have gone to Edmund Mortimer; and now his heir, Edward IV, has taken over and removed the usurper, Henry VI, "in whose time not plenty, peace, justice, good governance, policy, and virtuous conversation, but unrest, inward war and trouble, un-righteousness, shedding and effusion of innocent blood, abusion of the laws, partiality, riot, extortion, murder, rape, and vicious living have been the guiders and leaders of the noble realm of England."

No mention is made of the times under Henry V, though he too is called a usurper; all their spleen is reserved for Henry VI, who, "continuing in his old rancor and malice, using the fraud and malicious deceit and dissimulation against truth and con-science that accord not with the honor of any Christian prince," violated the agreement that he had made to consider the Duke of York his heir, and so Edward IV was perfectly justified in assuming the crown before Henry's death.[44]

The providential aspect of the Yorkist historical synopsis is more pronounced in *A Political Retrospect,* in which it is said

[44] *Rotuli parliamentorum* (London 1767–1777) 5.462–466.

that "unrightful heirs by wrong alliance/Usurping this royaume caused great adversity." Richard was the rightful heir, God's true knight, and there was prosperity during his reign. But Henry, "under the color of false perjury," came and put him in prison for life, where he pined away and died a piteous death. And holy Bishop Scrope, the blessed confessor, "in that quarrel took his death full patiently." God smote Henry "for his great fierceness" with a leprosy that finally caused his death. Next came Henry V, who is acknowledged as the best of that line, and even though he reigned unlawfully, yet he upheld England's honor. But through the great folly of his son, Henry of Windsor, "all hath returned unto huge languor." Since Humphrey of Gloucester was treacherously put to death, England has been full of troubles, a situation traced directly to the misrule of the land; and in explanation, the author goes on to say, mistakenly attributing his proverb to the Bible:

> Scripture saith, "Heritage holden wrongfully
>   Shall never chieve ne with the third heir remain,"
>   As hath be verified late full plain.
> Whereas three kings have reigned by error,
>   The third put out, and the right brought again,
> Whose absence hath caused endless languor.

The poet continues with another appeal to divine revelation:

> Also Scripture saith, "Woe be to that region
>   Where is a king unwise or innocent";
> Moreover it is right a great abusion,
>   A woman of a land to be a regent.

And he prays God to send Margaret and her followers an early end.[45]

The Emergence of the House of York

When the Yorkist or quasi-Yorkist chronicles discussed above take up contemporary events, they supply Richard of York and his sons and associates liberally with providential aids in the form of grace and miracles (or "wonders"). It will be instructive to cite the dedication that Capgrave makes to Edward IV in his chronicle, where he says to the new king: "Now will I make you

[45] *A Political Retrospect*, ed. Wright 267–269.

privy what manner opinion I have of your person in my privy meditations. I have a trust in God that your entry into your heritage shall and must be fortunate for many causes." He draws much fruit from the fact that Edward entered in 1460, since six is a perfect number. Then he gathers more fruit from the "four" in Edward's name: "He that entered by intrusion was Herry the Fourth. He that entered by God's provision is Edward the Fourth. The similitude of the reparation is full like the work of the transgression, as the Church singeth in a preface: 'Because Adam trespassed eating the fruit of a tree, therefor was Christ nailed on a tree.' We true lovers of this land desire this of our Lord God, that all the error which was brought in by Herry the Fourth may be redressed by Edward the Fourth. This is the desire of many good men here in earth, and, as I suppose, it is the desire of the everlasting hills that dwell above. God, for his mercy, fulfill that he hath begun; send our King Edward good life and good governance; and, after his labor, good reward in the bliss of heaven. Amen." [46]

For a more detailed introduction to this period, let us examine the Whethamstede Register referred to above. This work was influential in later times through its use by Holinshed, and it resembles earlier as well as later chronicles in a feature that we have often noted before — the ambiguity or contradictory nature of its politico-providential themes in connection with dynastic upheavals; that is, moral and divine support is sometimes bestowed upon the reigning party, and sometimes invoked against it. The register deals with the second abbacy of John Whethamstede in the Monastery of St. Albans, and the narrative extends from 1451 to 1461. It was written in its present form by another monk of the abbey some time after the later date, although this author apparently made some use of contemporary materials, part of them perhaps by Abbot Whethamstede himself.

The author of the register attributes the cause of the quarrel between York and Somerset, which resulted in the first battle of St. Albans and Somerset's death, to Somerset's supplanting of York as governor of Normandy, and to York's subsequent desire for revenge. For York shared the common fault of the nobility: they are unwilling to leave vengeance to God, to whom it properly belongs and who will avenge every wrong in good time,

---

[46] 2Capgrave 2–4. He seems to be referring to the Preface for Passiontide, though he may have been using a text different from that of the present liturgy, which was standardized in the sixteenth century.

and instead are overcome with passion and presumptuously take up the sword of vengeance themselves. So it was with York, who would not accept the mediation of the pious King Henry.[47]

York, however, was forced to submit at first; but later, when Henry fell ill, he was named protector, and after obtaining a release from the oath of future allegiance to Henry which he had been required to make, he imprisoned Somerset. But when the latter was freed upon Henry's recovery, York was compelled to flee to the North, where he confederated himself with Salisbury and Warwick. Here we are subjected to one of the author's incredibly pompous and learned set speeches, which are rather similar in style to the ones that Hall was to compose later. In the present speech, York draws on the Absalom and Achitophel themes — King Henry, like King David, was a good and upright man, but was impeded by the impious Somerset.[48]

At the first battle of St. Albans, the king's forces eventually fled, but it was not known whether their terror was sent by heaven, or came from their own inadequacy. At any rate, York attributed his victory to the grace of God because of his just cause against Somerset, and he bade Henry to rejoice with him.[49] And in the Parliament that followed a declaration was made establishing the innocence of York and his followers, thereby leaving no legal remedy for those they injured, so that every transgressor could, like Pilate, wash his hands of his crimes.[50]

Three years later, in 1458, by the prompting of the Holy Spirit, Henry attempted to reconcile the rival factions in a great council at Westminster.[51] But in the next year, the three great lords (York, Warwick, and Salisbury) rose in rebellion, even though not against the Lord, certainly against his anointed one, that is, the lord king.[52] Concerning the insurgents, some said they wished only to displace some of Henry's counselors, or, as others said, to punish his betrayers. But there were still others who maintained that they wanted to place York on the throne. Henry agreed that this last-named was their true motive, and soon collected an army, in order that God, who dwells in the

[47] Whet 160–162.
[48] Whet 162–166.
[49] Whet 168–170.
[50] Whet 183–184.
[51] Whet 296.
[52] "Etsi nequaquam adversus Dominum, adversus tamen christum suum, serenissimum, scilicet, dominum regem" (Whet 337). The reference here is obviously to Psalm 2.2: "Quare fremuerunt gentes, et populi meditati sunt inania? Astiterunt reges terrae, et principes convenerunt in unum adversus Dominum, et adversus christum ejus."

heavens, might ridicule them, and that he himself, their earthly lord, might also put them to scorn.[53]

After this account, which has been favorable to Henry, we are given a speech by Warwick, in which he states his reasons for declining Henry's terms.[54] One is that in spite of the king's letters he was not allowed freedom in working for the good of the realm, and in fact there was a plot against his life when he was at the council in Westminster, which was only averted through help sent him by God, rather than through any human power or in virtue of the royal pardon.[55]

Warwick and his companions fled into exile, where they prospered. According to the author, it was God himself who sent the grace to make this possible; it was as if he directed their steps wherever they went, for they were received graciously by all. York in Ireland was treated like another Messiah, and Warwick and Salisbury were warmly welcomed in Calais. The two latter nobles are pictured as giving a speech of praise and thanksgiving in unison, in which they again express their good intentions and their confidence that they will be safe there until divine grace inspires them, and God rises up to scatter their enemies.[56]

York was finally victorious and appeared in Parliament in no small exaltation of spirit; and coming to the throne, he placed his hand on it for a moment, "like a man about to take possession of his right." [57] When his intentions became apparent, however, the people cried out against him, because he had repeatedly sworn not to seek the crown and was now perjuring himself. He therefore modified his pretensions, and was satisfied with being

---

[53] "Cum quibus dominus rex in opinione conveniens, mox ut ille Deus, qui habitat in caelis, irrideret eos, ipseque dominus, qui moras trahit hic in terris, etiam subsannaret eos, associavit sibi exercitum magnum," etc. (Whet 337–338). The author here is drawing a further analogy to Psalm 2, the fourth verse of which reads: "Qui habitat in caelis irridebit eos, et Dominus subsannabit eos."

[54] When the register moves into direct address like this it seems to be a sign of the final redactor's presence.

[55] Whet 340.

[56] Whet 367–369. As usual these outbursts are full of scriptural phrases; the last clause referred to here, "quousque habebit idem Deus exsurgere et dissipare inimicos nostros," recalls Ps. 67.2: "Exsurgat Deus, et dissipentur inimici ejus."

[57] Whet 376–377. Cf. Davies 99–100, where York is said to remember the whole history of his lineage and the usurpation of Henry IV as he makes his challenge and claims the crown. We might mention also a pair of prodigies that were recorded in Brut 530 and passed on to Caxton and later chroniclers. While York was claiming his right in Parliament at Westminster Abbey and the Commons were discussing the question, the crown that hung in the midst of the hall fell down. And also the crown that stood on the highest tower of the Castle of Dover fell down the same year.

declared heir to the crown. Then, with King Henry's sanction, he marched against Margaret in the North. But the Northerners and their leaders, following a long-standing tradition of treachery, broke their faith and attacked before the agreed day, and thereby succeeded in capturing York and Salisbury.[58] They crowned York with swamp grass, "just as the Jews did to the Lord," and, after many insults, beheaded him. This, then, was York's return to England, and his final departure, "with Fate playing the step-mother, from the terrestrial and transitory realm to, it is hoped, the heavenly one that lasts forever without end." [59] This characterization of Fate is usually applied to Fortune, and it is in fact Fortune and Chance who are blamed for York's downfall in the verses that follow on the battle of Wakefield, and also in Edward's speech in Parliament.[60] This illustrates a tendency we have noticed before, whereby an author describes in providential terms only what seems favorable from his own viewpoint, and describes "unfortunate" occurrences in literary or classical terms (or else, at times, as engineered by the devil).

In order to clear our minds of any doubt about York's honesty, the author reminds us that he had been absolved of his oath to King Henry, and that therefore the charges mentioned above, which the people made against him on this score, "did not seem to have much efficacy against the aforesaid lord duke." [61] This reminder looks like an afterthought, and is perhaps placed here because the final redactor neglected to include it in a previously written report of York's entrance into Parliament, the account of which, as it stands in the register, is not particularly favorable to York.

There follows the fullest treatment of prodigies that is to be found in these English histories, and it may permit us some insight into the lost and unlamented science of reading the future from cosmic irregularities in the present.[62] The whole seems to have been written after the battle of Towton in 1461 by a man who recognized Edward IV as king. First, he says, it should be recalled that in the year he speaks of (presumably 1460), God, as if having been offended for forty years with this generation

---

[58] The battle of Wakefield, 31 December 1460.
[59] Whet 377–383.
[60] Whet 407.
[61] Whet 383–384.
[62] It may no doubt be assumed that Walsingham had some similar providential philosophy with regard to portents, in spite of his occasional diffidence in interpreting them (see above, Chap. I, n. 36). Abbot Whethamstede himself began his first abbacy at St. Albans while Walsingham was still writing his history.

and having decreed in his wrath to destroy it and the kingdom with it, and to send a new Deluge upon the earth, opened the cataracts of heaven.[63]

Secondly, since rare and unusual events that happen beforehand are signs to the wise of the evils that are to come, it should therefore be recalled, and recalled again and again by all the people, that that God who is said to be just and merciful, he, namely, who when angry is always careful to remember his mercy, showed us this year not only prodigies in the heavens above but signs on the earth below as well, so that we could thereby more fully conjecture the evils that would come upon us, if we should be unwilling to humble our souls in sackcloth and ashes like the Ninevites, in weeping and mourning and lamentation before the Lord.[64]

The signs that God showed were, first, a sharp sword hanging in the air in the regions of Norfolk, signifying that God would draw the sword of vengeance in those parts in the coming year. Secondly, "near us," in the area of Bedford, a bloody rain fell out of the skies, which led the wise to the manifest conclusion that blood would be shed like water in the environs "circa typicam nostram Jerusalem" (St. Albans); and so it happened soon afterwards. And in the third place God showed, if it is allowable to believe the report made by the common people, a triple sun in the sky, in testimony of the fact that just as there are three who give testimony of peace in heaven, namely, the Father, the Word, and the Holy Spirit (cf. 1 John 5.7), so on earth there are also three who shall provide matter for dispute in the realm in the coming year, namely, the king, the queen, and the Duke of York. It is also to be remembered, the author continues, that though there were no earthquakes this year, still the North rose against the South, first in the battle of Wakefield, then in that of St. Albans, and thirdly in a battle in the county of York under King Edward IV.[65] The last-named encounter refers to the skirmish at Ferrybridge and the battle of Towton. In other chronicles, the triple sun appears on 2 February 1461, on the morning of the battle of Mortimer's Cross, and is taken by Edward as a sign of success sent by God.[66] The prior who contin-

---

[63] Whet 384–385. The author is adapting Ps. 94.10–11 and Gen. 6.

[64] Whet 385.

[65] Whet 385–387.

[66] CLgaird 77; Davies 110. In the latter account Edward interprets it as representing the Father, Son, and Holy Ghost.

ued the Croyland Chronicle, like the author of the Whethamstede Register, takes the three suns as well as the bloody rain as terrible prognostics, but discusses them in a later context with political or military applications. He does note that the relaters of these and other prodigies were strictly examined by the Archbishop of Canterbury.[67]

After the queen and her Northerners won the second battle of St. Albans, according to the register, Henry uttered a prayer of praise to God for bestowing on his queen the power to be reunited to him. At Abbot Whethamstede's request, Henry ordered the Northerners not to plunder, but to no avail; and the author prays the God of vengeance to give them the reward they deserve; and he goes on to ascribe to the abbot a long lamentation over the evils done by the lawless troops of the North, and follows this with a versified attack against them.[68]

But soon the divine pity rescued the people, raising up the spirit of another Neoptolemus, that is, Edward, son and heir of the Duke of York, through whom God worked a sudden and almost unhoped-for deliverance in the midst of the people. Edward addressed his followers, telling them of his confidence that the Lord would be strong in his support, and that for three reasons: first, there was no human judge to settle the matter; second, his cause was just, because he had the closer title to the crown; and third, he had good intentions, since God, "who searches hearts as well as reins," knew that he intended nothing other than to recover his right.[69]

At Westminster, Edward publicly laid claim to the crown, and in doing so reviewed the history of the Lancastrian usurpation in the manner described above.[70] And upon being elected king, he went to London rejoicing and thanking God for his speedy success. He then led his army to Ferrybridge in Yorkshire; and in addressing his men, he pointed out that Gideon won with only a few men, and thus it was evident that victory did not consist in numbers but came from heaven. The author then compares Edward's confidence in God and his subsequent victory to the similar confidence of Theodosius the Great and his victory over Eugenius and Arbogastes.[71]

The captains of Edward's army forced the Northerners to flee,

[67] Croy 444.
[68] Whet 393–401
[69] Whet 401–404; cf. Rev. 2.23.
[70] At n. 43.
[71] Whet 408–409.

because, "like other sons of Ephraim," they were unwilling to keep the covenant of the Lord and to walk in his law, which required that the elder son must always precede the younger.[72] So Edward won at Towton by the aid of divine grace, no less than by the cooperation of human might. And back in London he was crowned king to the praise and glory and good pleasure of God Almighty, as many believed, because thereby the royal line was rectified, which had remained diverted for sixty years and more before this.[73]

In the verses that follow, as has been pointed out before,[74] the author declares that the saying is verified which asserts that ill-gotten gains scarcely last through the third generation. However, he does not explain Henry's fall explicitly in providential terms but in the classical terms of personified chance:

> O rota versatilis nimis! Oque rotabilis axis!
> Sorte novercante, Fatoque modum variante,
> Corruit Henricus, isto sub nomine sextus,
> Et casum tulerat; titulus sibi deficiebat.
> Defecitque bonus, heus! pro moderamine sensus,
> Proque bono campi cor defuit Herculis illi.
>
> . . . .
>
> Hic fuit in verbis rex mitis, rex pietatis,
> Attamen in factis nimiae vir simplicitatis.
> Hinc postquam triginta novem rex praefuit annis,
> Caeca suam Fortuna rotam, quasi fortis in armis,
> Volverat, et regimen rapiebat regis eidem,
> Compulit ac subito sic dicere, "Sum sine regno." [75]

The author here considers the Yorkist restoration as providential,[76] and yet he sympathizes with Henry's unfortunate fall. That is, he apparently does not wish to emphasize that Henry was being punished by God as the possessor of ill-gotten goods, even though this notion would follow as a corollary from his

---

[72] Whet 410. The allusion is to the sons of Ephraim who were routed in the day of battle for not keeping God's covenant (Ps. 77.9–10).

[73] Whet 410–412.

[74] Above at n. 16.

[75] Whet 414–415.

[76] When he comes to speak of Edward in his verses further on, he combines the notion of *sors* with that of grace and the gift of God:

> O sors prosperior! O gratia sorteque major!
> Qui diuturna nimis fuit expectatio plebis.
> Sed mittendus erat. Jam, dante Deo, veniebat
> Hic Martis suboles, et nomine Martius heros.

analysis. He did not make this conclusion explicit even in the speech he gave Edward in reviewing the troubles of the usurping Lancastrian kings.[77]

The register's treatment of the Yorkist theme agrees strikingly with that of Hardyng in the concluding portion of his revised history, although Hardyng expressly repeats the notion of his prologue that Henry VI was providentially born simple-minded, in order that the Yorkists might take advantage of it and regain their right. But Hardyng too treats Henry gently and begs Edward to do the same:

> O gracious lord, now of your sapience
> Consider well this sixty year and three
> Your kin and ye by all intelligence
> Have been divorced of all the royalty,
> To now that God, of his speciality
> Hath granted you grace your rights to recover
> And your enemies all to rule [all] over.
> Consider well the benign innocence
> Of King Henry, that now is in Scotland,
> By God's doom of small intelligence,
> For your prevail, as men can understand.

He goes on to advise Edward to restore Henry to his rights as Duke of Lancaster and attempt to win his loyalty.[78] He points to the example of Henry IV, who, after having been made king not for any personal merit "but only for the castigation/Of King Richard's wicked perversation," treated the Earl of March well, as did Henry V, thereby gaining his love and avoiding strife.[79]

Providential Vicissitudes under the Sun of York

As in the case of Henry IV's coming to power, so too with Edward IV's coup in 1461: the contemporary English chroniclers as a whole welcomed the change and saw in it a manifestation of God's justice. Just as the Continental writers who were sympathetic to Richard II sadly acquiesced in the change as brought about by God's providence (since everything is under his rule), but for reasons incomprehensible to the minds of men, so now

[77] See above at n. 43.
[78] 2Hard 410–411.
[79] 2Hard 409–410.

Comines in his *Memoirs* records that in his opinion and in the opinion of the world, Henry VI was the lawful king of England: "But, in such cases, the disposal of kingdoms and great states is in the hands of God, who orders them as he pleases, for indeed all things proceed from him." [80]

The contemporary chronicle accounts of the two decades of Edward IV's reign (1461–1483) are few in number, and in general favor the Yorkist point of view. The most extensive of these are the second and third continuations of the so-called Chronicle of Ingulph of the Benedictine Abbey of Croyland. The second continuation was finished in 1469 and was written by the prior of the abbey. The third was written in April 1486, almost certainly by John Russell, Bishop of Lincoln, though his account was apparently edited by one of the monks of the abbey.[81] Russell was one of Edward's most intimate advisers and was chancellor under Richard III, until shortly before the latter's overthrow. Since the Croyland Chronicle as a whole may have influenced Polydore Vergil in the revision of his manuscript *Anglica historia,* it may be well first to give a brief account of the second continuation from the time of Richard II.[82]

The prior's treatment of the events in the century is typical of many of the other Yorkist-flavored chronicles of this time that we have seen. That is, he draws on Lancastrian histories without entirely removing the Lancastrian bias. Richard II is pictured in an opprobrious light, whereas Henry IV is described as a welcome reformer, and no mention is made of any irregularity in his taking possession of the crown. Furthermore, Henry is said to have knowledge of the conspiracy of the earls through the providence of God.[83] However, we are told that it was due to the malice of the devil against the saints that the Minorite friars were put to death; but there seems to be no criticism of Henry implied here. Again, in the account of Archbishop Scrope's rising,

---

[80] Comines 2.85–86.

[81] Paul Murray Kendall, *Richard the Third* (London 1955) 432. See also H. A. Kelly, "Canonical Implications of Richard III's Plan to Marry His Niece," *Traditio* 23: 269–311, esp. 271–273 (1967).

[82] The first continuator, pseudo-Peter of Blois, covers only the first part of the twelfth century. The second continuation is fragmentary until 1388, well into Richard II's reign. See Chapter IV, n. 16, for Vergil's possible use of the chronicle.

[83] Croy 352–355. Conviction is added to this sentiment by the fact that one of the conspirators, Thomas Holland, Earl of Kent, was an oppressor of the monastery of Croyland; and by the sudden judgment of God on his wickedness, he was beheaded, it is said, on the very day on which he had planned to make an attack on Croyland.

nothing is said against Henry, even though the author points out that God worked great miracles in favor of the archbishop in aftertimes.[84]

The prior gives an interesting account of Henry IV's last days, in that he discusses the king's preparations for going to Jerusalem as being inspired by a deceitful prophecy. And when he was attacked a short time after by a fatal malady, he died in Westminster Abbey in a room called Jerusalem, "thus fulfilling the above idle prophecy." [85]

We have already discussed the prior of Croyland's treatment of the reburial of Richard II, which he says was motivated by Henry's desire to make reparation for his father's offense.[86] And the prior continues to regard Henry in a favorable light, considering him to have been providentially guided and protected in the affairs of the Lollard insurrection, the plot of the Earl of Cambridge, the taking of Harfleur, and the victory at Agincourt.[87]

In the prior's own time, after the death of the Duke of York at Wakefield, he tells of the descent of the Northerners upon the South and the plundering and sacrileges they committed, and he blesses God for not allowing them to attack Croyland. He describes the situation thus: "Wherefore, the Lord of Mercy, who, our sins so requiring it, hath oftentimes permitted the wickedness of the unrighteous to prevail, to minister to our punishment, being desirous to put an end to evils of so disastrous a nature, raised up for us a defender in Edward, the illustrious Earl of March." [88] He points out that Edward is a lineal descendant of Edward III (however, he does not say that he has a prior claim over Henry, just as he did not treat of the deprived line of March earlier in his history); and therefore, since the people had been abandoned by Henry, who had besides fallen into imbecility through sickness and ruled in name only, they chose Edward for their king. And by God's clemency, Edward was victorious over Henry's army in the North; peace was thereby brought to the kingdom, and all the people gave thanks to Almighty God for the triumph granted them by heaven over their enemies.[89]

[84] Croy 356–357.
[85] Croy 364.
[86] Above at n. 42. In recounting Henry's disapproval of Richard's dethronement and death, perhaps the prior is expressing his own disapproval as well.
[87] Croy 364–366.
[88] Croy 422–423. The prior goes so far as to tell us that Edward was of unblemished character (424).
[89] Croy 424–426.

The prior of Croyland Abbey concludes his continuation with a rather confused account of Warwick's first moves against Edward IV in 1469. He tells of Warwick's defeat of the Welsh led by Lord Herbert, Earl of Pembroke; the latter were supposedly fighting on behalf of Edward, but the author then proceeds to speak as if the Welsh themselves were rebelling against English rule:

The truth is, that, in those parts and throughout Wales, there is a celebrated and famous prophecy, to the effect that, having expelled the English, the remains of the Britons are once more to obtain the sovereignty of England, as being the proper citizens thereof. This prophecy, which is stated in the chronicles of the Britons to have been pronounced by an angel in the time of King Cadwallader, in their credulity, receives from them universal belief. Accordingly, the present opportunity seeming to be propitious, they imagined that now the long-wished-for hour had arrived, and used every possible exertion to promote its fulfillment. However, in the providence of God, it turned out otherwise, and they remain for the present disappointed of their desires.[90]

This report is significant in that it shows the Cadwallader prophecy to have been in current circulation before it was applied to Henry VII. In fact, according to Tito Livio, this prophecy or a similar one had been applied earlier to Henry V by the Welsh themselves, in virtue of his having been born in Monmouth.[91]

Bishop Russell, if we may so identify the author who added to the prior's continuation in 1486, begins by remarking that some review of the material covered by the prior is necessary,

[90] Croy 446–447. Hall 273 also speaks of Welsh prophecies at this point, but with reference to the outcome of the battle.

[91] TLTrans 8; PsElmham 4. Perhaps the prophecy alluded to in the tripartite convention of Glendower, Mortimer, and Northumberland (Giles 40) may have some connection with the Cadwallader prophecy. Cf. the Welshman, Adam of Usk, who says that Glendower claimed descent from Cadwallader, and also claimed that according to the prophecy he would be delivered from English tyranny by the help of Scotland; and he relied on God's help for his eventual triumph (Usk 240). Hardyng in the early part of his chronicle also alludes to the oracle given to Cadwallader, and says Welshmen still foolishly await its fulfillment (2Hard 178–179). Fabyan 126 says the same for Welshmen of his day; and we must remember that Fabyan wrote shortly after the prophecy was supposedly fulfilled in the accession of Henry Tudor. The legend of Cadwallader and his heavenly instructions was first recorded by Geoffrey of Monmouth at the end of his *Historia regum Britanniae,* and was probably invented by him from details found in Bede's *Ecclesiastical History.*

because his laudable ignorance of secular matters led him to overlook many of the implications of the events which he recorded. He points out, among other things, that in the Parliament of 1460 York claimed the crown as the true heir. And furthermore, after the second battle of St. Albans, the council declared that Edward's oath of allegiance to Henry was no longer binding, because of Henry's association with the queen and her followers, who had murdered York.[92]

Early in 1470, Warwick took Edward into custody, Russell says (in his continuation proper), but he escaped in a manner almost miraculous, and returned to London.[93] Later in the same year he was forced to flee to the Continent, and Henry was restored to the throne. "You might then have heard," he tells us, "persons innumerable ascribing this restoration of the most pious King Henry to a miracle, and this change to the working of the right hand of the Most High;[94] and yet, behold! how incomprehensible are the judgments of God, and how inscrutable are his ways![95] for within six months after this, it is a fact well known, that there was not a person who dared own himself to have been his partisan."[96]

In describing Edward's victorious recovery of his realm, though he does so with obvious approval, the author does not give it a providential setting, except for what is implied in the passage just quoted.[97] He does attribute the success of the Londoners' resistance against the Bastard Falconbridge to God's assistance; the reason given, however, is that God did not wish the capital of England to be plundered by such wretches.[98]

When he comes to the murder of Henry VI, he says:

I would pass over in silence the fact that at this period King

[92] Croy 453–456.

[93] Croy 458.

[94] This expression, as we have seen before, is taken from Psalm 76.

[95] This is another reference to an important and much used passage of Scripture: "O altitudo divitiarum sapientiae et scientiae Dei! quam incomprehensibilia sunt judicia ejus, et investigabiles viae ejus! Quis enim cognovit sensum Domini? aut quis consiliarius ejus fuit? Aut quis prior dedit illi, et retribuetur ei? Quoniam ex ipso, et per ipsum, et in ipso sunt omnia; ipsi gloria in saecula" (Rom. 11.33–36). This passage itself is full of echoes of the Old Testament, especially the Book of Job.

[96] Croy 462–463. Cf. the long eulogy of Henry's piety which the Great Chronicle of London inserts after telling of his restoration (CLgreat 212).

[97] Edward is given abundant divine aid in the History of the Arrival of Edward IV in England, which was used by Stow, and, indirectly, by Holinshed. Besides his providential victories, he is favored with a miracle through the intercession of St. Anne (Arrival 13–14; Waurin 5.655–656; Recovery 273–274).

[98] Croy 467.

Henry was found dead in the Tower of London; may God spare
and grant time for repentance to the person, whoever he was,
who thus dared to lay sacrilegious hands upon the Lord's
anointed! [99] Hence it is that he who perpetrated this has justly
earned the title of tyrant, while he who thus suffered has gained
that of a glorious martyr[100] . . . How great his deserts were, by
reason of his innocence of life, his love of God and of the
Church, his patience in adversity, and his other remarkable virtues, is abundantly testified by the miracles which God has
wrought in favor of those who have, with devout hearts, im-
plored his intercession.[101]

Concerning the execution of Clarence in 1479, the author says
he believes that Edward inwardly repented of this deed, but
outwardly he acted with a high hand and was dreaded by all.[102]
And the worst manifestation of this high-handedness in the mind
of the author, it would seem, was Edward's request that he be
given the next tithes by the clergy, just as though the prelates
were to do anything the king asked:

Oh, deadly destruction to the Church, which must arise from
such servility! May God avert it from the minds of all succeeding
kings, ever to make a precedent of an act of this nature! lest,
perchance, evils may chance to befall them, worse even than can

[99] The author here seems to be alluding to the episode in the Old Testament
in which David refuses to kill Saul, in spite of all his transgressions. The passage
does much to explain the attitude of many at this time who support Edward's
right but at the same time sympathize with Henry: "Et dixit David ad Abisai: Ne
interficias eum; quis enim extendet manum suam in christum Domini, et in-
nocens erit? Et dixit David: Vivit Dominus! quia nisi Dominus percusserit eum,
aut dies ejus venerit ut moriatur, aut in praelium descendens perierit, propitius
sit mihi Dominus ne extendam manum meam in christum Domini." And later
David tells Saul: "Dominus autem retribuet unicuique secundum justitiam suam
et fidem; tradidit enim te Dominus hodie in manum meam, et nolui extendere
manum meam in christum Domini. Et sicut magnificata est anima tua hodie in
oculis meis, sic magnificetur anima mea in oculis Domini, et liberet me de omni
angustia" (1 Sam. 26.9-11, 23-24). This biblical episode was also drawn upon by
the official Tudor homilists in their polemic against rebellion.
[100] Riley subjoins here that this sentence appears to be a hint of Edward's
complicity in the affair. But it seems also possible that the author is referring to
Richard of Gloucester.
[101] Croy 468. There follows the account of the embassy to the Duke of
Burgundy, on which Edward sent a doctor of canon law, identified by a marginal
note as the author of this history (p. 469).
Another contemporary account of Henry VI's virtues, that by John Blakman,
will be taken up in the chapters on Vergil and on Holinshed. But we may note
here that Blakman records that Henry defended his right to be king on grounds
of long and uncontested possession (p. 44).
[102] Croy 480.

be conceived, and such as shortly afterwards miserably befell this same king and his most illustrious progeny.[103]

The author explains his meaning by saying that Edward was suddenly and inexplicably seized with a malady and so brought to his deathbed. Perhaps he is also hinting at the providential destruction of his two sons because of his own sins, but if so the notion was probably not fully thought out in the author's mind, since he offers no further explanation. His chief emphasis in any case is upon the lesson Edward's fate has for others and not upon the eradication of his line. Polydore Vergil will deal more fully with the same idea, but will assign different reasons for Edward's punishment in his children.

It is noteworthy that after his somber meditation on the disastrous results of interfering with the rights of the Church, the continuator concludes his estimate of Edward on a more favorable note: "This prince, although in his day he was thought to have indulged his passions and desires too intemperately, was still, in religion, a most devout Catholic, a most unsparing enemy to all heretics, and a most loving encourager of wise and learned men, and of the clergy." He truly repented for his sins on his deathbed, and there is no doubt in the author's mind that his soul attained salvation, for God looks to intentions, not to actions.[104]

We may sum up this portion of our history by saying that the York myth in its unadulterated form completely reversed the Lancaster myth and pictured the Lancastrians as usurpers at last providentially deprived in favor of the divinely supported Yorkist claims — this in spite of the occasional instances of divine beneficence bestowed upon the Henrys.

The Croyland continuations do not fit neatly into this pattern, yet both consider the Yorkist accession to be providential. The prior sees Edward's victory as permitted by God to bring peace to the land. Bishop Russell also sees the hand of God in Edward's final replacement of the saintly Henry VI but finds the reason for it hidden in the inscrutable mind of God.

[103] Croy 483.
[104] Croy 483-484.

III

The
Tudor
Myth

In this chapter we shall discuss only the authors who wrote under Henry VII, the first Tudor monarch, and reserve for Part II the historians who wrote under Henry's successors in the sixteenth century.

We may take up again with the third continuation of the Croyland Chronicle. We have ascribed at least part of this continuation to Bishop John Russell, who, according to the fragmentary fourth continuation, was at Croyland during the last part of April 1486,[1] the time in which the third continuator declares he wrote his account.[2] This was just six months after Richard's defeat by Henry at Bosworth Field — time enough for the author to have switched his allegiance to the Tudor regime. Such a transfer of sympathies could provide an explanation for the basically unfavorable way in which he describes Richard's ascent to the throne. However, we may note the similar views found in Dominic Mancini's *De occupatione regni Angliae per Ricardum tertium*. Mancini was an Italian cleric who came to England in the latter part of 1482, and left in July of 1483, just after Richard's coronation. He completed his account of Richard's usurpation in December of the same year.[3] This is not to say that all the evil things said about Richard are true, but only that bad opinion about him existed independently of Tudor bias or intimidation.

[1] Croy 511–515.
[2] Croy 510.
[3] Cf. C. A. J. Armstrong, Mancini 5–6.

The Providential Interchange of Richard III and Henry VII

According to the Croyland account, at the time of Buckingham's revolt, a rumor spread that the two sons of Edward IV had met with a violent death, but it was uncertain how.[4] Therefore all thoughts became centered on Henry Richmond, and a message was sent to him by Buckingham, on the advice of John Morton, Bishop of Ely.[5] Meanwhile, everyone in England took an oath to support Edward, son of Richard III, as heir to the throne. "However, in a short time after, it was fully seen how vain are the thoughts of a man who desires to establish his interests without the aid of God." For Edward soon became ill and died, and Richard and Queen Anne nearly went mad with grief.[6]

Then follows the account of Queen Anne's death and Richard's abortive plan to marry his niece Elizabeth, Edward IV's eldest daughter.[7] Richard was soon diverted to other matters. It was said by some persons "endowed as it were with a spirit of prophecy" that Richmond would land at Milford, and Richard accordingly concentrated his forces there; but Richmond landed instead at another Milford, the one in Wales.[8]

Before the battle of Bosworth Field, Henry enjoyed the ministrations of the clergy who had been exiled and who returned with him. But the same was not true of Richard:

At daybreak on the Monday following there were no chaplains present to perform divine service on behalf of King Richard, nor any breakfast prepared to refresh the flagging spirits of the king; besides which, as it is generally stated, in the morning he declared that during the night he had seen dreadful visions, and had imagined himself surrounded by a multitude of demons. He consequently presented a countenance which, always attenuated, was on this occasion more livid and ghastly than usual, and asserted that the issue of this day's battle, to whichever side the

---

[4] Mancini also reports about the same time that the suspicion was abroad that young Edward had been done away with (115).

[5] Croy 485–491.

[6] Croy 496–497. Cf. Comines 1.397–398, who indicates that the death of his son was part of God's punishment upon Richard for the murder of his nephews.

[7] See Kelly, "Canonical Implications of Richard III's Plan to Marry His Niece," *Traditio* 23 (1967).

[8] Croy 500.

victory might be granted, would prove the utter destruction of the kingdom of England.[9]

It is noteworthy that Richard is not said to feel remorse of any sort. The author considers Henry's victory to be providential, and yet he has some praise for Richard: "At length a glorious victory was granted by Heaven to the said Earl of Richmond, now sole king, together with the crown, of exceeding value, which King Richard had previously worn on his head. For while fighting, and not in the act of flight, the said King Richard was pierced with numerous deadly wounds, and fell in the field like a brave and most valiant prince." Many insults were heaped upon his dead body, and it was mistreated "not exactly in accordance with the laws of humanity." But only Catesby and two others of the captured enemy were executed, as far as is known; and on account of this clemency on Henry VII's part, "he began to receive the praises of all, as though he had been an angel sent down from heaven, through whom God had deigned to visit his people and to deliver it from the evils with which it had hitherto beyond measure been afflicted." [10]

The author then delivers an *apologia* for the veracity of all that is contained in his account, and adds some verses on the fate of Richard III, and draws an analogy between the three Richards who were kings of England; they were alike in three things — they died without heirs, they led violent lives, and suffered violent deaths.[11] In further verses on peace, he points out that God has united both factions of England through the marriage of Henry to Elizabeth, and therefore all should be content and receive the timely blessings of the Lord with grateful hearts. Thus he indicates his agreement with the people who consider Henry the providential savior of England from its troubles. But he adds that if the wars continue (as in fact they did), they should be borne patiently as trials sent by God.[12]

[9] Croy 502–503.
[10] Croy 503–505.
[11] Croy 505–506.
[12] Croy 510. The verses in the original (p. 578) read:

Nunc victi, nunc victores, heu quomodo regni
Regnum vastavit! sed cum Deus ultima primis
Jam junxit, pariterque duo confecerat unum,
Contenti simus; melior fortuna sequetur,
Si volumus tam grata Dei modo munera recto
Acceptare animo; sin autem pendeat ensis
Et nondum Jupiter sua spargere fulmina sistat,
Turbam quam mittet Deus, aequa mente feramus.

Another important chronicler of this time is the chantry priest John Rous, who resembles John Gower in his attack upon a King Richard he had earlier supported, and in the supernatural dimensions of the praise he bestows on a King Henry who violently replaced him. In the pageant history of the Earls of Warwick that Rous finished before Richard III's fall in 1485, and apparently before the death of Queen Anne, he describes Anne of Warwick as first the spouse of Prince Edward, and then carried up by the wheel of Fortune to be the wife of the most victorious Richard III, who by the grace of God was king of England and France, by true descent from Henry II. Richard ruled well and merited the gratitude of God and love of all his subjects.[13] We may compare this view with that of one of Richard's partisans, Thomas Langton, Bishop of St. David's, who wrote: "On my truth, I liked never the conditions of any prince so well as his; God hath sent him to us for the weal of us all." [14]

Another favorable report is to be found, of course, in the Parliament Roll justifying Richard's title to the throne, which was suppressed by Henry VII when he took over. There it is said that the marriage between Edward IV and Elizabeth Grey was made "by sorcery and witchcraft committed by the said Elizabeth, and her mother Jacquetta, Duchess of Bedford, as the common opinion of the people and the public voice and fame is throughout all this land, and hereafter, if the cause shall require, shall be proved sufficiently in time and place convenient." Furthermore, it is stated that Edward's marriage was not legally solemnized, since he had been married to Elinor Butler, and that he had been living with Elizabeth in sinful adultery, "against the law of God, and of his Church; and therefore, no marvel that, the sovereign lord and head of the land being of such ungodly disposition, and provoking the ire and indignation of our Lord God, such heinous mischief and inconveniences as are above remembered were used and committed in the realm amongst the subjects." There follows a prayer on behalf of Richard III:

Our Lord God, King of all Kings, by whose infinite goodness and eternal providence all things have been principally governed in this world, lighten your [Richard's] soul, and grant you grace to do as well in this matter, as in all other, that which may be

[13] 2Rous 62–63.
[14] *Christ Church Letters*, ed. J. B. Sheppard (Camden Society 2.19, London 1877) 45–46: Letter of Langton to the Prior of Christ Church, Canterbury, 1483.

according to his will and pleasure, and to the common and public weal of this land. So that after great clouds, troubles, storms, and tempests, the sun of justice and of grace may shine upon us, to the joy and comfort of all true-hearted Englishmen! [15]

Rous managed to alter one of the copies of the Warwick Roll after Richard's downfall,[16] and attacked him in his *Historia regum Angliae,* written after the birth of Princess Margaret in 1489 and before his own death in 1491. Because this history seems to have been used by Polydore Vergil (and perhaps by More), it may be well to mention the brief passages of interest which occur in it before the reigns of Richard III and Henry VII.

Rous seems to have been the first to apply to Richard II the biblical theme of putting violent hands upon the king anointed by God. But since he gives the account of death by enforced starvation, he says simply that those responsible for his death were unwilling to raise a hand against the anointed of the Lord, so that they starved him to death instead of killing him violently. This account is followed immediately by words of praise for Henry IV.[17]

Rous has great admiration for the Archbishop of York, St. Richard Scrope, as he calls him;[18] and after he was executed, it is said that Henry IV was never well, but was stricken with a white leprosy. And similarly it is said that his son and heir, Henry V, was afflicted with the same infirmity.[19]

It might be expected that Rous would go on to develop a theme of retribution on the house of Lancaster, but he does not do so, nor does he suggest that the crown was unlawfully possessed by these kings. He has great praise for Henry V, and though he does say he died by the hand of God in France, the

[15] *The Chronicles of the White Rose,* ed. J. A. Giles (London 1845) 274–277.

[16] See William Courthope, introduction to 2Rous.

[17] 3Rous 206: "Noluerunt mittere manum in unctum Domini; major [igitur] sibi poena fuit. Erat iste rex Henricus miles laudatissimus, Christianismo et paganismo peroptime probatus."

[18] See 1Rous 4 (Rous's earlier *Pageant of Richard Beauchamp, Earl of Warwick*) for the same designation of the archbishop.

[19] "Similiter et filius et heres suus futurus eadem, ut dicitur, infirmitate involutus est" (3Rous 207); he goes on to say that a multitude of miracles declared the glorious merits of the archbishop. We may also mention here that Rous takes the comet that appeared early in Henry IV's reign to signify the Glendower disturbances, and he proceeds to describe a stone that Glendower possessed that could render him invisible (206–207).

emphasis is no doubt upon the fact that he died a natural death and was not killed in battle.[20]

In treating of Henry VI, Rous describes his great sanctity, and states that this most holy man was vilely put to flight from the kingdom, and was finally imprisoned again and crowned with martyrdom, thus passing to the eternal fellowship of the elect of God; he was wonderfully illuminated with miracles and conquered all adversity by his patience, thereby leaving an example for all.[21]

Rous also speaks of the death of the two sons of Edward IV as martyrdom, and he goes on to indicate that Richard's origins portended the evil he would commit during his life — he was two years in his mother's womb, and was born with teeth and with hair down to his shoulders; he was born when Scorpio was in the ascendant, and he acted like a scorpion, mild in countenance, but with a sting in his tail. In describing his personal appearance, Rous says he was small of stature, with a flat or mutilated ("curta") face, and with the right shoulder higher than the left.[22]

After stating categorically that Richard poisoned Queen Anne, Rous says that what was most detestable of all, both to God and man, and to foreigners as well as to Englishmen, was his murder of the most holy King Henry VI by the hands of others, or, as many believe, by his own hand. And this murder was in fact the fulfillment of a prophecy that the Duke of Gloucester would kill Henry VI, and it is said that it was because of this prophecy that Humphrey, Duke of Gloucester, was put to death, just as George of Clarence lost his life because of another prophecy that found its fulfillment in Richard of Gloucester.[23]

[20] 3Rous 207, 210.

[21] 3Rous 210. Edward IV is described as a most victorious prince, whom Fortune cared for in all circumstances (210–211). Rous also cites an interesting ballade on the contrariness of Fortune, allegedly written by Anthony Woodville, Earl Rivers, before his execution under Richard III (213–214).

[22] 3Rous 215–216. In the pictures of 2Rous 17 and 63, Richard is drawn of normal height and appearance, and far from having a higher right shoulder, it is his left shoulder in both cases that appears slightly higher. In Armstrong's view, it is almost impossible that Mancini would have failed to mention Richard's deformity if it were obvious and a matter of common knowledge (Mancini 25–26).

[23] 3Rous 215: "Et quia erat quaedam prophetia, quod post E, id est, post Edwardum quartum, G regnaret, sub hoc ambiguo Georgius dux Clarenciae, medius amborum fratrum Edwardi et Ricardi regum, dux ob hoc Georgius peremptus est. Et alter G, scilicet Gloucestriae, usque prophetiam finiret praeservatus. Simili prophetia Humfridus, dux Gloucestriae, funditus peremptus dicebatur, nempe quod dux Gloucestriae ipsum [Henry VI] interficeret, et totum completum est in isto misero rege Ricardo tertio prius Gloucestriae duce." Rous here seems to connect Humphrey's death with the alleged plot of his wife,

8

Rous does admit that Richard III was praiseworthy for the buildings he erected,[24] but his only other praise for him is that he behaved like a noble knight in spite of his small body and weak strength, and defended himself illustriously to his last breath, crying out repeatedly that he was betrayed, and shouting, "Treason! Treason! Treason!" and so, "tasting the cup he had frequently given to others, he miserably ended his life." [25] Just before this, he compared the length of Richard's reign with that of the Antichrist who is to come.[26]

In addressing Henry VII, he gathers together various prophetic materials that perhaps are a provincial reflection of the more definite prophecies applied to the Tudor reign by other authors. He first points out that Henry is only the sixth Henry to rule Ireland, and that many prophecies are current that greatly honor such a king.[27] Furthermore, according to certain ancient prophecies of the highest respectability many praiseworthy things are to be done by such a one, as God knows.[28] "We know well," he says, "that God has now given you the crown of England, and we receive you as our king, since the more ancient ones have been removed from the world." [29] He

---

Eleanor Cobham, to effect Henry VI's death by witchcraft. Rous's chronology is quite fluid, and his account of Henry VI's death in the context in which it is told gives the impression that Richard killed him after Clarence's death and after he had become king.

Rous goes on to describe the translation of Henry VI's body to Windsor in the month of August, after Buckingham's execution, but there is no allusion to the fact that this event could not have taken place without Richard's approval. Rous says that the body was very fragrant, and that this odor could not have been caused by any spices that had been placed in his tomb, since his enemies and torturers had buried him without taking any such pains. Furthermore, the body was mostly incorrupt, and his face had its normal expression, except that it was a little more emaciated than usual. And immediately afterwards, miracles attested to the sanctity of the king, as is fully evident from the written reports there — presumably at Windsor (p. 217).

[24] 3Rous 215.

[25] 3Rous 218.

[26] He says that Richard reigned a little over three years, as will the Antichrist (cf. Rev. 11.2; 12.6; Dan. 12.7, 11–12), and in this Rous demonstrates once more his faulty chronology, since Richard reigned only a little over two years.

[27] These prophecies may have had some connection with the prophecy of Henry VI with regard to young Henry Richmond, which was first explicitly reported by Bernard André, as we shall see below.

[28] "De quodem sexto Hiberniae multa vaticinia currunt ad maximum honorem sonantia et multa laude digna sunt per quendam talem, Deus novit, fienda, secundum antiqua vaticinia non mediocria, sed in superlativo gradu maxima"; he adds, "et ad summum honorem cunctis futuro seculis memoranda," which could refer to the praiseworthy deeds, but more likely refers to the closer antecedent, the "vaticinia" (3Rous 219).

[29] "Tibi coronam Angliae bene novimus Deus nunc donavit. Te nostrum in regem accipimus, antiquioribus regibus mundo sublatis ad tuam nunc celsitudinem pervenimus." If Rous were referring to Henry VII's immediate predecessors, the

goes on to say that it is unknown what will be conferred on
Henry in the future, to the praise of God; but undoubtedly
there is reserved in the secret counsel of God, to be revealed at
his will in the time to come, the excellent things that their age
is constantly hoping for with the greatest avidity. The chief
pontiff and vicar of Christ, Pope Innocent VIII, conferred on
him, "in bonum omen," the sword and cap and other insignia,[30]
prophesying his future glory. God has bountifully blessed him
with children of both sexes. For from his loins has sprung a new
Prince of Wales, an illustrious Arthur, his firstborn son, who,
as future heir of England, "Deo ordinante," will undertake the
deeds of another great Arthur under divine providence.[31]

The Report of the Court Poets

Of the court poets discussed by James Gairdner in his *Memorials of King Henry the Seventh,* by far the most important is
the blind Augustinian friar, Bernard André of Toulouse, who
in his *Historia regis Henrici septimi* (written *ca.* 1500–1502) calls
himself poet laureate and historiographer royal. But the works
of two other poets, which for the most part precede in time those
of André, can be dealt with first.

In the *Epithalamium* on the marriage of Henry VII and
Elizabeth by Giovanni Gigli,[32] who afterwards became Bishop
of Worcester, Parliament is represented as proclaiming to Henry
that the kingdom came to him through the gift of God, and that
Richard placated the shades of his nephews by being sent to the
Stygian waters, to black Dis, the avenger of crimes. The realm
belongs to Henry by right of his uncle, Henry VI;[33] or if one

---

use of "antiquiores" would seem strained. Perhaps then he is alluding to the loss
of the kingdom by the Britons, which he treated on p. 65; and on pp. 218–219,
just before mentioning these prophecies, he stresses Henry's Welsh grandfather
and his own birthplace in Wales. We have already seen that the prophecies of
the coming Welsh rule were long in the air (see above, Chap. II at nn. 90–91).

[30] Referring to the "sword of justice" and "cap of maintenance" conferred on
Henry in 1489. See André 46–47.

[31] 3Rous 219.

[32] *Epithalamium de nuptijs serenissimj et clementissimj principis et dominj,
Domini Henrici Dei gratia Anglie et Francie regis et eius nominis septimj, et
serenissime Domine Elisabet, eius uxoris, regine, anno salutis M° cccc° lxxxvi°* per
Johannem de Giglis, British Museum MS. Harley 336, foll. 70–82. The excerpt
(foll. 73–74) printed by Gairdner (André lviii–lix) contains most of the material
of interest to our discussion.

[33] Of course, Henry's right had nothing to do with the fact that his father was
Henry VI's half brother, since it was the wrong half (Henry V's widow, Queen
Katherine, married Owen Tudor). His Lancastrian title stemmed from his mother,
who was granddaughter of John Beaufort, Earl of Somerset, son of John of

desires to trace the line from the forefathers of Brute's blood, Henry is equally able to lay just claim to the title. The members of Parliament pray for peace and an end of evils, and suggest that Henry achieve this by marrying the virgin heiress of the house of York. And if any presages of truth can influence pious hearts, a sure peace will follow.[34] The Parliamentarians go on to describe the holier time and the Golden Age that will result.[35] As the wedding took place, Gigli tells us, "the Father of the gods nodded approval of the solemn ceremonies from his lofty heavenly seat; wonderful to say, he made their two bodies one flesh, and sanctified and united their minds; the high heaven gave a sign." [36]

Gigli also wrote epigrams on the name of Arthur to celebrate the birth of Henry's first son, born late in 1486, and here the prophecy that the glorious King Arthur of old would come again is said to have been accomplished in this boy.[37]

A similar sentiment is also to be found in the *Suasoria laetitiae ad Angliam pro sublatis bellis civilibus et Arthuro principe nato epistola* of Pietro Carmeliano of Brescia, who had been in England since the time of Edward IV. But before looking at this poem, we may glance at something that Carmeliano wrote earlier, namely, a versified life of Saint Catherine of Alexandria. He first dedicated it to Bishop John Russell (the prelate whom we discussed in connection with the Croyland Chronicle) when Russell was acting as Edward V's chancellor in 1483;[38] but after

---

Gaunt and Catherine Swinford. His title was somewhat weakened because it was thought that when the Beauforts were legitimatized under Richard II, they were specifically excluded from the royal succession; but this exclusion was specified only in the patent confirming their legitimation in Henry IV's time.

[34] Si qua pias moueant mentes presagia ueri,/Pax nos certa manet (fol. 74).

[35] *Ibid.* In a letter to Innocent VIII dated 6 December 1485, Gigli says that "it is persistently asserted that Henry will marry Elizabeth, which everyone believes will be most beneficial for the realm. The king himself is considered a very prudent man, and also one of great clemency; everything seems designed for peace, as long as the minds of men remain constant. For nothing has ever been more injurious to this realm than ambition and insatiable greed, which is the mother of all infidelity and inconstancy; and if God has liberated us of it, the affairs of this kingdom will be tranquil" ("a qua si Deus nos liberavit, res regni hujus quietae erunt"). See *Materials for a History of the Reign of Henry VII*, ed. William Campbell (Rolls Series 60.1, London 1863) 198–199.

[36] Gigli, *Epith.* fol. 79:
Solempnesque modos diuum Pater annuit alta
Celorum sede; gemino mirabile dictu
Efficiens vnam sacrauit corpore carnem
Coniuxitque animas; signum dedit arduus ether.

[37] Given in Gairdner, André lx.

[38] Gonville and Caius College, Cambridge, MS. 196; see R. Weiss, *Humanism in England during the Fifteenth Century*, 2d ed. (Oxford 1957) 171.

Richard III's accession, he rededicated it and addressed himself to Robert Brackenbury, keeper of the Tower of London. He speaks of Richard in the highest terms:

If, in the first place, we consider religion, what prince is there in our time who is more religious? If justice, who do we think is to be preferred to him in the whole world? If we look for prudence in fostering peace and waging war, whom do we judge ever to be his equal? But if we regard wisdom and largeness and modesty of mind, behind whom shall we place our Richard? Indeed, what Christian emperor or prince can be found more liberal and munificent towards the well deserving? None, certainly, none. To whom are theft, robbery, pollution, adultery, manslaughter, usury, heresy, and other abominable crimes more hateful than to him? Obviously, to no one.[39]

In the "persuasive letter" that he addressed to England on the birth of Prince Arthur, Carmeliano shows himself to have been won over to the Tudor cause, and we hear no more words of praise for Richard. He portrays the marriage between Henry and Elizabeth, which supposedly united the rival factions of York and Lancaster, as literally having been made in heaven. For God became impatient of the internecine slaughter that was being committed in England, and called for a moderation of the madness. He summoned a meeting of the saints and addressed them, detailing the background of the strife, and asking their advice on how he could bring about a long-lasting peace.[40]

The saints modestly reply that they cannot hope to contribute anything to his omniscient grasp of the problem, but that if anyone were to offer advice, St. Henry VI is the best qualified, for he himself was a victim of the conflict.[41]

Henry says that the two branches of the royal family must be united, and that the opportunity for doing so is at hand; for after the death of Edward IV, his ferocious brother made away with his sons and took over the rule himself (Henry interjects: "He is the accursed one who, ready for any crime, likewise ran me through by thrusting his sword into my entrails"); as a result, no male heir survives, and the right rests with Elizabeth, Ed-

[39] Pietro Carmeliano, *Beatae Katerinae aegyptiae, Christi sponsae, vita,* Bodleian Library, Oxford, MS. Laud misc. 501, foll. 1v–2. The text of the entire dedicatory letter will be found in Appendix B below.
[40] P. Carmeliano, *Suasoria laetitiae,* British Museum Additional MS. 33,736, foll. 2–3v. The whole poem is reproduced in Appendix C below.
[41] *Ibid.* 3v–4.

ward's eldest daughter. As for the Lancastrian side, Henry himself and his son were killed, but God has saved Henry's nephew, the Earl of Richmond, from Edward's sword, and has strengthened him by dangers to endure still greater dangers. "If, therefore, supreme Father," Henry concludes, "you are concerned to bring a peace to the English that will never die, release my nephew Henry from prison in due time and command him to be armed and to seek his rights; let him return to his native kingdom and drive out the vicious tyrant and restore his fatherland. Let him take as his bride Edward IV's daughter Elizabeth, who possesses her father's title. Thus let one blood be made of two, and hereafter let one house seek the rule." [42]

God agrees to carry out Henry's suggestions to the letter, and to bring it about that the wicked tyrant who raised a sacrilegious hand against Henry will undergo the punishment he deserves for the crime. The divine plan is put into action immediately; Henry gathers an army, and God signals the time for the departure of his fleet with a flash of lightning.[43]

When word of Henry's arrival reaches Richard, he readies his forces, but in vain; "for who would think himself able to win a war against saints or the counsel of God?" [44]

Henry and Elizabeth willingly marry, and soon a child is born of these two royal lines, who is to be the salvation and eternal glory of the realm.[45] "Arthur, who has lain buried for so many centuries, has returned." [46] The poet bids England to give incense and praise to God for so great a gift, which will remove civil wars and bring concord to the whole earth.[47]

Friar Bernard André was Prince Arthur's tutor, a position he acquired after, and no doubt partly because of, writing a hundred poems in honor of his birth.[48] He refers to him, before his death, as Arthur II, ruler of the Welsh.[49] Even after Arthur's death, André continues the theme of his potential greatness, for it was evident, he says, that not only England but the whole world would have had reason to rejoice eternally over such a great pledge of love, if only the Fates had given him longer life on earth; but God, who rules all things, and in whose hands

---

[42] *Ibid.* 4–6.
[43] *Ibid.* 6v–7.
[44] *Ibid.* 8.
[45] *Ibid.* 10.
[46] *Ibid.* 10v.
[47] *Ibid.* 11.
[48] André 41.
[49] André 10.

are the scepters of kingdoms and the measures of the lives of kings, ordained otherwise for him.[50]

André begins his history of Henry VII by discussing his British ancestry, treating him as the legitimate successor, after a long lapse of time, of Cadwallader. Following the lead of Geoffrey of Monmouth, he describes Cadwallader as being guided by God when he left England and as dying in Rome after a holy life; and thereupon, he says, the sanctity of his life was verified by widespread miracles, and he was canonized by Pope Sergius and the "College of Cardinals." [51] But André strangely neglects to draw upon Geoffrey's account of Cadwallader's vision, with its prophecy of the Celtic recovery of the realm.

He closes his account of Henry's Celtic pedigree by saying that after a great length of time, Henry came by divine and human right in the wake of countless wars and internecine struggles to liberate the land from a most savage enemy, namely, Richard III, the cruel murderer of his two nephews. With the aid of the divine power and vengeance, Henry ended the tyrant's career and slew him as his deeds deserved, to the untold benefit of the country; and thereupon he began to reign himself.[52]

In discussing the state of England during the youth of Henry Richmond, André not only treats Henry VI as a saintly and perfect ruler, but as one whose peaceful rule was overthrown by the evil spirit, in the same way that he overthrew the ancient Britons by arousing the Saxons against them. In other words, the Yorkists are portrayed implicitly[53] as having no right whatsoever to the crown, but as seeking it through diabolical instigation; and we are to conclude that the country was saved from them only by the divine grace which was operative in the young Earl of Richmond from his earliest years, and whose consequent piety, especially as manifested by his devotion for the recitation of the divine office, was taken as a presage of his future probity and felicity.[54]

He goes on to tell of an incident that takes on great importance in later historical works. Henry VI one day was pre-

[50] André 39.
[51] André 9–10.
[52] André 10–11.
[53] André's views on this question become explicit a little later when he says that Edward was influenced by some unknown Fury to aspire to the tyranny of the realm, and began to pursue Henry with his hatred, at first clandestinely, and then openly. But God did not allow Henry to be deceived by him: "Sed Deus omnium speculator et aequissimus judex non passus est sanctum virum insidias latere" (p. 18).
[54] André 12–14.

paring to join the nobles of the realm at a banquet, and while his hands were being washed, young Henry Richmond was summoned to him, and the king predicted that one day he would take the rule of the realm upon himself and possess all as his own; accordingly, he advised him to flee the savage grasp of his enemies, and the boy was therefore secretly sent to France.[55] André comments that Richmond's flight was thus decreed by a divine oracle, through the holy king's command.

When treating of the death of Henry VI, André has many interesting comments concerning fate and divine providence. After observing that the snares of Edward were not concealed from Henry, because it was not permitted by God in his justice, he goes on to say that pallid Tisiphone (who, as a note in the manuscript informs us, is one of the Furies, the avenger of slaughter) provoked Edward and his allies into breaking their oaths to Henry. Civil war resulted, and destruction was prepared for the king. André then exclaims in wonder at the power of hidden fate, by which some are carried headlong to good, others to evil. Seneca has justly said that the Fates drag the unwilling man, but the willing man is simply led by them. As an example of the latter, André points to Richard of Gloucester, who was decreed to kill this innocent king, and who delighted in bloody deeds from his earliest youth.[56]

Here again we have an instance of the literary presentation of the supernatural or ultimate causes of events unfavorable to the author in terms of Furies and Fates; but André proceeds a little further on to deal with the problem in religious terms. He first addresses God somewhat after the fashion of an apostrophe to Fortune ("modo illum humilias, modo istum exaltas," etc.), except that he assumes, like the authors of similar passages in the Bible, that there is a just reason for all that God has ordained to happen; and now he asks him what it could have been about the realm of England that moved him from eternity to permit these evil men to rejoice unpunished in a time of great upheaval and turbulence. André objects that, by allowing a prolonged impunity to malefactors, he leads others into a state of stupefied doubt. For when they see every criminal obtain his wicked desires, they begin to wonder, and indeed to suspect that he has little concern for things here on earth. For the good and harmless are punished, and the evil become presumptuous. He

---

[55] André 14.
[56] André 18–19.

instances this just, pious, and innocent king who had always obeyed his commandments; yet he permitted the scepter of his realm to be torn from him by a man of evil ambition with no lawful claim whatever. The cruel death of such a good king who was so pleasing to God disturbed André, and yet because of this, his love of God brought him to him (to seek an answer). And he finally says it is God's pleasure that we should all come to him at last through a multitude of anxieties in this life. This is found to be the case with the saintly King Henry, who was falsely deposed from an earthly throne only to be crowned with a celestial diadem among supernal kings. Furthermore, those who tormented him are paying the penalties their crimes deserved.[57]

In the sentiments and prayers that André puts in the mouth of Henry VI, he stresses the benefits as well as the sufferings he has received from God, who makes the sun to rise on good men as well as evil, and the rain to fall on the just and unjust alike;[58] he has received all things willingly. He tells himself that if he bears his evils patiently, they will all redound to his merit; and that the only evil death is the one that follows death, not the one that is preceded by a good life.[59]

Again, we notice that there is no doubt about Henry's right to the crown, and no sign of any of the other Yorkist charges against the Lancastrian dynasty. Henry thanks God for his royal parents, the victories of his father, and his most virtuous queen, Margaret.

André then proceeds to detail the evils that followed upon Henry's death. It is not specifically stated that these events are to be considered providential acts of retribution, but perhaps it is implied, at least in those he discusses first. He begins by pointing out that in spite of the fact that Edward IV was the most magnificent and powerful of kings, yet he was punished in his children, who were murdered by the brother to whom he committed them for protection. And even while he lived he was in constant fear that Henry Richmond would succeed him. In explanation of this, André says only that Edward was terrified by the prophetic testimonies of certain persons, and perhaps he is referring to the Welsh forecasts of Celtic recovery applied

[57] André 20–21. Since André is using the present tense ("luunt") of dead malefactors, we are to presume he is speaking of the punishments of purgatory or hell.
[58] Cf. Matt. 5.45.
[59] André 21–23.

to Henry even at this early date. In summing up Edward's failure to capture Richmond, Friar Bernard says that the wiles of mortal men have never prevailed against God; and on this account the king was finally seized by ill health and brought to his end.[60]

It may be wrong for us to stress a supernatural connection between the murder of Henry VI and Edward's failure to capture Richmond, or between Edward's failure and his death. It is clear that Richmond was providentially protected, but since no providential punishment is mentioned at this point for Richard, the actual perpetrator of Henry's murder, it may be that André's purpose here is simply to describe the natural effects or chronological sequels of the murder.

While Richard is progressing with his sinister plots in England, we are shown Richmond's movements abroad and his preparations for return. There is much piety involved in Richmond's words and actions, as we might well imagine, and in his prayer and speech before his invasion of England, he draws on many of the themes we have seen before in righteously portrayed usurpers or invaders; he comes with pure intentions, by God's command, to liberate the country, and to gain his rights; God has helped him in the past, and victory does not depend on numbers but on trust in God, as with God's people in the Bible. He knows that God will give him sufficient power if his claim is valid, and if not, he prays him to direct his efforts to something in keeping with his will. He tells his men that the time is now approaching when God, the just judge, will punish Richard through his hand, and though he is personally disinclined to war, yet it is better to obey God's command than to spend the rest of his life in exile. He directs the priests to pray continually until success is granted. And on landing he warns his men to do no plundering; if they follow his instructions God will be propitious to them, "since the unlawful usurper does not long rejoice in the goods of others." [61]

When Richard learned of Henry's landing to claim the rights his blood entitled him to both on his father's and his mother's side, he was told also of Henry's assertion that the time of

---

[60] "Verum nec praevaluit unquam in Deum mortalis astutia; quare posthaec adversa valetudine correptus obiit" (André 23).

[61] André 25–31. The last sentence referred to ("Si ita feceritis Deus erit nobis propitius, quippe alienis diu non gaudet illicitus usurpator") sounds like a variation on the proverb of third-generation loss of ill-gotten goods (see above, Chap. II at n. 18).

vengeance against Richard had arrived, and that God avenged with slow step, but at length his punishment descended all the heavier upon those defiled with guilt. André then gives the tyrant's raging speech ("tyranni in suos furibunda oratio"), in which he tells his men to kill Richmond without any respect for his blood or nobility, or better yet, to capture him so that Richard himself might slay him with new and unheard-of tortures. As for the battle of Bosworth, André leaves a blank, to be filled in when he is better informed. He makes one of his frequent apologies for having to rely solely on the oral testimony of others because of his blindness.[62]

But the victory at any rate was given to Richmond through the divine disposition, and the tyrant slain as he deserved. The churchmen who were present poured out their prayers of thanks to God, and Henry himself prayed at length, thanking not only God but the Blessed Virgin as well, and the other saints by whose intercession he won the battle; and he begged them to pray to God that his succeeding fortune might correspond to such felicitous beginnings.[63]

When he comes to describe Princess Elizabeth, André stresses her great piety from earliest childhood, and gives her prayer of thanks to God for Henry's victory. In a maidenly circumlocution, she told him she would like to marry Henry, and that she placed her trust in him to effect it. And God heard and answered her prayer, we are told, and permitted the prince's heart to be moved to love her.[64]

In treating of the risings of Lambert Simnel and John de la Pole (Richard III's heir) and Perkin Warbeck, as well as of the king's invasion of France, André plays upon the themes that we became familiar with in the Lancastrian chroniclers when dealing with Henry IV and Henry V. Divine aid is invoked,

---

[62] André 31–32.

[63] André 33–34. On Henry's reception into London, the blind André, who was present, remarks that "you might have heard the voices of all, praising and blessing the angelic countenance of the prince, and extolling the royal name of Henry to the stars" (p. 36). Compare this with the Croyland chronicler's statement that the people began to regard Henry as an angel sent from God (above, 67). Compare also the illustration at the beginning of Carmeliano's *Suasoria epistola*, showing two angels in the midst of red and white roses holding up the royal coat of arms (see Appendix C). The normal supporters of Henry's shield are the silver greyhound and the red dragon, which in this illumination are pictured below and to the right of the shield, respectively. The heraldic device of supporters was introduced during the time of Richard II, and it is for this king's shield alone, of all the monarchs preceding Henry VII, that angels fulfill the function.

[64] André 37–38.

received, and gratefully acknowledged in detail that need not be pursued here. (There is even an incidence of false prophecies concerning the mission of Perkin Warbeck.)[65] There are similar interpretations of the whole of Henry VII's career up to 1497 in a poem called *Les douze triomphes de Henry VII,* which was probably written by André,[66] and neither in this nor in his history nor in the two volumes of his annals that have survived (1504–05, 1507–08)[67] is there any indication of disaffection from the king on Andre's part (in contrast to the chroniclers under Henry IV, when the latter executed Archbishop Scrope). We have therefore in André and his fellow poets the unadulterated party line of the first Tudor monarch, together with all the "mythology" that it involved. In sum, it pictured the Lancastrian line as divinely vindicated and restored in the person of Henry VII, and the Yorkist usurpation and tyranny providentially punished, but with its royal pretensions appeased (by way of largesse), in having its heiress joined in marriage to the inheritor of the Lancastrian prerogatives, who by a startling divine coincidence also inherited the ancient Celtic rights to the throne.

[65] André 66.
[66] André 133–153 (trans. pp. 307–327).
[67] André 79–130.

Two

The
Syntheses
of the
Sixteenth-Century
Prose
Chroniclers

IV

Polydore Vergil

To obtain an ordered view of the main directions of sixteenth-century interpretations of the events of the previous century, we shall concentrate on the accounts of Vergil, Hall, and Holinshed, and draw on other sources only when they have something to contribute to our knowledge of these central works.

The first important synthesizer of fifteenth-century English history in the sixteenth century was Polydoro Vergilio of Urbino, a secular priest who came to England in 1502. Soon after his arrival he began to collect materials at the request of Henry VII for a complete history of England. He did not finish writing his history until four years after Henry's death, in 1513, and it was only after another twenty-one years, in 1534, that he finally published it, after having subjected it to massive revision. This first printed version was employed by Grafton and Hall for fifteenth-century material, and consequently was the version that exerted influence on later English historiography. But in order to observe the development of Vergil's thought and to assess his opinions, we shall refer at pertinent junctures not only to this first edition, but to the manuscript and also to the second edition of 1546, which contains significant variations from the 1534 text. It will furthermore be possible at times to discern layers of alteration in the manuscript itself, in terms of additions and deletions.

In our survey of the earlier sources, we noticed that the providential patterns tended to repeat themselves in accordance with the political alignment of the authors. Accordingly, we found that the establishment of each of the three royal houses that reigned in England in the fifteenth century, those of Lancaster, York, and Tudor, gave rise to a corresponding "myth." We have used the term "myth" to refer especially to the supernatural causation alleged to be behind specific visible events; such allegations are largely founded upon pious conjecture (and, we might add, rash judgment and libel) concerning the moral standing of prominent figures, and the consequent activity in their behalf or in opposition to them that supernal or infernal powers are assumed to initiate. Conjectures of this kind are usually elevated to the rank of the categorical as a result of the authors' conviction of the righteousness of the causes they support.

We have also seen a tendency in many authors to neglect the earlier portions of their history, which have no immediate or at least a less immediate bearing on the present situation, and to absorb the providential interpretations of former generations either unchanged or imperfectly modified, even when this involves a contradiction to the world-views that the authors are creating.

Polydore Vergil as a foreigner enjoyed the position of a man who was not committed to any partisan view of English history by reason of family ties or local patriotism, and he could therefore more easily bring himself to call into question traditions of dubious historicity, such as those of Brute and Arthur (thereby arousing, of course, the great wrath of the English antiquarians who had a native affection for such stories).[1] But since Vergil lived under the patronage of the Tudor monarchs, like the court poets of Henry VII's early reign, he would have had at least the occasion to be motivated by considerations of prudence, gratitude, or favor-seeking with regard to those particular elements of English history which would be of vital concern to Henry and his successor; and we shall of course have to weigh this possibility when discussing Vergil's treatment of pertinent events. But our survey of the earlier Tudor writers should help to guide us in forming our estimate of precisely what events and interpretations are to be considered peculiarly Tudor or of important concern to the mythological foundations of the house of Tudor.

Vergil stresses heavily the exemplary aspect of history, and frequently draws morals of universal application from events in England; but these lessons in the original (manuscript) version of his work are mostly ethical, and his explicitly providential observations are for the most part afterthoughts inserted marginally into the manuscript or added to the first or second edition.

[1] See Sir Henry Ellis, 2PVt xx–xxviii.

Moreover, Vergil was not a slavish copyist of the annalists who preceded him, unlike many of those who followed him; and as a result a great many of his providential reflections are original with him, in content as well as in style. The opinions he does take over are in general given a reportorial character, and even when they are his own or adopted as his own, they are frequently of a hypothetical rather than categorical nature.

Vergil accepts some aspects of the Lancastrian and Yorkist points of view, as well as portions of the Tudor position, and thus he modifies to some extent the Tudor picture of history that was presented to Henry VII's view by André and his fellow writers at court. For instance, Vergil upholds the prior claim of the Yorkists to the throne throughout his history, beginning with the declaration of the Earl of March as Richard II's heir in 1386, at which point he indicates that the present monarch, Henry VIII, has his claim through his mother, Elizabeth of York, and not through the Lancastrian (or Welsh) claims of his father, Henry Tudor.[2]

The Lancastrian Usurpation

Vergil's treatment of Richard II and Henry Bolingbroke remains almost entirely on the natural or ethical level. For instance, he takes Richard to task for his foolishness in choosing and following unworthy advisers, but he does not believe that what he did was worthy of the fate he received; for if he did anything wrong it was rather through youthful error than from ingrained malice, and the cause of his overthrow is to be attributed in large measure to the fickleness of the people, who deserted Richard and ran to Bolingbroke's support; and Bolingbroke himself perhaps had never even dreamed of taking the crown upon himself before this time. This consideration is offered as a great lesson to rulers, to be aware of and take precautions against the tendency of all mortals to oppose present conditions in the hope of better ones to come.[3] And when Richard was starved to death by Henry's order at the time of the rising of the earls, Vergil remarks that even though Richard was innocent of their con-

[2] oPV 107–108v; 1PV 406–407; 2PV 1046–1048. Vergil believes that it was the elder Edmund Mortimer, husband of Philippa, who was declared heir, and not his son Roger. Roger in turn passed on his right to his son Edmund upon his death in 1398; see above, Chap. I, n. 89.

[3] 1PV 419–420; 2PV 1079.

spiracy, yet he received an end similar to theirs, which was in fact the fruit of their evil pleasures.[4]

It is interesting to note that Vergil is not particularly harsh with Henry IV, either for his deposing of Richard, his taking the royal leadership upon himself, or finally for his doing away with Richard. There is certainly no word of the providential punishment of his deeds in the difficulties he had in keeping his realm and quelling rebels. Far from using the incident of the execution of Archbishop Scrope as an occasion for this sort of reflection, as many previous chroniclers had done, he simply alludes to the expeditious way in which Henry put down the revolution; and furthermore he specifies as Scrope's motive the desire to avenge the death of his brother, William Scrope, whom Henry had put to death as one of Richard's evil counselors; and in his eagerness to achieve this purpose, he says, the archbishop imprudently let news of his movements get to Henry.[5]

The over-all lesson taught by Richard's misfortune is that such falls happen most often to those princes who, while they are standing, believe no downfall is to be feared.[6] The fact that Henry IV was chosen over Roger Mortimer (who Vergil believes was still alive at the time) is just another example of what often occurs in such instances where might equals right ("vis jus vicit").[7] As for the rebellions against Henry, it is characteristic of human nature that many of the nobility should come to pity Richard after he was cast into so many evils, and to envy Henry, suddenly risen to such a height.[8] And, as is usual with the common people, who had hated Richard when he was alive, they desired him when he was dead, and there was much cursing and vilifying of Henry, which led, among other things, to the condemnation and execution of a number of Franciscan friars.[9]

When Vergil comes to the end of Henry's reign, he says that once the king was freed from the "civil war," in which it was shameful and degrading for Christians always to be involved,[10]

---

[4] 1PV 426; 2PV 1095.

[5] 1PV 429; 2PV 1104; cf. 0PV 126v, where he says that he read in an old codex of annals that the archbishop was brother of William Scrope, the treasurer, whom Henry beheaded, and therefore the archbishop and relatives of Thomas Mowbray gathered an army to avenge former wrongs. Actually, William Scrope was the archbishop's second cousin.

[6] 1PV 423; 2PV 1088; cf, 0PV 121v–122.

[7] 1PV 423–424; 2PV 1089–1090. (Cf. 0Pv 122v, where the moral is not drawn.)

[8] 0PV 121v; 1PV 422–423; 2PV 1087.

[9] 0PV 124v; 1PV 427; 2PV 1097–1098.

[10] The civil war here doubtless refers to the French-English conflicts, which have been the subject of discussion immediately preceding this passage; it is

and remembering that man had no more ancient duty than to direct all his efforts to the fulfillment of justice and to the benefit of mankind, he resolved upon several things for the good government of England, for taking up the war against the common enemy of Christianity, and finally for recovering Jerusalem, for which he was already preparing a fleet; but in the midst of all these plans and preparations he chanced to fall ill of an incurable ailment, of which he died at Westminster.[11]

It should be noted that there is no mention of any repentance on Henry's part for usurping the realm, nor indeed any mention at all of the fact that Henry was holding on to stolen property. This is all the more significant when we consider that Vergil was drawing upon Monstrelet constantly at this time;[12] and yet he does not cite the conversation which that author gives between Henry IV and Prince Henry, and which found its way into Hall and Shakespeare. Perhaps Vergil rejected its historicity for the same reason that he rejected Froissart's version of Richard's death, namely, that he was not likely to have had firsthand information on this subject.[13]

In the printed editions, Vergil does add as a sort of after-thought to the mention of Henry V's reburial of Richard that "Henry did it, I believe, for the purpose of expiating the faith that his father gave to Richard and afterwards violated." [14] This giving and breaking of faith most probably refers to Richard's request that he be allowed to live as a private citizen; although Vergil does not say that Henry gave his word to this, he does say that Richard was deprived not only of his majesty but of his liberty and his life by the "perfidia" of his enemies.[15]

Vergil may have been inspired to make the remark about

obvious from the context (especially in the MS) that Vergil is speaking more in terms of the City of God than in national terms, and that accordingly a war between Christian nations would be a civil war when compared to the war against the infidel.

[11] 1PV 433; 2PV 1112–1113; cf. oPV 129v, which lacks the phrase about the good government of England that appears in the editions; but this phrase in no way implies that Henry was preparing his crusade in order to prevent internal opposition in England. The MS does state at the very end of the chapter on Henry IV that after the civil wars and the various betrayals of his subjects, Henry showed himself a good ruler (fol. 130).

[12] Vergil often cites him by name (Engarranus) in the MS: e.g., foll. 128, 129v, 131v.

[13] oPV 120v (marginal addition); in 1–2PV the reference to Froissart is omitted, but his opinion is even more emphatically dissociated from Vergil's own view. Vergil's general attitude toward Richard and Henry, however, resembles that of Froissart in many respects.

[14] 1PV 423; 2PV 1088 (lacking in oPV 122).

[15] 1PV 423; 2PV 1087 (oPV 121rv reads "iniuria").

Henry V's motive in reburying by the similar remark in the Croyland Chronicle, which Vergil apparently read after making the first draft of his manuscript.[16] If this is so, it is interesting to note that whereas the prior of Croyland and Vergil both exculpate Henry V from the guilt of Richard's imprisonment and death (and possibly Vergil also intends to second the prior in dissociating Henry from Richard's dethronement as well), Vergil is aware of the Earl of Cambridge's family ties, and he makes a conjecture as to the principal motive of the Cambridge plot, namely, the restoration of the legitimate line to the throne. The story of the French bribe was invented by Cambridge, Vergil believes, to prevent Henry from lashing out against his children. And in the first edition, he adds the reflection that if Henry had cast his eye back upon the fire that was licking at his house, he would have seen its walls burning with a flame that would eventually destroy the whole of it; and he might have extinguished it then and there at its beginning, if he had realized Cambridge's intentions. And instead of his own manuscript lecture against rulers of state who, like Cambridge, are corrupted and commit treachery,[17] Vergil prints a speech of Henry to his men directed at staving off further treachery by appealing to their support of his campaign to avenge their ancestors in France; "however," he said, "if you do not wish it so, you will eventually suffer for it in every way, God so willing it." [18]

Far from condemning Henry V in any way for his possession of the throne and his intention of keeping it from the true or

[16] Although this point will be of more importance later, it may be well to present the evidence for it here. The incidents that are peculiar to the Croyland continuations and Vergil are usually treated in marginal or extrapaginal inserts in the later books of Vergil's MS. This is not so with the passage cited above, but if Croy 364 was an influence upon it, it was most likely added in a revision of the book on Richard II made on another copy of his history, after 1513, perhaps during the rewriting that Denys Hay places about 1521–1524 (PVh xvi). Later in the MS, however, Vergil marginally adduces and refutes the Croyland assertion that Warwick defected from Edward because he was angered over Edward's alliance with Burgundy (Croy 457; oPV 191v). Similar is the rejection of the "fama" that Doctor Shaw charged in his sermon that Edward's children were bastards (Croy 489; oPV 219v). And fol. 233 of the MS is a later insert dealing with Richard's dream before Bosworth, related in the terms of Croy 503. Furthermore, a marginal note on fol. 228v and an additional page (fol. 240) discuss the reconciliation of Queen Elizabeth with Richard (cf. Croy 496). One later addition, which appears in the first edition, may also have been influenced by Croyland; namely, the notion that Edward was punished in his children (1PV 517; cf. Croy 483; see above, Chap. II at n. 103). See also below at n. 47.

[17] oPV 132v.

[18] "Sin nolueritis, illud vobis modis omnibus aliquando fraudi erit, ita volente Deo" (1PV 436–437; 2PV 1122–1125). Vergil was no doubt following Monstrelet for his treatment of this episode (see above, Chap. I at n. 101).

closer claimant, therefore, Vergil praises Henry unequivocally in all his actions. His youth had been for the most part full of lasciviousness and insolence,[19] but warned perhaps by the sad examples of Edward II and Richard II, he put aside his companions, the authors of his evil pleasures, and selected good counselors; and since he intended to do many great deeds, while realizing that all our affairs are governed by God, and that human efforts are of no avail in the face of celestial power, he determined in his piety to build two religious houses, which he called Bethlehem and Sion, "in order that he might perpetuate in his realm the memory of that holy land whence our salvation proceeded." [20]

In his negotiations with the French, Henry was careful that no laws or rights should be violated,[21] and his minature expedition against the Lollards on behalf of the faith of Christ could without doubt be taken as a forecast of the victory which he won afterwards in France.[22] In his manuscript account he adds a parenthetical "ut placuit Deo" concerning Henry's knowledge of the Lollard plot. The fact that Vergil omitted this phrase while unquestionably retaining the sentiment in the printed texts would suggest that the presence or absence of such phrases is often simply a question of style.

Vergil gives a favorable view of Henry's French campaigns throughout, but when he comes upon the report of the small number of Englishmen slain at Agincourt, he becomes more critical. In the manuscript, he first reported that "about four hundred" ("quadringenti fere") English were killed along with the Duke of York. But then he crossed out this figure (which he got from Gaguin) and wrote in the margin, "scarcely one hundred," adding that this report would be strange if it were not done by divine intervention,[23] apparently allowing for the possibility or perhaps even the probability of such an explanation. But in the other margin he adds that some French writers set the figure of English fatalities at five hundred, and others at six hundred. And in the printed editions he says that the English figure is acceptable only if we believe those who write miracles; as for himself, he willingly aligns himself with the French

[19] The MS in contrast says Henry had shown good hope from the earliest age (fol. 130v).

[20] 1PV 433–434; 2PV 1115–1118; cf. oPV 130v.

[21] 1PV 435; 2PV 1118; cf. oPV 131.

[22] 1PV 436; 2PV 1122; cf. oPV 132rv.

[23] oPV 137.

estimates, since it is highly likely that in a strenuous battle that lasted three hours, the English as well as the French would receive many wounds. He records Henry's gratitude to God and to Saints Crispin and Crispinian for the victory, as in his original version, but he omits his manuscript moral that God thus aids those who fight with right on their side, and those who fight with a sure faith in the divine majesty.[24] He retains that part of Henry's speech before the battle encouraging his men to trust in God, who does not favor pact-breakers like the French, nor those who retain possession of what rightfully belongs to others.[25] This reflection on Henry's part is apt to strike the reader as highly ironic, but it is clear that Vergil is unconscious of the irony, for, as has been mentioned above, Vergil never treats Henry as a wrongful possessor of the crown, in spite of the fact that he discusses those who had a prior claim to it.

In describing the first operation of Henry's second French invasion of 1417, the siege of Caen, Vergil notes that after winning the town proper, Henry entered the local church and thanked God, as was his custom;[26] but later on, with reference to his capture of the citadel of the town, he adds an incident, which, as he tells us in the manuscript, he found in a biography of Henry, and which he does not think should be omitted.[27] Henry saw a cross shining in the air over his troops, a sign of his victory. Vergil adds that experience shows that divine aid is wont to be present to those who pray as they should and who wage just wars.[28]

[24] oPV 137rv; 1PV 441; 2PV 1135. Vergil also omits a MS sentiment of this tenor before the battle of Agincourt, specifically emphasizing Henry's trust in God (oPV 133v), as well as the moral attached to the pyx-stealer's punishment, that it was befitting for a warring prince to act in this way, and to seek above all the grace of God (oPV 134; cf. 1PV 439; 2PV 1128). But he does preserve for later chroniclers his declaration of Henry's determination to await what God sends him, and to fight it if it is his will (oPV 134v; 1PV 439; 2PV 1128–1129; cf. PsElmham 55).

[25] oPV 135; 1PV 440; 2PV 1131. In giving Henry's reasons for taking heart in spite of the large numbers, however, Vergil does omit the MS sentiment that a victory would be ascribed first to God, then to their own prowess. In print, Henry says simply that if they win it will be assigned to their own prowess.

[26] oPV 140v; 1PV 445; 2PV 1144.

[27] "In quodam Commentario uitae huius regis reperi quod praetereundum non puto." In the later versions, as usual, he omits the specific references to his source and says only "dicitur" and "ferunt." The incident of Henry's thanksgiving to God in church appears in TLTrans 91, PsElmham 112, and Gesta 114 (continuation); and the miraculous or quasi-miraculous apparition occurs at TLTrans 94 and PsElmham 114. The cross described resembles that seen over the army of Charles VII during the siege of Bayonne in 1451, where the miracle is alleged in favor of the French ("Mons" 2.198; CdeNorm 176).

[28] oPV 141; 1PV 445; 2PV 1145.

The Fall of the House of Lancaster

Henry V died as he had lived, in an extremely edifying fashion, and Vergil praises him as the unique glory of his time and the light of his country, whom no one could excel.[29] But when speaking of the death of Charles VI of France later in the same year, he says in his published texts that thereupon great changes occurred for the better in France (that is, everyone united behind the Dauphin), as if God was solicitous for their conservation.[30] This sentiment seems slightly strange when we remember his previous asseverations of the justice of the English effort in France. But he continues to speak in this new strain later when telling of the numerous towns that defected back to the French in order to regain their liberty, and of their confidence that God would deliver France from its troubles. For, Vergil says, God is pleased by prayers and wont to relieve the needs of the afflicted.[31]

It is evident from these remarks that Vergil at least did not consider England's loss of its Continental possessions the catastrophe that most Englishmen felt it to be. Another evidence of this is his admiring view of Joan of Arc.[32] Accordingly, he had no preconceptions against Henry VI's queen, Margaret of Anjou, from a nationalistic point of view, and his treatment of her is in general encomiastic.

Vergil did some reflecting on the fate of Henry VI and the house of Lancaster (and on that of the house of York) between the time he wrote his manuscript and when he finally issued his first edition, and again before 1546, the date of his second edition. In general the number of providential interpretations increases throughout his work, but not all of these interpretations have an important bearing on our main interests, even when it is a prominent figure like the Duke of Suffolk who is visited with divine retribution. It is fitting to believe this was the reason for his death, Vergil says, for among his other crimes he is said to have machinated the death of Humphrey of Gloucester, so that in this way the innocent blood of the one was avenged by the guilty blood of the other.[33]

[29] oPV 145v–146v; 1PV 453; 2PV 1164–1166.
[30] 1PV 454; 2PVt 2.
[31] 1PV 466; 2PVt 29.
[32] oPV 161v–162; 1PV 470; 2PVt 37–39.
[33] 1PV 491; 2PVt 83.

In the manuscript, Henry's fall is first characterized in terms of fortune and fate. When he was crowned king in his eighth year at Westminster in 1429, Vergil says that Fortune began by smiling on him, but his felicity did not last long. It gradually changed into calamity, which eventually compelled him to undergo a cruel fate, and the English people to suffer great oppression.[34] Later he says of Somerset's valiant but futile attempts to stop the Duke of York's schemes against Henry, that the necessity of fate could not be interrupted by any human efforts.[35] This expression is retained in the printed editions, along with the unfavorable view of York, whose hypocrisy is delineated even more clearly.

When Henry was disinherited by Parliament in favor of York in 1460, Vergil speaks of Henry in terms not of providential punishment but of providential discipline and reward. "It so pleased God," he says, "that the holy man Henry, who was most patient in bearing so many calamities, should because of them be deprived of an earthly realm, and soon enjoy a celestial one." The first edition adds to this that "a good man can never but be blessed, though he suffer a thousand afflictions." [36] All three versions also add the belief that the disinheritance was portended by a prodigy, for a little while before when Henry was sitting in state in Parliament, the crown fell from his head to the floor. This seems to be a variant of the prodigy recorded in the *Brut*.[37]

In accord with his usual practice in the printed editions, Vergil dissociates himself from interpretations of prodigies — he says here that the belief was current "apud vulgus." By the time he was ready to publish his work, he had come to discount the importance of unusual occurrences (not to be confused with miraculous signs of God's favor, like the cross in the sky seen by Henry V), and he includes a general repudiation of belief in prediction-phenomena early in his work.[38]

Already in the manuscript there is noticeable the theme of reparation in connection with Henry's sufferings. In the eulogy he gives the king after his murder in the Tower, Vergil says that he declared openly that he was oppressed with so many sufferings partly because of his own sins and partly because of

[34] oPV 155.
[35] oPV 180v; 1PV 494; 2PVt 89.
[36] oPV 188; 1PV 503; 2PVt 108 (cf. André, above, Chap. III at n. 57).
[37] Above, Chap. II, n. 55.
[38] 1PV 34; 2PVt 1.70–71.

the sins of his ancestors.[39] This, of course, is said in praise of Henry, and with no indication on Vergil's part that he thought Henry deserving of punishment in any way, though he no doubt would have agreed that Henry's merits were more than sufficient to atone for the sins of his ancestors, let alone for his own impeccable life. Furthermore, there is no indication that Vergil at this time had in mind either specifically or inclusively Henry IV's usurpation of the throne. He is simply drawing what seems to be an authentic picture of the king's humble attitude, something of which can be seen in one of Henry's own prayers, published in 1510 (when Vergil was working on the first version of his history) by John Blakman in his devotional biography of the king.[40]

When treating of Henry's restoration in 1470, Vergil says that he was brought back only to be ousted again after a few months, and he gives his own view of the principal reason for this ("credendum imprimis est"), namely, that the holy man completely minimized the importance of his kingdom. He devoted all his efforts to attaining the celestial kingdom by means of his pious works, and considered this earthly one as of little value.[41]

In the first edition Vergil expands upon this reason, saying that the command of a nation rarely follows after a person who flees from it. But he represents this reason now not as his own opinion, but as the opinion of many persons at that time ("jam tum multorum ferebat opinio"). He adds that Henry's enemies gave another reason, namely, that he was stupid, and a man of

---

[39] oPV 206; cf. 1PV 525 and 2PVt 156–157, where the same sentiments are slightly expanded. Earlier, the remark of oPV 173v–174 that Henry bore all human vicissitudes patiently is expanded in 1PV 485 and 2PVt 70–71 to include the idea that he took all afflictions in such good part that it was as if he had justly deserved them in punishment for some offense.

[40] Henry's prayer reads as follows: "O Lord Jesu Christ, who didst create me, redeem me, and foreordain me unto that which now I am, thou knowest what thou wilt do with me; deal with me according to thy most compassionate will. I know and confess in sincerity that in thy hand all things are set, and there is none that can withstand thee; thou art Lord of all. Thou therefore, God almighty, compassionate and pitiful, in whose power are all realms and lordships, and unto whom all our thoughts, words, and works, such as have been, are, and shall be, are continually open and known, who only hast wisdom and knowledge incomprehensible, thou knowest, Lord, what is profitable for me, poor sinner; be it so done with me as pleaseth thee and as seemeth good in the eyes of thy divine majesty. Receive, O compassionate Father and merciful God almighty, the prayer of me thy most unworthy servant; and let my supplications, which I offer before thee and thy saints, come unto the ears of thy mercy. Amen." — Blakman 24.

[41] oPV 197. Cf. Blakman 42.

no experience or ability. Thus it is, Vergil says, that whoever contemns what the mob admire is regarded as insane, when the truth of the matter is that their wisdom is foolishness in God's eyes.[42] "However," Vergil goes on to say, "there were certain others who believed that this misfortune should be ascribed to the divine justice, because the realm that had been acquired through force by Henry IV, this Henry's grandfather, could not be possessed overlong [perdiu] by that family, and so the sin of the grandfather redounded upon the grandchildren." [43]

It is in this form that Vergil's comments on the house of Lancaster were passed on to Hall. But it is interesting to note that all three of these opinions as to the family's or Henry's downfall were omitted in the third version, that is, the second edition of 1546; but the third reason given is placed in adapted form after the discussion of Edward IV's exceedingly fortunate encounters with his enemies in recovering the throne in 1471. In the first edition, Vergil merely added to this the notion that in all things, and in war especially, everything depends on good fortune, as the *vulgus* phrases it. But in the second edition, he goes on to say that perhaps it came out this way because of the misfortune of the house of Lancaster, which wise men at that time believed should be ascribed to divine justice, etc. (the sentence is completed as above, with the sin of the grandfather coming down upon the grandchildren).[44]

Vergil at this point obviously admits the possibility of this opinion and approves of those who formulated it, and perhaps it may be inferred from this that when he included it in the first edition he was similarly admitting the possibility, or, it may be, even the likelihood of this opinion. In support of this surmise, perhaps, is an observation that Vergil added to the first edition when speaking of the escape of Edward IV from Warwick's hands in 1470. "This was part of the infelicity of King

---

[42] "Cum revera talis sapientia, velut vulgo dicitur, stultitia apud Deum sit." Cf. 1 Cor. 3.19: "Sapientia enim hujus mundi stultitia est apud Deum."

[43] 1PV 514–515. Vergil may be referring to the generally Yorkist application to the house of Lancaster of the proverb concerning ill-gotten gains not remaining with the third generation (see above, Chap. II at n. 12). The concept is perhaps also reminiscent of Exod. 34.7, which Vergil adds to the 1546 edition (though in the wording of Num. 14.18) with reference to Egbert and his son Lothar (2PVt 1.135). In this instance, the son suffers because of the father's sin; but in the case of Henry and his son, the sin of the father is visited literally upon the third and fourth generations. We should note too that the question of the restoration of the realm to its rightful owners is not mentioned explicitly.

[44] 2PV 1347–1348 (2PVt 154); cf. oPV 205; 1PV 524.

Henry," he says, "since it can surely be seen from this that the final fate of his house had arrived, which could not be averted by any human plans or resources, so that perhaps it was the will of God." [45] However, at this point Vergil does not assign a reason for the supposed providential fall of Lancaster. He goes on to say that Warwick and his allies had staked everything on Henry's restoration, and they knew that this could not really be effected so long as Edward was alive; yet they let him slip from their grasp. He draws a Comines-like moral from this, namely, that when our affairs are going to come to nothing, our ability to think straight is taken away from us, at one time by fear, at another by foolishness or anxiety. The manuscript simply states that when Warwick heard of Edward's escape, he was dumfounded. He thought it was as if God were manifestly opposing his efforts; but since he possessed a high spirit, he prepared for war once more.[46] We may recall that the Croyland account speaks of Edward's escape as almost miraculous, and discusses subsequent events in terms of the incomprehensibility of God's ways.[47]

Vergil's final view of Henry is certainly not one of a man punished by God. He seems to have felt, eventually at any rate (as we have seen), that it was necessary for the realm to go out of his family's hands because it was wrongly acquired, though through no fault of anyone then alive. When he comes to sum up Henry's character after his murder, he says that, because of the spirit of reparation in which Henry received his afflictions, "he did not greatly dwell on or grieve over the dignity, the honors, the state of life, the son, or the friends he had lost; but when there was anything that offended God, that was what he cared for and mourned and grieved over. These and similar acts of true sanctity brought it about while he was still living that miracles were worked by God in his name." [48] The manuscript version is in much the same vein. But in the account that follows of Henry VII's efforts to have Henry canonized, the printed versions omit the clause saying that he committed the project to Henry VIII at his death. They also omit his manuscript statement that many of the witnesses of Henry VI's miracles were still testifying to them.[49]

[45] "Ita fortasse Deo cordi erat": 1PV 510; 2PVt 124.
[46] oPV 194rv.
[47] Above, Chap. II at n. 95.
[48] 1PV 525; 2PVt 156–157.
[49] oPV 206.

While no one could deny the sincere admiration Vergil felt for this saintly king, it has been suggested that his reference to his miracles can be explained as politically motivated, on the grounds that it is "the only example of a miracle in the later books." [50] This, however, is not the case, for Vergil even inserts references to miracles not in his manuscripts into the later books of the printed editions — specifically, the miracles at the tomb of St. Osmund, mentioned in connection with his canonization in 1457, and the miracles that have sanctified the shrine at Walsingham.[51] It seems probable, in other words, that Vergil believed in Henry's miracles. The unqualified assertion of political motivation with regard to Vergil's mention of Henry's miracles, therefore, needs a qualification — namely, that the political consideration may perhaps have been an added reason for his not omitting the reference.

The Punishment of the House of York

As we have seen, Vergil came, perhaps by the time of his first edition and certainly by the time of his second edition, to consider it likely that Edward's successes were due to the workings of divine justice in removing the crown from the family that had acquired it wrongfully. But Vergil is never sympathetic to the pretensions of the Yorkist claimants nor to the methods by which they sought to realize them. And in the manuscript itself, he meditated upon the possibility that Edward was providentially punished for his various crimes. He says that Edward had begun finally to act like a good and useful prince, when suddenly he fell into a terrible sin, the execution of his brother, George of Clarence.

He says that he was able to ascertain nothing certain about the reasons for this tragic fratricide, in spite of his questioning of trustworthy authorities. He first deals with the "fama in vulgo" (as he calls it in the editions), which he may have found in Rous's history, concerning the prophecy playing on the letter G, at which Edward was allegedly terrified and had his brother removed as a consequence. Before dismissing this reason, Vergil remarks that "because demons are thus accustomed to employ their wonders in entangling the minds of those who delight in

[50] Denys Hay, *Polydore Vergil: Renaissance Historian and Man of Letters* (Oxford 1952) 111.
[51] 1PV 497; 2PVt 96–97; 1–2PVh 21 (see below at n. 83).

such vain illusions," men said afterwards that the prophecy was a true one, since Gloucester reigned after Edward.[52]

"But it should rather be believed," Vergil goes on to say, "that it happened by reason of God's anger, either because of Edward's perjury at York . . . or because of the slaughter of so many nobles who had perished in the rival factions, or finally because of the murder of Henry VI and his son Prince Edward; and he consequently permitted it to happen that one brother should inflict a cruel death upon another, and an uncle upon his nephews . . . whereby the most noble house of York, stained by its own blood, should finally cease to reign." We have here an early example in Vergil of dynastic retribution, of the divine justice eliminating a whole family, including the innocent children (though the fact of their innocence is not remarked upon here). But Vergil deleted this whole passage from the manuscript, perhaps because such an extension of providential justice was not in keeping with his general line of thought at this time.[53]

In the first edition, he conjectured that Clarence's end was the effect of divine retribution for abandoning Warwick, for, as he says, "it seemed that God did not forgo the punishment the duke had earned for the violation of his oath, which the miserable man later underwent by a cruel death." [54] But perhaps this opinion did not seem so likely as time wore on, for he omitted it in the 1546 edition.

If Vergil deleted the specific reference to the providential punishment of Edward in his children, he did preserve and pass on to the printed versions of his history the notion that the three York brothers, Edward, Clarence, and Richard of Gloucester, for their murder of Henry VI (but not for their seizing of the crown from him, apparently), "clearly paid the penalty for their crimes; for when they no longer had enemies to lash out against, they turned their cruelty upon themselves . . . and polluted their hands with their own blood." But he omitted the specifically providential moral of the manuscript at this point: "Thus mortals should fear God, the just avenger, and believe that he is mindful of both good and evil deeds." [55]

[52] oPV 210rv; 1PV 530; 2PVt 167. See above, 70.

[53] oPV 210v. See Appendix D below for the text of the canceled passage.

[54] 1PV 518. Cf. oPV 211 for a similar judgment, but without explicit mention of God's punishment.

[55] oPV 205v; 1PV 525; 2PVt 155–156. The printed versions also omit naming the three brothers, beyond mentioning the common report that Gloucester personally did the deed; but when Vergil speaks of "whoever it was that struck the blow," and of "the murderer as well as the authors of the murder," it is clear to whom he is referring.

As for Edward himself, Vergil returned in the first edition to the suggestion he had canceled in his manuscript, namely, that Edward was punished later by the death of his sons. It is not explained how such a punishment could affect Edward himself, since he was already dead and suffering in the next world whatever his deeds merited; and we are led to suspect that Vergil's chief emphasis is upon the exemplary value of the moral for those who might be tempted to imitate Edward's actions. In reflecting on Edward's false oath at York, when he swore in the most solemn way that he intended to claim only his duchy, Vergil in his manuscript had lamented the general tendency in all of us to be so overwhelmed by greed for possessions that we do not hesitate to swear to God what we immediately forswear as soon as we obtain what we covet. "But God is a just judge who soon punishes such offenders in his own time; and there is not a single example of such a one who has not sooner or later received the punishment he deserves." [56] He indicates here that Edward was in fact providentially punished, but it is only later, in the first edition, that he specifies what the punishment may have been. Perhaps he was encouraged to make the point because of the Croyland author's belief that Edward was punished in his children.[57] At any rate, when he returned to the subject while rewriting his history, Vergil altered his remarks, and pointed out that "men of both high and low degree who are blinded by desire and forgetful of all religion and uprightness are accustomed to swear their faith by the immortal God, though they know that they intend to break their word before they give it. But as familiar examples go to show, they suffer the merited punishment of their perjury at one time or another, so that the dishonor often comes even to their descendants [ita ut ea labes saepenumero eorum etiam nepotibus veniat]. And it may not be without profit to return to this subject in the life of King Edward IV, where perhaps it will be permissible to see that Edward's progeny as well did not escape punishment for this perjury." [58]

Accordingly, after the murder of the young Edward and Richard by Richard III, Vergil asks "what man would not be

[56] oPV 199v.

[57] See above, n. 16. Vergil, however, is unconcerned with Edward's taxation of the clergy, which so outraged the Croyland chronicler, and seems to accept Edward's reason for requiring monetary aid from the churchmen in his proposed war with France, because they could not bear arms themselves (oPV 213v; 1PV 532; 2PVt 171). Cf. also André's opinion, above, Chap. III at n. 60, of Edward as being punished in his children.

[58] 1PV 517; 2PVt 139.

terrified and overcome with pity and grief at the shameful death inflicted upon such children? And yet," he says, "very few are moved by such examples, for people little consider that sometimes it is because of the sins of their ancestors that these things happen, when the punishment due to them redounds upon their descendants. That perhaps was the case with these two innocent boys, because their father Edward committed the crime of breaking the oath . . . he had sworn in the holiest possible way when he was at the gates of York; for, as soon became obvious, he had in mind to do the very opposite of what he swore to; and later by the death of his brother Clarence he assured himself of a heavy punishment from God." [59]

Richard III and Henry VII

Vergil accepted the villainous view of Richard III that he found in the histories written before him, and seems to have had this characterization confirmed by the contemporaries he spoke with upon the subject. And like his sources, all the versions of his history picture Richard as providentially punished for the enormities he committed.

He speaks with some skepticism of Richard's attempt to reform his life but seems to accept his motives as plausible — first of all he wished to gain pardon from God for his offenses, and secondly to win the favor of his people.[60] But, as the manuscript notes, Richard was unable by his works of piety to slow down his approaching punishment. And in the margin it is added that "Richard was not able to change his savage nature, and did not long persevere in goodness, but immediately returned to evil and did everything thenceforward, as is evident in the case of his wife's death, under a cloak of hypocrisy." [61] In rewriting this episode, Vergil substitutes for these remarks the simple observation that since his goodness was counterfeit to begin with, he soon grew cold again.[62] But he also inserts a reflection after the fashion of Comines to account for Richard's overthrow. He says that when Richard was at length relieved of most of his

[59] 1PV 540; 2PVt 189-190.

[60] oPV 221v-222; 1PV 541; 2PVt 192.

[61] oPV 222. The MS is also explicitly providential with regard to Richard's failure to capture Richmond in Brittany; it was prevented by God, who wished Richard shortly to pay the penalty of his offenses (fol. 227). The printed version says simply that the fortune of England prevented this deadly pact from succeeding (1PV 548; 2PVt 206).

[62] 1PV 541; 2PVt 192.

molestations, he began to be less alert. And the ultimate or supernatural reason for this was to prevent Richard from "averting the omen," that is, from avoiding his catastrophe, by any diligence on his part. "For the power of divine justice," he says, "causes a man to be less discerning, less providential, less cautious, when he is approaching the time of payment for his crimes." [63]

The time of payment, of course, came at the battle of Bosworth Field, and it is not surprising for us to learn that it was the divine justice that urged Richard on to meet his doom there.[64] After reading the account of the Croyland Chronicle, it would seem, Vergil inserted an extra page into his manuscript describing the reported dream that Richard had had the night before the battle, in which he saw "the terrifying images as it were of evil demons, which would not let him rest." But Vergil adds his own belief that it was not a dream but a warning from his conscience to repent before he died.[65]

Vergil returns once more to Richard's fate, in the following chapter or book (on Henry VII), when discussing Parliament's action against the Queen Dowager Elizabeth for reconciling herself to Richard's plans. He admits that she committed a great crime in doing so, but he does not agree that the result of it was one that should be avenged in this way by the law; for far from injuring anyone, it was of great benefit for everyone, and in particular for Henry, since because of it Richard dared to commit even more crimes than before and to neglect religion to the extent of seeking to marry his niece; this in turn made God more incensed with him, and resulted in his ruin. "We may surely be allowed to conclude from this," Vergil says, "that wicked men are not moved by human counsels but by the will of God, as though hastening of their own accord to their merited end." [66] Richard seems to be acting here in accordance with a general law, but one that is explicitly described in terms of the will of God. Perhaps therefore we should consider the same

[63] 1PV 551; 2PVt 214. Earlier Vergil also added that whenever a bad storm occurred the people remembered Richard's evil deed (presumably, the murder of the princes), and laid the blame for the storm on him, saying that God was revenging his wickedness on the English people (1PV 541; 2PVt 191). But Vergil does not develop in his own name, as Comines does, the notion that the people suffer providential punishment because of the sins of their rulers. We might note that Vergil does not seem to have read or used Comines.

[64] 0PV 232v; cf. 1PV 555, which adds that the divine justice was calling the man to pay the penalties his crimes had merited. But surprisingly the whole reference to divine justice is omitted in 2PVt 221 (2PV 1426).

[65] 0PV 233; 1PV 555; 2PVt 221–222.

[66] 1–2PVh 18.

notion as implicit in passages of similar tenor, especially in the rewritten versions of Vergil's history.[67]

The counterpart to Richard's providential fall, the providential rise of Henry VII, undergoes some interesting mutations in the three versions of Vergil's history. We may begin with his account of Henry VI's prophecy concerning the young Earl of Richmond, which he no doubt derived from Bernard André's *Vita*. After silently contemplating the exalted nature ("alta indoles")[68] of the boy for a while, the king is reported to have said: "This is he who will in time possess all." [69] Vergil remarks that "thus the holy man predicted that this boy would one day possess the realm, as it later came to pass." It is obvious that Vergil's chief emphasis here is the sanctity of Henry VI and not the providential aspect of Henry VII's acquisition of the realm. But just a little earlier, when he first began to speak of young Richmond, he says that "this Henry is the one who after conquering Richard III, Edward's brother . . . obtained the crown of England, of whom it should be believed that he was providentially sent [de quo illud credendum est, ut diuinitus ad regnum peruenerit] to extinguish the factions of Henry VI and Edward IV, which had been so destructive above all to the English nobility; for beyond a doubt this is what he accomplished." [70]

This sentiment is found both in the manuscript and in the first edition, but strikingly, it is completely omitted from the second edition. A somewhat similar development can be observed again when Vergil returns to the subject of Henry VI's prophecy after Henry VII's accession. But first it might be remarked that though Vergil's providential interpretation concerning Henry Richmond seems to be presented as his own opinion in the passage just quoted, it does not necessarily demand to be read in a sense expressing full divine approval of Henry, since the primary accent is upon the cessation of the civil conflicts in the realm.[71]

[67] The MS in this instance sees the matter simply as an example of the inconstancy of human affairs, whereby the prosperous (in this case, Queen Elizabeth) become miserable (oPVh 19).

[68] This expression could perhaps be rendered "noble birth" as well as "high spirit."

[69] oPV 198; the printed versions say: "This indeed is he to whom both we and our adversaries will yield the possession" (1PV 515; 2PVt 135).

[70] oPV 197v: "quod haud dubie fecit"; for this last phrase 1PV 515 reads instead, "quando nihil fuit, quod potius fecerit," which can be rendered, "since there was nothing that he more ably (or more willingly, or more surely) accomplished."

[71] Similarly, in the providential foiling of Richard's plot to capture Henry mentioned above (n. 61), it is Richard's punishment that Vergil is stressing. In the versions of 1–2PV, the substitution of the phrase, "the fortune of England," is more inclusive, perhaps, but it is also more vague.

And, as was the case in the heavenly council of Carmeliano's poem, it is providential mercy that is stressed here, with no hint that the troubles England has suffered are a providential punishment.

After completing his manuscript account of Henry VII's conquest and coronation, as an afterthought Vergil inserted on an extra page[72] the remark that Henry's rise to power could have been known beforehand by many centuries and also again during his lifetime. He then recalls the divine vision of Cadwallader and the prophecy about the eventual return of his race, which Vergil recorded in the third book of his history. They say ("ferunt") that this prophecy was fulfilled in Henry, who traced his line back to Cadwallader.[73] He recalls also that Henry VI predicted the same thing.

In the first edition he says that Henry's conquest seems to have been accomplished and provided for by the will of God ("quod Dei nutu atque consilio gestum et provisum videtur"). But in the 1546 edition he changes the "seems" to "seemed" ("visum est"); and this may strike us as being of some significance if we recall that this edition also suppressed the statement which says that Henry's arrival should be considered providential. It is possible that Vergil had become slightly disillusioned with the divine nature of the Tudor vocation. Already in the first edition he seemed to emphasize that the application of the Cadwallader prophecy was an early opinion and not an accepted fact. He says that "men had already been persuaded for a long time that Henry was led by the fate of this [prophetic] voice in obtaining the kingdom; and Henry VI had also predicted that this would come to pass." [74]

This interpretation may be reading more into the text than is warranted, but it is interesting to note that the published

---

[72] Fol. 236v (the recto side is blank), which is an addition to fol. 237.

[73] Vergil said earlier that Owen Tudor claimed descent from Cadwallader (oPV 171 margin; 1PV 481; 2PVt 62). We may remember that Owen Glendower made a similar claim, and that among Glendower's partisans were William ap Tudor and Rhys ap Tudor (Usk 226, 240). The form and perhaps also the content of Vergil's present statement may have been influenced by the similar passage in John Rous, who remarked that both contemporary and ancient prophecies foretold good things about Henry (see above, Chap. III at nn. 27–28). Vergil does not refer to the Arthur prophecies, for, aside from the fact that "Arthur II" had died, he seems to have treated the existence of King Arthur with skepticism. Perhaps he was also skeptical of the Cadwallader prophecy, since it first appeared in the suspect Geoffrey of Monmouth.

[74] 1–2PVh 4: "Istius vocis fato Henricum ductum regnum obtinuisse, opinio per animos hominum jampridem persuaserat, quod et Henricus sextus futurum praedixerat."

editions also eliminate the providential aspect of Henry VII's marriage to Elizabeth. In the manuscript Vergil said that we may be permitted the belief that the marriage came about by the aid of God ("quod diuinitus factum credere licet"), since by it all the causes of those pernicious factions were eliminated, and the houses of Lancaster and York united; and from it was born the true and certain royal heir, the presently reigning king. In print Vergil says simply that "from that time peace seemed [visa est] to be born to the English people," since the two houses were finally united.[75] He retains the statement that Henry VIII, the issue of the marriage, was the true royal heir, but it must be remembered that he based this judgment on his mother's Yorkist heritage, and not on his father's Lancaster or Tudor pretensions.[76]

Vergil does, however, record and preserve various acts and indications of Henry's piety. When he was informed of the plan to supplant Richard, he thanked God, believing that it could not have happened without God's special providence.[77] He rejoiced that Oxford was enabled to join him through God's assistance.[78] He prayed to God for a prosperous voyage across the Channel and over to Wales,[79] and thanked God at length for his victory at Bosworth.[80] He also mentions that after Henry was received into London, honor was given to God during several days of public prayer. The people believed for certain that the source and breeding grounds of the factions had at last been exhausted.[81] Such was not the case, of course, as Vergil soon points out,[82] for Henry was troubled with rebellion all his life.

Vergil also details the devotions that Henry performed to God and the Blessed Virgin in the shrine at Walsingham before and after his expedition against John de la Pole, the Earl of Lincoln, in 1487; and in the published editions he even adds, as was pointed out above, the detail that the place was sanctified by the miracles that were performed there.[83] This addition may be a lesson aimed at Henry VIII, as may the expanded accounts of

[75] 0–2PVh 6–7.
[76] With regard to Elizabeth herself, Vergil added to the first edition the notion that God aided the chaste mind of the virgin, and defended her from the crime that her uncle Richard III was planning to force on her by marrying her (1–2PVh 2).
[77] 1PV 544; 2PVt 197; cf. oPV 223v.
[78] 1PV 549; 2PVt 208; cf. oPV 228.
[79] 1PV 552; 2PVt 216.
[80] 1PV 557; 2PVt 226.
[81] 1–2PVh 3.
[82] 0–2PVh 9.
[83] 0–2PVh 21, 27.

Henry VII's religious fervor that Vergil gives at the end of the chapter dealing with him, where he adds that it cannot be doubted that his soul is in heaven, because he was such a zealous promoter of religion on earth; and Vergil goes on to speak of the houses of Franciscan Observants that he established.[84]

At the beginning of his manuscript chapter on Henry VIII, Vergil gives a summary of English history during the fifteenth century, where he recalls "how King Richard II entirely lacked male heirs, and how not long after the whole population of England was split into two factions, Lancastrian and Yorkist, and how a bloody struggle ensued for over a hundred years, indeed until our own day, till at last the houses of Lancaster and York were united." And from this united family, he says, was born Henry VIII, in whom the true progeny of kings was restored.[85] The providential fall of the original house of Lancaster (Henry IV — Henry VI) was an afterthought which appeared in the first edition; but it was never regarded by Vergil as a prerequisite on the supernatural level for Henry Tudor's providential arrival. Far from incorporating this afterthought into the summary just quoted, Vergil had another afterthought and dropped the whole summary.[86] Furthermore, the providential aspect of the Tudor accession is somewhat weakened in the first edition, and even more so in the second edition, as we have seen, whereas the providential disinheritance of Lancaster for its wrongful acquisition of the realm, which was first reported as a contemporary opinion in the 1534 text, received Vergil's own partial endorsement in 1546. The providential punishment of York is strengthened in the first edition, where the notion of dynastic retribution

---

[84] 1-2PVh 144-145, enlarged over oPVh 147. Vergil also praises the charitable works of Henry VII's saintly mother, Margaret, done at the urging of John Fisher, Bishop of Rochester, "viri summa doctrina, summa gratia, summa integritate" (1-2PVh 145), and in the third edition (1555) also adds a determined defense of Henry VIII's marriage to Catherine of Aragon (3PVh 149). He ceases to deplore the fact that Henry VII became avaricious toward the end (oPVh 131, 147), saying later that this was simply a charge of the people against him; he now seems to accept Henry's proclaimed motive of disciplining the people, and he says he finally took mercy upon them and directed that the oppression it caused be corrected (1-2PVh 134, 144). Vergil's own motive in making this change may have been a prudential respect for the reputation of his sovereign's father, but it may also have been connected with a desire to present to Henry VIII a portrait of his father that he should strive to imitate in every respect.

[85] oPVh 149.

[86] The only reference to Richard II in the later books is Richard III's charge against Buckingham that by seeking the Duchy of Hereford he was intending to repeat the pattern of usurpation followed by Henry IV (oPV 222v; 1PV 542; 2PVt 193). A similar story is given by More, but labeled as rather dubious (More-Hall 382 [89-90]).

is added; and the alterations of the second edition do not noticeably affect this presentation.

The providential interpretations concerning the three houses
are at their strongest in combination, therefore, in the 1534
edition, the one that chiefly influenced later sixteenth-century
English historiography. Of this version, it may be said in general
that Vergil accepted the Tudor myth in regarding the Yorkists
as punished for their crimes against the Lancastrians, and in
seeing Henry VII as the divinely sent pacifier and unifier of
England, and the providential instrument of vengeance upon
Richard III. He alters the received myth by tracing the legitimacy
of Henry VIII's kingship to his Yorkist blood, and by adopting
or at least recording the York myth of the divine dispossession of
Henry VI,[87] although there is no question of his accepting any of
the Yorkist aspersions against Henry himself, which were, in
fact, very few and indirect. And he accepts the Lancaster myth
of Henry IV's pious end and of God's glorification of Henry V
and Henry VI.

There is no hint in Vergil's thought of divine punishment
upon the people or upon England as a whole because of the
sins of the rulers, nor is there any concept of a divine curse that
involves several generations of expiation until payment is at last
fully exacted. There is the notion of descendants suffering for
the crimes of ancestors, but in the case of Henry VI it is a question of the restitution or at least the giving up of stolen property.
The young princes of York suffer, it is true, for something they
had no control over; but they die not in expiation of Henry IV's
sins (it is not even suggested that Henry VI *died* in expiation of
Henry IV's sins), but as a result of their father's sins. Edward IV
is not said to be punished for usurping the throne, for it was due
to him by his blood; he is punished, rather, for engineering the
murder of Henry VI. He is punished by the destruction of his
own family, including the death by his own command of his
brother Clarence; he is punished in his children also because
of his fratricide and because of his perjury at York. And Clarence
and Richard are punished in their own persons for their personal crimes.

[87] As we have seen, when he speaks in his own name in the first edition, Vergil
gives no reason for the fall of Lancaster in connection with fate and the will of
God. He does say that Henry was deposed because God wanted him to go through
tribulations before receiving his final reward; and he also says that Henry received
his sufferings for his own sins and those of his ancestors; but he only reports as
the opinion of some in Henry's time the theory that he lost the realm because of
Henry IV's unlawful possession of it.

A devious connection between the providential retribution meted out to the houses of Lancaster and York might be found in the consideration that Edward would not have committed his perjury at York if Henry IV had not usurped the throne in the first place. This is true, perhaps, but in Vergil's mind Edward's sin was a lapse committed of his own free will; and in any case the kingdom was being providentially restored to the York line through the misfortunes of Lancaster. If the Yorkists committed sins to further this process, they must be expiated. There is continuity in this century's events, of course, a chronological and political continuity in the realm of natural cause and effect. And there is also a moral and providential continuity, in the sense that all sins are eventually paid for and righteousness vindicated. But the sufferings from which the Tudor advent providentially relieves the country are not depicted in the context of providential punishments. The only attribute of God emphasized in these passages (except with regard to Richard III) is mercy, not justice.

V

Edward Hall

Hall is unusual among sixteenth-century chroniclers in beginning with the period of history which we have been studying. He starts with Henry IV's usurpation, and takes as his chief interest the division that this usurpation caused, along with the union that was finally achieved in the policy of Henry VII and in the person of Henry VIII.

Hall put his plan into operation by using Vergil's history as the framework of his own, and much of his own is nothing more than a pompous translation of Vergil's Latin. But he also makes extensive additions from other chronicles, and not infrequently adds his own interpretations. Unlike most other English chroniclers and antiquarians of the sixteenth century, Hall never attacks Vergil, either directly or indirectly. Perhaps this reserve was due to the great debt he owed him, which is never acknowledged.[1] Sometimes he takes over Vergil's opinions so completely that he translates "credo" as "I think"; but at other times he records Vergil's views by representing them as the opinions of several writers — "some men think," etc. But when Vergil's sentiments go counter to Hall's religious or patriotic opinions, he simply omits them or attacks the similar views of other authors — although he sometimes translates without comment or per-

[1] Vergil's name does appear in the list of authorities given at the beginning of Hall's work, but this list was probably compiled by Richard Grafton, who printed the history in 1548, after Hall's death in 1547. The list is probably based on the contents of Hall's library, but it does not include several authors that are explicitly alluded to in the body of the work (e.g., Aeneas Sylvius, p. 229; John Baker, p. 210). In his continuation to Hardyng, published in 1543, Grafton himself had used both More and Vergil without acknowledgment. But in his edition of Hall's work, he inserted marginal acknowledgments of More's authorship. It might be mentioned that in his *Chronicle at Large* (1569), Grafton used Hall's more "spacious" translation of Vergil rather than his own terse rendering.

sonal commitment some of Vergil's remarks that are not in exact accord with his own views.[2]

Hall was a great admirer of Henry VIII, and, unlike Polydore Vergil, a vigorous supporter of his religious reforms. As a consequence, he is vehement in his opposition to papal interference in England and to the abuses of the landed clergy, which he believed Henry reformed in dissolving the monasteries and reorganizing the ecclesiastical hierarchy. And naturally enough, Hall displays a more intense feeling for England and against France than Vergil could claim. It is in these areas, therefore, that Hall chiefly modifies Vergil's themes; otherwise, he accepts and intensifies Vergil's lines of thought, upon his stylistic principle that if a thing is worth saying at all, it is worth saying two or three times in a row. This policy resulted in the inflated texture that Ascham condemned as "indentured English," or legal tautology. The same failing can be found much earlier, however, as in Chaucer's prose translations.

Hall is fairly original in the insistence upon the blessings of unity with which he begins his history, when he makes the rather ingenuous remark that a union cannot be understood except with respect to a division, and therefore he says he will describe the division that existed in England, beginning with the deposition of Richard II.[3] And he is certainly original in choosing to restrict his history to the account of this one period of discord and union. But since he is also writing a general history of England from the time of Henry IV to his own day, and a much fuller one than had ever been written before, he includes many events and discussions which have nothing to do with his theme of union, and in fact the theme is often lost sight of. But he does follow the example of Vergil in recalling the whole history of the houses and claims of York and Lancaster, both at the beginning and at the time of the Cambridge plot,[4] as well as in places that Vergil does not.[5]

But it should be noted that in setting forth his theme, Hall

[2] Hall describes his procedure in the dedicatory letter (whose change of address from Henry VIII to Edward VI was probably made by Grafton), where he says that he has compiled and gathered (and not made) the contents of his simple treatise out of various writers, foreign as well as English (p. vii).

[3] Hall 1–2.

[4] Hall 2–3, 61. In the latter passage, Hall introduces his translation of Vergil's analysis by saying: "Divers write that," etc.

[5] For instance, in speaking of the Percy-Glendower support of Mortimer, pp. 27–28. (Hall mistakes Sir Edmund Mortimer here for the son and heir of Roger Mortimer, Earl of March, whereas he was only Roger's younger brother; see above, Chap. I, n. 89).

does so on the purely ethical level, with no explicit reference to the providential order. He is emphasizing the benefits of union and the evils of discord, with the view of encouraging his readers to avoid dissension and work for concord. The providential will eventually appear in the picture, but only at the urging of Polydore Vergil. It may be noted too that whereas Vergil emphasizes the prior claim of the Yorkist blood in Henry VIII by giving only the York lineage, Hall is vague on this subject, and seems more inclined, perhaps from a sense of drama, to regard the two lines as having an equal claim.

The Establishing of the Lancastrian Line

In summarizing the events that led to Richard II's downfall, Hall gives a long speech to Archbishop Arundel of Canterbury, in which the prelate asks Bolingbroke in exile to take the kingship upon himself; and in the course of his remarks some of the providential elements of the Lancastrian myth are reflected. Arundel says that Henry should come home so that the people can receive him as a king sent from God, and that he would thereby obtain the gratitude of his Creator and the love of his people. Before this Hall himself said that if Bolingbroke thanked God for this development, it should surprise no one.[6]

Thus at the very beginning of Hall's history we are introduced to a problem we have met with before, but one that makes itself felt more acutely in Hall — and that is the question of the value to be placed upon the providential notions expressed in the reported speech of historical characters. The problem will be even more vital, of course, in Shakespeare, where the speeches of the characters are all we have.

In the case of an historian like Hall, who records his own views as well as those he finds or invents for his characters, it might be thought a good rule to assume that he agrees with the providential sentiments of the characters he treats sympathetically. But a rule like this is dangerous, and implies a consistency and depth of thought that is not evident in Hall. Much of his characterization is not his own work, and much that is his own is influenced by considerations which have nothing to do with his main theme of the division and union of York and Lancaster. The speeches he gives his characters seem to be constructed primarily with a view to their rhetorical effectiveness, rather

[6] Hall 6–7.

than from any consideration of their place in a coherent thematic structure. Accordingly, in the speech of the Archbishop of Canterbury, we must assume that Hall's primary purpose was to make it a good speech. And although his view of Arundel is not unfavorable, what little expression of it there is, we can hardly conclude from this that Hall is agreeing with him in considering Henry IV as the providential punisher of Richard (which is at least plausible) and the divinely appointed king of England (which is scarcely plausible).

Hall repeats Vergil's comment that any offense Richard might have committed was due to the frailty of his wanton youth rather than to malice, and that the cause of his overthrow was principally the fickleness of man in being perpetually dissatisfied with the present.[7] He does not indicate that God was involved in Henry's accession either on his side or against him, and in fact he does not comment on whether or not Henry was justified in claiming the crown. Although he does indicate (rather obliquely) that the Earl of March had a prior claim by blood, he omits Vergil's remark that Henry's might overcame March's right, and simply says that March and his brother-in-law, the Earl of Cambridge, were not pleased by these proceedings, and that the opposition between these two branches of the family, started here, did not stop until the male heirs of both were wiped out.[8]

Hall's implicit position, one perhaps that was never explicit even to himself, seems to be that once Henry IV was elected by all his subjects and after he received their sworn allegiance, he was the true king, and that it was treason to rebel against him, either in favor of Richard II, or in favor of the Earl of March. Certainly in his accounts of the rebellions against Henry IV, he treats the rebels with undisguised hostility — though much of his hostility is due to the blameworthy motives the rebels had in wanting to change kings, apart from the just claims that their candidates might be thought to have had. Observe, for instance, his treatment of the Abbot of Westminster. According to Hall, the devil used this hypocritical monk to organize the earls' plot, and his motive for rebelling against his lawful prince was a fear that Henry would encroach upon the possessions of the spirituality.[9]

[7] Hall 8–9.
[8] Hall 13–14. He is, of course, conjecturing history here. As we have seen before, the Earl of March was only eight years old at this time (1399). Richard, Aumerle's younger brother, did not become Earl of Cambridge until 1414, and did not marry Anne Mortimer (March's elder sister) until 1408, when she was nineteen years old.
[9] Hall 15–16. He uses this opportunity to denounce the partiality of the monkish

Hall follows Vergil in saying that Richard was innocent of the earls' plot,[10] but he does not pass judgment on Henry's role in his death. He says that he "was by king Henry adjudged to die," to remove the ground of Henry's fear; some authors say he commanded Richard to be killed, others that he condescended to have him killed, still others that it was done without his knowledge, but that he confirmed it when he found out.

No matter which of these versions Hall preferred, it is difficult to see how he could consider Henry as completely free from blame, and yet he refrains from accusing him of any guilt in the matter; and, when telling of Henry V's reburial of Richard, he even omits Vergil's belief that Henry did it to expiate for his father's breach of the faith he gave to Richard.[11] He also fails to report Fabyan's elaborate description of the penances Henry IV received from the pope, which Henry V fulfilled. Presumably Hall would object primarily against the idea of papal jurisdiction in England, but perhaps he also had some reservation about the doctrine of purgatory, which would also help to account for the omission of Vergil's remark. The moral he draws is simply one of mutability, showing us that Fortune weighs princes and paupers alike on the same scales.[12]

During his first year as king, Henry IV was molested by internal sedition, French craft, and Welsh invasions, all of which Hall sees simply as a fulfillment of the old proverb that one evil commonly follows another; and besides all this, Fortune envied Henry's fortunate proceedings, and armed the Scots against him.[13]

In discussing the rebellions of the Percys and their allies against Henry, Hall takes up the tripartite compact, drawing on an account now lost, and places it before the battle of Shrewsbury, when Hotspur was still alive to participate in it. He is extremely severe with the participants, because they believed in the vain mouthings of a Welsh prophesier who convinced them that a prophecy of Merlin's foretold Henry IV's destruction at their hands. But what actually came to pass was not prophesied, namely, their own destruction. But though Hall goes on to say

---

chronicles, which praise and sanctify whichever kings bestowed privileges upon them and damn to the lowest hell any ruler who dared suggest some diminishing of their possessions or liberties, even for the most just and worthy purposes.

[10] Hall 19; 1PV 426; but Vergil includes Richard among the companions who received the fruit of their former evil life.

[11] Hall 20; 1PV 423.

[12] Hall 20–21.

[13] Hall 22–23.

that Mortimer's heirs succeeded where he failed, he does not raise the question of right or wrong with regard to the possession of the crown, either here or earlier where he discusses Henry's refusal to ransom Mortimer and his wish to see him and all his line in heaven, thereby leaving the king with an unquestioned title.[14]

Furthermore, Hall translates from Hardyng the articles that the Percys charged against Henry, devised by the advice of Archbishop Scrope, in which Henry was accused, among other crimes, of perjury, regicide, and usurpation. But Hall certainly does not share Hardyng's enthusiasm (in his Yorkish phase) for the archbishop or the cause of the Percys. The providential appeal of the articles in addition throws this cause into an embarrassing position when judged by the outcome of the battle of Shrewsbury, for the Percys said that they intended to prove their case that day in battle by the help of Almighty God.[15] When Henry saw these articles, he made a similar claim of divine aid; and after his victory, he duly thanked God.[16]

As for Glendower, he was dismayed by this victory and fled into desert places, "where he received a final reward meet and prepared by God's providence for such a rebel and seditious seducer," namely, death by starvation. "This end," Hall says, "was provided for such as gave credence to false prophecies. This end had they that by diabolical divinations were promised great possessions and seigniories. This end happeneth to such as, believing such fantastical follies, aspire and gape for honor and high promotions."[17]

In opposing Welsh prophets, Hall must not be thought to oppose the prophetic arts in general; for though he has a similar animus against French astrology and prophecy,[18] he sometimes accepts the findings of local efforts. For instance, he expands Vergil's comment about the comet that appeared at this time, and points out that, as the astronomers affirmed, it signified great effusion of human blood, "which judgment was not frustrate, as

[14] Hall 23, 27–28. He says Henry pretended he would not ransom Mortimer because he was willingly taken by Glendower, and Hall calls this device a fraud and a "cautel" in speaking of the Percys' angry reactions to it. If this is to be taken as an expression of Hall's own disapproval of Henry's actions, it is a very slight one.
[15] Hall 29–30.
[16] Hall 30–31. Henry's assurance of God's assistance is perhaps an echo of 1Wals 362–363 or an account derived from it. We should note that Hall 31 and 1Wals 368 (= 3Wals 2.258 and 4Wals 401–402) agree in saying that Douglas broke a testicle in fleeing from Shrewsbury.
[17] Hall 31.
[18] Hall 125, 164; see also his remarks on Joan of Arc (148–159).

you shall perceive" (referring to the battle of Shrewsbury).[19] He also quotes with seeming approval the prophecy that Shakespeare will also employ, connecting Somerset's death with castles.[20] And, as we will see, he gives wholehearted support to the prophecies of Tudor dominion, in spite of their Welsh overtones.

As for Archbishop Scrope's rising, Hall follows Vergil's succinct summary. Henry advanced to York before the rebellion could get under way (there is no word of any trickery involved in capturing Scrope), and the archbishop was executed. But Hall goes on to deny vehemently the story that Henry was punished by God with leprosy for this action. He uses Fabyan's version of this alleged providential punishment, and finds it an example of the kind of distortion practiced by the monkish chronographers: "Here of necessity," he says, "I ought not nor will not forget how some foolish and fantastical persons have written, how erroneous hypocrites and seditious asses have indited, how superstitious friars and malicious monks have declared and divulged, both contrary to God's doctrine, the honor of their prince, and common known verity, that at the hour of the execution of this bishop, which of the executioner desired to have five strokes in remembrance of the five wounds of Christ, the king at the same time sitting at dinner had five strokes in his neck by a person invisible, and was incontinently stricken with a leprey — which is a manifest lie, as you shall after plainly perceive. What shall a man say of such writers which took upon themselves to know the secrets of God's judgment? What shall men think of such beastly persons, which, regarding not their bounden duty and obeisance to their prince and sovereign lord, envied the punishment of traitors and torment of offenders? But what shall all men conjecture of such, which, favoring their own worldly dignity, their own private authority, their own peculiar profit, will thus juggle, rail, and imagine fantasies against their sovereign lord and prince, and put them in memory as a miracle to his dishonor and perpetual infamy? Well," he concludes, "let wise men judge what I have said." [21]

While making due allowance for Hall's bias against the corrupt practices of the clergy, we may take this passage as a further instance that he did not consider any of Henry's troubles during his reign to be a manifestation of God's displeasure, at least when

[19] Hall 27; cf. 1PV 427.
[20] Hall 233; cf. Davies 72.
[21] Hall 35; cf. Fabyan 572 (the pertinent passage is omitted in the Protestantized editions of Fabyan, issued in 1542 and 1559).

he wrote this early part of his history; nor is there any indication that he thought Henry deserving of any punishment from God at all. Furthermore, he indicates his personal belief that it is impossible to know God's mind in these matters. He goes on to say that Henry was further disquieted about this time, since the people bore such a cankered heart toward him that they let no opportunity of removing him pass them by; for now some unknown person started the rumor that Richard was still alive and in Scotland, and if it had not been for Henry's prudent action in anticipating its effects, it would have started a blaze that could not easily have been put out in a short time.[22]

And finally, after all of his fortunate undertakings, including the French campaigns, Henry piously turned to the betterment of his realm and the preparation of a crusade. Hall is giving a rather exact paraphrase of Polydore Vergil here,[23] but in speaking of the illness that interrupted these plans, he first draws the lesson in his customary proverbial way that our ways are not God's ways,[24] and he goes on to deny once more that the disease was a leprosy inflicted by the hand of God, as foolish friars had previously maintained; and he proves this by saying that Henry would not have undertaken or been able to undertake such a great crusade if it had been true. The fact of the matter is, he says, that he was stricken with apoplexy.[25]

Hall then proceeds to give the crown scene from Monstrelet, though strikingly he not only omits Monstrelet's condemnation of Henry for usurping the crown,[26] but modifies Henry's admission of guilt ("My fair son, what right have you to it? for you well know I had none") and omits his prayer for mercy from God. Instead, he has Henry say (though still with the great sigh taken over from Monstrelet): "What right I had to it and how I en-

[22] Hall 36. In the seventh year of Henry's reign, Hall adds an incident in which the king aboard ship was almost captured by the French; but by God's provision "and fortunate chance," he escaped.

[23] However, with regard to the civil dissension, by translating "omisso civili bello" as "being now delivered of all civil division and intestine dissension, with the which almost all Christendom was infected and disturbed," Hall probably has in mind the rebellions in England rather than Henry's dealings in France. But as in Vergil, there is no suggestion that Henry is forming his crusade in order to avoid more civil war at home.

[24] He says: "But see the chance, whatsoever man intendeth, God suddenly reverseth, what princes will, God will not, what we think stable, God suddenly maketh mutable, to the intent that Solomon's saying might be found true, which wrote that the wisdom of men is but foolishness before God" (p. 45).

[25] Hall 44-45.

[26] Hardyng has similar expressions, which Hall likewise omitted. Both Hardyng and Monstrelet speak of Henry's leprous condition.

joyed it God knoweth." [27] This extremely ambiguous statement could perhaps be taken to mean the same as Monstrelet's, namely, that Henry is saying he had no right; if this is so, the expression "God knows" is taken in its meaning, "God knows, I don't." Or it could be taken more literally to mean anything from positive affirmation of his right to an expression of doubt concerning it or of trust in God to set it right. The same ambiguity can be seen in the word "enjoyed," and Henry could mean either "how I possessed it" or "how I failed to find any joy in it." At any rate, it is clear that Hall has toned down the theme of usurpation, perhaps to avoid showing Henry V in a bad light (that is, as determined to hold on to stolen property).

Hall concludes his portrait of Henry IV by saying that after he had resolved all the dissensions in his realm he showed himself so gentle to everyone that he won more love from the nobles in his latter days than he had malice and ill will from them in the beginning.[28]

Hall follows Vergil rather closely in his depiction of Henry V, with a few adjustments made in accord with the changing times. Thus, Henry gets off to his pious start not by founding religious houses, as in Vergil, but by commanding the clergy to preach the word truly and to live by it, and the laity to serve God and obey their king, urging them not to commit adultery or perjury, and exhorting both estates to live together in amity.[29] Hall gives an ambiguous picture of Oldcastle, in which he seems to approve both of him and of Henry's action against him. Of the Lollard rising, he does not admit it was inspired by Lollardry, but says there are so many conflicting reports about what really happened that he prefers not to conjecture which is correct.[30]

Regarding the English claim to France, Hall takes over the version of his contemporary, Robert Redmayne, who saw it as

[27] The whole passage reads, after Henry IV asks his son why he had so misused himself:

The prince with a good audacity answered, "Sir, to mine and all men's judgments you seemed dead in this world; wherefore I as your next and apparent heir took that as mine own and not as yours." "Well, fair son," said the king, with a great sigh, "what right I had to it, and how I enjoyed it, God knoweth." "Well," quoth the prince, "if you die king, I will have the garland and trust to keep it with the sword against all mine enemies as you have done." "Well," said the king, "I commit all to God and remember you to do well," and with that turned himself in his bed and shortly after departed to God, in a chamber of the Abbot's of Westminster called Jerusalem, the twentieth day of March (Hall 45).

[28] Hall 45. This is the very opposite of the conclusion of 2Hard 371, but corresponds to that of Vergil's MS (oPV 130).

[29] Hall 47. Cf. Henry V's exhortations in PsElmham 16 and Redmayne 13–14.

[30] Hall 48–49. Cf. the favorable treatment of Oldcastle in Redmayne 15–22.

a project inaugurated by the clergy to keep the Parliament and Henry from encroaching on their temporalities.[31] The clergy's spokesman is Henry Chicheley, Archbishop of Canterbury, of whom Hall says that before becoming archbishop he was a Carthusian monk, a man who had professed voluntary poverty, and yet when he came abroad, he greatly desired honor; he describes him as a man who put great store in God's law, but who loved his own lucre more.[32] It seems that we are to conclude from this last sentence and from all that follows that Hall regarded the case that Archbishop Chicheley put forth against the French and in support of the English claims as a perfectly sound one, even though he was prompted to elaborate it from unworthy motives.

In his treatment of the Cambridge plot, Hall translates Vergil precisely for the discussion of Cambridge's real motives, and, as in Vergil, there is no suggestion that Henry was wrong in possessing the throne, nor that he would have been at fault for wiping out the house of York if he had realized what was afoot.[33]

Hall is more elaborate than Vergil in his account of the battle of Agincourt, and he draws on previous accounts to enlarge upon the providential aspects of his victory; he includes also an editorial comment that God, who never forsakes those who put their confidence in him, sent him this glorious victory, one that could hardly be believed possible, were it not for the similar instances we read of in the Book of Kings. But he uses Vergil's words in rejecting the report of infinitesimal loss on the English side (that is "if you will give credit to such as write miracles," and so on).[34]

Hall also adapts from Monstrelet the interview between Henry and Montjoy, the French herald, in which Henry told him that this victory was not won by their power but was given by God himself, and given, Henry believed, because of the sins of the French. But Hall glosses this statement, interpreting the sins in question as the injuries they had committed against the English.[35] And he adds as his own view that the efforts of the Emperor

---

[31] Redmayne may have based his long account on a similar opinion reported in Caxton's *Polychronicon* (2Caxton 529). Hall may have taken his inspiration for the archbishop's scriptural arguments (p. 51) from 2Hard (see above, Chap. II at n. 11).

[32] Hall 49.

[33] Hall 61.

[34] Hall 64–72. He rejects a lower figure than Vergil's "scarcely a hundred," however. He gives the estimate of not over twenty-five, in addition to four mentioned by name.

[35] Hall 70.

Sigismond to make peace fell through by reason of "the evil chance" of the French nation, because they were predestined to suffer still more plagues from the hands of the English than they had already borne.[36]

He has an interesting variation on the note of foreboding recorded by Vergil on the birth of Henry's son. Hall says that he first thanked God for giving him an heir. But when he heard that he was born at Windsor, whether he was influenced by some old blind prophecy, or had some foreknowledge, or else simply judged what his son's fortune was to be, he said to his chamberlain, Lord Fitzhugh, that he, Henry of Monmouth, would reign but a short time and win many possessions, but Henry of Windsor would reign long and lose everything. Then the king resigned himself to God's will.[37] We should note that Hall condemns the prophecy (if it was a prophecy) as old and blind even though it was verified.[38] He admits also the possibility that Henry was favored with some kind of premonition (no doubt sent by God), or that he had a foreboding from natural causes; at any rate, he uses it as an illustration of Henry's submission to God and his confidence in him.

The first two chapters of Hall's work have ended, therefore, with no indication that he believed that God was angered at the house of Lancaster or the English people. Rather the opposite is true, for the evidences of God's favor to Henry IV and especially to Henry V and to England as a whole are abundant.

The Troublous Season of Henry VI

In treating of French-English affairs after the death of Henry V, Hall of course does not follow Vergil's suggestion that God would have had reason to help the French liberate themselves from the English. Hall's position on this subject, while admittedly chauvinist, would seem nevertheless to be more logical than Vergil's, since if the English were justified in conquering France

[36] Hall 74. We may note here that in his account of Henry's second expedition to France, Hall follows Vergil in having Henry thank God for his victory at Caen, but he omits the miraculous apparition of the cross in the sky (p. 78). For the siege of Rouen, Hall takes over some of the pious and providential aspects of John Page's poem, which perhaps he found in one of the MSS of the *Brut* (pp. 83–89).

[37] Hall 108. Vergil simply reports a popular tradition that Henry V took his son's birth at Windsor as a bad omen (1PV 451). Hall seems to have used another source for the circumstances of Henry's remark.

[38] Holinshed was more logical, perhaps, when he omitted the derogatory words "old" and "blind" (1–2Hol 3.129).

under Henry V, they were justified in holding their acquisitions under Henry VI.

The Duke of Bedford sums up what perhaps may be assumed to correspond to Hall's own view of the providential aspects of the situation in the speech that Hall expands from Vergil's account of Henry VI's coronation in Paris in 1431. Bedford assures the French that Henry V was set up by God himself as a great scourge of their nation for the sole purpose of punishing those who had wrongfully usurped the rights of others and had taken possession of what did not belong to them; and by the will of God, the Holy Ghost illumined the heart of Charles VI with the realization that Henry was the true heir of his realm. Furthermore, God was not willing to permit such an illustrious prince as Henry V to be barren, and so he sent him a son, Henry VI, who has come here today to be crowned, with no misgiving in his heart, because he knows that they have it preached to them daily that they should fear God and honor their king, and that anyone who balks at obeying his king is thereby disobedient to God; for the prince on earth is God's vicar, the head and shepherd of Christ's flock, to whom both clergy and laity are subject in all affairs of government.[39]

Hall accordingly considers Joan of Arc as a sorceress sent by the devil rather than by God; and it was the devil, he says, who persuaded Charles to make use of her;[40] furthermore, the devil himself, in order to disrupt Anglo-French relations still more, "did apparel certain catchpoles and parasites, commonly called titivils and taletellers, to sow discord and dissension" between the Dukes of Bedford and Burgundy.[41] And he discusses the loss of Normandy in terms of worldly mutability and the unknown purposes of God's will, much as he did in speaking of the frustration of Henry IV's projected crusade. "But who can prevent Fortune's chance," he asks, "or have spectacles to see all the things to come or the chances that be present, seeing God disposeth that man purposeth, and that all worldly devices and man's cogitations be uncertain and ever unperfect." [42]

But later Hall does pick up a providential reason for the loss

---

[39] Hall 162–163. Cf. 1PV 471, where Bedford simply says the French are noted for obeying their king in the place of God.

[40] Hall 148, 157.

[41] Hall 173.

[42] Hall 186. He makes a similar remark later in regard to Edward IV and the Woodville family, who were at first enemies, and then related by affinity: "But who," he asks, "can know the secrets of God, or without him declare the chance that after shall ensue?" (p. 243).

of the French possessions as well as for the trouble in England that led ultimately to Henry's deposition, his son's death, and his queen's exile. It is that given by Fabyan, elaborated from Caxton and the *Brut*. It would seem, Hall says, that God was not content with the marriage of Henry to Margaret of Anjou (apparently because it involved breaking an agreement to marry the daughter of the Earl of Armagnac). But the lesson Hall draws from this, especially with reference to Margaret's fall from prosperity to adversity, is one emphasizing worldly unstableness and the wavering ways of false and flattering Fortune.[43] He thereby mutes the suggestion that God was punishing Henry (or the English people).

In treating of the emergence of the house of York, Hall in general follows Vergil word for word. But he inclines to be more favorable to York than Vergil was; perhaps he was influenced in this direction by the allegiance to York of his ancestor, Sir Davy Hall, whom he describes as York's chief counselor, and from whom he may have derived some of his information.[44]

With regard to providential themes relating to the two houses of Lancaster and York, Hall translates those of Vergil wherever he comes upon them. But he also makes a striking contribution of his own; and, as is the case with many of Hall's original additions, it occurs in an oration, which in this instance is given by Richard Plantagenet, Duke of York, when he claims the crown of England as his own in the House of Lords in 1460.

He tells the lords that the realm of England is sick, and that the root of its sickness is to be traced back to the usurpation of the throne by Henry IV, who attacked and imprisoned Richard II, and finally put him to death, in violation of the allegiance he had sworn to him and the homage he had paid him as his sovereign lord. After Richard's death, the realm belonged by right to the Earl of March, who passed the right on to York himself. But when the Percys, along with the Welsh rebel Glendower, attempted to assert March's claim, it cost both these noble persons (that is, Northumberland and Hotspur) their lives. The same was true of York's father, the Earl of Cambridge, whose death was due more to the exercise of power than to impartial justice. And

---

[43] Hall 205. Fabyan 618 brings in the fortune motif in support of the statement that God did not appear pleased with the marriage; for, he says, after it, the fortune of the world began to turn from Henry. See above, Chap. II, n. 8. Hall follows Fabyan in designating the jilted girl as Armagnac's daughter rather than his sister.

[44] See Kingsford, *English Historical Literature* 262–263.

he himself, York says, has also been compelled to use force in asserting his right, but not, he insists repeatedly, for his own personal emolument and private advancement, but with a view to restoring the peace to the realm that has been banished from it ever since the first ungodly usurpation of the above-named Henry, untruly called Henry IV. What manslaughter and iniquity, he exclaims, have been committed since the doleful death of King Richard! And to this very day, he asks, who is there that dares to petition for his right if it goes contrary to the will of the counselors who now bear the swing and rule the roost? He continues:

Well, well, although almighty God slackly and slowly do proceed to the punishment of sinners, yet the deferring of his scourge is recompensed with the greater pain when his rod striketh, yea, and oftentimes he leaveth the very malefactors apparently unpunished, and scourgeth their blood and punisheth them in their heirs by worldly adversity. Such is his mercy when it pleaseth him to show it, and so sharp is his whip when he list to strike.[45] For although Henry of Lancaster, Earl of Derby, took upon him the scepter and crown and wrongfully bare the name and style of a king, and was not much tickled with mine uncle, the Earl of March, at that time being within age, yet was he never in surety of himself, nor had any or enjoyed any perfect quietness, either in mind or in body; for surely a corrupt conscience feeleth never rest, but looketh when the sword of vengeance, will descend and strike. His son also, called King Henry V, obtained notable victories and immortal praises for his noble acts done in the realm of France — yet God for the offence of his untrue parent suddenly touched him, unbodying his soul in the flower of his youth and in the glory of his conquest. And although he had a fair son and a young apparent heir, yet was this orphan such a one as preachers say that God threatened to send for a punishment to his unruly and ungracious people, saying by his prophet Isaiah, "I shall give you children to be your princes, and infants without wisdom shall have the governance of you." The prophet lied not, if you note all things in an order. For after this Henry the Fifth — whose fame no man can justly reprove or deface — succeeded his son, whom all we have called our natural prince, and obeyed as his heir; in whose time and wrongful reign, I require you diligently to consider with what great

---

[45] Holinshed, following 2Grafton, omits these first two sentences in this paragraph (1–2Hol 3.263). The 1550 text of Hall has been used here in omitting a superfluous "the" between the words "do proceed" in the 1548 and 1809 editions.

torments and afflictions God hath whipped and scourged this miserable isle, yea, with such and so many scourges and plagues as no nation, the Egyptians only except, were ever tormented or afflicted withal.

I will not speak of rebellious murders and oppressions, which of late hath been done and exercised here among us; but I will declare and manifest to you how the crown and glory of this realm is by the negligence of this silly man and his unwise council, minished, defaced, and dishonored. Is not Normandy, which his father gat, regained, and conquered again, by the insolency of him and his covetous council, is not the whole duchy of Aquitaine by two hundred and odd years peaceably possessed by the kings of this realm, in one year and a little more, gotten out of our hands and seigniory? What should I speak of Anjou and Maine, or the loss of the Isle of France with the rich city of Paris? [46] Alas, my heart sobbeth, mine eyes water, and my tongue faltereth, either to speak or think of the losses and misfortunes that this our native country hath of late sustained. But as the preachers say, evil-gotten goods do not long continue, nor usurped power hath no prosperous success.

I will not molest you with the rehearsing of the calamity which fell amongst the Israelites, when Athaliah slew all the blood royal except little Joash and tyrannously usurped the crown, nor trouble you with the continual warfare which happened among the Romans when Julius Caesar took upon him without law or authority the name and style of emperor; but I put you in remembrance of our own nation, what mischief, strife, and misery succeeded in this realm by the injurious usurpations of Harold, son to Godwin, Earl of Kent, and Stephen of Blois, Earl of Boleyn, the one being the cause of the conquest of this realm, and the other the occasion of infinite troubles and domestical dissension within the same. Yet all these vexations and scourges be but a shadow or counterfeit light in comparison of the great calamities and miseries which all we here present have seen and experimented. Yet[47] in the midst of this affliction, and to make an end of the same, God of his ineffable goodness, looking on this country with his eyes of pity and aspect of mercy, hath sent me in the truth, to restore again this decayed kingdom to his ancient fame and old renown. Which[48] here in open Parliament, according to my just and true title, I have and do take

---

[46] Holinshed, again following Grafton, omits the following material.

[47] Holinshed's text resumes at this point.

[48] "Which" seems to refer to York himself, an unusual construction that looks like a literal translation from the Latin. Grafton and Holinshed, however, change the construction and the meaning, reading "whereof" for "which" and making it refer to the kingdom.

possession of this royal throne, not putting diffidence but firm hope in God's grace, that by his divine aid, and the assistance of you, the peers of the realm, I shall decore and maintain the same to the glory of him, honor of my blood, and to the public wealth of all you here present as of all the poor commons and subjects of this kingdom and regiment.[49]

"When the duke had thus ended his oration," Hall says, "the lords sat still like images graven in the wall or dumb gods, neither whispering nor speaking, as though their mouths had been sewed up. The duke perceiving none answer to be made to his declared purpose, not well content with their sober silence and taciturnity, advised them well to digest and ponder the effect of his oration and saying; and so, neither fully displeased, nor all pleased, departed to his lodging in the king's palace."

We too may well sit stupefied before this rhetorical display, and wonder how much of it Hall believed himself. The fact that he could write such a speech is a sufficient indication that he had considered the various claims and interpretations that York alleges, and beyond a doubt he believed that York was a closer heir to the throne than Henry. But whether he agreed that York was justified in rising up in arms against the king to whom he had sworn allegiance is doubtful, since he did not approve of any of the risings against Henry IV. York's characterization of Richard II and the Percys is also at variance with Hall's own treatment, nor would he agree that Henry V unjustly executed Cambridge or that Henry VI lost his possessions abroad

---

[49] Hall 245–248. The substance of this remarkable speech resembles that of the Yorkist works examined in Chapter II, especially *A Political Retrospect* and the second version of Hardyng's *Chronicle* (Hall unquestionably used the latter). But it also resembles the speech given by Edward in the Whethamstede Register. However, if we discount certain similarities in the stylistic gigantism and bombast of their formal speeches, there is little indication that Hall knew of the register. But he has succeeded in making a more elaborate case for York than any of the Yorkists who lived in the days of which he treats. Since Hall often expands speeches that he finds in his sources, he may have had access to a tradition of such a speech made by York at this time; and a likely source would be Sir Davy Hall, who, however, was slain along with York later in the same year, in the battle of Wakefield. R. L. Storey, *The End of the House of Lancaster* (London 1966) 3n, is no doubt correct when he says that Hall was drawing upon the official Yorkist manifesto issued by Parliament under Edward IV (above, Chap. II at n. 44). It is important to notice that this Parliament speaks of a defense of his claim that York made in October of the previous year, in which he "showed, opened, declared, and proved his right and title to the said crown tofore the Lords Spiritual and Temporal and Commons, being in the same Parliament, by ancient matters of sufficient and notable record undefeasible; whereunto it could not be answered or replied by any matter that of right ought to have deferred him then from the possession thereof" (*Rot. parl.* 5.465).

through insolence, nor that York's motives were as pure as he maintained. And as for York's claim that all the troubles that had recently befallen England were punishments sent by God, Hall was aware that most of them were caused by the secret machinations of York himself; with regard to Cade's rebellion, for instance, Hall maintains at some length that York's party definitely engineered it, whereas Vergil merely suggested this explanation as a possibility, leaving open the other possibility that it was a spontaneous rising.[50]

As for Hall's probable opinion of the Duke of York's claim to be sent by God to rescue England from its troubles, we may remark first of all that Hall portrays York two pages later as being killed in the midst of England's troubles;[51] and then too we may refer to the paragraph immediately following the account of York's speech for Hall's private view concerning those who claim to know the mind of God in his direction of human affairs. He says that while York was thus declaring his title in the House of Lords, a strange event happened in the House of Commons; for a crown that was hanging there as part of a light-fixture suddenly fell to the ground, without being touched by anyone or dislodged by the wind, and at the same time there also fell down the crown that stood on the top of the Castle of Dover, as a sign or prognostication that the crown of the realm would be changed from one line to another; this at any rate was the judgment of the common people, "which were neither of God's privity, nor yet of his privy counsel, and yet they will say their opinions, whosoever say nay." [52]

Hall no doubt takes his cue for mocking this providential interpretation from the slighting way in which Vergil reports a similar alleged portent,[53] for in general he follows the lead of Vergil in his providential remarks. For instance, on the next page he translates Vergil's comment that it was the will of God that Henry suffer the final adversity of the deprivation of his crown before being recompensed with a heavenly garland,[54] and the same is true with regard to Vergil's other providential statements referring to the houses of York, Lancaster, and Tudor discussed in the preceding chapter (and detailed below). Some-

[50] Hall 219–220; cf. 1PV 491–492.
[51] Hall 250.
[52] Hall 248.
[53] Above, Chap. IV at n. 37.
[54] Hall 249 (1PV 503); he also translates the three contemporary opinions given in 1PV 514–515 in explanation of Henry VI's final fall, including the one of inherited guilt and punishment (285–286).

times he even makes explicit implicit providential sentiments; for instance, where Vergil says the murderers of Prince Edward were punished under the *lex talionis* (that is, by being murdered), Hall says that some of the "actors" afterwards tasted the bitterness of this murder "by the very rod of Justice and punishment of God." [55] And occasionally he inserts a providential notion of his own by way of stylistic expansion.[56]

Perhaps Hall follows Vergil in many cases from force of habit, since so much of his history is taken over from him in the lump. But perhaps too he found Vergil reasonable and sufficiently hypothetical in his providential judgments; furthermore, he obviously admired Vergil's elegant Latinity as well as his own rendering of it into English. We have seen, however, that Hall is not as tolerant with regard to some of the earlier attempts at providential analysis (the crown prodigy and the leprosy attributed to Henry IV), and his expressions in dealing with them show a basic tendency in him, when expressing his own opinions and not handing on those of others, to cast doubt on the facile explication of God's motivations and to stress the mysterious and unknown factors in the movements of divine providence. We have seen him speak in this way also of the death of Henry IV and of the English losses in France.[57]

Other manifestations of this tendency on Hall's part appear further on. Although he accepted Fabyan's suggestion that God apparently was not pleased with Henry VI's marriage to Margaret as an explanation for the troubles that followed (rather interfering, by the way, with the opinion in the Duke of York's speech that these troubles were due to the crimes of Henry IV and the unlawful possession of the throne by the house of Lancaster), yet he rejects a similar explanation for the troubles that followed upon Edward IV's marriage to Elizabeth Grey. He says that afterwards many speculated that these disasters stemmed from the fact that God was not pleased with this marriage, or else that God punished Edward in his posterity for dissimulating with his faithful friend Warwick. But such conjectures, Hall says, for the most part are more the results of "men's fantasies than of divine revelation." [58] He is apparently drawing on some source or sources that have since been lost. It is striking, however, that

[55] Hall 301; 1PV 523.
[56] For instance, the favorable wind that brought Richmond safely back to Normandy was, according to Hall, "sent even by God" (Hall 396; cf. 1PV 546).
[57] Above at nn. 24 and 42.
[58] Hall 265.

he accepts a rather similar judgment of Vergil's with regard to Edward IV's perjury at York and the destruction of his children, and even sets it forth as his own opinion — "Of this thing," he says, "I may fortune to speak more in the life of Richard III as the cause shall arise, where it may evidently appear that the progeny of King Edward escaped not untouched for this open perjury." [59]

A bit earlier, Hall draws on the *Great Chronicle of London* for its report of the supernatural interpretations concerning Margaret's inability to return to England to join Warwick when he succeeded in putting down Edward IV in 1470. According to her enemies, it was by God's just provision that she who had caused so many battles and so much bloodshed in England should never return there again to do more mischief.[60] Her friends on the other hand said that she was kept away by sorcerers and necromancers.[61] Thus, Hall says, "as men's imaginations ran, their tongues clacked." [62]

Hall follows Vergil in regarding Margaret's misfortune as primarily one caused by human failing and misjudgment in allowing Gloucester to be killed by his enemies, rather than to any explicit providential action.[63] But earlier, in addition to adopting the Fabyan opinion concerning Henry VI's breach of contract, he remarks that there is an old saw which says that a man intending to avoid the smoke falls into the fire; so it was with Margaret, who, in her effort to preserve her husband in honor and herself in authority, consented to the death of the Duke of Gloucester, which brought about what she most desired to avoid; for if he had lived, York would not have dared to put forth his claim, the commons would not have revolted, and the house of Lancaster would not have been destroyed; but all these things came to pass by the destruction of this good man. Hall

[59] Hall 292. The "may evidently appear" should perhaps be interpreted hypothetically rather than categorically, to correspond with the "fortasse videre licebit" of 1PV 517 (1Grafton 452 translates: where a man may see that the progeny of Edward were punished for this offense). When Hall does return to this subject, interrupting More to translate Vergil once again, he reads his "fortasse . . . contigit" as "might so happen," and reads Vergil's positive judgment concerning Clarence's death as merely probable — because Edward killed Clarence, "he incurred, of likelihood, the great displeasure toward God" (Hall 380; 1PV 540).

[60] This judgment of course was refuted as soon as she did succeed in returning to cause more bloodshed.

[61] CLgreat 214 refers more explicitly to some sorcery or witchcraft performed by someone called in those days "Bungay," or by someone else. Fabyan 661 speaks skeptically of mists allegedly raised by Bungay at the battle of Barnet.

[62] Hall 287.

[63] See Hall 297–298 (1PV 521).

then adds to this sentiment, which is basically that of Vergil, the following remark: "This is the worldly judgment, but God knoweth what he had predestinate and what he had ordained before, against whose ordinance prevaileth no counsel, and against whose will availeth no striving." [64] Here, then, he has combined his own theme of the unknowability of God's ways (since he gives no reason for God's predestination in this case) with Vergil's themes of destiny and the will of God in the fall of Lancaster, which he translates elsewhere.[65] But the theme is no doubt derivable from Vergil's remarks also, since in the first edition Vergil does not associate himself with any providential reason for Lancaster's downfall, apart from the divine disciplining of King Henry VI.

In spite of the turmoil that led to Henry VI's brief restoration in the ninth and tenth years of the reign of Edward IV and the other disturbances met with during his twenty-two years as king, Edward's reign is on the whole considered a prosperous one, and the chapter in Hall dealing with it is so named. Hall makes a few observations and reservations concerning Edward's prosperity and lack of it that are not taken over from Polydore Vergil.[66] We have already discussed his rejection of the providential interpretations of Edward's marriage and his bad treatment of Warwick. He does speak of Warwick's escape from Edward effected by God,[67] but he says the same about Edward's escape from Warwick.[68] There are similar providences in favor of Warwick and Edward in Comines, whom Hall was using at this

[64] Hall 210.

[65] Hall 226 = 1PV 494 (Somerset's inability to stop York's scheming); Hall 276 = 1PV 510 (Edward IV's escape from Warwick's hands); Hall 297 = 1PV 521 (a reference to Margaret's destiny). In the second of these passages, Hall translates "extremum ejus domus fatum" as "the extreme point of decay of his house and estate" and "his unhappy predestinate chance." And he makes Vergil's conjecture ("ita fortasse Deo cordi erat") a fact ("well, such was God's pleasure"). Hall also applies his proverbial theme of "man proposes, God disposes" to Margaret when she fails to take control of London after the second battle of St. Albans in 1461 (252–253). He also translates Vergil's report that Henry himself considered his misfortunes God's punishment for his own sins and those of his ancestors (303–304), but as we saw, he did not include unlawful possession of the crown as one of these sins. Hall mentions the report that old men gave of Henry's miracles, but he goes on to explain that Henry VII desisted from his attempts to have him declared a saint because Rome charged too much for canonizing kings (Hall 303–304; cf. 1PV 525).

[66] He translates Vergil's remark on the punishment of the murderers of Henry VI (303, 1PV 525), as well as that on Clarence's divine punishment for perjury in abandoning Warwick and Henry VI (293, 1PV 518).

[67] Hall 282.

[68] Hall 284, 285.

point.[69] He carries over from him the divine favor on behalf of the French against the English,[70] as well as the report of the dove that alighted on Edward's tent, which gave rise to the opinion that the treaty between the two nations was effected by God.[71] Hall sarcastically leaves it to the reader to decide whether the dove sat there to dry herself or was a token given by God.[72]

In spite of his occasional disclaimers against providential interpretations, Hall can at times make an independent assertion of God's intervention; for instance, after Edward's victory at Hexham Field and his success in running down those who escaped, he says that it would seem from the outcome that God had ordained that everyone who rebelled against King Edward should eventually receive death as his reward.[73] But it is not at all likely that he is attempting to build up at this point a unified providential theme on political lines.

More's History of Richard III

Hall followed the example of his printer Richard Grafton in taking over as a whole the unfinished life of Richard III attributed to Sir Thomas More; he fits it into his chapters on the "pitiful life" of Edward V and the "tragical doings" of Richard III.[74] It is generally agreed that this work preserves many facts and opinions from a time contemporary to the events which are described in it, and that John Morton, Bishop of Ely and later Archbishop of Canterbury, exerted a direct or indirect influence upon its content.

In this highly literary essay in biography, there are numerous providential or supernatural references, but they are for the most part contained in speeches given to the various personages, and as such usually cannot be found to contribute materially to an authorial providential theme, except indirectly. Thus the

[69] Comines 1.189, 191.
[70] Hall 309, 313; Comines 1.251, 262, 324, etc.
[71] Comines 1.279–280.
[72] Hall 320.
[73] Hall 260. He also portrays Edward as thanking God for his success (pp. 254, 297, 301).
[74] That is, Hall took over the version that Grafton had printed in his continuation of Hardyng. Rastell later printed a different copy of the English along with some passages translated from the Latin version. See Richard L. Sylvester's introduction to his edition of More's History (New Haven 1963). But here we shall deal with the text as it appears in Hall, since it was in this form that it first influenced English historiography. The page numbers of the Sylvester edition will be added in brackets.

hypocritical piety of Richard and his appeals to God and divine providence serve as an ironic gloss upon the editorial indications that Richard incurred God's displeasure and felt the effects of his justice.

More's presentation of Richard's rise to the throne constitutes a parody of the usual supernatural apparatus that is brought into play whenever a king is forcefully overthrown and replaced by a newcomer, a pattern abundantly illustrated in the examples we have seen of the Lancaster, York, and Tudor myths. The theme of hereditary punishment is ingeniously employed in the sermon delivered by Doctor Shaw, shortly before Richard's accession. He takes for his text Wisdom 4.3: "Spuria vitulamina non dabunt radices altos." His thesis is that children born outside of the laws of matrimony ordinarily lack the grace God gives to legitimate offspring, and for the most part they are unhappy, as a punishment for the sin of their parents; and though some of them, because the truth of their origin is hidden from the world, inherit and enjoy for a time what does not belong to them, yet God always sees to it that it does not long remain in their line, but arranges for the truth to come to light and the rightful heirs to be restored, while the "bastard slips" are pulled out before they can root deep. And in confirmation of this view. Shaw adduces various examples from the Old Testament and ancient history.[75]

Shaw seems to be doing a variation here on the theme of ill-gotten goods not lasting through the third generation, a proverb which the Yorkists had used to good effect against the Lancastrians, and which Hall incorporated into York's speech, in addition to translating the allusion to it in Vergil. In his own name, More applies a similar adage to Richard, as André had done. He says: "As the thing evil gotten is never well kept, so through all the time of his usurped reign, never ceased there cruel murder, death, and slaughter, till his own destruction ended it." [76]

The standard claim that the new king is sent by God is utilized to great burlesque effect in the botched attempt of Shaw to time his words to coincide with Richard's entrance, and thereby to make it seem that the Holy Spirit was at work, and that Richard was chosen by God through a kind of miracle.[77] The same is true

[75] More-Hall 367–368 [66–67]. More follows the common opinion that Shaw died for shame after making this speech; but, while this death is considered very fitting, it is not explicitly denominated as providential (pp. 365, 368 [59, 68]).

[76] More-Hall 377 [82]; cf. also Sackville's tragedy of Buckingham, Mirror 326.

[77] More-Hall 368 [68].

of Buckingham's offices on behalf of Richard, when he portrays him to the citizens as the friend and ally of God, and appeals to the familiar *Vae terrae* of the Wiseman.[78]

This providential "anti-myth" is further advanced in the amusing scene in which Buckingham urges Richard to accept the kingship, to the praise of God. Richard declines, for, "lauded be God," his protectorship has begun well, since the enemies of the realm have been repressed, partly by good policy, and partly and more particularly by the special providence of God. When Richard is finally prevailed upon to accept, he says he hopes by God's grace to regain France, and he asks God to let him live only as long as he intends to govern well.[79] And after uncovering the witchcraft plot against him by Queen Elizabeth, Shore's wife, and Hastings,[80] "as a godly continent prince clean and faultless of himself, sent out of heaven into this vicious world for the amendment of men's manners," Richard has the Bishop of London put Jane Shore to open penance.[81] He gives it out that God helped them to discover Hastings' treachery in good time, and that by God's grace all the realm shall rest in "good quiet and peace." [82] The merchant who remarks that Richard's proclamation concerning Hastings was written by prophecy is perhaps being ironic rather than naive; but there is no doubt about More's irony.[83]

In speaking of the results of the murder of the two young sons of Edward IV, More details the misfortunes that befell those responsible for it, and seems to indicate that they were the effects of divine justice. He says that if one ponders well this affair, one must conclude that "God gave this world never a more notable example either in what unsurety standeth this world's weal, or what mischief worketh the proud enterprise of

[78] More-Hall 369–371 [69–74].

[79] More-Hall 373–374 [77–80].

[80] More-Hall 360 [47–48], also reported in 1PV 536. For similar instances of sorcery used against the life of the king, cf. the charges made against the Dowager Queen Johanna under Henry V (2Wals 123; 3Wals 2.331; CLk 73; CLn 107; Hall 132; 1–2Hol 3.106); against Eleanor Cobham under Henry VI (Brut 477–482, 508; CLgreat 175; CLgreg 183–184; CLf 102, 115; CLk 148–149, 154–155; CLn 128–130; Davies 57–60; 2Hard 400; Fabyan 614; 1–2Caxton 566–567; Giles 3.30–31; Hall 202; 1–2Hol 3.203–204); and against Clarence or Clarence's servant under Edward IV (Mancini 77, 134; cf. 1PV 530, Hall 326, and 1–2Hol 3.346). We have discussed above the theme of sorcery in connection with Henry IV, Edward III, and Richard II, Joan of Arc, and Queen Margaret. We have also seen that the Parliament under Richard III accused Queen Elizabeth and her mother of effecting the queen's marriage to Edward by means of sorcery.

[81] More-Hall 363 [54; not in the Latin].

[82] More-Hall 363 [53–54].

[83] More-Hall 363 [54; not in the Latin].

an high heart, or finally what wretched end ensueth such dispiteous cruelty. For first to begin with the ministers, Miles Forest at St. Martin's le Grand piecemeal miserably rotted away. John Dighton lived at Calais long after, no less disdained and hated than pointed at, and there died in great misery.[84] But Sir James Tyrrell was beheaded at the Tower Hill for treason. And King Richard himself was slain in field, hacked and hewn of his enemies' hands, harried on a horseback, naked, being dead, his hair in despite torn and tugged like a cur dog. And the mischief that he took within less than three years of the mischief that he did in three months be not comparable. And yet all the meantime spent in much trouble and pain outward, and much fear, dread, and anguish within." [85]

At this point, Hall interrupts More to translate Vergil's account of the reactions of the people and especially of Queen Elizabeth, and his views on hereditary punishment and on Richard's efforts to appear as a good king.[86] He takes up More again for his account of the breach between Richard and Buckingham, and stays with him until More breaks off in the midst of the encounter between Buckingham and Bishop Morton.

Morton tells Buckingham that he has resigned himself to God's will in allowing the sons of neither of his former masters (that is, Henry VI and Edward IV) to come to the throne; and yet he indicates that he is not resigned to Richard's reign, and that he wishes God had given Richard as many virtues for governing as he gave to Buckingham.[87]

In the passages that Hall added to Morton's conversation with Buckingham, there is every reason to suppose that he was carrying forward the characterizations of the bishop and the duke as he found them in More, and therefore it is not very likely that he was portraying Buckingham's sentiments as sincere, much less that these sentiments are automatically to be taken as exemplifying Hall's own feelings.

It seems clear that Hall intends Morton to hint at the plan of having Richmond marry Elizabeth, with the purpose of luring Buckingham into proposing and claiming the scheme as his own invention.[88] This, at any rate, is what the duke does. He says the

---

[84] The Rastell-Holinshed text reads that Dighton is still alive and is likely to be hanged before he dies.

[85] More-Hall 379 [86–87].

[86] Hall 379–381; see above, Chap. IV at nn. 58–63.

[87] More-Hall 383–384 [92–93].

[88] Hall 284–285.

Countess of Richmond had suggested that her son marry one of Edward's daughters, and when he recalled her words, he truly believed that the Holy Ghost prompted her to make her suggestion, without any realization on her part of its implications, or on his own part for that matter; "but such a lord is God, that with a little sparkle he kindleth a great fire," and therefore, Buckingham concludes, he (Buckingham) intends by this marriage to establish a clear line to the throne and so bring Richard to destruction.[89]

Morton was exultant at this prospective union of the two houses and the peace that could be expected to result from it. "And lest the duke's courage should suage, or his mind should again alter, as it did often before, as you may easily perceive by his own tale," the bishop set about hoisting all the sails that he had, so that his ship might quickly come to harbor. Accordingly he told Buckingham that since "by God's high provision and your incomparable wisdom and policy, this noble conjunction is first moved," it was necessary to spread the word to the right people. But when this was done, Morton escaped from Buckingham's detention.[90]

The Tudor Myth in Hall

While we cannot accept either Buckingham or Morton as a spokesman for Hall on the divine inspiration of the plan to promote the union of York and Lancaster, we can agree that Hall added to the Tudor myth by translating Vergil's reflections on this subject and by contributing a few points of his own, often, it seems, simply in the interests of style. Thus he adds to Vergil's account of Henry VI's prophecy of Richmond's coming reign the phrase, "so ordained by God"; and a favorable wind in Vergil is sent by God in Hall.[91] And when he comes to this subject again at the beginning of Vergil's chapter on Henry VII,

[89] Hall 385–389.

[90] Hall 389–390.

[91] Hall 287, 396; cf. 1PV 515, 546. Hall repeats the evidences of Richmond's piety recorded by Vergil (above, Chap. IV at nn. 77–81; Hall's corresponding passages are on pp. 392, 405, 410, 420, 433; on the last-named page, Hall has Henry VII pray for God's aid through the intercession of the Blessed Virgin, but he omits mention of the miracles at Walsingham). He also adds a few more prayers of his own; for instance, he has Queen Elizabeth praise God when she hears of the plot to marry her daughter to Richmond (p. 391); and Richmond thanks God for sending him so many good captains; and again, he speaks of his trust in God for victory when requesting aid of the Duke of Brittany (p. 397). Hall's translations of Vergil's remarks on the providential punishment of the Yorkists (pp. 292, 293, 301, 303, 380) can also be regarded as an element in the Tudor myth.

before giving the prophecies of Cadwallader and Henry VI, he does not say, as Vergil does, that Henry "seems" to have succeeded by divine aid, but rather he asserts this as a fact: "Which kingdom he obtained and enjoyed as a thing by God elected and provided, and by his especial favor and gracious aspect compassed and achieved." He goes on to say that Henry was crowned and proclaimed king "by right and just title of temporal inheritance, and by provision of divine purveyance." [92]

Hall also made a substantial addition by giving long speeches to Richard and Richmond before the battle of Bosworth. Richard admits to his men that in acquiring the throne he was instigated by diabolical temptation into committing a detestable act. But he is confident that he has sufficiently expiated it by repentance and penance, and he asks them out of friendship to forget it as completely as he himself remembers and laments it. They doubtless know, he proceeds, how the devil, the perpetual enemy of human nature and the disturber of concord and sower of sedition, has entered into the heart of an unknown Welshman and excited him with a desire to seek the crown for himself, thereby dispossessing Richard and his heirs. But the enemy are not to be feared, for when these traitors and renegades ("ronnegates") behold their banner advancing against them, they will remember the oath of fidelity they swore to him, their sovereign lord and anointed king, and their consciences will be so stricken with remorse and dread of divine punishment that they will either shamefully retreat or humbly submit themselves to his mercy.[93]

Before Richmond's speech, Hall remarks that he seemed more an "angelical creature than a terrestrial personage";[94] he tells his men that "if ever God gave victory to men fighting in a just

---

[92] Hall 423. He also gives more details on the prayers of thanksgiving and celebration held in London after Bosworth (p. 423); and with regard to Henry's prayer immediately after Bosworth, he says that he not only thanked God heartily, but besought him to send his grace to advance and defend the Catholic faith, and to maintain justice and concord among his subjects, who had now been committed by him to his care (p. 420). And in speaking of the marriage between Henry and Elizabeth, he says that peace was thought to have descended from heaven (p. 425), instead of simply having been born, as in Vergil. He also takes over an interesting item from 1Grafton 544, according to which Henry got lost the night before the battle of Bosworth, and feared that it was a prognostic of bad fortune for him (p. 413).

[93] Hall 415. Richard's remark about the devil entering into the heart of Richmond is a recollection of Satan's entering into Judas to betray Christ (John 13.2, 27; Luke 22.3; cf. Acts 5.3).

[94] We have seen Henry VII referred to in angelic terms in the Croyland account and in André (above, Chap. III at nn. 10 and 63).

quarrel, or if he ever aided such as made war for the wealth
and tuition of their own natural and nutritive country, or if he
ever succored them which adventured their lives for the relief
of innocents [and] suppressing of malefactors and apparent
offenders, no doubt, my fellows and friends, but he of his
bountiful goodness will this day send us triumphant victory
and a lucky journey over our proud enemies and arrogant adversaries." Richmond emphasizes the righteousness of their cause,
and is confident that God would rather fight on their side than
aid those who have no respect for him or his laws. Richard
wrongly keeps him from the crown, but he firmly believes that
God will deliver him and his allies to him as a punishment, or
cause them to fly because of the prick of their corrupt consciences.

"For surely," he says, "this rule is infallible, that as ill men
daily covet to destroy the good, so God appointeth the good to
confound the ill. And of all worldly goods the greatest is to
suppress tyrants and relieve innocents, whereof the one is ever
as much hated as the other is beloved. If this be true, as the
clerks preach it, who will spare yonder tyrant," who untruly calls
himself king, who has violated the laws of God and man and is
a Tarquin and a Nero combined.

He lists Richard's crimes, among them his attempt to violate
his niece, whom he himself has sworn to marry. Thank God,
he says, they have survived the secret treasons in Brittany, and
have finally found the furious boar whom they have sought for
so long. And now, he tells them, they are to advance forward, as
"true men against traitors, pitiful persons against murderers,
true inheritors against usurpers, the scourges of God against
tyrants." [95]

We may with a fair degree of safety assume that Hall approves
of the sentiments he gives Richmond here, and that he disap-
proves of those he has Richard speak. He brings in the motif
of the devil again, this time in his own name, when he deals with
the pretenders set up by Edward IV's sister, Margaret of Burgundy, against Henry VII,[96] and he follows Vergil in assuring
us that Henry's soul must be in heaven, though he omits entirely Vergil's elaborate praise of his religious practices.[97]

It is strange that Hall has no original summary or concluding

[95] Hall 416–418.
[96] Hall 428, 430, 459, 462. He takes over from 1Grafton 583 the notion of Perkin
Warbeck's death as providential punishment (p. 489).
[97] Hall 505; 1Grafton 590 also ends the life of Henry VII in this fashion.

sentiment to offer on the Tudor union of York and Lancaster. He is satisfied with a translation (slightly distended, as usual) of Vergil's two brief sentences on the subject — one on Henry's marriage with Elizabeth, and another on the expected heir of both houses.[98] As we have pointed out,[99] Vergil omitted his manuscript summary of the century of strife after Richard II's death and its final resolution in the person and reign of Henry VIII. The fact that Hall does not make a summary of his own suggests that he has lost sight of the theme expressed so forcefully in his title and preface and in the early part of his history. For from discoursing on peace, he speaks at great length and with great bitterness concerning the discords of Henry VII's reign after the union of York and Lancaster, most of it aroused by Yorkists who did not agree that a satisfactory union had been achieved.[100]

As we noted, Hall's theme of discord and union as set forth by him does not have a providential dimension. The reigns of Richard II, Henry IV, and Henry V are portrayed without reference to divine justice in the matter of Richard's overthrow and Henry's usurpation. When the providential element does appear, it is to the benefit of the Lancastrian kings; Glendower (and implicitly the Percys) are providentially punished for their rebellion; Hall denies that Henry IV was providentially punished for his just execution of Archbishop Scrope, and he condemns those who presume to know the secrets of God's judgments; and finally, God aided Henry V in his enterprises. In general, Hall enhances even more than Vergil the Lancastrian myth of the unrighteousness of Richard II and the righteousness of Henry IV and Henry V. As for Henry IV's consciousness of wrongdoing toward Richard, Hall omits Vergil's reference to Henry V's act of expiation in reburying Richard; but this mission is no doubt counterbalanced by his adaptation of Monstrelet's deathbed scene, if Henry IV's remarks are taken as an expression of remorse — as they were by Holinshed.

[98] Hall 423, 424–425; 1PVh 3, 6–7. See above, Chap. IV at n. 75 (and n. 92 above for Hall's rendering of the statement about the marriage).

[99] Above, Chap. IV at n. 86.

[100] See especially Hall 430. On p. 426 he translates Vergil's comments on the sweating sickness, emphasizing his contempt for the "fantastic" judgments of the common people, and giving a hypothetical support to the alternate reading of the portent (adding Vergil's disclaimer: "if vain superstition can set forth any truth"), namely, that it signified that Henry should never have his spirit and mind quiet to the end of his life, considering that now in the very beginning of his newly obtained reign he was "troubled, vexed, and unquieted" with the sedition and commotion of his people.

The providential destruction of the house of Lancaster, then, has the appearance of an afterthought, and it is largely Vergil's afterthought. The analysis of Vergil's treatment therefore applies in general to Hall also. As in Vergil's 1534 edition, Hall only reports, as the opinion of certain men at the time of Henry VI's final fall from power in 1470, the theory of the inherited guilt and punishment of the house of Lancaster; and no opinion is offered by anyone of an intrinsic connection on the providential level between the downfall of Lancaster and the punishment of the Yorkists. Hall's own observations do not promote the notion of dynastic or hereditary retribution, but in general follow the rather simple providential pattern of seeing God's favor in fortunate events and his disfavor in unfortunate ones.[101] However, the speech he gives to the Duke of York shows that he was familiar with the literature of such concepts and could employ them for dramatic purposes. His contributions to Vergil tend as a rule to reinforce all three myths, Lancaster, York, and Tudor; but his occasional expressions of doubt as to the possibility of making valid judgments about providential motives tend to weaken the force of the judgments he himself supports; and a further weakening factor is the contradictions involved in the conjunction of these three myths. Finally, the use of providential themes and the creation of anti-myths or pseudo-myths by characters of dubious sincerity, such as York, Buckingham, and Richard III, might lead us to accept one of Hall's conclusions as inclusive of himself: "As men's imaginations ran, their tongues clacked."

[101] He does, however, draw an interesting moral to Vergil's observation on Queen Elizabeth's parliamentary dispossession. Vergil merely stressed worldly mutability; but Hall adds that the purpose of this mutability is to teach those who are prosperous not to be overconfident, and to prevent those in adversity from losing confidence in God, and to help them live in hope of a better day (Hall 431–432; 1PVh 18). Hall also treats the problem of restitution (on a human level) briefly at one point, where he criticizes Richard III for promoting his sister's daughter, to whom he was in no way bound to make restitution, instead of preferring his brother's daughters, whom he had disinherited (p. 402).

VI

Raphael Holinshed
and
Abraham Fleming

It is generally agreed that Shakespeare used only (or primarily) the 1587 edition of Holinshed's *Chronicles*, which was issued several years after the author's death. But it will be necessary at times to distinguish between this second edition and the earlier edition of 1577/78, which we may accept as expressing Holinshed's own views (as regards fifteenth-century English history), even though he was working under the direction of Reginald Wolfe until the latter's death in 1570.

The second edition was put in charge of John Hooker (alias Vowell), but Abraham Fleming, a very Protestant clergyman and copious moralizer, did most of the actual editing, at least for our period of English history. There are occasional contributions from Hooker (usually introduced by Fleming) and Francis Thynne; and also an editor who identifies himself as W.P. makes frequent comments up to the middle of the fifteenth century. But it is Fleming's tedious and often puerile comments that are the most significant for the theme of divine providence; and it is probably a safe enough assumption that the unidentified additions are also by Fleming, or at least approved by him.[1]

Fleming seems to have possessed or compiled a commonplace book of pithy Latin verses, and he omitted no occasion to point up morals with them; he often invented occasions by prosing in bridges between harmless reports or comments by Holinshed and the verses that he wished to inflict upon his readers. His

---

[1] However, to be perfectly safe, we shall not identify the editor as Fleming in any particular addition unless he does so himself. For recent appraisals of Fleming, see Sarah C. Dodson, "Abraham Fleming, Writer and Editor," *University of Texas Studies in English* 34:51–66 (1955); William E. Miller, "Abraham Fleming, Editor of Shakespeare's Holinshed," *Texas Studies in Literature and Language* 1:89–100 (1959).

usual method is first to paraphrase what the poet has said as if it were his own sentiment, and then to add, "as the poet very well saith," etc., giving the verses.[2]

One of Fleming's favorite works is Christopher Ocland's versified textbook *Anglorum praelia;* but this work and the other new sources used by Holinshed and Fleming will be dealt with only as occasion arises in the course of our treatment of the two editions of Holinshed. Fleming's most valuable new source is John Stow's *Chronicles of England* (1580); Stow is important however, not for his own comments but for the chronicles and official documents which he uses. Holinshed himself drew on one of the editions of Stow's earlier *Summary of English Chronicles.*[3]

The Fall of Richard II and the Rise of the Lancastrians

In his account of Richard II, Holinshed uses a variety of contemporary sources like Créton (the French pamphlet owned by Master John Dee), the *Traïson* (John Stow's French pamphlet),[4] and Walsingham,[5] as well as Polydore Vergil, Caxton, and Fabyan. And with the beginnings of Henry IV's rise, Hall begins to emerge as a primary source.

With all the various viewpoints that these sources represent, it can easily be imagined that the final picture that emerges of Richard and Henry often presents unresolved conflicts in their characters and destinies. But the most flagrant of these contradictions are created by the intrusive moralizations of the second-edition editor.

With regard to Richard, Holinshed repeats Hall's (really

[2] At at least one point this method is followed in the course of an insert by W.P. (2Hol 3.212–214). But Fleming may have added the verses to W.P.'s material. W.P. identifies the time of his writing as 1585 in one of his additions (2Hol 3.75).
[3] Stow's *Summary* was issued in 1565, 1566, 1570, 1574, and 1575 (and once more in 1590).
[4] 1–2Hol 2.836, 850, etc. (For Richard II's reign, all references to 2Hol will be to the second volume of Ellis' edition.)
[5] Fleming specifically cites the *Ypodigma Neustriae* (4Wals) as his source, but 1Hol seems to have used the *Historia anglicana* (3Wals); Stow saw both works through the press for Archbishop Parker in 1574. In the account of the aftermath of Richard's execution of the Earl of Arundel, for example, we read not only that Richard was greatly troubled by his conscience in horrible dreams, but also that he had Arundel's body exhumed. This latter point is not mentioned in 4Wals 377, but both are mentioned in 1Wals 219 and 3Wals 2.225–226 (1–2Hol 842). Holinshed usually refers simply to "Wals." but in one instance at least (1–2Hol 3.13) his note reads: "Chr. S. Al.," i.e., the Chronicle of St. Albans.

Vergil's) statement that if Richard had any offense it ought rather to be imputed to the frailty of wanton youth than to the malice of his heart; and then he goes on to give Vergil's indictment of the fickleness of men in always desiring the overthrow of the present state of things.[6] The second edition then adds this comment: "But in this dejecting of the one and advancing of the other, the providence of God is to be respected and his secret will to be wondered at. For as in his hands standeth the donation of kingdoms, so likewise the disposing of them consisteth in his pleasure, which the very pagans understood right well; otherwise one of them would never have said,

> Regum timendorum in proprios greges,
> Reges in ipsos imperium est Jovis
>   Cuncta supercilio moventis." [7]

In this comment on the rule of Providence over nations, the editor seems to assume the validity of Polydore Vergil's argument that Richard did not deserve to be overthrown, and is simply indicating that this is one of the instances in which the reasons for God's disposition of events are not apparent, and that the righteousness of his providence is to be taken on faith.

Somewhat later, Holinshed inserts the reported abuses of Richard's time, citing Hardyng, but actually drawing on the doctored-up citation of Hardyng in the Protestantized 1542 and 1559 editions of Fabyan. According to this source, Richard promoted many ignorant men to bishoprics and other livings. And furthermore, lechery was very prevalent, and was much indulged in by Richard, but even more so by the prelates. As a result, the whole realm was so infected by their evil example that the wrath of God was daily provoked to vengeance for the sins of the prince and his people.[8]

At this point the editor of the second edition asks: "How then could it continue prosperously with this king? against whom for the foul enormities wherewith his life was deformed, the wrath of God was whetted and took so sharp an edge that the same did shred him off from the scepter of his kingdom and gave him a full cup of affliction to drink, as he had done to other kings, his predecessors, by whose example he might have taken warning.

[6] 1–2Hol 855.

[7] 2Hol 855. A side note refers to Horace, *Odes* 3.1.

[8] 1–2Hol 868–869; see Fabyan 544 and 2Hard 346–347. Hardyng does not charge Richard with lechery, nor does he say anything about the wrath or vengeance of God.

For it is an heavy case when God thunders out his real arguments either upon prince or people." [9]

Aside from the fact that this sentiment contradicts the judgment upon Richard cited earlier, it intrudes upon Holinshed's text at a particularly unfortunate point, especially since its character as an addition to the text is not indicated (such additions are often marked by brackets or side notes or both in the 1587 edition). For Holinshed proceeds immediately after this insertion to condemn the opinions he has just cited from writers with an unfavorable view of Richard. He says:

Thus have ye heard what writers do report touching the state of the time and doings of this king. But if I may boldly say what I think, he was a prince the most unthankfully used of his subjects of anyone of whom ye shall lightly read. For although through the frailty of youth he demeaned himself more dissolutely than seemed convenient for his royal estate and made choice of such counselors as were not favored of the people, whereby he was the less favored himself, yet in no king's days were the commons in greater wealth, if they could have perceived their happy state; neither in any other time were the nobles and gentlemen more cherished, nor churchmen less wronged. But such was their ingratitude towards their bountiful and loving sovereign that those whom he had chiefly advanced were readiest to control him (for that they might not rule all things at their will), and remove from him such as they misliked and place in their rooms whom they thought good, and that rather by strong hand than by gentle and courteous means, which stirred such malice betwixt him and them till at length it could not be assuaged without peril of destruction to them both.

The Duke of Gloucester, chief instrument of this mischief, to what end he came ye have heard. And although his nephew, the Duke of Hereford, took upon him to revenge his death, yet wanted he moderation and loyalty in his doings, for the which both he himself and his lineal race were scourged afterwards, as a due punishment unto rebellious subjects; so as deserved vengeance seemed not to stay long for his ambitious cruelty,[10]

[9] 2Hol 869. Earlier, after repeating Holinshed's summary of Archbishop Arundel's sermon on *Vir dominabitur* (the providential justification of Henry), the editor of the second edition gives the whole sermon, as it appears in Fabyan. The reason he gives is that the scope of this volume calls for such matters to be set down at large (pp. 865–867). Both editions record the statement of Parliament that Richard's misrule would have completely ruined the realm if God had not provided a remedy (1–2Hol 864).

[10] He seems to mean: So that the vengeance Henry's ambitious cruelty deserved did not seem long in coming.

that thought it not enough to drive Richard to resign his crown and regal dignity over unto him, except he also should take from him his guiltless life.[11]

It is possible that Holinshed is referring to a kind of natural consequence that follows upon evil deeds, but he may also be implying a retribution more specifically providential. When he says that deserved vengeance "seemed not to stay long," he is no doubt pointing to the troubles of the early part of Henry's reign and not to the troubles of Henry VI, for in the latter case it would indeed seem like a long time for due punishment to fall. However, Henry VI's trials would be included in the reference to Henry IV's lineal race.

Though Holinshed draws on Hall for his account of the earls' plot against Henry IV, he does not attack the conspirators as Hall does. The devil plays no part in the rising, and Holinshed takes only a passing swipe at the abbot, who, he says, feared that Henry would encroach upon the clergy's possessions, and thus remove the great beam that grieved his eyes and pricked his conscience.[12] However, he does attribute the failure of the armed revolt to the decree of the mighty Lord of Hosts, who disposes all things at his pleasure.[13] But this is perhaps not a defense of Henry's righteousness, as it was in Walsingham and Gower, but is more akin to Froissart's view and to that of the editor of the second edition of Holinshed cited above, where the incomprehensibility of God's ways is suggested.[14]

After giving the various accounts of Richard's death, Holinshed proceeds to discuss the further troubles of Henry's reign. When he comes to the incident of the trap laid in the king's bed, he betrays the Lancastrian origin of his source (probably Walsingham), for he says that it was planted by wicked traitors, but, as God willed it, Henry perceived it in time.[15]

---

[11] 1–2Hol 869. The editor of the second edition then inserts a tirade against Henry, which takes its cue from the immediate context of Holinshed's comment, rather than from the context of the editor's previous insertion (according to which Henry should be regarded as the scourge of God upon Richard).

[12] 1–2Hol 3.9. All further references to 2Hol will be to the third volume unless noted otherwise.

[13] 1–2Hol 11.

[14] Frois 678; 2Hol 2.855. At the point where Holinshed begins to speak of the earls' plot, 2Hol also adds that if this conspiracy had not been hindered, Richard might have been restored. But God, who, as the poet says, revolves human affairs like dust in a whirlwind, had prepared a disappointment for their plot, and therefore it was no wonder that the outcome of their labors was unfortunate (2Hol 8–9).

[15] 1–2Hol 18; 2Hol expands upon the notion that Henry must have been ill at

In general, Holinshed follows Hall in his treatment of the Percy-Glendower-Mortimer revolt;[16] but after mentioning that the Percys appealed to the great number of men who were well affected to Richard II, he adds the significant comment that it was no wonder if many envied Henry's prosperity, since it was evident enough to the world that he had wrongly usurped the crown and not only violently deposed Richard but also cruelly procured his death, for which undoubtedly both he and his posterity were afflicted by troubles that constantly endangered them, until their direct line was completely destroyed by the opposing faction.[17] Once again, it is conceivable that Holinshed here is implying no more than a purely natural cause-and-effect series of events, but it is perhaps more likely that some kind of providential punishment for sin is implied in the statement.

Holinshed gives briefly Walsingham's favorable view of Archbishop Scrope's rising against Henry in 1405, according to which Westmoreland tricked him into dismissing his army; but he also mentions the version of one Eiton, which has it that Westmoreland simply intimidated the archbishop in his interview with him, upon which Scrope submitted to Henry's mercy. At any rate, Holinshed says, both the archbishop and Mowbray were beheaded.[18] He implies no censure for Henry IV in all this, even though he does seem to treat Scrope with respect, saying that he suffered his death with great constancy. He goes on to say that as a result of this constancy, the common people regarded him as a martyr and affirmed that miracles were worked for him. Holinshed here is no doubt being critical of these views of the people, as is more evident when he proceeds to say that they began to worship the dead carcass of him whom they had loved so much when he was alive, until the king's friends forbade it, and they became frightened and desisted.[19]

Following the pattern set by Vergil and Hall, Holinshed describes Henry's projected crusade as undertaken from motives entirely unselfish. He also follows Hall in denying that Henry's

---

ease at all times, seeing that even his bedroom was invaded by the hate and envy of the people; Horace expressed very well the state of such a king, etc. (2Hol 18–19).

[16] He does, however, add a side note saying that Henry's suspicions of Mortimer were grounded upon a guilty conscience (1–2Hol 20).

[17] 1–2Hol 24.

[18] 1–2Hol 37–38.

[19] 1–2Hol 38.

illness was a leprosy, and in discoursing upon the unknowable ways of God in his dealings with men.[20]

The crown scene then follows as in Hall, except that at Henry's ambiguous words ("what right I had to it, God knoweth") Holinshed places a side note: "A guilty conscience in extremity of sickness pincheth sore." [21] He then adds from Fabyan the story of his being brought to the Jerusalem Chamber; when he heard its name, he bade praise to be given to the Father in heaven, for he knew he would die there, according to the prophecy. Holinshed says he will leave it to the reader to decide whether Henry really spoke these words, like a man who gave too much credit to foolish prophecies and vain tales, or whether the whole story was made up, as frequently happens in such cases.[22] At any rate, it is clear that Holinshed himself did not put any stock in such reported prophecies — unlike Fleming, who added from Walsingham the prophecies of the deaths of Archbishop Scrope and Northumberland.[23]

In resuming with Hall's commentary, Holinshed repeats that chronicler's opinion that Henry IV in his latter days showed himself so gentle that he won more love from his people than he had purchased malice and ill will in the beginning.[24] But then Holinshed proceeds to contradict this view; the truth of the matter is, he says, that after Henry IV had attained the crown, he resorted to such severe measures in raising the money he needed and in punishing those who resented his usurpation of the crown in violation of the oath he took on return from exile, and who rebelled against him at various times, that he won for himself more hatred than would have been possible for him to weed out in a much longer lifetime than he had. And yet, Holinshed continues, his subjects no doubt got what they deserved when they tasted that bitter cup, since they were so ready to join him in deposing Richard, their lawful king, whose chief failing consisted only in being too bountiful to his friends and too merciful to his foes.[25]

Once again, then, Holinshed vindicates Richard II and condemns Henry IV and the people who joined him in rebelling

[20] 1–2Hol 57. Just above, he says (drawing on Walsingham) that it pleased God to let Henry recover his strength somewhat over the Christmas holidays.

[21] 1–2Hol 57.

[22] 1–2Hol 58. This criticism of the prophecy resembles that of 2Elmham 122 and Croy 364; see above, Chap. I at n. 83; Chap. II at n. 85.

[23] 2Hol 38, 45.

[24] 1–2Hol 58.

[25] 1–2Hol 58.

against Richard, thereby contradicting the opinion of the second edition that Richard was being punished by God for his sins when he was overthrown. We are mercifully spared an interruption from Fleming at this point, and so we leave the life of Henry IV with the seemingly implied suggestion not only that Henry himself was punished by God for his usurpation but also that the people who partook in the revolts and who were cut off by Henry were being punished for aiding Henry in the first place, even though they were now ostensibly attempting to remedy the situation by appealing to Richard's memory and putting forth the lawful heir to the throne. This judgment would apply only to men like the Percys, of course, and not to those who never approved of Henry's rise to power.[26]

Holinshed repeats the gathered data concerning the sudden reform of Henry V on coming to authority, though the second edition is consistently concerned with making his early wanderings seem less reprehensible than they were generally portrayed.[27] Holinshed follows Hall in characterizing Henry's pious start and dependence upon God not by the works of founding religious houses but by his exhortations to the clergy and laity to live well. He also follows Hall in his brief account of the reinterring of Richard II.[28] Fleming gives as his motive his abhorrence of obscure burial, and describes the cortege as given in the *Polychronicon,* adding that many other solemnities were had at his interment, according to the customs of the time.[29] There is no allusion to the *Polychronicon's* elaborate description of the penances Henry V was performing on behalf of his father for his guilt in procuring Richard's death.[30] Holinshed's account of the English claim to the French crown follows Hall's history in general, except that he omits Hall's attack on Archbishop Chicheley.[31]

With regard to the Cambridge plot, Holinshed repeats the Vergil-Hall account, including the opinion that if Henry had known Cambridge's real motives, he would perhaps have been

[26] Archbishop Scrope should perhaps be included in the group that aided Henry to the throne, since he is listed as one of the witnesses of Richard's renunciation of his rule (1–2Hol 2.862); but nothing is made of this fact in Holinshed's subsequent account of Scrope. He also omits any mention of revenge as the archbishop's motive.

[27] 2Hol 61, as contrasted with 1Hol 1165; see also the addition of 2Hol on pp. 54–55 (after the reference of 1–2Hol to Eiton).

[28] 1–2Hol 62.

[29] 2Hol 62.

[30] Above, Chap. II at n. 40.

[31] 1–2Hol 64–65.

able to quench at that time the fire that was to destroy his house.[32] But then he proceeds to cite the official indictment against the conspirators, which fully details their plan to replace Henry with Mortimer as the legitimate heir to the throne. He concludes that their purpose was apparently well enough known at the time, although perhaps not widely promulgated for various considerations.[33]

Holinshed himself repeats the orations of Henry V to the conspirators and to his men as he found them in Hall. But the second edition strangely changes them and intensifies the impression that Henry was aware only of the bribery motive, in spite of the fact that this edition carries over Holinshed's demonstration that Cambridge was known to be attempting to bring the heir of Richard II to the throne. The editor even goes to the extent of having Henry claim that the great mercy of God graciously revealed to him the treason that was at hand. And the king proceeds to appeal to God's mercy for his French expedition, declaring that the justice of his demand was well known to him; and he commends the success of all his labors to his mercy alone.[34]

Holinshed, then, follows the practice of historians before him in side-stepping the issue of possible culpability in Henry V's tenure of the throne in place of the rightful heir, and follows them also in not adverting to the incongruity of urging the God-sanctioned right of females to inherit upon the French, when this very right was what entitled Mortimer to all that Henry V claimed for himself both in England and in France.

Henry's piety and reliance upon God in his French campaigns are portrayed in Holinshed according to the traditional patterns, with reflections of Tito Livio, Monstrelet, the Chaplain's *Gesta*, Vergil, and Hall. After the battle of Agincourt, Holinshed details Henry's prayers of thanksgiving to God as in Hall, saying that he gave all the credit to God and did not boast of any power of his own. It should be noted that Holinshed himself nowhere attributes the victory to God, but it is evident that he approves of Henry's actions, and in a side note he commends the splendid example given by this devout prince.[35]

[32] 1–2Hol 71.

[33] 1–2Hol 71–72.

[34] 2Hol 70–71 (as contrasted with 1Hol 1173).

[35] 1–2Hol 82. Holinshed adds that "divers clerks" of Paris saw divine persecution of the French in this defeat, in punishment for the way the nation was being misruled (1–2Hol 83). And he explicates Hall's statement that the French were predestined to suffer yet more plagues from the English by saying that their evil

Holinshed repeats the story of Henry's foreboding of his own early death and of the final ruin of his son, along with Hall's commentary.[36] And on his deathbed, Henry is said to have justified his French campaigns by saying that he did not carry on these wars out of vain ambition or other unworthy motives, but only for the recovery of his lawful title; he wished only to establish a perfect peace after acquiring his rightful inheritance; before beginning the wars he was persuaded by wise and holy men that upon these premises he might and ought to proceed by force until he arrived at a just conclusion, and that he could so act without any danger of God's displeasure or peril to his soul.[37]

The Downfall of Lancaster

As a rule, Holinshed accepts Hall's account of the divisions that took place in England during the latter part of Henry VI's reign.[38] He paraphrases Hall's qualification of Vergil's judgment that Henry VI's ruin could have been avoided by preserving Gloucester in power, namely, that God's judgments are unsearchable, and that no human counsel prevails against his decree.[39] Also repeated is the Fabyan-Hall supposition that God

---

hap, as of men appointed by God's providence to suffer yet more damage at English hands, would not permit the emperor's peacemaking attempts to succeed (1–2Hol 85).

[36] 1–2Hol 129.

[37] 1–2Hol 132–133. Holinshed cites Titus Livius for this account, but it does not appear in TL or Trans.

[38] J. P. Brockbank, "The Frame of Disorder: *Henry VI*," in *Early Shakespeare* (Stratford-upon-Avon Studies 3, London 1961) 81, mistakenly says that Holinshed attributes the continuance of internal troubles in England to the fact that the God of love and peace was not among the jarring nobles. In fact, the comment referred to is made by Fleming, and he is speaking of the failure to bring about a peace between England and France, not between the English factions (2Hol 183).

[39] 1–2Hol 211 (cf. Hall 210). Holinshed also follows Vergil-Hall in seeing divine punishment in Suffolk's death, but it is interesting to note that the second edition modifies Hall's elaboration (Fortune would not let Suffolk escape; Hall 219, 1Hol 1279) by substituting "God's justice" for "Fortune" (2Hol 220). There are other instances in which the editor of the second edition has deleted the reference to Fortune in the first edition (Fortune is mentioned in 1Hol 1218, 1237, 1241, 1276, 1297, 1305, but not in 2Hol 134, 159, 163, 216, 253, 270). These instances might indicate a certain prejudice in the editors against the use of personified Fortune, but if so, the prejudice is not universally operative, for a personified Fortune sometimes appears in both editions (e.g., 1–2Hol 280, 281, 296, *bis*), and sometimes such references are introduced by the second edition from other sources; e.g., from Hall (2Hol 297) and Fleming from Stow (2Hol 325). Perhaps the prejudice is that of W.P., for the remark on Fortune at 1Hol 1241 is replaced by a short comment of W.P.'s at 2Hol 163, and references to Fortune begin to appear only after W.P.'s contributions have ceased.

was not pleased with Henry's marriage, as well as the Vergil-Hall comment on the failure of Somerset to stop York, to the effect that destiny cannot be prevented by any human effort.[40]

The principal additions or changes that Holinshed makes in Hall's history derive from the Whethamstede Register, which Holinshed cites as if Abbot Whethamstede himself were the author, and Fleming in the second edition also makes extensive insertions of documents from Stow's 1580 *Chronicles*. For instance, Holinshed mentions the solemn oath that York made at this time (1451), citing Whethamstede;[41] and Fleming supplies the text of the oath from Stow, according to which York swore absolute loyalty to Henry VI, placing his hands on the Gospels and the cross, and receiving the sacrament of the Eucharist; he stated that by the grace of God he would never attempt anything against Henry's royal majesty, but if he should, he was to be considered forsworn and deprived of all his estate and degree.[42]

At the first battle of St. Albans in 1455, Fleming inserts the formal appeal that York made to Henry VI, in which he protested that God knew his intentions were honorable toward the king; and he ended by calling upon God to be his defense. Included also is York's address to his men, which involves an even more extended appeal to God to help them in their just cause against the malice of those who opposed them.[43] Similar pious appeals are made by York, Warwick, and Salisbury after fleeing the country in 1459.[44] Holinshed discusses the Parliament in which these fugitives were declared guilty of high treason, and, quoting from a part of Whethamstede favorable to Henry VI, says that the king's modesty and zeal for mercy was so great that he had inserted a clause permitting him to forgive the attainted lords without consulting Parliament.[45]

Holinshed thought it good to set down in his history the speech of the Duke of York in Parliament after Henry's defeat in 1460, even though he found it odd that Whethamstede, who

[40] 1–2Hol 208, 233 (Hall 205, 226). In the latter passage, Holinshed adds an explanatory side note: "Destiny, or rather God's providence, cannot be avoided" (1Hol 1284). But 2Hol rather surprisingly omits the explanatory words, "or rather God's providence."

[41] 1–2Hol 233.

[42] 2Hol 234–235. No mention is made at this time of any concession to York as next in line to the throne (but, historically, it does seem that he was so regarded until an heir was born to Henry VI in 1453, i.e., Prince Edward).

[43] 2Hol 239–240 (Stow via Fleming).

[44] 2Hol 254–256, 256–258 (Stow via Fleming).

[45] 1–2Hol 256.

was probably present at the Parliament, made no mention of such a speech.[46] He gives the speech as abbreviated by Grafton, however, thereby omitting much of the element of providential punishment;[47] but he retains the notions that God cut off Henry V in his prime because of his father's offense, and that he punished the unruly and usurping people of England by sending them a ruler without wisdom in Henry VI, during whose unlawful reign God scourged the kingdom with great afflictions, until out of his great pity and mercy he desired to put an end to it all by sending York himself.[48]

Holinshed also repeats the two crown incidents, which he says were considered to be signs that the crown was to change lines; but he omits Hall's contemptuous rejection of this kind of attempt to read the mind of God.[49] Later on Fleming inserts a confused dissertation in which he takes great pains to defend such prognostications, or at least to defend the notion that such prodigious accidents have a significance that is verified as time goes on, and that therefore they are not to be omitted from history as a matter of course. There are various examples of such prodigies in this present book, he says, among which this crown episode is especially memorable.[50]

Fleming quotes the official articles of the settlement entailing the crown on the Duke of York and his heirs, in which it is said that this solution was arrived at through the direction of Christ; included also is the oath sworn by York never to agitate in any way against Henry VI.[51] When York was killed by the forces of the queen at Wakefield, Holinshed says that many believed this miserable end came upon him as a due punishment for breaking his oath of allegiance to his sovereign lord, King Henry. But others (no doubt by "others" Holinshed means Whethamstede) consider him discharged of it, because he obtained a dispensation from the pope on the grounds that it was taken unadvisedly, to the prejudice of himself and all his posterity.[52] Holinshed himself no doubt shared the former view and regarded the pope's action as of no import; and this is

---

[46] 1–2Hol 262.

[47] See above, Chap. V, nn. 45–47.

[48] 1–2Hol 262–264.

[49] 1–2Hol 264.

[50] 2Hol 534–535.

[51] Fleming from Stow, 2Hol 266. Holinshed omits the sentiments of Vergil-Hall that it pleased God to let the holy King Henry suffer the loss of his crown, etc.

[52] 1–2Hol 269.

presumably the implication of his side note: "Mark the Pope's dispensation." [53] It is certainly the interpretation of the second edition, where the side note reads: "A purchase of God's curse with the pope's blessing." [54]

Drawing on Whethamstede, Holinshed says that Henry VI thanked God for enabling the Northerners to restore his queen to him.[55] He repeats from Hall the maxim that God disposes what man proposes, referring to Margaret's failure to hold London, and also gives his account of the prayers of Edward upon being elected king.[56] But significantly he omits the pro-Edwardian sentiments of the Whethamstede Register which regards his victories as divinely achieved, as well as Hall's comment at the battle of Hexham Field that it would seem that God had ordained death for rebels against Edward, and also leaves out the long observation of Vergil-Hall that Edward's escape from Warwick in 1470 was God's will and signaled the final fate of the house of Lancaster.[57] He likewise drops the notion that God provided Edward with a place of refuge with his brother-in-law Burgundy, but the second edition picks it up again.[58] Furthermore, he omits the three opinions men had of Henry VI's final fall, as recorded by Vergil-Hall, including the one that considered it a divine punishment for Henry IV's usurpation of the crown.

In speaking of the first appearance of Henry Richmond, Holinshed omits the Vergil-Hall declaration that we should believe Richmond was sent from God, etc., just as Vergil does in his second edition, though it is obvious that Holinshed is drawing on Hall and not any edition of Vergil; for he includes Henry VI's prediction of Richmond's coming reign in the language of Hall's translation (specifically, with Hall's addition: "so ordained by God").[59]

[53] 1Hol 1304. This reading seems to be verified in Holinshed's final remarks on the destruction of the house of York, given below.

[54] After giving the traditional report that York was killed during the battle, Holinshed adds that some (meaning Whethamstede) note that he was captured and crowned and mocked as Christ was by the Jews (1–2Hol 269).

[55] 1–2Hol 271.

[56] 1–2Hol 271, 272, 276.

[57] Holinshed also makes no mention of the opinion, scoffed at by Hall, that God was displeased with Edward's marriage or his treatment of Warwick. With regard to the tempest that frustrated Burgundy's attempt to capture Warwick, Holinshed reduces Hall's work of God to Fortune's doing, and this explanation is kept by Fleming (1–2Hol 296). And Holinshed omits the opinions mocked by Hall concerning Margaret's inability to return to England.

[58] 2Hol 297; cf. Hall 285.

[59] 1–2Hol 302. Fleming adds: "So that it might seem probable by the coherence of holy Henry's predictions with the issue falling out in truth with the same that

Holinshed draws on the Yorkist *History of the Arrival of Edward IV*, as modified by Fleetwood, the recorder of London, to observe that Edward landed at Ravenspurgh when he returned to England in 1471 to regain his crown, the very place where Henry Bolingbroke landed when he came to deprive Richard II of the crown and to usurp it himself;[60] and he uses the same source to record the praise given to God by those witnessing Edward's reconciliation with Clarence.[61] But he does not record the elaborate miracle in the church at Daventry (he says simply that he heard services there)[62] nor the prayers that Edward makes here and elsewhere during the course of his reconquest, nor the authorial attribution of his successes to divine aid.[63] One exception is the report of Edward's thanksgiving to God in the abbey church for the victory it had pleased God to give him at Tewkesbury, with the added report that Edward pardoned those who fought against him.[64]

The 1587 editor at this point makes a typically "disintegrated" intrusion, for he takes no regard for the total context of Holinshed's narrative and proceeds to sing Edward's praises: "Oh the patience and clemency of this good king, who, besides the putting up of wrongs done to him by violence of foes without vengeance, freely forgave the offenders, and did so honorably temper his affections!" [65] For just above on the same page we have Holinshed's account of Edward's promise to spare Prince Edward's life if taken alive, and of the subsequent capture and murder of the prince, quite obviously, it would seem, with the king's approbation; Holinshed concludes by saying in Hall's words that the greater number of his murderers suffered a similar death through God's just punishment.[66]

Earlier Holinshed describes Edward's oath at York as willful perjury, for which, he says, "as hath been thought," Edward's children suffered for their father's offense in being deprived not only of their worldly possessions but of their lives as well, at the

---

for the time he was indued with a prophetical spirit." He goes on to praise Henry's piety.

[60] 1–2Hol 303; Arrival 2.

[61] 1–2Hol 308; Arrival 11.

[62] 1–2Hol 309.

[63] He does draw on Hall to say that Edward offered his standards at St. Paul's after the victory at Barnet (1–2Hol 314), and earlier he repeats Hall's noncommittal report of the alleged sight of the threefold sun at Mortimer's Cross ten years before (Hall 251; 1–2Hol 270).

[64] 1–2Hol 320; cf. Arrival 30–31.

[65] 2Hol 320.

[66] 1–2Hol 320.

hands of their cruel uncle King Richard III.[67] It seems possible that Holinshed agrees with this conjecture of Vergil-Hall, at least as a probability.[68] There is no doubt of the second edition's concurrence, which adds: "And it may well be; for it is not likely that God, in whose hands is the bestowing of all sovereignty, will suffer such an indignity to be done to his sacred majesty and will suffer the same to pass with impunity." [69]

Holinshed goes on to describe Henry's virtues, abbreviating Vergil-Hall; and he then proceeds to refute the opinion of the *Arrival*. He says that these virtues of Henry make it unlikely that he died of any wrath, indignation, and displeasure because the business about keeping the crown on his head had no better success; unless perhaps one could say it grieved him to think that the slaughters and mischiefs which had come about in the land were due solely to his own folly and inadequacy as a ruler; "or (that more is)[70] for his father's, his grandfather's, and his own unjust usurping and detaining of the crown." But however it was, he continues, it pleased God to work miracles for him in his lifetime, "as men have listed to report." [71]

It should be observed that Holinshed does not seem to imply in the foregoing that Henry or the country was being punished by God. He admits that the Lancastrians were holding the crown illegally, and he suggests that Henry's awareness of it and of the bloody deeds it led to was a source of pain to him. But it is interesting to note that in the abridgment of the Vergil-Hall account of Henry's virtues, just referred to, he omits Henry's sentiment that his troubles were caused by his own sins and those of his ancestors (though, as we saw, there was no suggestion that he considered the Lancastrian possession of the crown to be a sin; rather the contrary was indicated). He simply says that he was extremely patient in all his adversities, never desiring

---

[67] 1–2Hol 305. Holinshed does not promise to return to this subject nor does he return to it, for unlike Hall he does not interrupt More's history to record Vergil's reflections.

[68] It is difficult to judge the force of the "as" in the parenthetical expression, "as hath been thought." Holinshed may be dissociating himself from this opinion and merely reporting it as an opinion, or he may mean to signify that it is the opinion of others as well as his own.

[69] 2Hol 305.

[70] This parenthetical expression seems to mean "what is more likely," or, "what is even more true"; or it could mean, "which is more of an offense to God."

[71] 1–2Hol 324–325. In inserting the report of the *Arrival* at this point, Holinshed omits the Vergil-Hall declaration that those responsible for Henry's murder later received their deserved punishment. He goes on to give an account of Henry VII's abortive attempt to have Henry canonized, toning down Hall's sarcastic references to Rome.

vengeance, and accepting them as reparation for his sins; he never made any account of his losses, but if anything were done that seemed offensive to God, he sorrowed over it with great repentance.[72]

In the second edition Fleming adds the remark that because princes "princely qualified" cannot be too highly praised, he will set down a number of incidents that contribute to Henry's everlasting renown, and offer examples worthy of imitation by all men. Fleming cites Stow's quarto *Chronicles* (1580) as his source, and Stow in turn is drawing on John Blakman's devotional biography of Henry, though without citing him. Aside from the events illustrating the king's devout and innocent life (omitting the alleged miracles detailed in Blakman), he includes the incident in which Henry was asked why he held the crown of England unjustly for so long; Henry's reply was that both he and his father inherited it without dispute, and that therefore he could say with King David: "The lot is fallen unto me in a fair ground; yea, I have a goodly heritage, my help is from the Lord which saveth the upright in heart." [73]

The Fall of the House of York

At the end of his life of Edward IV, Holinshed tells us that, God willing, he will reproduce Thomas More's unfinished history word for word as printed among his other works (including portions found only in the Latin version). His text then is taken from Rastell's edition and is considerably different from that used by Hall; but for the most part these differences are of little significance for the themes concerning the supernatural.[74] He makes no insertions of his own into More's account, except for Hall's description of the coronation of Richard III, an addition which he indicates in marginal notes.[75] The editor of the second edition is not as scrupulous, however, and he proceeds to beautify More's text with his platitudes, leaving no indication of his interpolations (aside from the telltale Latin verses). Most of these additions are of no concern to us, but the one commenting on the execution of Hastings deserves notice. By this deed,

[72] 1–2Hol 324.
[73] 2Hol 325–326 (Blakman 44); Henry here is citing Ps. 7.11 and Ps. 15.6.
[74] 1–2Hol 358. One interesting variation is that in Richard III's appearance at Baynard Castle, he is not flanked by bishops in 1–2Hol (Rastell) as he is in Hall and Shakespeare.
[75] 1–2Hol 397–400.

we are told, Richard began to establish his kingdom in blood; by it he increased the hatred of the nobles and shortened the length of his rule; for God will not have the days of bloodthirsty tyrants prolonged, "but will cut them off in their ruff," as David says, etc.[76]

When More's account gives out, Holinshed reproduces Hall's continuation. The second edition makes some additions, especially in the way of side notes. And in the midst of Morton's speech, the editor introduces the sentiment that Richard's kingdom could not last for long, that the Lord would not permit him to go on desecrating the holy office of kingship with deeds of tyranny — "For such he will overthrow, yea he will bring most horrible slaughter upon them, as it is prophesied,

> Impius ad summos quamvis ascendat honores
> Aspice quas clades tempora saeva vehent." [77]

Holinshed follows Hall in general for the history of Richard's overthrow by Richmond. But Fleming introduces an account received from Hooker, his general editor, of an incident that occurred in Exeter. When Richard came there to the Castle of Rougemont and learned its name, "suddenly he fell into a dump, and, as one astonied, said, 'Well, I see my days be not long.'" He was speaking, we are informed, of a prophecy which declared that once he had come to Richmond he would not have long to live; and in fact the prophecy turned out to be true concerning a different Richmond, namely, Henry, Earl of Richmond, who defeated Richard at Bosworth Field in the following year.[78]

Holinshed takes over the Vergil-Hall observation that divine justice causes a criminal like Richard III to be less provident at the very time when his punishment is nearest at hand, and that Richard came to Bosworth by the appointment of God's justice and providence. The second edition adds that though God forbore a while, his forbearance was not an acquittal, but rather a time for preparing whatever was lacking in the plagues that he had determined to rain upon him for his offenses.[79]

After he repeats Hall's final remark on Richard III, that he leaves his punishment to God, who knew his thoughts at the

---

[76] 2Hol 381, citing Buchanan's versified rendition of Psalm 55.
[77] 2Hol 406.
[78] 2Hol 421.
[79] 1–2Hol 432, 438; 2Hol 432–433.

hour of his death,[80] Holinshed proceeds to report that Henry VII set up a tomb over the place where Richard was buried in the Franciscan church at Leicester, with a picture in alabaster representing his person. He did this honor to his enemy out of "a princely regard and pitiful zeal," whereas Richard himself, when he did a similar service for Henry VI, whom he had cruelly murdered, was putting on "an hypocritical show of false pity." [81]

"And now to conclude with this cruel tyrant King Richard," Holinshed says,

we may consider in what sort the ambitious desire to rule and govern in the house of York was punished by God's just providence. For although that the right to the throne might seem to remain in the person of Richard, Duke of York, slain at Wakefield, yet may there be a fault worthily reputed in him, so to seek to prevent the time appointed him by authority of Parliament to attain to the crown entailed to him and his issue;[82] in whom also, and not only in himself, that offense, as may be thought, was duly punished. For although his eldest son, Edward the Fourth, being a prince right provident and circumspect for the surety of his own estate and his children, insomuch that, not content to cut off all his armed and apparent enemies, he also of a jealous fear made away with his brother Clarence, and so thought to make all sure, yet God's vengeance might not be disappointed; for, as ye have partly heard, he did but further thereby the destruction of his issue, in taking away him that only might have stayed the cruelty of his brother of

[80] Hall 421.
[81] 1–2Hol 447. He says that in the second year of his reign, Richard had Henry's body solemnly reinterred at Windsor; cf. Rous, above, Chap. III, n. 23.
[82] Holinshed seems to be confusing the incidents in the life of Richard, Duke of York, in view of his previous account. In his discussion of York's death at the battle of Wakefield, he mentioned the opinion that York was punished for breaking the oath he took in 1451 not to seek the crown, from which he was dispensed by the pope. He took another oath (as 2Hol shows) after seeking the crown and getting it entailed to him, to the effect that he would let Henry live out his reign. This latter oath was not broken by York, for according to Holinshed's own account he died not in an attempt to anticipate the time set by Parliament, but in opposing Queen Margaret, who disallowed this action of the Parliament (Edward IV, however, did anticipate the time allotted, on the grounds that Henry had violated his end of the compact). But in this concluding section, Holinshed seems to be drawing not on his own version of the events of York's life, but on the account of Thomas More, which he reproduced in his chronicle; according to More, York first used peaceful means to attain the crown, and succeeded in getting it entailed to him after Henry's death. "But the Duke, not enduring so long to tarry, but intending under pretext of dissension and debate arising in the realm to prevent his time and to take upon him the rule in King Harry his life, was with many nobles of the realm at Wakefield slain, leaving three sons, Edward, George, and Richard" (More 6).

Gloucester, who, enraged for desire of the kingdom, bereft his innocent nephews of their lives and estates. And, as it thus well appeared that the house of York showed itself more bloody in seeking to obtain the kingdom than that of Lancaster in usurping it, so it came to pass that the Lord's vengeance appeared more heavy towards the same than towards the other, not ceasing till the whole issue male of the said Richard Duke of York was extinguished. For such is God's justice as to leave no unrepentant wickedness unpunished, as especially in this caitiff Richard III, not deserving so much the name of a man, much less of a king. most manifestly appeareth.[83]

In this summary of providential punishment from the time of Richard II to Henry VII, Holinshed becomes the first to suggest that Edward IV and his children were punished not for Edward's own sins, but for a crime committed by his father. However, when he says that the house of York was punished for its bloody methods in achieving the crown, he is no doubt including the deeds of Edward IV as well as those of Richard III; for in saying that God's punishment of unrepentant wickedness in the house of York was especially manifest in Richard, he implies that it was also manifest in other members of the family. And the only other bloody deeds mentioned here are Edward's execution of his brother Clarence and the destruction of his armed enemies.

In contrasting the fates of the house of York and Lancaster, Holinshed makes it clear that he considers each house to be punished for the faults of its own members, and certainly there is no suggestion that York is being punished for the sins of Lancaster. York has its own sins, and though the ultimate occasion for these sins could be said to be Lancaster's usurpation of the crown, York is not thereby relieved of the responsibility for its sins, in Holinshed's view, especially since the crown could have been obtained without them.[84]

There is no indication that Holinshed considers England to have lain under some kind of providential curse, or that the people were being punished for the crimes committed by their rulers. Holinshed did indicate something of this sort, as was noted above, with regard to the people who suffered under

---

[83] 1–2Hol 447–478 (*sic;* the pagination in Ellis' edition goes awry and omits pp. 448–477).

[84] Sir John Hayward has a similar providential analysis in his *Life of King Henry IV*. The Lancastrian kings were punished by God for Richard II's murder, and the Yorkists also suffered, apparently for the murder of Henry VI and his son (Hayward 133–134).

Henry IV's repressive actions; but he also indicated that they were deserving of this punishment for helping Henry to the throne. He does not suggest that the people's guilt was passed on to succeeding generations.[85]

Holinshed notes that the house of Lancaster was also punished by God, though not so severely as the house of York. It would seem to be straining his words too much to find in them a suggestion that Henry V and Henry VI harbored "unrepentant wickedness"; they are not included in this censure any more than the young children of Edward IV. It could hardly be applied even to Henry IV, for Holinshed interprets his deathbed words as expressing repentance for seizing the crown.[86] The question of restitution is not brought up at this point, nor, strictly speaking, is it brought up at all — though when speaking of Henry VI's virtuous abhorrence for all kinds of sin, Holinshed does say that all three Henrys unjustly usurped the kingship, and the obligation of restitution is seemingly implied; but perhaps he considered the obligation to have been adequately met by having the kingdom entailed to York.

Holinshed does not detail in his summary precisely what the punishment of the house of Lancaster consisted in; but in the earlier part of his work in which he treats of Henry IV's actual usurpation, he says that he and his lineal race were scourged for it, until the direct succeeding line was completely destroyed. (In this sense, therefore, Lancaster was punished at least as severely as York.) Holinshed differs from his predecessors, Vergil and Hall, in that he interprets Henry IV's troubles as a punishment for his crimes against Richard II. In this instance, the logic of providential justice has overcome the force of the Lancaster myth, though some elements of this myth are carried over in his account, especially where influenced by Walsingham.

Holinshed ignores the problem involved in Henry V's inheritance of the throne before its legal heir, and negates the Yorkist myth to the extent of deleting most of Hall's references not only to the providential overthrow of Henry VI and the house of Lancaster but also to the providential rise of York.

[85] Holinshed does partially record from Hall the Duke of York's assertion that God was punishing the whole of England for Lancaster's wrongful tenure of the throne, but there is no indication that he agreed with this view, any more than he agreed with the duke's assertion that God was sending him there to bring an end to all England's troubles. Furthermore, as we noted above, Holinshed questioned the authenticity of this speech.

[86] Edward IV is also pictured as religiously making ready for his passage into another world (1-2Hol 355); 2Hol 355–358 adds his dying speech from Hall.

And he returns to the subject at the end only to assert that the house of Lancaster was punished less than the house of York. Furthermore, the piety of Henry V and Henry VI is emphasized throughout.

It is to be noted that Holinshed also greatly diminishes the Tudor myth, for he omits not only the Vergil-Hall belief that Henry was sent from God to put an end to the civil wars, but also the Vergil-Hall treatment of Henry's advent as divinely prepared for and predicted in the time of Cadwallader (with the recollection of Henry VI's prophecy).[87] Fleming restores the latter passage from Hall, however, and amplifies it by repeating the whole incident of Henry VI's prophecy, and adding that "so it came to pass by the appointment of God, to whose government, gift, and disposing, all realms and all dominions are subject, as King David confesseth, saying: 'Omnia sunt regno subdita regna Dei.' ".[88] Fleming substitutes this statement for Hall's assertion that Henry VII was crowned by just title of inheritance and by provision of divine purveyance. Holinshed himself reflects the Vergil-Hall notion that God preserved Princess Elizabeth from Richard's incestuous intentions;[89] and an editor of the second edition (still Fleming, no doubt) remarks on the great sufferings caused by the warring factions; he says they were all ended in the blessed union of Henry and Elizabeth, which was authorized by God, as the *Anglorum praelia* says:

Hoc Deus omnipotens pacis confecerat author,
Civilisque habuit tandem contentio finem

— this in spite of the fact that further down on the same page appears a contradiction of this view that Henry VII's marriage put an end to civil contention, for Holinshed repeats in modified form the Vergil-Hall discussion of the sedition that occurred during Henry's reign.[90]

With these final examples of Flemingesque moralizing, we

[87] He does, however, copy most of the prayers and the acts of piety recorded of Henry VII in Hall.

[88] 2Hol 481, citing "Gu. Ha. in psal. 103."

[89] 1–2Hol 479.

[90] 1–2Hol 482. Holinshed remarks that the sweating sickness was judged by some to be a token of a troublous reign for Henry, "as the proof partly afterwards showed itself" (1–2Hol 482). Here Holinshed seems to admit some kind of validity for the prediction. But he omits the premonition Katherine had of Arthur's death (reinstated by 2Hol 529 from Hall 497, who got it from 1PVh 128; cf. oPVh 123). In general Holinshed seems noncommittal on the subject, as opposed to Fleming's definite support of the predictive character of prodigious phenomena.

may attempt to assess as a whole the influence that Fleming's supervision of the second edition had upon the providential picture that Holinshed drew of fifteenth-century events. It seems that he dealt with Holinshed's material in much the same way that Hall dealt with Vergil's history. Neither Hall nor Fleming offered any concepts or reflections of their own concerning dynastic providential retribution arising out of the internal dissensions over the crown in England; instead they took over in undigested form the views of their respective models. Furthermore, each of them made a practice of promiscuous moralization, which resulted in lining the text with a number of providential morals side by side with those already contained in the authors they were adapting (namely, Vergil and Holinshed). Often these new morals are found to supplement the views appropriated from Vergil and Holinshed, and sometimes they are irrelevant to these views; but at other times they are in contradiction to them. One example in Fleming's edition of Holinshed noted above was the providential condemnation of Richard II which the editor inserted immediately before Holinshed's vindication of Richard.

All the writers we have been considering, Vergil and Holinshed as well as Hall and Fleming, had a tendency at times to be influenced in their editorial statements by the contradictory opinions of previous writers with varying political ideologies or moralizing syndromes. Vergil and Hall differ from the Holinshed syndicate in that they follow the classical practice of composing orations for historical characters, and often draw upon providential formulations for this purpose.

In presenting a coherent providential view of the century, Holinshed seems, in a sense, to be more successful than Vergil. With Vergil it was largely an afterthought, and as a result the concepts remain largely unintegrated in his work. It is especially true with regard to the house of Lancaster, for the speculation on providential ruination of that family centers on Henry VI rather than on the guilty Henry IV. The account of Henry IV's reign remains free of any consideration that he was punished or punishable by God. The opinion is recorded (and more or less adopted as his own in the second printed edition) that Henry VI's deposition was brought about by God's justice, because of his grandfather's unjust acquisition of the realm. This opinion as it stands might seem unfair, since the innocent grandson suffered for the guilty grandfather; but the justice of it is implied in the consideration that the family of Lancaster was retaining possession of what was rightfully due to another. The situation is mollified further by Vergil's view that Henry VI's troubles were not divine punishments of the king but rather divine proofs of his sanctity. However, these considerations do not help much with regard to Prince Edward, Henry's son (but then the reasons for his fate are never really discussed), and they do not apply at all in the case of the sons of Edward IV, whose deaths are explained as a providential *exemplum*.

Holinshed avoids the problems inherent in the concept of hereditary retribution by keeping his references to it vague and general and by concentrating upon the punishment dealt out to the guilty parties. Thus he places his speculation on the punishment of Henry IV and his line in the chapters on Richard II and Henry IV.

Neither Vergil nor Holinshed regards the troubles of the Wars of the Roses as a punishment sent by God upon England; nor do they regard the advent of Henry Tudor as reflecting a decision on God's part to bring an end to the punishment he had been dealing out to England.[91] It is true that the troubles that beset the principal nobles of the realm are at times considered to have been God's punishment upon them for past sins; but in the context in which Vergil speaks of Tudor's providential advent, the evils that he is to end are not viewed as providential scourges; rather God is pictured as mercifully bringing to a close the sufferings that men have inflicted upon each other.

Also it may be recalled that Vergil and Holinshed independently reduced the providential role in Henry Tudor's rise to power. Vergil modified his own 1534 history in his 1546 edition, and Holinshed altered in a similar fashion Hall's rendering of Vergil's 1534 version. At the same time both Vergil and Holinshed reworked the concepts of the providential punishment of Henry VII's predecessors. Perhaps these authorial processes are a further confirmation of the judgment that the divine punishment of the Lancastrians and Yorkists was not regarded as intimately bound up with Henry's rise, except for the obvious instance of Richard III, where Henry was the instrument of his punishment.

[91] We saw a notion similar to this exploited to some extent by Gower for the Lancaster myth; cf. also *A Political Retrospect* (see Chap. II at n. 45), where something of the same may be implied for the York myth. It is explicitly developed in the speech that Hall gave to York.

Three

The
Views
of the
Elizabethan
Poets

VII

A
Mirror
for
Magistrates

There are three important poetic surveys of fifteenth-century English history, namely, the tragedies of the *Mirror for Magistrates,* Daniel's *Civil Wars,* and Shakespeare's history plays.

There are other poems and plays that touch upon portions of this period's events and make some use of the providential themes evolved by the chroniclers. But for the most part they do not reflect any important advances in thematic development, and they can easily be put into perspective when considered in relation to the works that will be dealt with here. At times, however, relevant parallels to minor works will be noted in the course of our discussion.

The form and didactic method employed by William Baldwin and his associates in compiling *A Mirror for Magistrates* in the reign of Mary Tudor resemble in many ways those of a fifteenth-century work printed in 1543 by Richard Grafton, namely, the *Chronicle* of John Hardyng. Hardyng used verse as his main vehicle, but the prose chapter headings are similar in function to the tragedy titles and prose links in the *Mirror,* and his policy of addressing and instructing those in power (or likely to be in power) concerning their rights and the best ways to promote them corresponds to the *Mirror's* method of lessoning all governmental officials. But whereas Hardyng is explicit about those to whom he directs his advice, Baldwin found it necessary to keep his counsels general — ostensibly, at least — since the association of fallen princes with magistrates in power could easily be taken as a matter of accusation and threat rather than one of friendly advice. And to judge from the difficulty Baldwin had at the hands of the government censors, he aroused a certain amount of official resentment in spite of his precautions.

However, there is little indication that the authors of the *Mirror* were familiar with Hardyng's history. Their chief historical authority was another work recently published by Grafton, Hall's *Chronicle*. Hardyng's constant insistence upon the evils of division and the blessings of peace is also found in Hall, of course, as has often been pointed out, and the *Mirror* may have received some of its inspiration along these lines from Hall. But there is no sign of the over-all pattern that Hall stresses in his title and preface, which traces the division begun with Henry IV's usurpation and ending with the marriage of Henry VII. The view of the *Mirror* is definitely a short-range one. Nor is the scope of Hall's work the reason for the *Mirror*'s beginning with the reign of Richard II. As George Ferrers tells Baldwin in the preface, it was the printer's idea to start at this time because it is where Lydgate's version of Boccaccio's *Fall of Princes* leaves off. Otherwise he would apparently have preferred to have started, like Hardyng and Fabyan, "from the first beginning of the inhabiting of the isle." [1] As it is, they are forced to rely on Fabyan for the earlier part of Richard II's reign, and they continue to use him as a subordinate source for the matter covered by Hall.[2]

The form of the individual chapters or tragedies is, of course, based on Lydgate-Boccaccio, and so is the tone of general moralizing, as well as the type of biography chosen for treatment and the variety of lessons that are drawn from each. This kind of historiography specializes in minatory didacticism, and stresses negative reinforcement. Pains and punishments are dwelled upon to great length, and rewards (in the stories themselves) are relegated to the realm of what might have been, or what can never last, or what cannot be in this world. The first requirement then is to select a historical personage who ended his life in adversity, and this usually involves a violent or untimely death. The personage is then made to lament his fate and to draw universal morals or formulate universal laws of life, most of which are contradicted by the universal maxims arrived at by fellow unfortunates. Thus we see that the wicked always end badly, that God never suffers the unjust to continue happily, and that rebellion never prospers, all of which indicates that the only way to get ahead is to be good; but at the same time, Fortune is always unfair, the good are always oppressed, and prosperity never fails to turn to adversity.

[1] Mirror 70.
[2] See Lily Campbell, Mirror 10.

Counterexamples to the general laws are usually ignored within each tragedy, though at times an effort is made to analyze the discrepancies involved in different kinds of tragedies. The effort is ordinarily not very successful, and often results in contradictions within the same tragedy, and identical misfortunes are successively blamed entirely upon punishment for sin, bad luck (or the malice of Fortune), and the triumph of evil over good.

Obviously the prevailing fault in this type of literature is its invalid generalizing. The one general truth that can be drawn from stories of falls is that nothing temporal is lasting. No universal morals beyond this can be adduced concerning the reasons for disasters; and certainly no satisfactory lessons can be propounded on the subject of avoiding the unavoidable. People in a religious society could perhaps without contradiction be urged by such tales to look upon life in this world as a preparation for eternity, and sometimes we find this theme stressed. But the avowed purpose of the *Mirror for Magistrates* is to teach people how to get ahead or stay ahead in this world.

Baldwin and his friends could have achieved their purpose in a valid and coherent way only by restricting themselves to certain kinds of falls (those, namely, that could have been avoided by a more prudent or moral course of action), and further, by speaking in terms of probabilities rather than in universals. But their literary antecedents were too strong for them, and as a result they dealt not only with all kinds of falls, but with the accumulated falls, including death, of all kinds of persons;[3] the sentiments appealed to are not only satisfaction and approval in response to poetic justice but also sadness at poetic injustice and mixed emotions in mixed cases. And whereas the practice of drawing untrue absolutes from particular cases was a mere peccadillo in most of the moralizing historiographers we have thus far considered, with the authors of the *Mirror* it assumes the proportions of an uncontrollable vice.

These circumstances preclude any consistent view of the specific events we have been dealing with in English history of the fifteenth century. But coherency was dealt a further blow by having each episode narrated by one of the historical characters. This situation would not be of great moment if it were true, as John Dolman has Hastings say, that naked ghosts like himself tell only what the real nature of events was.[4] In most

[3] Only in the Ferrers tragedy of Eleanor Cobham is the protagonist represented as still living.
[4] Mirror 268.

cases, except for the outright villains like Richard III, we have obvious instances of special pleading; self-love is not drowned in Lethe's flood, and the ghosts do not recount only what time has found to be true, as is evident when two ghosts give contrasting analyses of the same event. The matter becomes even more complicated when we consider the multiplicity of authors of the *Mirror* and the various times in which the different sections were composed and issued. And we must also take into account the dramatic nature of the work. Each tragedy of course is conceived and executed as a dramatic monologue, but in addition the authors are pictured as discussing the tragedies in the prose links. The links were probably written by Baldwin (as were no doubt the anonymous tragedies and perhaps also most of the titles of the contributed tragedies).[5]

With regard to suprahuman causation in the tragedies as a whole, it may be said that recourse to God and his justice and providence is rather sparing in comparison to the number of times that Fortune is accused of misdeeds. And when a man accuses Fortune of his downfall, there is usually a connotation of the undeserved in his analysis of ensuing adversities. But in his general dedication, Baldwin attempts to bring all the tragedies within the scope of providential justice. Rulers, he says, are the representatives of God himself. He permits evil rulers to rule, however, in order to punish the people. But on the other hand, he must also in justice punish the impudent presumption and hypocrisy of the evil tyrants themselves by sending them shameful death, disease, or infamy. Lydgate shows how God plagued evil rulers in other countries and times, and the *Mirror* does the same for latter-day England. In fact this is the chief end of the book, to illustrate how vice has been punished in others, in order to teach its readers to avoid similar disasters.[6]

But he adds as a kind of afterthought that though his princely readers will find that some of God's officers have been envied and murdered for their virtue, yet he urges them not to slacken in the virtuous fulfillment of their offices. "Punish sin boldly," he exhorts, "both in yourselves and other, so shall God, whose lieutenants you are, either so maintain you that no malice shall

---

[5] Baldwin will be cited by name only for the tragedies definitely assigned to him by the text, in the signed prefaces, and in the prose conversations in which he identifies himself as speaking. Miss Campbell (Mirror 24–25) says that only the tragedies of Cambridge, York, and Clarence are consistently ascribed to Baldwin; but he also seems to take credit for the Mowbray story in Prose 3 (Mirror 101).

[6] Mirror 65–66.

prevail or, if it do, it shall be for your good and to your eternal glory both here and in heaven, which I beseech God you may covet and attain. Amen." [7]

Baldwin could have tightened up this qualification of the universal rule that goodness results in worldly success by saying that evil suffered for good in this world brings eternal glory *at least* in heaven; and he could have added another qualification of the rule he expressed so clearly above (that God must punish all evil rulers with shameful death, etc.) by saying that if he fails to do so in this life, he will make up for it later. But even these qualifications would leave unaccounted for the large body of men, many of whom are treated in the *Mirror*, who fall or die for nothing sinful and for nothing virtuous (or for neither wholly or chiefly).

Perhaps Baldwin felt constrained to preface the *Mirror* with his otherworldly qualification because of a curious characteristic of the format followed in the tragedies which makes any consideration of reward or punishment after death practically impossible. Although the tragic figures are pictured as telling their tales after death, they are abstracted from the Christian concepts of the afterlife — that is to say, they are not pictured as rewarded or punished in the states of heaven or hell. They are in a poetic never-never land, and are in a position only to lament the disasters of their life. The disasters outweigh the blessings, of course, because they are dead, and death from their peculiar point of view is always a disaster, though occasionally it is welcomed as putting an end to greater evils. Therefore, any stray references in the text to the redress of evils in the afterlife have no direct connection with the tragedies under discussion.[8]

The Fall of Richard II and the Reign of Lancaster

The fall of Richard II obviously implies the rise of Henry of Lancaster. But since success is never treated in the *Mirror* except as a foil to immediate disaster, Henry IV's crimes are referred to extensively, but there is never a word about any punishment he undergoes for them, providential or otherwise, and the Vergil-Hall remarks about the providential downfall of the house of

[7] Mirror 67.

[8] For instance, Ferrers has Tresilian instruct magistrates to keep God, "the just judge supreme," before their eyes and to keep in mind their "reckoning at the day extreme" — which obviously refers to the punishment or reward to be allotted after death or on the day of the general judgment (Mirror 80).

Lancaster in the third generation are never utilized or hinted at. But the theme of the deprived line of March-York is rather prominent in the *Mirror*'s treatment, especially in the tragedies of the two Mortimers, Cambridge, and York, and, on the Lancastrian side, in those of Somerset and Henry VI.

The first providential interpretation in the *Mirror* occurs in Ferrers' tragedy of Thomas of Woodstock. Ferrers introduces the chapter by saying that Woodstock was a man who was miserably made away with, or, as the title puts it, unlawfully murdered.[9] Accordingly Woodstock takes on an injured tone throughout most of his monologue. His analysis of the effect of his death upon Richard resembles that of Hardyng's; he says that Richard's method in having him killed was an act odious to God and man, and by it he hastened his own tragic fate. For "blood axeth blood," and vengeance is just reward for vengeance. The judgments of the righteous God are unerring, and everyone will be dealt with as he has dealt with others. He warns princes to learn by the examples of the past that "blood will have blood, either first or last." [10] All these scraps of morality are applied to Richard, however, and it never occurs to Woodstock (or Ferrers) that the death which he admittedly inflicted upon Richard's counselors had come home to roost.

All the providential teaching of this tragedy then is restricted to the divine punishment of unjust kings, and there is no sign of the notion of the divine character of the king's office nor of the Tudor doctrine of divine retribution against all rebels, even though the doctrine receives great stress elsewhere in the *Mirror*.

Of course, God's punishment of evil kings is what is stressed in Baldwin's preface, and the strongest assertion of God's unending war against rebels does not appear until the second edition of 1563, in Cavyl's tragedy of the Blacksmith, and in the prose piece that follows.[11] It might be thought therefore that the 1559 edition contains remnants of an anti-Marian stress on the punishment of rulers, and the 1563 edition emphasizes a pro-Elizabethan view against self-appointed reform. This is hardly the case, however, since the 1563 prose passage attacks those who "disable our queen, because she is a woman, and our king, because he is a stranger," [12] which is obviously referring to Mary and Philip, a reference that remains unchanged in all the suc-

---

[9] Mirror 91.
[10] Mirror 98–99.
[11] Mirror 412, 419–421.
[12] Mirror 420.

cessive editions. Furthermore, the tragedy of Cade in the first edition along with the prose links before and after lays stress on both these aspects of providential government.[13] So that it would seem that the complete doctrine (namely, that God always punishes evil kings and always brings rebels and rebellions to a bad end) with all its theoretical and factual inconsistencies was supported by the authors of the *Mirror* in the reigns of both Mary and Elizabeth.

The failure of Ferrers and Baldwin to point out the providential justice in Woodstock's fall, therefore, would seem to stem not from any doubt of the doctrine but from an inability to keep all the aspects of their theme in mind at once, even where the facts bear the doctrine out. For example, in this instance, Woodstock could be considered to have been punished for presuming to rebel against God's lieutenant, and Richard himself to have been punished for being a bad lieutenant. It is understandable, of course, that they should be silent on the exasperatingly unorthodox career of Henry Bolingbroke, who twice rebelled successfully against his lawful king (he accompanied Woodstock in his early action against Richard), and further succeeded as a usurper king in beating down all the rebellions initiated against him. But theoretically it was only these latter rebellions that had any chance of success:

For whatsoever man, woman, or child is by the consent of the whole realm established in the royal seat, so it have not been injuriously procured by rigor of sword and open force, but quietly by title, either of inheritance, succession, lawful bequest, common consent, or election, is undoubtedly chosen by God to be his deputy; and whosoever resisteth any such, resisteth against God himself, and is a rank traitor and rebel, and shall be sure to prosper as well as this blacksmith and other such have done.[14]

Richard himself is not explicitly said to have come to divine retribution in the tragedy devoted to him by Thomas Chaloner, except in a variant reading of 1578, namely, "that God, though late, at last will surely smite." [15] All the editions agree in saying,

---

[13] Mirror 170–179.

[14] Mirror 420–421 (from the final prose comment in the edition of 1563, following the tragedy of the Blacksmith). It is made clear on p. 419 that the only valid way for a ruler to be appointed in England is inheritance by lineal descent, with the female line included.

[15] Mirror 118.

in Richard's words, that lawless life always draws to lawless death, referring to Henry's illegal execution of Richard.[16] Once again, of course, Henry's crime is tacitly exempted from these irrefrangible laws of retribution. His killing of Richard is not his only crime specified in this account; for when Richard tells of York's treasonable support of Bolingbroke, he says that the latter cruelly put to death anyone who showed the least inclination to favor Richard; and after Richard was betrayed into his enemies' hands, he was kept in prison until Bolingbroke's pride caused him to give up his crown.[17]

In the anonymous tragedy of the Earl of Salisbury, who was slain while valiantly fighting in the French wars during the time of Henry VI, there is an interesting review and analysis of the unsuccessful attempt of the earls to replace Richard II on the throne shortly after Henry IV's usurpation. Salisbury is trying to clear the name of his father, John Montague, also Earl of Salisbury, who was one of the conspirators. He objects against judging men by their end, and against assuming that any violence or misfortune suffered, especially when it results in death, is the merited punishment of some sin. Instead, he says, men should be judged from the nature of the cause they were pursuing at the time. His father is an instance in point; he has been defamed by his end, and yet his cause was obviously just. He sums up the lesson thus:

> When deeds therefore unluckily do frame,
> Men ought not judge the authors to be naught
> For right through might is often overraught.[18]

But instead of leaving well enough alone, Salisbury goes on to analyze the problem at greater length and makes a remarkable about-face, committing the very fault he has been warning against. He says that God allows this kind of thing to happen, but why he does so, his wit is too feeble to say, unless it is to heap up wrath and woe on the heads[19] of those "that injuries devise." For, he says:

> The cause why mischiefs many times arise
> And light on them that would men's wrongs redress,
> Is for the rancor that they bear, I guess.

[16] Mirror 117–118.
[17] Mirror 115–116.
[18] Mirror 143–145.
[19] The editions of 1571–1587 say "wicked heads."

God hates "rigor" even though it furthers right, he continues, for sin is sin, no matter what the circumstances are. And therefore God punishes the offenders with shame and death, even though they themselves are greatly offended against. For the end does not justify the means, and every sin receives its due reward.[20]

In other words, Salisbury's feeble wit can explain disasters only as God's due retribution for sin, and therefore his father and his associates must have committed a crime proportionate to their punishment. This rigorous view (which, significantly, he does not apply to his own unfortunate death while using rigor against the French) leaves one wondering why God did not punish the greater sinner, Henry, with a similar or greater disaster; and instead of inclining readers to applaud God's justice it tempts them to complain of its unfairness. Salisbury would have done better in appealing to Baldwin's original qualification (especially since Baldwin is probably the author of the Salisbury tragedy), namely, that some men have been envied and murdered for their virtue, and that even though malice prevails it is for the good of the virtuous and will result in their eternal glory both here and in heaven. Or at least in heaven.

In the confused and often contradictory tragedies that follow, Owen Glendower is the only other enemy of the Lancastrians whose story takes on a providential dimension (unless we count Cade and his fellow rebels). In the words given to him by Thomas Phaer, Glendower, like Hall, inveighs against the crafty Welsh deceivers, and adds the notion that false prophecies are "plagues for divers crimes/Which God doth let the devilish sort devise/To trouble such as are not godly wise." [21] Perhaps then Glendower's own deception by such prophecies is regarded as God's means of bringing him to the miserable end his sins deserved.

The Misfortunes of Lancaster and York

In his tragedy of the Duke of York, Baldwin resorts to a different method, namely, the dream vision. He says he dozed off, and York appeared to him in his sleep and told his tale; and when he was awakened he recited it to the others.[22] The lack of

[20] Mirror 145.
[21] Mirror 127.
[22] Mirror 181.

appeal to Providence in York's recital is striking; Baldwin is obviously drawing on Hall, but he makes no use of the elaborate providential claims in the speech that Hall provides for York during his appearance in Parliament.

However, he does parallel the speech in Hall by running through the history of the deprivation of his line by the Lancastrians; he even attacks Henry V as Henry IV's "cursed son." He attributes his own disastrous end to the malevolence of Fortune; but in a moralization that follows, he says that it would be better to lose "a piece of right" than to lose limbs and life in struggling for it. It is not the force of friendship "but God that causeth things to fro or frame." [23]

It is clear that by this providential reference York does not mean to assign any special reason for God's action in causing him this particular loss (such as punishment for his sins); he is simply referring to the unpredictability of events, and to our inability to make things go the way we plan. He explains this in the next line, where he says that "not wit, but luck doth wield the winner's game." Therefore, he adds, if we would repress our follies, time would redress all wrongs, and we would be free from pain. And for this reason princes should be warned not to engage in war for any cause except the realm's defense; their troublesome titles are not worth the bloodshed they lead to. He points to his own experience:

> Of friends and foes behold my foul expense,
> And never the nere; best therefore tarry time,
> So right shall reign, and quiet each crime.[24]

In having York express this naive belief that time will automatically right all wrongs, perhaps Baldwin means to imply the explicit judgment that God in his providence eventually restored the right line to the realm of England. But if so, neither Baldwin nor any of his associates seems to develop this idea further in other parts of the *Mirror*.[25] And it must be remembered that York's son Edward got the crown by fighting for it, thus going against York's advice here.

In George Ferrers' delayed tragedy of Somerset (it did not ap-

---

[23] 1578 version: "But God above that kingdoms set in frame."

[24] Mirror 183–184, 189–190. In the alternate version (1578), the last part reads, "Best then to tarry low by the ground, than overhigh to climb." "Never the nere" presumably means "never nearer to my goal."

[25] As will be seen below, however, Baldwin does have Clarence say that God's providence kept the March-York line supplied with heirs.

pear until the 1563 edition), Somerset describes York's rise to power in the most unfavorable terms. He was an outright rebel, and yet was declared heir to the crown and given control over his king, which was a monstrous breach of the order of nature.[26]

Ferrers then has Somerset answer the chief objection against his own view. Some, perhaps, he says, will allege a prior right for York's side. He calls this a brainless objection; for when the passage of time has firmly established a regime and left the realm in peace, it would be far better to forget about such rights than to convulse the whole country in forwarding them. He states the facts of the case: York and his sons came from the female heir, and the Lancastrians came from the male heir, "of whom three kings in order did succeed,/By just descent." This, he says, "is no feigned tale"; but he draws no further conclusion from it. His meaning, however, would seem to be that Henry had an even stronger hereditary claim to the throne than York did, given its long possession by the Lancastrian line. He then says:

> Who would have thought that any storm or gale
> Our ship could shake, having such anchor-hold?
> None, I think sure, unless God so would.[27]

This last sentence could mean that no one would have thought that their house could have fallen without the special (or miraculous) intervention of God, and yet it did. But it could also mean that it was God's will that their house should fall. However, if this latter meaning is the intended one, he does not assign a reason for God's providential decision. There is no hint that he is punishing their family for any crimes they have committed, let alone for crimes committed by their forebears. And there is certainly no indication that Somerset believes that God approves of York's title; he consistently denies that York was anything but a traitor.

In the unassigned tragedy of the Lancastrian Clifford, we are told that he was killed for his cruel slaughter of young Rutland and for beheading the body of York. He says it was God's just award in which "due justice plainly doth appear." By this he means the poetic justice of being struck by a headless arrow (for beheading York), and losing his voice and being unable to ask for pardon (for not listening to the pleas of Rutland).[28]

[26] Mirror 398.
[27] Mirror 398–399.
[28] Mirror 192 (title); 194–195.

Although the tragedy of Clifford has its share of contradictions and invalid maxims, a principle is enunciated that may explain a certain consistency in the *Mirror*, namely, the omission of all references to hereditary providential retribution. Clifford says (in his own condemnation) there is no denying that it is good to punish sin; but avenging the father's fault on his kin does not avenge sin but merits vengeance.[29] Therefore, since this type of revenge is judged to be bad form for human beings, perhaps Baldwin and the others considered it so much the less to be ascribed to God.[30]

Henry VI is given an interesting lament in a modified poulterer's-verse stanza.[31] It is introduced in the prose link by the remark that Henry was the cause (which seems to mean "occasion" here) of the destruction of many noble princes, and was himself the most unfortunate of all. And the title of his tragedy describes him as a virtuous prince who was cruelly murdered after having suffered many other miseries.[32]

Henry first discourses on the magnitude of the troubles he experienced; he wishes he had died young, and then his friends would not have been killed and his subjects oppressed and he himself "washed in waves of worldly woe." But death or cruel destiny denied him this escape.[33]

He goes on to explain his view of the cause of tribulations in general. The dolts, he says, who believe that everything happens by chance say that disasters are caused by lack of prudence; they thereby attribute to man a power that belongs to God alone. For it is the power and knowledge of God that guides every event, and his will can bring to nothing what our own minds and wills strive to preserve with the greatest of care.[34]

He denies that we are determined by our bodily humors; they do operate, however, as incentives to sin, and together with sin they bring God's vengeance on the infected soul. As for the stars, they are the indications of our fate, and fate (or destiny) is the same as God's will.[35] In this analysis of the suprahuman causes of human hardships, Henry restricts fate to mean the action of God's love by which he chastises the good; this and punishment for sin

[29] Mirror 193.
[30] For the possibility that Edward IV was punished in his children, see the discussion of Clarence's tragedy, below.
[31] a(6)a(6)b(6)b(7), with abundant alliteration. The author is not specified.
[32] Mirror 211–212.
[33] Mirror 212–213.
[34] Mirror 213.
[35] Cf. the similar treatment in Cade's tragedy (Mirror 171).

are the two principal reasons for our suffering, and all other causes are subordinated to them. And although Henry humbly admits that his "sundry sins" place him among the worst, yet the events of his life make him hope to be among the first (that is, the highest in God's favor), because the Eye that searches all and sees all knows how thoroughly he hated sin and sought after virtue. He considered his kingdoms of no worth, and was concerned only with heaven.[36]

Henry would seem to be assuming here that he was chastised rather by God's love than by his wrath; yet he does not return to this idea. He goes on to say that no other man had so many misfortunes piled on him as he did, but why this was so, he says, God knows, not he, unless it was to show the brittleness of worldly honor by demonstrating it in a prince.[37] Now it is true that this reason can easily be linked to the motif of God's love, and at the same time it is a denial that his sufferings were a punishment for sin. But in the rest of his monologue, it is precisely punishment for sin that he adduces as the cause of his mishaps. In doing this, however, he is not drawing on the opinion recorded in Vergil-Hall that God was punishing him for Henry IV's crimes, nor on the Vergil-Hall belief that he had decreed an end to the house of Lancaster; rather he repeats the Fabyan-Hall judgment that God was not pleased with his marriage to Margaret because it involved a breach of contract with the Earl of Armagnac's daughter. This action was, Henry says, the cause of many a death, first of Gloucester, who opposed it, and then of Suffolk, the flatterer who arranged the marriage and who received the just reward of those who advise their princes badly. And Henry himself bore the brunt of all; for God punishes this sort of double-dealing even though one feels no guilt in it at the time. He himself was deluded into thinking he acted rightly, Henry says; his clergy assured him he could go ahead, but he has since found out that their word is not Gospel.[38]

In Henry's description of York's persecution, it is important to note that he considers himself to be the true king. For he says York forced him to resign his crown and titles, which were "due unto my father's line." [39]

His queen rescued him and slew York, but still his sorrows

[36] Mirror 214–215.
[37] Mirror 215.
[38] Mirror 215–216.
[39] Mirror 217.

returned like the heads of Hydra. Warwick finally restored him; but what does human effort avail when destiny decrees otherwise? His friends only came to worse trouble for helping him, for he was ordained to be plagued with wretchedness. He was soon deprived again, and Warwick and his allies were slain at Barnet. "O Lord," Henry exclaims, "that ever such luck should hap in helping right." And when Margaret defied Edward, their young son was taken and murdered by Edward in his rage, and he himself was stabbed by "his brother's bloody blade." He sums up by saying,

> Lo here the heavy haps which happened me by heap,
> See here the pleasant fruits that many princes reap,
> The painful plagues of those that break their lawful bands,
> Their meed which may and will not save their friends fro
>   bloody hands.

In this stanza Henry reiterates the idea that he was punished for his marriage, and he alludes for the first time to a responsibility for failing to save Gloucester's life, for which also he was plagued by God.[40] He ends with a prayer to God to let his "woeful haps" teach persons of all callings the brittleness of worldly honors, "that warned through my fearful fate, they fear to do amiss." [41] At first he seems to have returned to the position that the only reason God troubled him was to demonstrate the vanity of the world; but his conclusion shows that he is still on the subject of the punishment of sin, with the implied moral that if men avoid sin, all will go well for them, together with the corollary that whatever goes wrong is a punishment for sin.

In the Earl of Warwick's tragedy, Warwick takes an entirely favorable and self-congratulatory view of himself, which contradicts the report of Worcester in the preceding tragedy. While his "uncle dear," the Duke of York, was living, Warwick says, he himself was successful in all that he tried. God gave him fortune, and his good behavior stole the people's hearts away from Henry VI.[42] He briefly runs through his astonishing career, and imparts to Baldwin the secret of his success — he was no hypocrite, but practiced what he preached, and sought to aid

---

[40] Raleigh in his *History of the World* (Preface xi) uses these two faults of Henry (along with hereditary punishment of Henry IV's sins) to explain his fall.

[41] Mirror 217–218.

[42] Mirror 206.

the people and not to gain glory for himself. He had been assured that God avenges the wrongs of the poor and oppressed, as Scripture says, for he had often seen proof, and witnessed the execution of their oppressors. It made him always deal justly; and the people, who realized it, supported him, since they knew that he always had their interests at heart. They were correct in this assumption; for when the realm went to pieces because of good King Henry's evil counselors, Warwick aided the king's enemies in an effort to bring order to the land. But when Edward refused to leave his sinful ways, he restored Henry, as the better of the two. He was finally slain in the latter's cause, which he thinks was just.[43]

The moral Warwick points has nothing to do with his fall, but rather concerns his rise. He tells Baldwin to teach those who want the love of the people to do as he did, practice the principles they profess; give liberally, he says, and you will gain all hearts. And in the prose link that follows, someone remarks that all this that Warwick said was very true; for if he had not been such and acted such, the people would never have loved him as they did.[44] Hence, in giving this favorable account of Warwick, the *Mirror* writers have forgotten once more one of their most cherished lessons, that it is always forbidden to rebel against the king, and that God will always punish severely such affronts to his authority.

In Baldwin's tragedy of George Plantagenet, Duke of Clarence, there is a discussion of the "famous house surnamed Plantagenet," as there was in Ferrers' Somerset tragedy; but whereas Somerset meant chiefly the house of Lancaster, Clarence means exclusively the house of York. He says that Dame Fortune "frowardly did frown" at it when Bolingbroke unjustly deprived Richard II of the crown; but though it was obscured for a long time, "God so preserved [it] by providence and grace" that it never lacked legitimate heirs. From Lionel the line descended to the Duke of York, and York had four sons. But the fourth, Richard, was "born to be the mischief of us all."[45]

This last statement could be construed as connoting providential predestination, perhaps, though there is little in the immediate context to warrant such a reading. For Clarence has not indicated that God was anything but favorably disposed to-

[43] Mirror 208–209.
[44] Mirror 210–211.
[45] Mirror 221–222.

ward their house, and he does not expand upon Richard's "innate" role. However, as we shall see, Richard's destruction of his brother and his nephews is said to be ordained and a divinely revealed "fact-to-be."

He goes on to say that God draws good out of evil and works everything for our good; for through the death of those two noble peers. Warwick and Montague, Clarence's brother Edward lived and reigned in peace, whereas otherwise the Lancastrians might have kept the "careful crown," and the Yorkists been put down for good.[46] Once again Clarence pictures the house of York as saved by divine providence from being "quite put down." Yet it was put down within a very short time. He speaks here as if he had no knowledge of his own destruction and the destruction of Edward's children at Richard's hands, and yet he obviously alluded to it at the beginning.

He then discusses Edward's two sons who were "born to be punished for their parent's sin." [47] This could be a simple statement of fact on the natural level — their fate was to be destroyed because of the sin of their father (the sin presumably being the dispatching of Clarence, which cleared the way for Richard to plot against his nephews).[48] Of course, Baldwin may also be drawing on the Vergil-Hall opinion that Edward was being punished by God not only for doing away with Clarence, but also for his perjury at York. But if so, he avoids attributing directly to God the inflicting of punishment on persons innocent of all guilt for the sin in question.

Clarence goes on to explain his downfall. The fortunes of Edward's sons were calculated (astrologically), and the king was greatly disturbed at the result, because a prophecy made him believe that "G" was to succeed him, which he took to mean George of Clarence. But "G" could stand for anything, Clarence points out, and this ambiguity is a sign that it was a false prophecy. He proceeds to expound the bizarre doctrine that God does not make use of riddles to foretell the future, but employs the natural qualities of animals (for instance, a hare signifies a cowardly man). This is the way Merlin prophesied, for God inspired him, like the Jewish prophets, to foretell the deeds of future kings. But his predictions were distorted in being referred to the arbitrary animal symbols of heraldry. Clarence says he

[46] Mirror 225–226.
[47] Mirror 227.
[48] Mirror 232.

learned this lore from one of his servants, who by God's gift could utter true prophecies. He knew, for instance, that Richard was the boar that would kill Clarence and Edward's sons.[49] By Clarence's own rule, however, he should have labeled this prophecy false, since it was based on Richard's crest, unless he were to say that the heraldic symbol chanced to coincide with his natural qualities in this instance.

Clarence was warned therefore long before the event; but, as he points out, "wit nor warning can in no degree/Let things to hap which are ordained to be." The same no doubt would hold for another item disclosed to Clarence by his household soothsayer, namely, that Clarence's wish to remarry would cause such strife between him and Edward that only Clarence's death could resolve it. And when the prophet objected against Edward's refusal to let Clarence marry because of his fears of false prophecies, he was executed on a false charge of practicing sorcery against Edward's life.[50] Yet it would seem that the prophet acted irrationally in trying to prevent Edward from acting on false prophecies when he knew by a true prophecy that Edward's actions along this line were inevitable anyway.

In drawing the moral, Clarence tells Baldwin first of all to warn princes to eschew dark and doubtful (that is, false) prophecies.[51] However, if Clarence thinks that the observance of this counsel would have saved his life, he is sadly mistaken, for his death was inevitably predicted by not one but two clear and true prophecies. In fact, even now he unwittingly proceeds to give characteristics not of false but of true prophecies: "What God hath said, that cannot but ensue," and any attempt to fly one's fate may simply further it. Princes therefore should not resort to murder in an attempt to avoid what is prophesied, for by this means they may only aggravate their troubles, and cause God's vengeance to be heavier when it alights. "Woe worth the wretch," that strives against God's foresight. "For if we think that prophecies be true," we must believe that what God foreshows in them must necessarily come about, since his decrees are immutable. And this, Clarence says, both his brothers found to be true; therefore other rulers should learn by their example.[52]

Apparently Baldwin has illogically assumed for the moment

[49] Mirror 227–231.
[50] Mirror 230–232. See above, Chap. V, n. 80.
[51] Mirror 234.
[52] Mirror 234.

that both Edward and Richard were trying to forstall the G-prophecy (now implicitly regarded as true) by murdering Clarence, but only made matters worse for themselves in so doing. As for the general statement that attempts to foil prophecies by murder may cause God's vengeance to be all the more heavy, he may, of course, be referring specifically to the tragic fate of Edward's children; but then again, he may have nothing specific in mind. He has obviously not thought out the implications of his moralizing when he includes Richard in the category of those who attempted and failed to forestall prophecies from coming true. A simpler reading would be that Baldwin had merely a vague idea in mind that the affairs of both Richard and Edward came to no good end, and that it would be good to point it out as a moral to others.

At any rate, even if it is maintained that Baldwin intends to say here that God punished Edward in the destruction of his children, it would not be grounds for assuming that he says it elsewhere, or that it was a permanent viewpoint of his. As we have seen, consistency was not the hobgoblin of Baldwin's little mind. As for Edward himself, the title that introduces John Skelton's verses on him attributes his sudden death to his "surfeiting and untemperate life."[53] This tragedy marks the close of the first edition of 1559, and there is no further mention of any punishment of Edward in person or in his posterity in any of the prose or verse added in subsequent editions.

The treatment of Richard III himself is very simple. His tragedy is placed after the tragedy of Collingbourne, who was executed under Richard for making a foolish rhyme,[54] and in the intervening prose section someone says that Richard and his associates should have listened to men like Collingbourne instead of getting rid of them; for they would then have been warned of their sins, which continually call for God's vengeance — vengeance that never fails to fall unless deterred by heartfelt repentance. But as the commentator proceeds, he would seem to be suggesting that wicked men never get the chance to repent. For, he says, as everything turns out well for good men, so even good things turn out badly for the wicked, and lead to their eventual

[53] Mirror 236. Skelton, of course, says nothing of this or any other sin as the cause of Edward's death; he says simply that the king went the way of all flesh, for God has ordained all dust to return to dust.

[54] Mirror 347 (title). Collingbourne's tragedy is an exasperatingly silly and contradictory piece, in which, among other things, Collingbourne tries to say he meant no disrespect to Richard and the others by calling them hog, dog, rat, etc. (356–357).

ruin. For after persecuting Collingbourne in this shameful way ("the common reward of best endeavors"),[55] the eternal destruction of this tyrant and his fellow tormentors followed dirrectly.[56] According to the title of Richard's tragedy, Richard was deservedly deprived of his life and kingdom after murdering his nephews and usurping the crown.[57]

The author of the tragedy, Francis Seager, has Richard say that in dispatching the young princes, he offended God and provoked his just wrath.[58] When he heard Henry Richmond had landed in Wales, he regarded it as a punishment for his sins; but still he hoped all would be well. But "fickle Fortune" frowned and gave the victory to Richmond. Richard concludes by saying that we may behold in him the just reward of tyranny and treason, "which God doth most detest," and he urges others not to attempt to overcome right with wrong, for God has promised to redress every wrong.[59]

Since this passage contains the only mention of Henry Tudor in the *Mirror,* only the bare essence of the Tudor myth is provided, namely, the conviction that the defeat of Richard III was a judgment of God upon him for his wicked life.

As for the Lancaster and York myths, it is suggested at least that Richard II's downfall was not only deserved but providential, although Henry's part in it is generally considered reprehensible. But since the peculiar outlook of the *Mirror* calls for here-and-now punishment of sin, no reference is made to any providential destruction of his line. The pious Henry VI sees himself as the legitimate king and as punished not for his ancestors' but for his own sins, in breaking his marriage precontract and in not preventing Humphrey of Gloucester's murder. Perhaps Somerset suggests that it was God's will for the house of Lancaster to fail, but if so it was not a question of divine retribution.

The York line, according to Clarence, was providentially preserved, but York admits that it would have been better to let their title pass unclaimed than to have started civil wars over it. The destruction of the house of York is said (again by Clarence) to have been providentially ordained, although no reason

---

[55] In other words, things do not ordinarily work for the best in good men, contrary to what he just said.
[56] Mirror 359.
[57] Mirror 360.
[58] Mirror 361.
[59] Mirror 368–370.

is given for it; it would seem to be a matter of *de facto* necessity; it happened, and therefore it could be said to have been ordained by God. In Worcester's tragedy, we read that Edward IV was punished by God's vengeance in being forced to flee his realm, because of his bloody policy in rooting out his enemies[60] (Hall says it was a penance for his wantonness and negligence). And Clarence says that God restored Edward again; but he also says that Edward's children were punished (possibly divine retribution is meant) as the result of Edward's effort to save them by executing Clarence. Originally, of course, the providential destruction of the whole house of York was a part of the Tudor myth. But the stray references to God's punishment of Yorkists in the *Mirror* (with the exception, naturally, of Richard III) have nothing to do with Henry VII's rise to power. As we saw, this is also often the case in Vergil and the prose chroniclers who followed him.

Given the actual approach of the authors of the *Mirror,* it would be a fallacy to attempt to find any consistent or over-all philosophy of providential punishment or reward derivable from their treatment of fifteenth-century events. They are concerned not with the large view, but with the lessons that can be drawn from one life story or even from part of a life story, whether or not they are valid for all time or even for the whole life of the historical personage under observation.

[60] *Mirror* 199–200.

VIII

Daniel's
Civil Wars

The *Civil Wars* of Samuel Daniel seems to have been influenced by Hall's conception of the period from Richard II to the Tudor union as providing invaluable lessons on the evils of discord and the blessings of concord, with the glorification of the contemporary regime a primary aim. This view is strongly emphasized in the dedications to the second and third editions (1601 and 1609),[1] but it can also be gathered from the body of his work. In fact, his emphasis on dissension is much clearer and more single-minded than Hall's, for the latter undertook to write a complete history of the country as well as to trace themes of strife and union. There is greater accent on reflection and commentary and a smaller amount of historical facts in Daniel than in any of the historiographers we have treated thus far, although Daniel professes to follow historical data scrupulously. He does, however, revert to the classical practice of composing characteristic speeches for historical personages, a usage discontinued by contemporary historians like Grafton, Stow, and Holinshed.

From the providential viewpoint, Daniel makes a significant

---

[1] Daniel speaks of the blessed union that redressed the wounds of war, that sacred concord which prepared the way of glory for Elizabeth alone to enjoy (2Dan 65). And in the 1609 version, he says he wanted to show the deformities of civil dissension and the miserable results of rebellions, conspiracies, and bloody deeds of revenge which followed "as in a circle" upon that breach of the due course of succession effected by the usurpation of Henry IV, and thereby to make the blessings of peace and the happiness of an established government in a direct line appear the better. He says he planned to extend the history up to the glorious union of Henry VII, from which their present happiness descended (3Dan 67).

The first edition of the *Civil Wars* appeared in 1595, and it is likely that it was known to Shakespeare while he was writing the "first" tetralogy (*Richard II–Henry V*). Significant similarities between the two authors will be noted in the chapter on Shakespeare.

addition to sixteenth-century treatments of the fifteenth century. For the first and last time we meet here with views that include the entire period from Richard II to the Tudor dynasty in over-all providential patterns. These patterns, however, do not greatly affect Daniel's treatment of the individual events within the period; and since he never came to the end of his history, where he might conceivably have made similar long-range observations, we may deal with all the allusions to these themes at the outset.

Daniel begins his poem by stating his theme, the civil wars of a mighty land and the unnatural strife of brother against brother, in which all right was overthrown while right was claimed by all. He asks England what fury possessed her to act so, when otherwise France could have been won. But he adds that she has no reason to complain, since by it came the calm she enjoys:

> The bliss of thee, Eliza, happy gain
> For all our loss; for that no other way
> The Heavens could find then to unite again
> The fatal severed families, that they
> Might bring forth thee; that in thy peace might grow
> That glory, which no age could ever show.[2]

In this stanza he may be saying that the principal purpose of the Heavens was to bring forth Elizabeth, and that the only way in which they could do this was to unite the severed families. This reading would take the lines as an explanation of his statement that England's present calm came by means of the civil wars, with the implication that the calm which resulted from the union could not have taken place without the wars. Following this line of reasoning, we should perhaps see the Heavens as inaugurating the wars in the first place in order to produce Elizabeth. And perhaps Daniel meant to imply this. But it would seem more likely on the face of it that he is merely repeating one aspect of the original Tudor myth, that God wished to put an end to the strife and the injuries that the English were inflicting upon themselves, and that therefore he arranged the marriage between the warring families, with no suggestion that

[2] o–3Dan 1.1–3. The undated MS (oDan) extends only into the second book and shows little significant divergence from the first edition of 1595. All quotations will use the 1595 variants unless otherwise specified. In the text cited, the later reading is "whenas" for "for that" in the second line, and "find but" for "find then" in the third line ("then" here seems to mean "than"). The last line reads "few times" for "no age."

he was responsible for the previous suffering, or was now calling a halt to divine punishment.

It would no doubt be wisest to content ourselves with the most obvious meaning in this kind of adulatory verse, and not look for far-reaching concepts underlying such slight suggestions. However, Daniel does intimate elsewhere that the disasters of the civil wars grew out of a providential design. Later in the first book, when lamenting the deaths of the Black Prince and Edward III, he says that the scepter was left to a child, Richard II, who was ordained by fate to stay the course of what might have grown too great. Such oppositions, he explains, are placed in the way to prevent "great fortune" from becoming overly presumptuous.[3]

He goes on to say that too many governors breed factions in the court, that is, when the head is weak and the members have grown out of proportion. This is what "transports" kingdoms, and it is the plague that the Heavens threaten as a punishment for injustice, namely, child-rulers who lose what their ancestors acquired.[4] In the 1609 edition, he modifies this analysis to say that factions arise when children rule, and that they are the plague that God threatens against those kingdoms that he intends to "transport to other lines, or utterly defeat." [5]

We have here then three providential accounts of the disasters that befell England beginning with the reign of the child-ruler Richard. They were ordained by fate as a check upon the presumptuous greatness (present or future) of the nation; they were the result of a plague sent by God for injustice;[6] or, in place of this latter reason, they were the result of a plague God sent because he desired (for unspecified motives) to transfer the government to another line or to bring the kingdom to ruin. According to these accounts, therefore, the usurpation of the throne by the house of Lancaster would have to be regarded as a result or as a part of divine punishment, or of an unaccounted-for providential policy.

As in the section that dealt with the providential union of the factions, so in this portion dealing with their providential origin,

---

[3] 0–3Dan 1.21.
[4] 0–2Dan 1.28.
[5] 3Dan 1.28.
[6] Daniel perhaps specifies later the injustice he has in mind, when he distributes the guilt for the troubles of Richard's reign. He says they were all at fault, the ambitious uncles, the indiscreet young king, the greedy council, the "minions naught," and the times that were filled with all injustice; in short, the state was spoiled by youthful counsel, private gain, and partial hate (0–3Dan 1.33).

there is no explicit link with the other terminus of the process, and perhaps once again we should not "presume too far" and find wholes where there are only pieces; that is, perhaps Daniel did not have the Tudor union in mind at all at this point, at least not from a providential point of view.

However, there is one more treatment of a large providential view that does include both termini of the process from concord to concord through the discord of the fifteenth century. But if it is viewed as a seriously proposed explanation of English history, it is probably the least satisfactory of all Daniel's reflections on the subject. It concerns his fantasy in the sixth book on the invention of gunpowder. Before the use of guns and the printing press, he informs us, everything was just right in Europe; no countries were excessively large, and wars were only petty squabbles of short duration. This state of affairs lasted only until Nemesis came out of the Orient, "fierce Nemesis, mother of fate and change,/Sword-bearer of th'eternal Providence," who had long scourged the pride and glory of Asia with manifold afflictions and incited the barbarians to prey upon it. But finally she turned to the West, and was filled with resentment at the happiness she found there. She told Pandora that these states were so well off that they seemed to have made a pact with fate to be exempted from the pain that came to others.[7]

To put an end to their peace, she instructs Pandora to release all the swelling sciences, in order to make men learn everything except what is right; she is also to foster religious disputes and make sin attractive by providing two fatal instruments, printing and gunpowder. She is to have the large states devour the small, and is to begin by dividing the fairest land of all (England, of course) into factions, thereby creating a strife that will not end until the greater part of her inhabitants are destroyed. While these bloody tragedies are being acted here, the neighboring states can take the opportunity to grow so great that no force except their own can defeat them. And when their power falls in upon itself, England may in turn watch their tragedies, at a time when peacemaking Hymen has united the warring English parties and set the crown upon one head.[8]

Out of this blessed union, Nemesis continues (with somewhat more warmth than befits her character), there will arise a sacred branch blessed with grace and glory, whose virtue will so benefit

[7] 1–3Dan 6.28–32.
[8] 1–3Dan 6.35–44.

her land that all the power of Nemesis and Pandora will not affect her.

> For she, fair she, the minion of the Skies,
> Shall purchase of the Highest to hers such rest,
> Standing between the wrath of Heaven and them,
> As no distress shall touch her diadem.

But Pandora is not to be discouraged, for only she (Elizabeth or England) will have the grace to be kept free from all disturbances and to fulfill her role so gloriously; for she alone, being privileged from on high, has this "patent of eternity." [9]

If this poetic flight is to be given any weight as a metahistorical analysis of world events, it tells us only that the pain and turmoil which are the providential lot of all men are the explanation for the strife that tore England apart in the fifteenth century, and that England was exempted from this lot during the sixteenth century because of the favor its queen found with God. It can hardly be thought, however, that the alleged ideal of small states represented Daniel's true feelings, especially with regard to England, or that this passage would support the early explanation he gave for the civil wars, namely, that they were a providential curb to overweening greatness. For he constantly laments England's loss of France, and he conjures up with great regret what might have been England's glory had she not spent herself in intestine conflict. This is especially true of the passage toward the end of the second book, in which he wished that Henry Bolingbroke's cause had been as lawful as he himself was fit for the kingship and born for government. For then the blood of thirteen battles fought on this account, which proved fatal to their land, would have been reserved for glory, for bringing nations and kingdoms under their command, and all that he and his son Henry V acquired would still be in their hands, and that great worthy last Henry (the Eighth) would have joined to it the Western Empire. And Elizabeth, his great imperial daughter, now indeed the admired glory of the earth, would thereby have had all the adjacent world at her feet; then Spain would not have been seeking to attain to a falsely conceived monarchy, but would have been kept within its barren bounds and not made its vain attempts to stain the seas with blood; and finally, England

---

[9] 1–3Dan 6.45–47 (the third edition ends the last-cited line with "of her dignity" for "of eternity").

would have moved its victorious armies into unknown regions and would have taken up the crusade against the infidel.[10]

Providence and Henry IV

We have not yet seen that Daniel makes any specific reference to Henry Bolingbroke's place in an over-all providential design. We did see what might have happened if he had had a right title. But it was fated not to be that way. In the first book, Daniel says that everything worked in Henry's favor, for the Heavens, fate, and Fortune were arranging for him an easy path to the throne. He was ordained by Providence to start a quarrel that would last longer than his days.[11]

Once again, therefore, Henry's usurpation must be viewed not as the cause but as the result of the providentially arranged civil wars. And since no further reason is given for this divine maneuver, we can only conclude that Daniel had no particular reason in mind at this point, or else that he meant this passage to reflect the themes we have seen discussed earlier in the first book. At the end of the first book, he describes various classical prodigies which he says the Book of Providence disclosed at this time. He first explains these fictitious events as the effort of Nature to warn men away from their ruinous course, and next he says that heaven and earth taught men to see but not to shun their fall. Then he asks whether the universe has this kind of regard for the deeds and misdeeds of men, or whether men's fear deludes them into thinking their faults the cause of such disturbances.[12] He continues the discussion for two more stanzas (which he deleted from the 1609 edition), where he concludes by saying that mortality is forbidden to search into the power that guides this frame. We must simply admire God's work and tremble at his will.

When Henry invades England, Daniel pictures him as receiving a vision from the Genius of England, who begs him to consider the bloodshed and turmoil he is commencing, which

---

[10] 1–2Dan 2.115–116 + (123–125). He omits the last part of this glimpse into what might have been in the third edition, which appeared after the Tudor dynasty had come to a close. (The plus sign in citations from Daniel indicates stanzas not contained in the third edition; in this case, for instance, the deleted stanzas 123–125 of the second edition are to be read after 3Dan 2.116.)

[11] 0–3Dan 1.84. Cf. 1.104, where Richard's return from Ireland is barred by tempests, winds, and seas, as if they too warred against him.

[12] 0–3Dan 1.113–117.

may last many generations; she tells him to desist while still
free of guilt;

> Injustice never yet took lasting root,
> Nor held that long, impiety did win.
> The babes unborn shall, oh, be born to bleed
> In this thy quarrel, if thou do proceed.

Henry says to let the sin be on the heads of those who first did
him wrong.[13] The Genius's warning may be a reflection of the
proverb on ill-gotten goods.[14]

In a long passage not in the manuscript, Daniel says that Fortune was guilty of Henry's deed and must bear some blame
for his great sin. He goes on to say that "we" will not think that
Henry meant other than what he swore on the Gospels in the
sight of Heaven at Doncaster, and that he came only with the
upright intention of putting order into the realm. Although we
might be inclined, he continues, to presume that the effect argues
the offense intended from the beginning, God forbid that we
should pry so closely into the deeply buried sins of the past;
therefore let us charitably believe that his oath agreed with his
intention, and that succeeding fortune forced him on to more.[15]

This analysis of Henry's actions is typical of Daniel's attitude
toward him, which became more pronounced with each succeeding edition. He does not deny his guilt, but he lays great stress on
mitigating circumstances.[16] Such sentiments do not encourage the
idea that Daniel had providential punishment in store for him.

There must have been present at the deposition Parliament,
Daniel reflects, the better few who disapproved of these actions
and divined tragic sequels from them. Time might have corrected these faults of Richard's, they said, since they were fatal
to greatness; and worse offenses had not been punished in this
way;

> But oh, in this the Heavens, we fear, prepare
> Confusion for our sins as well as his,
> And his calamity beginneth our;
> For he his own, and we abused his power.[17]

---

[13] 0–3Dan 1.87–90. Henry wakes and treats the vision as a mere dream (1.92).
[14] See above, Chap. II at n. 13.
[15] 1–3Dan 1.93–99.
[16] For details, see Michel's introduction.
[17] 1–3Dan 2.102–103.

This suggestion that the calamities inaugurated by Bolingbroke's usurpation were a divine punishment for the sins not only of Richard but also of his people is reminiscent of the notion in the first book that the reign of the child-king Richard was in itself a plague sent by God for injustice.

When Richard was required by Henry to give up his crown, he at first refused, saying that he would sooner lose his blood, "that blood that shall make thee and thine accursed." [18] This remark of Richard's could perhaps be taken to be a prediction that if Henry killed him, the vengeance of God would light upon him and his race.

But eventually Richard did resign, and absolved all his subjects of their oath and fealty to him, calling on heaven and earth and God and the saints to witness it. He did this only to be allowed to live, Daniel says, although in the final edition he omits this remark, and says instead that Richard professed to comply with the greatest willingness.[19] Earlier, when Richard delivered himself into Henry's power, he said he was pleased if his own disgrace would bring good to his country, for that was always his wish. Yet he asked God to grant that Henry's course in this matter would not cause succeeding ages to repent.[20]

In the Parliament held after Henry's coronation, Richard is sentenced to imprisonment, and to death if any revolt is raised on his behalf. The Bishop of Carlisle says he will never consent to such a judgment against their king, who has not even been allowed to plead his guiltless cause.[21] He goes on to say that the stain that they make sinks farther into their souls than all their blood can wash off, and he urges them not to link sin to sin, for heaven and earth will dash down this ill-accomplished work before long, for fencing wrong with wrong provides only a weak bulwark.[22]

Daniel accepts the report of Exton's murder of Richard, at Henry's subtle instigation. And he remarks in the final edition that Henry thereby added to the sin of usurpation and "intruding force" a greater crime, which made everything that went before seem all the worse.[23] He opened himself up to the assaults of

---

[18] 1–3Dan 2.106.

[19] 1–3Dan 2.109–110.

[20] 0–2Dan 2.60.

[21] 1–3Dan 3.20–23.

[22] 1Dan 324. In the second and third editions he alters this stanza to have Carlisle ask if they think that any means can secure so indirect a course, or any cunning build so strongly that it can hold off the hand of vengeance for long.

[23] 3Dan 4.1. He is speaking specifically here of Henry's difficulty in justifying his position to foreign powers.

those who, like himself in the past, undertook to censure the actions of a monarch, and they would have had the same pestilential results in him as in Richard, "had not the Heavens blessed thy endeavorings." [24] It would seem, then, that Henry's position on the throne was providentially maintained as well as providentially initiated.

However, when Daniel speaks of the battle of Shrewsbury, he says that Northumberland was reserved to raise another tempest against Henry (although he was requited for it later), as if wrong-revenging Nemesis intended to afflict Henry all his life. But he goes on to say that Northumberland "happely" failed to appear at Shrewsbury, with results greatly beneficial to Henry.[25]

If Daniel means Nemesis here to represent providential justice, as he does in the sixth book, then it would appear that God was punishing Henry for his former wrongs while at the same time not permitting him to be completely overcome. This explanation might seem to be a logical unification of Daniel's scattered allusions, but no doubt it errs in giving too much force to casual remarks by deducing a well-thought-out theory from them.

Daniel closes the fourth book with an account of Henry IV's death. In the third edition, he explains Henry's sickness as the last of the uninterrupted series of troubles he experienced. After the Earl of Northumberland was finally put down, Henry became suspicious of his son, thinking that he was growing too popular and ambitious, and unscrupulous advisers added to his suspicions to such an extent that he became sick from grief. When the virtuous prince, who was (Daniel tells us) the model of a glorious monarch, heard of this state of affairs, he dispersed his father's fears by his humble protestations and cleared his name; he thus put his detractors to shame and demonstrated that a heart so nobly formed as his could not contain an unworthy thought within it.[26] Prince Henry therefore had no faults, and Daniel apparently considers the reports of his wildness before his coronation as simply the result of slander.

The king was then able to enjoy some peace, but death was upon him. In the "crown scene," he asks his son why he is so eager to anticipate the miseries of kingship; his inheritance would be constantly challenged because of his father's sin in obtaining it

[24] 3Dan 3.90.
[25] 1–3Dan 4.35.
[26] 3Dan 4.81–82.

by force; and he tells him that if he could manage to prosper apart from this burdensome office, he should let it go.[27]

The prince answers with a demurral, saying that since Henry's fortune attained such a height, he does not intend to descend from it, as if he had not the spirit to defend what his father won. Time, he says, will appease those who complain now, and eventually rectify his position. What wrong is there, he asks, that mere length of time has not completely outworn? The passage of years makes right what was not born so.[28] The matter then is presented as a question not of Henry V's keeping what belongs to someone else, but of keeping what his father wrongly acquired.[29]

"If so," the king answers, "God work his pleasure." But he tells the prince that he must endeavor with all his might to perform virtuous deeds, in order to transform their wrong into right, and to manage the realm so well as to wipe out completely the blot of wrongful acquisition, so that the discontented may have no opportunity to wish it otherwise than it now is. He continues:

> And since my death my purpose doth prevent,
> Touching this sacred war I took in hand,
> An action wherewithal my soul had meant
> T' appease my God, and reconcile my land,
> To thee is left to finish my intent;
> Who, to be safe, must never idly stand,
> But some great actions entertain thou still,
> To hold their minds who else will practice ill.[30]

This is the first time that we have seen any personal motive attached to Henry's projected crusade (aside from his implied wish to fulfill the prophecy about dying in Jerusalem). According to all the sources, the king wished to free the Holy Land and to unite the forces of Christendom against the infidel, thereby preventing their scandalous wars with each other. But Daniel sees Henry undertaking it as an act of reparation for his offenses against God, and also as a means for uniting his own people.

Looking back, then, we may see that in the first three books of

[27] 1–2Dan 4.89.
[28] 1–3Dan 4.90.
[29] In an episode before the "crown scene," which Daniel omitted from the final edition, while his body is in a deathlike trance, Henry's spirit finds peace in resolving to give the crown to the one to whom it seemed to belong (1–2Dan 4.88 + [3.129–130]). But his conversation with his son after he wakes indicates that he is thinking of him and not of the Mortimer heir.
[30] 1–3Dan 4.91–92.

the *Civil Wars,* which cover the life of Richard II, including his death after Henry's usurpation, there is no mention whatsoever of the royal line that had priority over the house of Lancaster. The emphasis is entirely on the question of overthrowing a lawful king. We first hear of the Mortimer claim in connection with Henry's refusal to ransom Edmund Mortimer (whom Daniel takes to be the Earl of March) from Glendower. Daniel says that Henry much feared Mortimer, and well he might, for Edmund was the heir Richard had named to succeed him.[31]

The dispute over Mortimer's captivity led to the tripartite pact and the battle of Shrewsbury, and from there Daniel skips immediately to the deathbed scene that we have just discussed.[32] As we have seen, the question of Mortimer's right to the realm was not brought up.

At the beginning of the fifth book, Daniel says that Henry V seemed to appear to him and rebuke him for not describing the glorious feats of his time, instead of limiting himself to the deeds of sin and shame. Henry goes on to lament that there was no epic poet in his days to commemorate their achievements. For, he says, what is the glory worth that they attained to with all their labor if it is lost as soon as it is won?[33]

It is quite obvious that Daniel's conception of Henry V differs radically from that of the chronicles and Shakespeare; for in these treatments Henry appears not only as reformed from low living, but also as a king of the highest piety, who, though he might appeal to glory in urging his soldiers on, would attribute all the honor to God and none to himself. Daniel's honor-craving hero, on the other hand, is virtuous in function of his magnanimity rather than as an expression of piety. His magnanimity, in fact, was the cause of his son's misfortunes, for it prevented him from cruelly eliminating the "pretendant race" of March-York.[34] He has an extensive treatment of the Cambridge plot. At one point he says that even though Cambridge's cause seemed right and the title strong, yet it was made wrong by the time of acting upon it, because it would have frustrated English designs upon France.[35]

[31] 1–3Dan 4.20–22.
[32] In the third edition he adds an incident concerning the Mortimer children; according to Daniel, Henry IV was holding them as hostages to prevent their father Edmund from making an attempt for the crown (3Dan 4.70–73). He also adds an account of the Scrope uprising in terms entirely unfavorable to the archbishop (3Dan 4.73–80).
[33] 1–3Dan 5.2–8.
[34] 1–3Dan 5.33–34.
[35] 1–3Dan 5.29–30.

It would be a mistake, however, to interpret him as implying here that the Cambridge plot would have been right at some other time, or that he would have approved of any kind of attempt to dethrone Henry V.

Daniel sums up Henry's achievement by saying that where corrupted faith had made the people unfit for obedience, he infused order and discipline, and sent discontent abroad, dispersing ill humors in heroic actions, and uniting them in a single purpose by placing the goal of glory before them; as a result, the malicious had no leisure to dissent nor the envious time to practice treachery. The present action diverted thoughts from past madness; and pride, oppression, and usury, the cancerous evils of the state, were sent forth to prey upon the enemy.[36]

The Triumph of the House of York

After nearly sixty years had passed since Bolingbroke first attained to the crown, "God knows how just," his descendants were considered its legitimate possessors. But then the Duke of York began to contrast his title with theirs, and to point out the injury that had been done to his family. However, in order to prove his right, York had to disprove time, law, consent, oath, and allegiance. And there was no way for this but the way of blood.[37]

Daniel admits that the occasion that led York to make his attempt was at least a partial excuse; under the pusillanimous and inept rule of Henry VI, York's enemies were free to exercise their campaign of slander against him and to abuse the country in general; this, combined with the people's love for him and his apparent right, may seem to have been sufficient incitement.[38] He does not make clear here whether or not he believes York was justified by these motives. From what he has already said, it would seem that he treats York as he did Henry Bolingbroke; his main line of action was wrong, but there were mitigating circumstances. But he obviously likes Bolingbroke better than he does York. He goes on:

Besides, the now ripe wrath, deferred till now,
Of that sure and unfailing Justicer

[36] 1–3Dan 5.17–18. Daniel does not bother to examine the morality of this kind of war policy.
[37] 1–3Dan 5.45–46.
[38] 1–3Dan 5.48.

That never suffers wrong so long to grow,
And to incorporate with right so far
As it might come to seem the same in show,
T' encourage those that evil-minded are
By such success, but that at last he will
Confound the branch whose root was planted ill.[39]

Daniel never finishes the sentence he begins in this stanza, but presumably he means that God's deferred wrath finally took effect, as it always does eventually. Otherwise, he continues, the impious might spitefully suggest that God permits the great to do as they please, and that he plagues only the weak and wretched. In reality, however, Daniel says, God uses these mighty wrongdoers only to scourge others, and then at length he rids the world of them.[40]

This explanation hardly fits the facts, however, and Daniel seems to realize this, no doubt calling to mind that his hero Henry V and the pious and pitiful Henry VI could hardly be regarded as deserving to be purged from among mankind. "But could not yet," he asks, "for bloodshed satisfy/The now well-ruling of th'ill-gotten crown?" Must even the good receive the penalty of past sins committed by others? And must a just king's blood and misery pay for the overthrow of a bad one?[41]

He has avoided the real moral question at issue here (aside from his calling that well governed which he had just previously called badly governed). York's injury did not stem from the unjust overthrow of the bad king Richard II or from any blood shed in the Lancastrian acquisition of the crown, but rather from the Lancastrian refusal to allow the crown to pass to its rightful heirs. In such matters, as in cases of theft, no reparation is considered adequate unless restitution is made, if at all possible.

Daniel chooses instead to analyze the situation in terms of the primitive biblical notion that God visits the sins of the father upon the children — not so much, it seems, in order to punish wrongdoing as to prevent further wrongdoing: that is, God is said to be motivated by the desire to provide examples in order to restrain other men from sin. Daniel goes on, as we saw, to ask if it had to be this way. We are to suppose that he answers in the affirmative; for he says we see that "right in his course must

[39] 1–3Dan 5.49.
[40] 1–3Dan 5.50.
[41] 1–3Dan 5.51.

go,/And men, t'escape from blood, must keep it so." [42] That is, any deviation from the right order will bring bloodshed, and the only way to prevent it is not to deviate in the first place. The wording of this conclusion is perhaps meant to reflect the particular problem involved here, the hindering of a family from its due heritage.

The sixth book of the *Civil Wars* is taken up with the first battle of St. Albans (1455), and York is treated consistently with disfavor. It was his use of artillery in this battle that inspired (if that is the word) Daniel's long digression on the invention of gunpowder at the instigation of Nemesis and Pandora. The 1595 version ends with the remark that York's impious faction had not as yet enlarged its shameful designs to the extent of attempting anything directly against King Henry:

> Mischief was not full ripe for such foul deeds,
> Left for th'unbounded malice that succeeds. [43]

In the seventh book, which appeared in 1601, Daniel takes up York's appearance in Parliament in 1460 to justify his claim to the crown. He supports his position with such forcefulness that he seems to vanquish all opponents. First he argues the right due to his blood, which has so long been withheld by the usurpation of the Lancasters; for the right of a direct line, he says, has always been considered to be the sacred course of blood, as their ancestors, their laws, and their venerable customs have testified. And whenever it has been violated, horror and confusion have always resulted until the proper line is restored. [44]

It may be that York here is implying not only the natural chaos that follows upon disorder but also the divine punishment that is fully specified in Hall's version of this speech. If so, however, it soon becomes evident that Daniel considers York to be a fraud in his appeal to the troubles that England had suffered. For York does not point to past disasters but lists only the present afflictions. He bids his listeners witness the universal misery the realm stands in, as if accursed. The Church and the commons suffer violence, extortion, and robbery, and there is neither order

---

[42] 1–3Dan 5.51. This is the wording of the third edition, which seems to say more clearly what he meant to say in the earlier versions (the first edition says: "I see due course must rightly go,/And th'earth must trace it or else purchase woe").

[43] 1–3Dan 6.114.

[44] 2–3Dan 7.67–68.

nor respect for the laws. Thus, Daniel says, York complains of what he himself caused.[45]

York blames everything on the insolence of others, who, he says, exhausted the crown's revenues and were attempting to deliver Ireland and Calais to the French. And yet, he says, these traitors procured the attainders of faithful subjects like himself and his friends. And since this malice can have no end but the ruin of the country, and since the God of heaven seems to support his cause, as do the best men of the realm, and since his blood, so long menaced, seems reserved for some purpose, it rests upon the judgment of his listeners either to set the country upright or to ruin it completely. For they are to be sure of this, that he must pursue his right as long as life remains to him and his.[46]

York would seem to be making an indirect claim to God's protection here, implying that God appears to be on his side because his life has been preserved from all the attempts made upon it in the past, and that therefore he is no doubt preserving him to accomplish his purpose. Daniel described a similar appeal on York's part in the first edition, when he was detailing the subtle and indirect ways in which York won support for his claim. He urged Warwick and other lords to rescue the land from the disgrace it lay in. And no doubt God would approve of their actions, he told them, since he was aware not only of his right, but also of the misrule of those whose weakness was calling upon them to act, even though unwillingly. He protested that it was not for the sake of a crown that his soul was moved (though he added that if it were his right, he had no reason to refuse what was his), but only to correct these indignities. And what if God, whose judgments were unknown, had ordained him to come to the relief of the land? If so, in helping him they would be helping themselves.[47]

York appears more modest (or more politic) in Daniel than he does in Hall, for he speaks only of the possibility or probability of God's support, and not of its certainty. In both cases, however, the eventuality of his sudden end demonstrates clearly that God was not preserving him for the crown, in his own person at least.

After he describes York leaving the chamber to allow the Parliament to take counsel, Daniel gives at length the considerations

[45] 2–3Dan 7.69.
[46] 2–3Dan 7.71–73.
[47] 1–3Dan 6.20–21.

of the more temperate men among them (as opposed to the others, the majority, who were not inclined to run any serious opposition to York's demands). They admit that York's claim looks good in the abstract, but in the present circumstances they think it lacks "the right face of Right," since the crown has been possessed in act for sixty years in three descents of another line, and confirmed by all the nobles of the realm, as well as by the people's assents, oaths, parliaments, and many acts of state, both of their own and of all foreign governments; so that by order, wrong may have become right by this time, since right is nothing but the observance of order.[48]

From the tone of this speech, and Daniel's commendation of the character of the men who spoke it, it would seem natural to suppose that he agreed with its sentiments, and perhaps he did at the time. But in the 1609 edition he adds a gloss: "Non confirmatur tractu temporis, quod de jure ab initio non subsistit." He could mean by this that the mere passage of time does not make a thing right which was not right in the beginning, thus refuting the argument of the text. But on the other hand he could be offering a dictum in explanation and support of the text, and saying that nothing could be confirmed with the passage of time (as the Lancastrian possession of the crown was) unless it survived by right from the beginning. This latter interpretation, however, is perhaps less likely since the text admits that there was wrong in the beginning, and this was certainly Daniel's view; we need only recall the dedication to the third edition.

The minority report of the text continues, citing precedents from the past, in the cases of William Rufus, Henry I, John, and Edward II and Edward III. The crown was received with apparent wrong in all these instances, and yet it sat easily on their successors and passed for right. If therefore they could arrange everything to everyone's satisfaction in those days, it would seem best in the present case that the crown should remain where it is, in order to prevent the confusion of further mischief.[49]

Thus, Daniel says, did those ancient fathers of the Law, grave Baron Thorp and learned Fortescue, argue; and though they

---

[48] 2–3Dan 7.74–75. The last couplet reads:

> That Wrong, by order, may grow Right by-this;
> Sith Right, th'observer but of Order is.

"By-this" would seem to mean "by this time" rather than a repetition of "by order," especially in view of the third-edition gloss referring to the passage of time.

[49] 2–3Dan 7.77–78.

were not able to reverse the waywardness of the others, yet they were able to moderate it and to preserve some reverence for their pious king. And therefore it was agreed that he should remain king, and that York should be his heir.[50]

The people of the North, however, did not accept the validity of this action, and held out for the one whom they considered to be the true heir, namely, Prince Edward, Henry VI's son. They denied that Henry could will away the crown, because it was not his to give but only to use, and no act of his could divert it from his due successor. The entailment of the crown to York they considered an unnatural and insolent intrusion of attainted blood that must in justice be opposed by force.[51] York therefore was forced to undergo the final labor of his ambitious life; his excessive pride and confidence, accumulated from his past good fortunes, led him to a tragic end. He was "born not to wear the crown he wrought for thus." [52]

Daniel may be suggesting some kind of destiny at work here against York. He is more explicit regarding Queen Margaret, however, who failed to stop York's son Edward at Mortimer's Cross; for no plots, he says, can succeed in averting the mischiefs which the Heavens have decreed.[53] But Daniel would hardly have used the term "mischiefs" if he were thinking of a divine restoration of right to the house of York at this point.

It did not take long for Parliament to approve Edward's right to the government, and to declare Henry guilty of breaking his oath and the act of Parliament. For Edward pleaded with the sword, the speediest way to settle legal disputes.[54] He was crowned with all the appropriate rites, and what York could not achieve with all his travail was bestowed freely upon him. It was up to him to "make fair what foully was begun." [55] Edward had all the qualifications for kingship — "Both personage, blood, virtue, power, and wit"; and these things alone are what win the hearts of men, and only they were able to bring order to the realm. Daniel honors him in his verses, for, as he says, "this is my side, my muse must hold with kings." [56] And had the attainment of

[50] 2–3Dan 7.79.
[51] 2–3Dan 7.81–83.
[52] 2–3Dan 7.85–86. He adds that his son Rutland was made a sacrifice for the sins of others before he knew how to sin himself (7.88).
[53] 2–3Dan 7.103.
[54] 2–3Dan 7.106.
[55] 2–3Dan 7.109.
[56] 2Dan 7.109 + (6.113). Perhaps Daniel felt pangs of conscience in leaving poor King Henry in the lurch like this; at any rate, he deleted this stanza in the third edition.

this goal ended all the bloodshed still to follow, he says, the land would have been truly blessed. As it is, his muse is unwilling to proceed, and longs to see that glorious holyday of union, the final reconciliation of this discord.[57]

It would seem, then, that as far as Daniel is concerned the civil wars could have ended here, and England would have been more blessed than she was in fact. He no doubt forgets for the moment that the Tudor union would not have taken place if this had happened. And it would probably be safe to say that he did not have in mind at this juncture any supernatural or providential design that demanded the continuing of the wars. Nor is it evident that any such reason occurred to him or affected him in any discernible way when he wrote the additional book that appeared in 1609.

In this book, the eighth, Daniel first treats of the battle of Towton. He gives Edward a speech before the battle, in which he says that though right is on their side and is recognized by both God and man, yet it will do them no good if they cannot win there this day. For Justice is a proud virtue, which abandons weak misery and supports power.[58] He therefore does not claim divine aid in his fight, even though he does say that God approves of his cause.

It would seem that Daniel's enthusiasm for Edward or at least for his cause has cooled since he wrote the seventh book. In speaking of Henry's defeat he says:

> Thus, England, didst thou see the mightiest king
> Thou ever hadst in power and majesty
> Of state and of dominions, governing
> A most magnificent nobility,
> With an adventurous people, flourishing
> In all the glories of felicity,
> Chased from his kingdom, forced to seek redress
> In parts remote, distressed and succorless.
> Now, Bolingbroke, these miseries here shown
> Do much unload thy sin, make thy ill good.
> For if thou didst by wrong attain the crown,
> 'Twas without cries, it cost but little blood.
> But York by his attempt hath overthrown
> All the best glory wherein England stood,
> And did his state by her undoing win,
> And was, though white without, yet red within.[59]

[57] 2–3Dan 7.110–111. The 1601 version ends here.
[58] 3Dan 8.9–10.
[59] 3Dan 8.34–35.

For all practical purposes, these are Daniel's concluding remarks on the civil wars.[60] He regards the effort that York and his faction made to restore the crown to his line as a much greater wrong than Henry IV's usurpation. We can only conjecture whether he would have considered the final destruction of the house of York as divine retribution for this wrong. However, if Daniel's mind were bent in this direction, it is strange that he would have omitted such considerations when dealing with the tragic death of the Duke of York, who seemed to bear, in Daniel's view, the greatest burden of guilt in this matter.

At one point, as we have seen, Daniel considered the loss of the crown by the house of Lancaster to be the effect of God's justice, deserved because of the Lancastrian usurpation. It would perhaps be possible to deduce from this that York was an instrument, though unjust himself, in the hands of divine justice, and that all the troubles he caused both before and after his death constituted scourges of God's wrath upon England. But there is no indication that Daniel's mind worked this way. He could only with reluctance admit that the house of Lancaster was being punished in the person of Henry VI, and he shows no inclination to consider the people of his time as sharing in this punishment.

And in the books written after 1595, there is no return to or elaboration of the large providential designs of the 1595 version. In that first version, in addition to the possible suggestion that the wars were a necessary prelude to the Tudor union, he indicated that they were meant to rein in presumption, and that they were part of God's plague for sin, a punishment that began with his sending the child-ruler Richard II. In 1609 this latter reason was changed, and Richard was considered as a plague that God sent because of his intention to transfer the royal line or to bring defeat to the nation. And later on, the wars are explained simply as a sharing in the pain that God in his providence requires all men to suffer. The importance of these explanations is magnified, however, by lifting them out of context in this way; for in the actual development of the civil wars, regarded as a whole, these concepts do not seem to have been controlling influences on Daniel's thought. They do not even appear to be organically related to the remarks he makes concerning the providential establishment of Henry IV's regime. If he had gone on to finish the *Civil Wars* as he had first projected it, he might have

---

[60] He does say later that when Henry VI was captured, everything conspired for Edward's establishment. But soon a fire started that would engulf the whole state (8.44).

made the divine dimension of the work more consistent; but it is evident that any such consistency would have been an after-thought, and not the result either of a long-standing tradition or personal conviction.

IX

Shakespeare's
Double
Tetralogy

In all the works we have studied so far, our principal source of providential themes has been the commentary of the authors upon the historical personages and events they relate. But in Shakespeare's plays such commentary is completely absent, except perhaps for an occasional choric speech; and we will therefore be restricted to analyzing the sentiments of the characters and studying their own analyses of events. And from this investigation we may attempt to see what patterns emerge from the plays regarded as individual works as well as parts of a series. It is assumed from the outset that Shakespeare meant each play to be a self-subsistent unity. The plays then will be treated individually, and thematic relationships with other plays in the cycle will be considered from this viewpoint.

We shall begin with *Richard II* and end with *Richard III*, following the chronological order of the events, as we have done in previous chapters. There would be some merit in beginning with *Henry VI* and ending with *Henry V*, the order in which Shakespeare wrote the plays, for it would enable us more easily to trace the development of his handling of historical providential themes. But it is hoped that this development can be given adequate consideration in the present approach.

Richard II

As in our analysis of the contemporary sources concerning Richard II's overthrow, we can divide the providential themes of Shakespeare's play on the subject into pro-Lancastrian and anti-Lancastrian sentiments. We may begin, as the play does, with the Lancastrian appeals to God against Richard and his associates for the abuses they are charged with. The murder of Woodstock is chosen to inaugurate the action, and Bolingbroke cites this as his chief motive in opposing Mowbray, whom he accuses as the spiller of Woodstock's blood. This blood, like Abel's, cries out "for justice and rough chastisement"; but it is Bolingbroke and not God to whom it cries out.[1] Gaunt, however, in speaking with Woodstock's widow, places both the guilt and the duty of punishing the guilt upon Richard himself, and for this reason he says they should leave their quarrel "to the will of Heaven," which "will rain hot vengeance on offenders' heads" when the hour is ripe. It is God's quarrel, he says, for his own deputy, who was anointed in his sight, caused Woodstock's death. If he did so wrongfully, let Heaven avenge it, for he himself "may never lift/An angry arm against his minister." [2]

In these words of Gaunt, Shakespeare would seem to be setting up a code of morality by which subsequent events in the play are to be judged, if we can infer such a meaning from the nature of Gaunt's character, which is unalloyed with any unworthy motives. On this basis, Bolingbroke's rising and his subsequent dealings with Richard would stand condemned. On the other hand, it would by no means follow that Richard's misfortunes were the result of divine justice. In fact, just the opposite would be true, for in terms of Gaunt's code, Henry's actions would constitute the sinful usurpation of God's office of judge and avenger. It would, of course, be easy to consider Richard's fate as divinely intended even though the human instrument was acting unjustly. We have seen this kind of analysis employed frequently enough before in other works, but it seems hardly possible to

[1] R2 1.1.98–106. In the notes, Shakespeare's history plays are designated by the first letter of the king's name followed by the appropriate numeral, in arabic. In cases where a play has more than one part, the appropriate arabic numeral precedes the letter. For example, a reference to the *First Part of Henry the Fourth* would read 1H4; or, as here, Richard II would be R2.

[2] R2 1.2.4–41. In the contemporary play of *Woodstock*, which Shakespeare perhaps drew upon, Woodstock expresses sentiments resembling those of Gaunt in *Richard II*. He affirms his loyalty to the king, God's great deputy; he swears before his God he will never consent to any rash act against his state; he has always been true to him and will remain so. Their own sins have caused what is now amiss, and they must abide Heaven's will (4.2.144–150). When Green is killed, Richard laments and tells his friends that the fearful wrath of Heaven sits heavy on their heads for Woodstock's death. Blood cries for blood, and "that almighty hand" does not permit murder to stand unrevenged (5.4.47–50). But Shakespeare was no doubt influenced by Froissart in making Gaunt the spokesman of law and order. Hardyng also considered Richard's death as preordained for his murder of Woodstock, and the *Mirror for Magistrates* entertained similar views.

derive such a meaning from Gaunt's views and from the events that follow. Nor is it possible to find assurance of a sentence of divine retribution against Richard from the various omens of disaster to be found in the play, such as the queen's seemingly causeless sorrow,[3] or the incident of Richard's horse Barbary,[4] or the signs and prophecies noted by the Welsh.[5] Even if we are to agree with the Welsh captain that "these signs forerun the death or fall of kings," we would still not know the providential reasons for Richard's fall nor even know if his fall is being singled out as a special providence. We may recall the difficulty that Daniel had in interpreting the significance of the prodigies he invented just before Richard's deposition.

The characterization that Shakespeare gives Richard when Gaunt is on his deathbed corresponds to the Lancastrian view of him. Richard and his followers pray God to hasten his uncle's death so that his wealth can finance their projected Irish campaign.[6] But Gaunt's references to Richard's sacred and anointed character as king should no doubt be classified as belonging to the anti-Lancastrian tradition. This is an aspect of providential speculation that receives far more emphasis in Shakespeare, and especially in this play, than in any of the chronicle sources before him. We have seen from Gaunt's use of this consideration that it can easily be appealed to not only against an evil king,[7] but even on behalf of an evil king, against rebellious subjects; and where a good king is concerned the appeal against rebellion is of course all the more natural.

Now it is abundantly evident that in this play Richard by no means considers himself the opprobrious villain that his opponents make him out to be; he never refers to his offenses as any more than follies, as he does, for instance, when he is forced to renounce his crown in Parliament. And this is also the case with his supporters. Furthermore, there is some justification for their attitude in the objective portrayal of the king and his party. For instance, Bolingbroke charges Bushy and Green with keeping

---

[3] R2 2.2.1–40.

[4] R2 5.5.8–9, 76–94; cf. Froissart's story of Richard's greyhound, which abandoned Richard instinctively and went over to Henry.

[5] R2 2.4.7–11. Shakespeare seems to be drawing specifically on Walsingham's prodigy of the bay or laurel trees, which Fleming added to Holinshed (2Hol 2.850).

[6] R2 1.4.59–65.

[7] Cf. also Gaunt's chiding of Richard for committing his anointed blood to the physicians who first wounded him (2.1.97–99).

the king from the queen and causing her to weep over their "foul wrongs." [8] But this charge can scarcely be given much credit in view of the warm relationship that we have seen to exist between the queen and Richard's friends in the second scene of the second act, and the queen's attitude in the garden scene that follows is another counterindication. Green sums up their point of view eschatologically when he answers Bolingbroke's charges:

> My comfort is that heaven will take our souls
> And plague injustice with the pains of hell.[9]

Very early in the play, Richard appeals not only to his sacred blood, but also to the "unstooping firmness of my upright soul." [10] In the matter of confiscating Bolingbroke's inheritance, however, it seems fairly clear that Richard is meant to be objectively portrayed as being in the wrong. This is the opinion of York, at any rate, whose conscience urges him to right the injury done to Henry; but at the same time he indicates that his conscience has a greater obligation to Richard, his sovereign, whom he is bound by oath to defend.[11] It is on the basis of his bearing the power of the anointed king that he challenges Henry; but he soon admits that his power is weak.[12] Later he laments that "such a sacred king" as Richard should have to hide his head, and he warns Henry now not to take more than what is owing to him, "lest you mistake the Heavens are o'er our heads." Henry answers that he knows it, "and oppose not myself/Against their will." [13]

When Richard first returns from Ireland, he encourages himself by reflecting upon his kingship, asserting that the stones of his realm would turn into soldiers before its king would succumb to the power of rebels. Carlisle supports him by telling him that "that Power that made you king/Hath power to keep you king in spite of all." But he cautions him to make use of the means that God provides and not refuse his assistance. Aumerle translates this counsel — the bishop is saying that they should be preparing to defend themselves.[14]

[8] R2 3.1.11–15; for the significance of Bolingbroke's charge, see above, Chap. I, n. 6.
[9] R2 3.1.33–34.
[10] R2 1.1.121.
[11] R2 2.2.111–115.
[12] R2 2.3.88–105, 153–159
[13] R2 3.3.8–19.
[14] R2 3.2.24–35.

But Richard goes on to place all his confidence in his state alone, and he says that the treacherous Bolingbroke and his forces will collapse at the very sight of him.[15] Not all the water in the sea can wash the balm from an anointed king, he says: "The breath of worldly men cannot depose/The deputy elected by the Lord." And he asserts that God has an angel fighting on his side for every rebel mustered against him by Bolingbroke; "then, if angels fight,/Weak men must fall, for Heaven still guards the right." [16]

Shakespeare has Richard utter this absurd *Mirror for Magistrates* generality and then contradict it immediately afterwards when further bad news is brought. And he repeats once more this process of moving the king from overconfidence in his state to despair. In doing so, he has Richard follow a pattern we have noticed occasionally in earlier writers;[17] success is attributed to God, but misfortune is blamed on some personification. Here it is Time that has "set a blot" on Richard's pride.[18] Furthermore, in his deflated mood, the king recalls the histories of past kings, all of whom, far from being defended by God, were murdered.[19]

When Richard talks with Northumberland, he is once more confident of the divine authority backing him:

> We are amazed; and thus long have we stood
> To watch the fearful bending of thy knee,
> Because we thought ourself thy lawful king;
> And if we be, how dare thy joints forget
> To pay their awful duty to our presence?
> If we be not, show us the hand of God
> That hath dismissed us from our stewardship;
> For well we know, no hand of blood and bone
> Can gripe the sacred handle of our scepter,
> Unless he do profane, steal, or usurp.
> And though you think that all, as you have done,
> Have torn their souls by turning them from us,
> And we are barren and bereft of friends,
> Yet know, my master, God omnipotent,
> Is mustering in his clouds on our behalf
> Armies of pestilence; and they shall strike

[15] Cf. the similar notion expanded upon by Richard III in the speech given to him by Hall before the battle of Bosworth.

[16] R2 3.2.36–62.

[17] For example, see above, Chap. I at nn. 45, 69; Chap. II at n. 60; Chap. III at n. 56.

[18] R2 3.2.81.

[19] R2 3.2.145–170.

> Your children yet unborn and unbegot,
> That lift your vassal hands against my head
> And threat the glory of my precious crown.
> Tell Bolingbroke — for yon methinks he stands —
> That every stride he makes upon my land
> Is dangerous treason. He is come to open
> The purple testament of bleeding war;
> But ere the crown he looks for live in peace,
> Ten thousand bloody crowns of mothers' sons
> Shall ill become the flower of England's face,
> Change the complexion of her maid-pale peace
> To scarlet indignation, and bedew
> Her pastures' grass with faithful English blood.

Northumberland piously responds by praying the King of heaven to forbid any such attack against their king, and he says that Bolingbroke swears by everything swearable that his intentions are honorable.[20]

King Richard's words could perhaps be taken as a prediction of the whole century of intermittent strife over the crown that was caused by Bolingbroke's usurpation until the kingdom rested in peace under Henry VIII, so that all the suffering caused by this strife would be looked upon as the effect of God's retribution. If so, it would be the only appearance of such a theme in the historiographical works on this period that we have examined. However, it seems just as likely, or even more likely, in view of Richard's later prediction to Northumberland in the fifth act, that Richard is warning that Henry himself will go through much trouble before the crown he seeks rests in peace on his own head, and that those who have aided him in his rebellion will undergo the punishment of divine justice, which will be felt by their children as well as by themselves. The prediction that pestilence will strike their children yet unborn and unbegot might seem to contain long-range implications, but this is not necessarily the case. Henry V later warns that there are some "yet ungotten and unborn/That shall have cause to curse the Dauphin's scorn,"[21] but he is hardly envisaging a campaign outlasting his own lifetime.

Shakespeare has not given much validity to Richard's providential claims earlier in this act, and has allowed them to be

---

[20] R2 3.3.72–120.
[21] H5 1.2.287–288. Cf. the similar expression in Daniel, above, Chap. VIII at n. 13.

refuted as soon as they are uttered. The force of his prediction of future divine discomfiture for Henry and his allies is therefore somewhat weakened; and, as in the preceding scene, Richard follows up his assertion of providential backing with abundant words of self-abasement.[22]

We find out later, in York's narrative to his duchess, that Bolingbroke took Richard at his word to do with him as he wished, and led him to London in a debased state. He recalls how the people called God's blessings upon Henry instead of upon Richard; and they treated Richard with such scorn that they threw dust on his sacred head,

> Which with such gentle sorrow he shook off,
> His face still combating with tears and smiles,
> The badges of his grief and patience,
> That had not God, for some strong purpose, steeled
> The hearts of men, they must perforce have melted,
> And barbarism itself have pitied him.
> But Heaven hath a hand in these events,
> To whose high will we bow our calm contents.[23]

These thoughts of York resemble the sad reflections of Créton and Froissart upon the fall of their liberal patron, King Richard, which they explain in terms of the unfathomable judgments of God and the necessity of fate to follow out its course.[24] But York concludes by pledging his undying support to Henry.

Carlisle's defense of Richard in Parliament is based ultimately on the anti-Lancastrian author of the *Chronicque de la traïson et mort de Richart deux roy Dengleterre,* and Shakespeare expands upon it in keeping with the spirit of the original, as Hall had done. When Bolingbroke says that he will ascend the throne in God's name, Carlisle prays God to forbid it, and proceeds to condemn all their proceedings. Even thieves are not tried without a hearing, he says:

> And shall the figure of God's majesty,
> His captain, steward, deputy elect,
> Anointed, crowned, planted many years,
> Be judged by subject and inferior breath,
> And he himself not present? Oh, forfend it, God,

---

[22] R2 3.3.143–170.
[23] R2 5.2.1–38.
[24] Cf. also Créton's account of Henry's reception into London.

That in a Christian climate souls refined
Should show so heinous, black, obscene a deed!
I speak to subjects, and a subject speaks,
Stirred up by God, thus boldly for his king.
My Lord of Hereford here, whom you call king,
Is a foul traitor to proud Hereford's king;
And if you crown him, let me prophesy,
The blood of English shall manure the ground,
And future ages groan for this foul act.
Peace shall go sleep with Turks and infidels,
And in this seat of peace tumultuous wars
Shall kin with kin and kind with kind confound.
Disorder, horror, fear, and mutiny
Shall here inhabit, and this land be called
The field of Golgotha and dead men's skulls.
Oh, if you raise this house against this house,
It will the woefullest division prove
That ever fell upon this cursed earth.
Prevent it, resist it, let it not be so,
Lest child, child's children, cry against you "woe!" [25]

In this speech Shakespeare seems clearly to intend a prediction of the wars that would take place not only in Henry IV's time but in the days of Henry VI as well, since he speaks of "child, child's children," [26] and perhaps he even means the wars up to Richard III's reign and beyond, although Richard III's reign itself is concerned primarily not with a two-family feud, but with inter-familial strife. However, the bishop is not speaking in terms of divine punishment here, but in terms of a human situation — if they raise one house against the other, a terrible division will result. It will be their doing, and generations to come will denounce them for it. There is no suggestion that the sufferings of the future will be undergone in expiation of or as a punishment for the sins of the present.

When Carlisle mentions two houses here, he is making an oblique reference to the fact that there is another heir. This, and Richard's indignation at Bolingbroke's acting as if he were next in line to the crown,[27] are the only indications in this play that

[25] R2 4.1.113–149. Cf. Carlisle's warnings in Daniel.
[26] Miss Campbell believes that Carlisle's warning is fulfilled in the overthrow of Henry VI (Shakespeare's "Histories" 207); cf. Holinshed's sentiment, that Henry IV and his lineal race were scourged for his rebellion against Richard (above, Chap. VI at n. 10). But Carlisle is speaking of those who effected Henry's triumph, not Henry himself.
[27] R2 1.4.35–36.

there is anything more to Henry's accession to the throne than the dethroning of a lawful king. Richard's heir is never named, and not even York alludes to the existence of such a person.

In Parliament, Richard compares himself to Christ betrayed by Judas, as he had done upon his return from Ireland,[28] and he elaborates upon this comparison by accusing those who are showing an outward pity of being Pilates who wash their hands while delivering him up to his "sour cross"; and he warns them that water cannot wash away their sins.[29]

Richard tells Northumberland that if he were to read over a list of his own faults, he would find there the grievous crime of deposing a king and breaking an oath, "marked with a blot, damned in the book of heaven." [30] This is Richard's answer to Northumberland's demand that he read his offenses, in order to justify their action against him. Richard considers their crime of deposing him worse than any of the follies he has committed.

As before, he alternates between asserting his divine prerogatives and abdicating from them, sometimes ironically, sometimes in sorrowful earnest. He cries "God save the king!" even though he himself is not the king; and then he gives them to understand that he alone is king in the eyes of Heaven.[31] He says he washes off with his own tears the balm that he had previously declared not all the water in the ocean could remove. And he releases all the oaths made to him and repudiates all his acts, decrees, and statutes. He means this ironically, it would seem, for he goes on to pray God to pardon all the oaths made to him that are broken, and to keep all vows unbroken that are made to Henry. These prayers are also ironic, and his blessing proves more effective than a curse. He concludes by bidding God to save King Henry at the prayer of "unkinged Richard," and to send him "many years of sunshine days." [32]

---

[28] R2 3.2.132.

[29] R2 4.1.167–171, 237–242. Richard makes the same comparison in *Traïson*. Cf. Créton's account of Henry, who reminds him of Pilate trying to escape guilt by asking the crowd what was to be done with their king, and then turning him over to them to be killed. And in the refrain of his ballade on Henry's treachery, he says that he will go body and soul into perdition.

[30] R2 4.1.229–236. Richard's outburst a little later in which he characterizes Northumberland as one of the tormenting fiends of hell (v. 270) intensifies his portrayal of Percy as having committed a deed that deserves damnation. There is, of course, no implication in Richard's words ("Fiend, thou torments me ere I come to hell!") that he expects to go to hell himself. He tells his queen later that they must lead holy lives to win a new world's crown, since their "profane hours" lost them the one they had here (5.1.22–25), and in his dying words he says: "Mount, mount, my soul! thy seat is up on high!" (5.5.112).

[31] R2 4.1.172–175.

[32] R2 4.1.207–221.

Later he calls them all traitors, and includes himself in this number for consenting to dethrone himself; he denounces them all as thieves, who "rise thus nimbly by a true king's fall." [33] Richard has, unknowingly, been unfair in his characterization of the members of the assembly before him, for not all consented to his overthrow, as is made clear to us in the discussion that follows the Parliament. Carlisle, who was arrested and placed in the custody of the Abbot of Westminster, answers the abbot's remark concerning the "woeful pageant" they have witnessed by saying that the woe is yet to come; "the children yet unborn" will feel the sting of this day.[34] This expression is similar to the one Richard had used to Northumberland, but as it stands, it connotes a global sense of foreboding without specific indications of the length of time he expects the trouble to last.

But when Aumerle addresses them ("You holy clergymen") to ask if there is any scheme afoot to remove "this pernicious blot" from the realm, Carlisle must necessarily be portrayed as joining the abbot in his plans to bring them to a "merry day" and thus prevent the woe he has predicted.[35]

It is interesting to note that in Aumerle's expression, that he will attend the jousts at Oxford "if God prevent not," [36] it is possible to read the implication that God does prevent it, which would accord not only with the interpretations of Walsingham, Gower, and other Lancastrian chroniclers, but with that of Froissart and Holinshed as well.[37] Shakespeare seems to share in Holinshed's sympathy for the plotters rather than in Hall's absolute condemnation of them. According to Hall, the devil instigated the rising, but in Shakespeare it is Richard's murder that the devil inspires.[38]

York tells Henry that if he pardons Aumerle, more sins may prosper on account of this forgiveness. Henry considers Aumerle's offense a "foul sin," but he pardons him, "as God shall pardon me." [39] Perhaps Henry is speaking in anticipation as well as in retrospect concerning his own need for forgiveness; for one of the sins which follows (and not from his forgiving of Aumerle) is Richard's assassination, for which Henry feels morally responsible.

[33] R2 4.1.246–252, 317–318.
[34] R2 4.1.321–323.
[35] R2 4.1.324–334.
[36] R2 5.2.55.
[37] See above, Chap. I at nn. 19, 30, 38; Chap. VI at n. 13.
[38] After he has killed Richard, Exton says that the devil who convinced him that his deed was good now tells him that it is recorded in hell (R2 5.5.116–117).
[39] R2 5.3.82–131.

Shakespeare dramatizes it according to the account derived from the *Chronicque de la traïson,* as elaborated by Hall, Holinshed, and Daniel, and its damnable nature is emphasized by both Richard and Exton, as well as by Henry himself, who is exemplary in his remorse. In fact, of those who believed Henry guilty of his murder, Shakespeare is the first to suggest that Henry was repentant for the deed at the time it was committed. He is also the only one to picture him as projecting his crusade at this time with the motive of making reparation for his part in Richard's death.[40]

There are two passages in particular that look forward to the events beyond the scope of this play. The first is Richard's prediction to Northumberland that in a very short time "foul sin gathering head/Shall break into corruption," referring specifically to the discontent and dissension he could sense as inevitable between Northumberland and Bolingbroke. One who knows how to set up unlawful kings will know how to pull them down again; the love of wicked men changes to fear, fear to hate, and hate leads one or both of the parties "to worthy danger and deserved death." This prophecy, however, is based on a natural rather than a supernatural evaluation of the situation. But Northumberland's answer can easily be taken to have providential implications: "My guilt be on my head, and there an end." [41]

The other passage previewing events to come dramatizes Henry's concern over his unruly son. We may note especially his remark that "if any plague hang over us, 'tis he." [42] Perhaps some far-ranging irony is intended here; a number of plagues do hang over Henry's head, but his son is not one of them. This attitude of Henry's will be given explicit providential overtones in the next play. Meanwhile the present play ends on Henry's hope that he will be able to obtain forgiveness from God and wash Richard's blood from his guilty hand,[43] which is, after all, a rather reasonable attitude for a Christian to foster, since his religion assures him that the sinner's destruction is inevitable only if he fails to repent. We must believe that Henry is sincere in his evaluation of his conscience at this point; it is significant therefore that he expresses no sense of wrong in continuing to possess the kingship, as does King Claudius in *Hamlet.*

[40] Daniel portrays Henry on his deathbed as intending his crusade to appease his God and to reconcile his land.
[41] R2 5.1.55–69.
[42] R2 5.3.3.
[43] R2 5.6.45–52.

After viewing the providential themes in *Richard II*, we may ask if there is any indication that Shakespeare intended us to feel that God was active in bringing about any of the actions of the play, or in aiding any of the characters. It would seem that we must answer in the negative, for not even the characters themselves are dramatized as considering any of the play's vicissitudes to have been brought about by God. In the beginning there is much talk of leaving Richard's punishment to God. But when Richard comes to undergo his trials, he is presented as a wronged man, who utters his own predictions of divine punishment upon his enemies. Some of these predictions are immediately refuted, and the others refer to times outside the action of the play, except in the case of the abortive rising of the earls. It may well be that when Shakespeare wrote *Richard II*, he believed or meant to suggest that the afflictions which later befell Henry IV were providential scourges for his sins. But in order to discover his views concerning these events when he came to write about them, we must go on to the two plays named after that king.

I Henry IV

The First Part of Henry the Fourth opens with the king discussing the preparations for the crusade he desires to lead to Jerusalem. And since *Richard II* closed with a similar expression of desire to go to the Holy Land, it has often been assumed that Shakespeare intended the motive that Henry named in *Richard II* to carry over into *I Henry IV*. But it is not at all clear that such an assumption is justified. If Shakespeare had meant Henry to envision his crusade as a work of reparation for Richard's death, it is almost inconceivable that he would not have brought this motive explicitly to the fore, instead of relying entirely upon the recollection of those in the audience who had seen *Richard II*.

It seems much more likely that if Shakespeare assumed any knowledge in his audience of the historical events he was dramatizing, it would be the knowledge that they could have derived from the chronicle accounts of these events. It also seems highly probable that Shakespeare himself consulted the chronicles once more before writing *I Henry IV*. It is significant therefore that he dramatizes Henry as expressing only those intentions specified in the Vergil-Hall-Holinshed account of his motivations for the crusade, except that Shakespeare does not extend the notion of strife among Christians to include anything but the troubles of England; one reason for this is that he does not cover the French conflicts of Henry IV's reign; furthermore, he has Henry project the crusade early in his reign, before most of the rebellions against him take place.

According to the chronicles, Henry was motivated by sorrow at seeing Christians oppose one another, and also by his zeal to recover the Holy Land from the hands of the infidel.[44] Similarly, in the first act of the play, Shakespeare has Henry say that there will be no more civil war in England. No more will those eyes, which "like the meteors of a troubled heaven" are bred of one nature and substance, oppose each other, but everyone will march in one direction. "Therefore, friends," he continues:

> As far as to the sepulcher of Christ,
> Whose soldier now, under whose blessed cross
> We are impressed and engaged to fight,
> Forthwith a power of English shall we levy,
> Whose arms were moulded in their mother's womb
> To chase these pagans in those holy fields
> Over whose acres walked those blessed feet
> Which fourteen hundred years ago were nailed
> For our advantage on the bitter cross.

Preparations for the crusade are still in the planning stage, and Henry has called this meeting to discuss what is to be done. But the immediate needs of the Welsh and Scottish wars force him to set aside his "holy purpose" for a while.[45]

No other motives are given for the crusade here, and this is also true of *II Henry IV*, except in the deathbed scene, where, as we shall see, Henry alleges a more selfish interest for his expedition. But the motive of reparation for Richard's death is never returned to in this context, nor does Henry express the least remorse or show any signs of guilt for his treatment of Richard in the whole of *I Henry IV*. In fact, quite the opposite is true. He regards himself as the rightful king, supported by human and divine right against rebellion. And this is the viewpoint of the chroniclers in general, especially Walsingham, Vergil, and Hall, for the events covered in this play.

This characterization of Henry is made very evident in his

---

[44] See above, Chap. IV at n. 11; Chap. V at n. 23.
[45] 1H4 1.1.1–102.

dealings with his son. When he calls him in to give an account
of himself, the king addresses him as follows:

> I know not whether God will have it so,
> For some displeasing service I have done,
> That, in his secret doom, out of my blood
> He'll breed revengement and a scourge for me;
> But thou dost in thy passages of life
> Make me believe that thou art only marked
> For the hot vengeance and the rod of heaven
> To punish my mistreadings. Tell me else,
> Could such inordinate and low desires,
> Such poor, such bare, such lewd, such mean attempts,
> Such barren pleasures, rude society,
> As thou art matched withal and grafted to,
> Accompany the greatness of thy blood
> And hold their level with thy princely heart? [46]

In this remarkable speech we are told that Henry is not conscious of any sin that God could be punishing him for.[47] Furthermore, the audience is well aware that he is completely mistaken
in his analysis of God's dispositions toward him as far as the
prince is concerned; he has not bred revenge for him in his son;
if anything he has blessed him with the most glorious son and
successor that a king ever had.

Of course, it could be held that Shakespeare introduced the
providential theme here for its rhetorical effectiveness in its immediate context, in spite of the fact that it goes counter to a larger
theme in the play. Shakespeare rather frequently employs this
kind of rhetorical abstraction from the plot of his plays; for
instance, he has Hamlet declare that no one ever returns to this
world from the dead, just after he has received a rather convincing visitor from the other world in the person of his own father.
But the evidence for a "greater theme" of the providential
punishment of Henry IV is completely lacking in this play. And
if we are to assume that the theme is wholly taken for granted on

[46] 1H4 3.2.4–17 In the prince's reply, he asks his father to pardon whatever
faults he may have committed. Henry answers: "God pardon thee!" which could
mean, "Let God pardon you for I will not." But it seems more likely that this
is Henry's own expression of pardon: "I pardon you and therefore I ask God to
pardon you." Cf. the response of Henry V to Grey: "God quit you in his mercy!"
(H5 2.2.166).

[47] The only "sin" with which he connected himself earlier in the play is the
sin of envy of which he accused himself when he saw how blessed Northumberland was in his son, whereas he could see only riot and dishonor in his own;
he went on to wish that Hotspur were his son instead of Hal (1.1.78–90).

Shakespeare's part, we must protest that a speech like this one of Henry's would practically negate such an implied theme, unless one were to postulate an extraordinarily subtle kind of irony in the king's words.

A more plausible interpretation is that Shakespeare indeed introduced the providential theme for its rhetorical effect, but that it contradicts no other theme. It is simply Henry's way of saying that his son's conduct is absolutely inexplicable. It may be that he says this in despair of ever seeing him reformed, or that he is using these strong words to convince the prince of his error.

On the other hand, if irony were intended, the audience would be expected to believe that Henry is really suffering the pangs of a remorse he always feels but never acknowledges, even in soliloquy, and that he knows or suspects that God is punishing him for his crimes against Richard, in allowing or forcing his son to follow his disastrous course. Perhaps one could even make a case for saying that God is actually punishing Henry in allowing him to believe that his son is on the path to destruction; there is no doubt that the king does suffer much in this regard. But if so, we must also admit that God very shortly calls a halt to this punishment, for Henry realizes his mistake when the prince answers him. He now realizes what the audience already knows, that his son will turn out well, and that therefore God is not punishing him as he feared; the prince will have fulfilled his promise abundantly by the end of the play.

Furthermore, the theory that Henry is meant to be afflicted with remorse for his offenses against Richard throughout the play is decisively refuted in this very scene. The king is clearly thinking of the way he acquired the crown, but it is in terms precisely the opposite of remorse. He recalls his achievement with pride, and he chides his son for not imitating the deportment that enabled him to succeed as he did; he compares the prince's actions with Richard's and warns that a fall like Richard's may be his lot as well.[48]

[48] 1H4 3.2.29–88. As has been indicated, the audience realizes that there is no danger at all of this, for they have heard the prince explain his course of action (1.2.218–240). It is interesting to remark that although Hal uses different means from those employed by his father, his concept of government is the same — to base his rule upon an intimate knowledge of the popular mind and its reactions, and to maintain authority by an impressive demeanor. M. M. Reese, *The Cease of Majesty: A Study of Shakespeare's History Plays* (New York 1961) 315, thinks that Prince Hal refused complicity in Henry IV's ideas of statecraft in *I–II Henry IV*. But though the prince's policies differ from his father's, it is not evident

Henry goes on not only to compare Prince Henry to Richard, but to liken Hotspur to himself when he landed at Ravenspurgh; and he adds:

> Now, by my scepter and my soul to boot,
> He hath more worthy interest to the state
> Than thou, the shadow of succession.
> For of no right, nor color like to right,
> He doth fill fields with harness in the realm,
> Turns head against the lion's armed jaws,
> And, being no more in debt to years than thou,
> Leads ancient lords and reverend bishops on
> To bloody battles and to bruising arms.[49]

Once more, then, we see that Henry considers himself the legitimate king, and that the rising against him has no right whatsoever to commend it. He completely ignores or disallows the reasons brought up by the Percys, which in the sources derive from the Yorkist chroniclers like Hardyng, who wrote in the latter part of Henry VI's reign. In other words, Shakespeare has once again distributed the moral and providential judgments of the sources according to their political components; in this play, the Lancastrians speak from the viewpoint of the Lancaster myth, and their opponents voice the anti-Lancastrian objections assimilated into the York myth.

If Henry manifests no guilt about Richard's deposition and death, the Percys do — or at least Northumberland does; he prays God to pardon their part in his wrongs.[50] From this phrase, we can gather that Northumberland hopes to be pardoned by God for the crimes he committed against Richard, as did Henry at the end of *Richard II*. However, none of the three Percys is really thinking in terms of guilt and repentance, but rather in terms of dishonor and revenge.[51]

As for Henry's statement that Hotspur was taking to the field against him with no shadow of right, Hotspur does pretend to a

---

that Shakespeare means to have the prince regard his father's career as objectionable in any way. It is only in *Henry V*, in his prayer before Agincourt, that Henry refers to anything sinful in his father, and here he is speaking of his acquisition of the throne, not his methods in holding it (at least, not after the death of Richard II).

[49] 1H4 3.2.93–105.
[50] 1H4 1.3.149. The text reads: "Whose wrongs in us God pardon!" It could conceivably be referring to the wrongs Richard did to them, but this seems a less likely interpretation than the one adopted here.
[51] This is evident from their words in 1.3.153–186.

right in the person of his brother-in-law Mortimer, who was named by Richard as his heir.[52] We are told this in a rather awkward piece of exposition, in which Hotspur professes complete ignorance of Mortimer's title, although, as we find out later,[53] Hotspur's wife knows well enough about it, and so do the elder Percys.

There was no mention of Mortimer in *Richard II,* and after *I Henry IV,* he drops out of the picture again; and the existence of another claimant to the throne besides the Henrys is never again alluded to in this tetralogy, which constitutes Shakespeare's last words upon the subject. With regard to *II Henry IV,* it is perhaps debatable how conscious an omission this was on Shakespeare's part, since Mortimer does not figure in the prose chronicles for the incidents covered in that play; but it is beyond a doubt, as we shall see, that the omission of this consideration in *Henry V* was quite deliberate.[54]

Even in the present play, Henry never admits that Mortimer has any valid claim to the throne. In the chronicles it is conjectured that Henry deliberately wished Mortimer dead because of his prior right to the crown; but Shakespeare transforms this editorial view into a supposition made by Hotspur.[55] Further, the conviction of the chroniclers that Henry fabricated the charge of conspiracy against Mortimer is not at all clear in Shakespeare. In point of fact there is a conspiracy already under way, as Worcester later informs Hotspur.[56] And though it is not obvious from Worcester's account that Mortimer was in on the plot from the beginning, the fact that he has already married Glendower's daughter would seem to indicate this (Henry points this out), as would Kate Percy's suspicion that he is agitating for his title.[57] Furthermore, any appearance of right the Percys might

[52] For this mistaken identification, see above, Chap. V, n. 5. Richard's heir was Roger Mortimer, whose son, Edmund, was considered to have been named heir on Roger's death in 1398; the Edmund Mortimer who was Hotspur's brother-in-law was Roger's younger brother.

[53] 1H4 2.3.84–86.

[54] In the earlier plays of *I–II Henry VI,* two contradictory accounts are given of the fate of the composite Edmund Mortimer of sixteenth-century historians; as will be shown below, these accounts more or less correspond to the two Edmund Mortimers of history.

[55] 1H4 1.3.158–159; see above, Chap. V at n. 14; Chap. VI, n. 16. Shakespeare, of course, does make it obvious that Henry fears Mortimer and would like to be rid of him. We may take Hotspur's word for it that the king paled at the mention of Mortimer's name (1.3.141–144).

[56] 1H4 1.3.188–299.

[57] 1H4 1.3.84–85; 2.3.84–86. Cf. Charles Fish, "Henry IV: Shakespeare and Holinshed," *Studies in Philology* 61: 208 (1964).

have had in supporting Mortimer is rather decisively counter-
acted by their plan to divide the kingdom into three and to rule
one of the sections themselves.[58] On the other hand, Hotspur's
ridicule of Glendower's pretensions to magic and his interpretations of portents has the effect of undermining any serious
significance that might be attached to other allusions of this
sort, not only in Falstaff's jocular view[59] but also in Henry IV's
reference to him as "that great magician, damned Glendower." [60]
And it certainly goes counter to the providential implications
Hall found in their misfortunes, which he viewed as the result of
divine punishment for believing in false prophecies, since
Glendower is the only one who believes in them. Shakespeare
does, however, make functional use of this theme of prophecy
later, for he explains Glendower's failure to appear at Shrewsbury by his being overruled by prophecies.[61]

It is evident that Worcester does not have the highest estimation for the righteousness of their cause, when he expresses his
fears that the people will construe Northumberland's absence as
his disapproval of them; he says:

> For well you know we of the offering side
> Must keep aloof from strict arbitrament,
> And stop all sight-holes, every loop from whence
> The eye of reason may pry in upon us.[62]

This sense of the unlawful nature of their rising is reinforced by
Blunt's response to Hotspur's wish to have him on their side
instead of having him stand against them as an enemy:

> And God defend but still I should stand so,
> So long as out of limit and true rule
> You stand against anointed majesty.[63]

And of the motives of the "well beloved" Archbishop of York,
that "noble prelate," we hear only the one related by Vergil and
Hall, namely, revenge; for, according to Worcester, he "bears hard
/His brother's death at Bristol, the Lord Scrope." [64]

[58] 1H4 3.1.1–141.
[59] 1H4 2.4.369–372.
[60] 1H4 1.3.83.
[61] 1H4 4.4.18. For contemporary views of Glendower's use of magic against
Henry IV, see above, Chap. I at n. 65.
[62] 1H4 4.1.60–72.
[63] 1H4 4.3.38–40.
[64] 1H4 1.3.267–271. Hotspur says, however, that the archbishop commends the

The charges Hotspur and Worcester bring against Henry before the battle of Shrewsbury are in substance those reported by Hardyng and transmitted by Hall, concerning the king's rise to power in violation of his oath, his destruction of Richard, and his depriving the true heir, Mortimer, of the kingship; but it was Henry's bad treatment of the three Percys, Hotspur says, that caused them to raise this power for their own protection, and to examine his title, which they find "too indirect for long continuance." [65]

Worcester makes similar accusations later,[66] but it is evident that the Percys are not being completely honest in the declaration of their motives, for they do not mention the tripartite pact; and Henry does not answer their charges but exposes what he takes to be their true motive — they publish these reasons to give some appearance of justice to their rebellion, in order to attract the malcontents who welcome every change.[67]

The heavy emphasis upon the Percys as rebels is strengthened still more by Henry's prayer to God to befriend his side, because of the justice of his cause.[68] It is true that Hotspur also assures his men that their own cause is just,[69] but just before this his uncle Worcester characterized their action as treason.[70] It is evident that Shakespeare has put the burden of blame for this rebellion and the losses suffered in the battle upon Worcester, and no doubt Henry's closing sentiments are to be taken as an honorable summation of the play's events, especially since they reflect Prince Henry's victory and vindication as well as his own.

When therefore Henry speaks the *Mirror for Magistrates* maxim, "thus ever did rebellion find rebuke" [71] (his own career is a glaring exception), we are to interpret it to mean that right has triumphed, and perhaps also to see in it an implicit claim of divine aid. Henry rebukes Worcester and tells him that if he had reported the truth of his offer like a Christian, many would still be alive;[72] and we are to believe, it would seem, that he was

---

general course of the action (2.3.21–23), and this would no doubt include the formulation of the charges brought against Henry before Shrewsbury.

[65] 1H4 4.3.52–105.
[66] 1H4 5.1.29–71.
[67] 1H4 5.1.72–82.
[68] 1H4 5.1.120. Henry's appeal to God here has much the same flavor as that found in the accounts of Walsingham and Hall.
[69] 1H4 5.2.87–88.
[70] 1H4 5.2.1–11.
[71] 1H4 5.5.1.
[72] 1H4 5.5.2–10.

sincere in his offer of pardon before the battle. And his concluding words confirm the approval we are to give him:

> Rebellion in this land shall lose his sway,
> Meeting the check of such another day;
> And since this business so fair is done,
> Let us not leave till all our own be won.[73]

Shakespeare no doubt meant these words to indicate to the audience that Henry did succeed within a short time in putting down all further rebellion. And if he meant to imply divine support for any person in the play, in the light of the play's ending we must conclude that that person is Henry IV if it is anyone at all. We must keep in mind that when this play was written and first produced, there could be no question of supplementing its themes with those of the as yet unwritten *Second Part of Henry the Fourth*.[74]

II Henry IV

The moral situation of the second play on Henry IV reverts to that of *Richard II* in some aspects that were altered in *I Henry IV*. For one thing, it seems evident that Henry feels remorse for his treatment of Richard and seeks God's pardon for it. Then again, Richard's prophecy to Northumberland is picked up, and the theme of an alternate claimant to the crown disappears. There is no suggestion that Henry is keeping the realm from a rightful heir, and Archbishop Scrope's rising is for the reform of Henry's rule, not for his overthrow.

The archbishop's motives appear somewhat less worthy in the characterization they receive in Northumberland's camp than they do in his own person. In Morton's speech to Percy on the matter (deleted from the quarto edition of the play), he says that the gentle Archbishop of York binds his followers with a double surety. Hotspur had only their bodies, for their souls were frozen up in the belief that rebellion was unlawful;

> But now the bishop
> Turns insurrection to religion.

[73] 1H4 5.5.41–44.

[74] We need not enter into the dispute of whether or not Shakespeare intended to write a second part of *Henry IV* from the outset. But even if it is held that he did (which seems the less likely opinion), it can hardly be believed that he deliberately omitted themes from the first part with the intention of making them appear retroactively when he included them in the second part.

Supposed sincere and holy in his thoughts,
He's followed both with body and with mind
And doth enlarge his rising with the blood
Of fair King Richard, scraped from Pomfret stones;
Derives from heaven his quarrel and his cause;
Tells them he doth bestride a bleeding land,
Gasping for life under great Bolinbroke;
And more and less do flock to follow him.[75]

It would appear from Morton's tone that though the people suppose the archbishop sincere and holy, Morton himself does not believe it is so. This, of course, may be a wrong interpretation, and it may be that Shakespeare intended Morton and the others to look upon their cause as completely righteous. It is to be noted that there is no repetition of the revenge motive in Archbishop Scrope, either here or elsewhere in the play.

In Scrope's own analysis of the situation, he blames the fickle people most of all for the present troubles: "The commonwealth is sick of their own choice." The sickness he likens to that of a dog whose ravenous greed has left it nauseated. Whoever builds on the vulgar heart, he says, has an unsure foundation. He recalls the loud applause they sent up to heaven in blessing Bolingbroke before he became what they wanted him to be. And now this common dog seeks to cast him up just as it did King Richard; it wishes to return to its vomit and howls to find it. "What trust is in these times?" he asks; those who wanted Richard dead when he was alive are now in love with his grave. Those who threw dust on his "goodly head" when he despondently followed after the admired Bolingbroke through the proud streets of London now beg the earth to give them back their first king and to take this one away. "O thoughts of men accursed!" he exclaims. "Past and to come seems best; things present worst." [76]

Here Shakespeare seems to be reflecting an attitude similar to that of Vergil-Hall-Holinshed concerning Bolingbroke's first rise to power, and he parallels Vergil's remark that the people characteristically hated Richard when he was alive, and yearned for him when he was dead.[77]

The sickness of the commonwealth is matched by Henry's own illness and unrest, which is described by Falstaff.[78] The king's

[75] 2H4 1.1.189–209.
[76] 2H4 1.3.87–108. Cf. York's description of the entrance of Bolingbroke into London in *Richard II*.
[77] Cf. also Holinshed's concluding remarks on Henry IV.
[78] 2H4 1.2.118–134.

4

soliloquy at the beginning of the third act, his first appearance in the play,[79] is simply a dissertation on the worries and trials of kings in general, much in the vein of the one added in the second edition of Holinshed after the incident of Henry's providential escape from the trap in his bed.[80]

Henry tells Warwick of his conviction that the country is so diseased that its heart is endangered. Warwick replies that it is only distempered, and that it will soon be well.[81] In the event, it would seem that Warwick's diagnosis and prognosis are the correct ones; but it soon becomes evident that Henry is troubled by the prophecy Richard made to Northumberland. We may perhaps assume that he is remorseful over the way that he dealt with Richard, and fears that Richard spoke with a kind of supernatural prescience when he outlined the course of events to follow.

Henry begins his reminiscing speech ("O God! that one might read the book of fate") by saying that if the future were known,

> The happiest youth, viewing his progress through,
> What perils past, what crosses to ensue,
> Would shut the book, and sit him down and die.[82]

He is asserting here, it would appear, that he would never have returned from exile to oppose Richard if he had known what it would entail. When he goes on to recall the words that Richard spoke to Northumberland, it is evident that Shakespeare now envisages the prophecy as having been spoken well before the deposition of Richard, no doubt in the encounter at Flint Castle, in Bolingbroke's own hearing.[83] When he repeats Richard's characterization of Northumberland as the ladder by which he himself was ascending the throne, Henry says:

[79] 2H4 3.1.4–31.

[80] Above, Chap. VI, n. 15. Cf. also Hardyng's "unreformed" summation of Henry's life, with regard to the great torments he suffered at the hands of his subjects; he points out however that all the evil intended against him in their revolts fell on their own heads, and they were deservedly put to death. In the light of the outcome of II Henry IV, this is the impression we get in general of the persecutors of Henry (viz., that they deserved what they got). Archbishop Scrope's rising is exceptional, of course.

[81] 2H4 3.1.38–44.

[82] 2H4 3.1.45–56.

[83] Cf. Henry VI's prophecy of Richmond's future reign (3H6 4.6.68–76). When Shakespeare has Richard III refer to it in the next play, he pictures it as having been uttered in his presence (R3 4.2.98–104).

Though then, God knows, I had no such intent,
But that necessity so bowed the state
That I and greatness were compelled to kiss.[84]

It is possible that Shakespeare means this disavowal of premeditated usurpation to be a rationalization on Henry's part. But to judge from Henry's character in this play, it would appear more probable that this is Shakespeare's present view of Henry's state of mind when he came to England to claim his patrimony; and in fact it is at least tenable that it is also what Shakespeare meant us to think in the Flint Castle scene of *Richard II*.

In response to Henry's implied concern that Richard was prophesying his overthrow, Warwick gives a quite reasonable natural explanation of Richard's words:

There is a history in all men's lives,
Figuring the nature of the times deceased;
The which observed, a man may prophesy,
With a near aim, of the main chance of things
As yet not come to life, which in their seeds
And weak beginnings lie intreasured.
Such things become the hatch and brood of time;
And by the necessary form of this
King Richard might create a perfect guess
That great Northumberland, then false to him,
Would of that seed grow to a greater falseness,
Which should not find a ground to root upon
Unless on you.

Henry seems convinced by this account, and says that since these things are necessary, they are to be met like necessities.[85] That is, they are necessities that can be met and dealt with, and not, as he seemed to fear, the predestined working out of a prophesied retribution against him.

The meeting of the archbishop's forces with those of Lord John of Lancaster is no doubt meant to illustrate the way in which Henry's necessities are dealt with and his fears refuted. But the nature of the moral situation shifts ground again, as we move from the motives of Northumberland (which were chiefly in Henry's mind) to those of the Archbishop of York.

[84] 2H4 3.1.72–74.
[85] 2H4 3.1.80–93.

In giving an account of himself to Westmoreland, who asks why a man of peace like the archbishop should turn to war, Scrope returns to the theme of sickness. "We are all diseased," he says:

> And with our surfeiting and wanton hours
> Have brought ourselves into a burning fever,
> And we must bleed for it; of which disease
> Our late king, Richard, being infected, died.[86]

As before, York does not blame Henry for Richard's overthrow, but distributes the blame among all the people, including Richard and himself. He goes on to say that he does not come as an enemy of peace but only seeks to purge away the obstacles that have begun to stop up the very veins of their life. He has, he says, weighed in the balance the wrongs they suffer and the wrongs their rising may bring about, and he finds their griefs heavier than their offenses. He ends by repeating that his goal is to establish a true peace.[87]

It seems evident that the archbishop and his allies are sincere in declaring the sum and scope of their motives, since they agree to disband when they receive guarantees that their complaints will be honored and their wrongs remedied; and the expression of their intents when they discuss them among themselves in private remains the same as it is when they state them to the opposing captains.

This, however, does not necessarily mean that the insurgents are portrayed as justified in their rising; the answer that Westmoreland gives to the archbishop has behind it the weight of the commonly accepted doctrine of Elizabethan times. After denying that there is need for redress, he adds: "Or if there were, it not belongs to you." In other words, Westmoreland's characterization of York's action as sealing a "lawless bloody book/Of forged rebellion with a seal divine" and as consecrating "commotion's bitter edge" would stand no matter whether his complaints were justified or not.[88]

The archbishop is convinced that Henry will not force them to fight, but will accede to their just demands,[89] and perhaps the

---

[86] Cf. 1Dan 4.46 (referring to the battle of Shrewsbury):

> O that these sin-sick states in need should stand
> To be let blood with such a boisterous hand!

[87] 2H4 4.1.30–87.
[88] 2H4 4.1.91–98.
[89] 2H4 4.1.197–223.

king would have acted in this way had it been his decision (if we can judge from his offer of peace before the battle of Shrewsbury in *I Henry IV*). But, as it is, Westmoreland and John of Lancaster are the ones who engineer the overthrow of York and his allies, and who bear any opprobrium attached to the equivocation that brought this overthrow about.

It can be legitimately questioned, however, if any opprobrium at all is meant to arise from Lancaster's action. His sermon to the archbishop contains the same kind of approved doctrine that Westmoreland alluded to, and in it he dwells with even more emphasis upon the misuse the prelate makes of his sacred office. But when Lancaster accuses him of going against the peace both of Heaven and of the king, God's substitute, York defends himself by reasserting his claim that they act only in self-defense, to save themselves from being crushed by the "time misordered," and again he repeats that the granting of their "most just and right desires" will bring them back to true obedience.[90]

After Lancaster deceives the leaders of the rising into dispersing their army, he seizes them and orders his men to pursue their dismissed troops. He consigns Scrope and his companions to "the block of death,/Treason's true bed," remarking that "God, and not we, hath safely fought today." [91]

It is difficult to see how any audience could join with Lancaster in this righteous feeling of divine approbation and aid. Even if we were to admit that the archbishop, Mowbray, and Hastings were objectively in the wrong when they raised their army, we can hardly doubt that they did not believe themselves to be in the wrong, and, as has been pointed out above, we know for certain from their discussion alone together[92] that they were sincere in their determination to uphold the peace they agreed to. Lancaster could have achieved the same results of pacification by letting York and his allies return home, without resorting to a kind of deceit that could hardly be considered honorable in any age or under any circumstances.[93]

Shakespeare has more or less followed the Holinshed account

---

[90] 2H4 4.2.4–42.

[91] 2H4 4.2.116–123. We might also note that in the previous scene Westmoreland prayed God to let peace emerge (4.1.180).

[92] 2H4 4.1.183–223.

[93] Shakespeare did not have a very high regard for telling the truth if it was a question of a good cause that required a lie. Perhaps then the present scene should be looked upon as another example of this tendency. Lancaster, however, denies that he has lied or perjured himself, by pointing to the careful phrasing of his promise, which did not specifically include pardoning the insurgents.

of the archbishop (as modified from Walsingham), in giving a
generally favorable picture of his actions and motives, and a
fairly noncommittal dramatization of the way in which he was
captured.[94] And as he did in *Richard II,* he has sorted out the
moral and spiritual sentiments of the histories and given them
to their proper spokesmen; the Lancastrians speak from the
viewpoint of the Lancaster myth, and the archbishop speaks in
accordance with the York myth; but this aspect of the York myth
was taken over in part from Lancastrian chroniclers like Walsingham whose clerical allegiances influenced them against Henry
at this point.[95] Only the Lancastrian side appeals directly to God,
and it is this side that wins. But Shakespeare does not make it at
all clear that he believes either side to have God's full approval
or full condemnation.

Shakespeare moves from this battle immediately to the time
of Henry's last agony.[96] His suffering is increased by the unex-
plained (and perhaps unexplainable) fact that he has once more
lost confidence in Prince Henry's virtue,[97] and he has dire fore-
bodings of the ruin that his reign will bring.[98] The crown scene,
derived from the anti-Lancastrian Monstrelet, follows. When the
prince takes the crown, he calls it a "golden care" that keeps its
bearer awake at night,[99] which recalls Henry's own soliloquy in
the third act.[100] But when he believes the king is dead, he expresses none of the reluctance that one might suppose these
melancholy thoughts would have induced in him; rather he says:

> My due from thee is this imperial crown,
> Which, as immediate from thy place and blood,

[94] See above, Chap VI at n. 18.
[95] Above, Chap. I at n. 70. Vergil and Hall support a Lancastrian view of this episode.
[96] Shakespeare invents a few portents here which the people and Henry's younger sons interpret as a sign of the king's imminent death, alleging similar phenomena before the death of Edward III (4.4.121–128; cf. the signs that the Welsh believed signified Richard II's death, R2 2.4.7–11). Henry himself attributes the sudden worsening of his health to Fortune, to whom he also attributes the good news of the defeated rebels (vv. 102–110); but in vv. 1–2 he regarded the outcome of the civil war as in God's hands.
[97] We would have to phrase it this way if we assume that Shakespeare has in mind the events of *I Henry IV*. But it is not at all clear that he did. In fact, he seems quite clearly to be portraying the king as having no knowledge of any reform ever effected in his son, such as the one that Hal promised and carried out in *I Henry IV*, and he completely mischaracterizes the prince in his advice to Clarence on how to humor him (4.4.23–48). In this sense, therefore, *II Henry IV* can be regarded not as a sequel to *I Henry IV*, but as an alternate version of it.
[98] 2H4 4.4.54–66.
[99] 2H4 4.5.21–31.
[100] Above at n. 82.

Derives itself to me. Lo, where it sits,
Which God shall guard; and put the world's whole strength
Into one giant arm, it shall not force
This lineal honor from me. This from thee
Will I to mine leave, as 'tis left to me.[101]

It seems unquestionable that the prince has no doubt about his right to the crown, and that Shakespeare intends his audience to have no doubt about it either. The rest of the play (as well as the whole of *Henry V*) bears out this interpretation.

After Henry's rather tedious tirade against his son, the latter answers by praying God, who "wears the crown immortally," to keep it long with his father; and he goes on to say that if it caused any unworthy emotion in him when he took it, he asks God to keep it from his head forever and reduce him to the poorest vassal that kneels in awe before it. Henry is convinced, and says that God inspired him to take the crown away, in order that he might win his love all the more by pleading so wisely in excuse of the deed.[102]

With these preliminaries over, Henry gives his son his last advice:

God knows, my son,
By what bypaths and indirect crooked ways
I met this crown; and I myself know well
How troublesome it sat upon my head.[103]
To thee it shall descend with better quiet,
Better opinion, better confirmation;
For all the soil of the achievement goes
With me into the earth. It seemed in me
But as an honor snatched with boisterous hand,
And I had many living to upbraid
My gain of it by their assistances;
Which daily grew to quarrel and to bloodshed,
Wounding supposed peace. All these bold fears
Thou seest with peril I have answered;
For all my reign hath been but as a scene

[101] 2H4 4.5.41–47.
[102] 2H4 4.5.144–181.
[103] When Shakespeare has Henry contrast what God knows with what he knows, he surely does not mean to have Henry deny knowledge of the irregular and sinful way he acquired the crown, for he goes on to ask pardon for it; the expression "God knows," therefore, implies "and so do I," and Shakespeare follows Holinshed's reading of remorse into the ambiguous expression found in Hall. Cf. the views of Henry's death as given by Hardyng and Capgrave in their Yorkist phase.

Acting that argument; and now my death
Changes the mode; for what in me was purchased
Falls upon thee in a more fairer sort;
So thou the garland wearest successively.
Yet, though thou standest more sure than I could do,
Thou art not firm enough, since griefs are green;
And all my friends, which thou must make thy friends,
Have but their stings and teeth newly ta'en out,
By whose fell working I was first advanced
And by whose power I well might lodge a fear
To be again displaced; which to avoid,
I cut them off; and had a purpose now
To lead out many to the Holy Land,
Lest rest and lying still might make them look
Too near unto my state. Therefore, my Harry,
Be it thy course to busy giddy minds
With foreign quarrels, that action, hence borne out,
May waste the memory of the former days.
More would I, but my lungs are wasted so
That strength of speech is utterly denied me.
How I came by the crown, O God forgive;
And grant it may with thee in true peace live!

The prince responds:

My gracious liege,
You won it, wore it, kept it, gave it me;
Then plain and right must my possession be,
Which I with more than with a common pain
'Gainst all the world will rightfully maintain.[104]

At the risk of excessive repetition, let us stress once more that
the crown in *II Henry IV* is definitely regarded as the rightful possession of the Henrys; and these speeches are the strongest expressions of this view we have yet seen. Admittedly, the crown was
wrongfully acquired, but Henry prays (and, we presume, hopes)
for pardon for this offense. And he prays further for God to grant
that his son may possess it in true peace. He most certainly does
not ask for forgiveness for cutting off his former allies. Their assistance was wrong ("fell") in the first place, as was his ascent to
the throne. But their turning upon him was equally wrong, and
he only did what was right in putting them down.

Henry's remarks on the crusade he intended and his advice to

[104] 2H4 4.5.184–225.

his son to occupy unstable minds in foreign quarrels is strongly reminiscent of Daniel, who is the only author before Shakespeare to suggest that Henry was motivated to undertake his crusade in order to draw fire away from his crown. Shakespeare does not add here, as Daniel does, the motive of appeasing God, nor his commission of the project to his son.[105] For the latter point, Shakespeare substitutes the notion of foreign quarrels, in much the same way that Daniel speaks of Henry V's French campaigns.[106] But we may note here that this motive is never alluded to again, either in *II Henry IV* or in *Henry V*.

Henry spoke of his plan for a crusade twice before in this play; in the first instance, before the Northern rising, he says that if the civil wars could be brought to an end, "we would, dear lords, unto the Holy Land";[107] and in the second, before he gets word of the success in the North, he says:

> Now, lords, if God doth give successful end
> To this debate that bleedeth at our doors,
> We will our youth lead on to higher fields,
> And draw no swords but what are sanctified.
> Our navy is addressed, our power collected,
> Our substitutes in absence well invested,
> And everything lies level to our wish.
> Only, we want a little personal strength;
> And pause us, till these rebels, now afoot,
> Come underneath the yoke of government.[108]

In these two passages, there is no hint of the motive of protecting his crown; there is only the motive given in the chronicles, to engage in the holy war because it is holy. There is one final motive given, which is not specifically linked to that of piety, but whose pious nature is rather obvious. When Henry learns he fainted in the room called Jerusalem, he says:

> Laud be to God! even there my life must end.
> It hath been prophesied to me many years,
> I should not die but in Jerusalem;
> Which vainly I supposed the Holy Land.
> But bear me to that chamber; there I'll lie;
> In that Jerusalem shall Harry die.[109]

[105] See above, Chap. VIII at n. 30.
[106] Above, Chap. VIII at n. 36.
[107] 2H4 3.1.107–108.
[108] 2H4 4.4.1–10.
[109] 2H4 4.5.236–241.

Shakespeare presents this scene simply, as it appears in Fabyan, without any hint of the aspersion that Holinshed casts on the prophecy.[110]

We have witnessed the pious death of a good king, who is at peace with God. There is no indication at this point, in his references to the troubles he experienced during his reign, that they were in any way a punishment from God for his sins in acquiring the throne; and he expresses no qualms about punishment after death. The final act of the play is taken up with King Henry V's appearance as the worthy successor of his father. He says that he survives his father to frustrate prophecies and to refute the "rotten opinion" that has judged him according to appearances; and, "God consigning to my good intents," no one will have just cause to wish, "God shorten Harry's happy life one day!"[111] And the play ends with Prince John's surmise of Henry's eagerness to undertake the conquest of France.[112]

We must therefore conclude that in neither of the plays named after Henry IV are the Lancastrians dramatized as being punished by God for their acquisition and continued possession of the throne. Henry's uneasiness might be interpreted as a fear of God's punishment; but in the event this fear proves unfounded. And if his apprehension itself is to be considered a divine punishment (a rather forced interpretation), the punishment must be said to end whenever his fears are relieved — specifically, when he gains confidence in his son in *I Henry IV* 3.2 and *II Henry IV* 4.5, and when his enemies are defeated in *I Henry IV* 5.5 and *II Henry IV* 4.4.

Henry V

We have observed how Shakespeare has matched Daniel's effect of presenting a flawless character for Henry V, but by using a different strategy. Whereas Daniel denounces all the stories about the prince's subcurricular activities as slanders, Shakespeare accepts them as true but purifies the motives of the prince for indulging in his low pursuits.[113]

---

[110] Fabyan 576–577.

[111] 2H4 5.2.125–145; cf. 1H4 1.2.218–240, where Hal soliloquizes over his plan to falsify men's hopes; and in 1H4 3.2.36–38, Henry IV says to him:

> The hope and expectation of thy time
> Is ruined, and the soul of every man
> Prophetically do forethink thy fall.

[112] 2H4 5.5.111–114.

[113] The prince's striking the chief justice (Redmayne 11; Hall 46) might be

This theme is continued in the expository accounts of the new king by the Archbishop of Canterbury and the Bishop of Ely.[114] We are obviously to consider these churchmen sincere in their estimation and praise of Henry, and it would seem that we are also to believe the archbishop sincere in his declaration of Henry's right to the French crown. This right was unanimously asserted and assumed by the English chroniclers; and though Hall made a bitter attack on the archbishop's morals and motives, he allowed (sincerely, it would seem) that he had great respect for God's law. Holinshed omits Hall's aspersions upon the character of the archbishop and the other clergy; and Shakespeare, while showing them to be more concerned for the Church's possessions than would be considered proper in his time, does not evidently portray their concern as completely damning.[115]

At any rate, it can hardly be maintained that Shakespeare asks us to believe that Henry is being deceived by the archbishop in undertaking the war in France. It is clear that negotiations for claiming the French crown have already been opened, and that the effort of the archbishop to frustrate the attempt of the Commons did not consist in calling to Henry's attention his French title, but in offering him a great sum of money to finance what was already being deliberated upon "in regard of causes now in hand," as Canterbury phrases it; in fact, the archbishop's conversation with the king on this subject was interrupted by the arrival of the French ambassadors.[116]

A somewhat liberal view of the archbishop's character and of his advice to Henry is further strengthened by Henry's solemn admonition to him in the name of God to expound the case rightly, and by his warning that all the blood shed in a great war cries out against the side that is in the wrong.[117] And it is further

---

alleged as an exception, but this incident was not dramatized. Also one might adduce his tentative confession of some faults in 1H4 3.2.18–28. But this is largely a virtuous expression of humility.

[114] It is interesting to note that in agreeing with Ely's solution to the king's sudden change of character (that he had previously obscured his contemplation under the veil of wildness), the archbishop answers:

It must be so; for miracles are ceased,
And therefore we must needs admit the means
How things are perfected. (H5 1.1.67–69)

The assumption that miracles had ceased was a principle of the Reformation, which, however, still allowed for diabolical wonders and the providential disposition of events.

[115] For Hall, see above, Chap. V at n. 32.

[116] H5 1.1.72–97.

[117] H5 1.2.9–32.

confirmed by the rest of the play, in which Henry is motivated
by the assumption that he is fighting a just war.

The speech of the archbishop establishing the English right to
the kingdom of France is based on the one elaborated by Hall
from Redmayne.[118] When he refutes the so-called Salic Law,
there is no mention, either in the play or in the chronicles, of the
fact that if the Salic Law were not to be observed, neither France
nor England would belong to Henry, but both would go to Edmund Mortimer. But in this play Edmund Mortimer does not
exist. And though reference is made not only to Henry's great-
grandfather, Edward III, but also to his great-uncle, the Black
Prince (Richard II's father), his irregular title is ignored and he
is declared to be their heir, who sits on their throne.[119]

Henry responds that he is determined, "by God's help/And
yours," since France is his, to bend it to his will "or break it all
to pieces." [120] In response to the Dauphin's tun of tennis balls,
he says:

> We will, in France, by God's grace, play a set
> Shall strike his father's crown into the hazard.[121]

And he sends word to the Dauphin that his soul will be charged
with the "wasteful vengeance" that his mockery will cause, and
many that are yet unbegotten and unborn will have good reason
to curse him;

> But this lies all within the will of God,
> To whom I do appeal; and in whose name
> Tell you the Dauphin I am coming on
> To venge me as I may, and to put forth
> My rightful hand in a well-hallowed cause.

[118] See above, Chap. V at n. 31.

[119] H5 1.2.33–117. Shakespeare is even more emphatic in his portrayal of Henry as
the true heir in the scene in the French court, where King Charles points out
that Henry is a stem of the "victorious stock" of the Black Prince, and that this
should make them fear his "native mightiness and fate" (2.4.62–64). Exeter then
brings Henry's ultimatum, which entreats them in the name of God Almighty
to give up the dignities that belong to him and his heirs "by gift of Heaven,/By
law of nature and of nations." He sends his pedigree, by which they can find
him "evenly derived" from Edward III. He is coming in a tempest, "like a Jove,"
to use force, if necessary; and he bids him "in the bowels of the Lord" to deliver
up his crown, and to take mercy upon the poor wretches that the war will
destroy; for Charles will be responsible for all the suffering and sorrow it will
entail (vv. 77–109).

[120] H5 1.2.222–225.

[121] H5 1.2.262–263.

He tells his advisers that he has no thought in him now except for France, "save those to God, that run before our business"; "for, God before," he says, "We'll chide the Dauphin at his father's door." [122] His consciousness of the need for divine support, as well as his confidence in obtaining it, is all-pervasive.[123]

Shakespeare treats the Cambridge plot at great length, but he completely obscures the significance it had for the extinction of his dynasty, a point which is stressed by all his sources, and which was brought out in a completely different version of the episode in an earlier play in his own series (*I Henry VI*). But here the three conspirators are regarded simply as traitors, seduced by French bribery; this is not only Henry's view but that of the Chorus as well, in his prologue to the second act.

There are two extremely oblique references to the real business that the conspirators had in hand. Grey tells Henry that he thinks there is no one dissatisfied with his reign, for all of his father's enemies have "steeped their galls in honey" and serve him "with hearts create of duty and of zeal." And Cambridge says:

> For me, the gold of France did not seduce,
> Although I did admit it as a motive
> The sooner to effect what I intended.
> But God be thanked for prevention,
> Which I in sufferance heartily will rejoice,
> Beseeching God and you to pardon me.[124]

By this latter speech we are assured that Shakespeare of set purpose suppressed the theme of another claimant to the throne with a better pedigree than Henry's. Only the most erudite members of the audience could be expected to understand what Cambridge was referring to as his real motive. It is beyond a doubt that Shakespeare portrays Henry as having no knowledge of a conspiracy against his house.

Shakespeare's treatment of the episode is rather mawkishly melodramatic. The three plotters are first shown to advocate the extremest kind of cruelty in suppressing all opposition to Henry, and to express their own support of him with the greatest pos-

---

[122] H5 1.2.281–308.

[123] His confidence is no doubt supplemented by the words of the archbishop in greeting him:

> God and his angels guard your sacred throne
> And make you long become it! (1.2.7–8)

[124] H5 2.2.29–31, 155–160.

sible hypocrisy. They are unbelievably wicked, especially since they act only out of desire for French gold (which is avowedly the case with Grey and Scrope). Henry suggests at length that Scrope acted at the bidding of a cunning fiend from hell.[125]

The king hands them over to the law, and prays God to forgive them. Scrope answers that God has justly discovered their purposes; he repents his fault more than his death, and asks Henry's forgiveness. We have seen that Cambridge thanked God for preventing their attempt, and Grey too rejoices that he was kept from their "damned enterprise." Henry sentences them to death, not to avenge himself, but for the safety of the kingdom. Once more he prays to God on their behalf, asking that in his mercy he may give them patience to endure their death and true repentance for all their great offenses.[126]

Henry then tells his loyal followers that he has no doubt of the success of their war, since God so graciously brought to light the dangerous treason plotted against them at the outset; and he adds:

> Then forth, dear countrymen! Let us deliver
> Our puissance into the hand of God,
> Putting it straight in expedition.[127]

There is not the slightest indication here of the motive adduced by Henry IV on his deathbed as a reason for his son to engage in foreign wars, namely, to keep attention away from his throne and title; and we are no more to assume its unspoken presence in this play than we are to assume that Henry IV's motive for his pilgrimage in *Richard II* was silently carried over into the two parts of *Henry IV*.

With regard to the French campaign itself, the speech Henry gives before Harfleur[128] is a piece of rhetorical exuberance that perhaps can be justified theoretically within the whole play by reading it simply as a strategic threat made in order to win the town without bloodshed.[129] There is certainly nothing else in the play to justify the supposition that his soldiers would actually

---

[125] H5 2.2.100–142. Cf. PsElmham 36, where Henry says the consiprators plotted against him at the urging of the devil ("suggestione diabolica"); this was the view of the *Gesta*, as we saw.

[126] H5 2.2.143–181.

[127] H5 2.2.184–191.

[128] H5 3.3.1–43.

[129] Historically (according to Henry's Chaplain), the king before Harfleur made the offer of peace and listed the penalties for refusal outlined in Deut. 20.

commit the wide-scale atrocities he describes in gruesome detail: and if Henry or his officers were to notice any of their men acting in this way, they would without doubt shortly see to it that they would never be able to repeat their crimes. This is well illustrated by the incident of Bardolf's execution for robbing a church.[130]

On the march to Calais, Henry continues to reflect the traditions of the chronicles in telling the French herald that with God before them they will proceed even though two nations like France were to stand in the way; and he tells his brother Gloucester that they are in God's hands, not the enemy's.[131]

For the elaborate dramatization of the English camp on the night before Agincourt, the Chorus in the prologue to the fourth act sets the stage with a magnificent description of the noises of the night, a remarkable example of Shakespeare's ability to transform the pedestrian details of his sources. In contrast to the overconfident French, "the poor condemned English,/Like sacrifices," sit patiently by their watch fires and ruminate upon the danger that morning will bring.

Henry gives a little sermon by drawing upon homely *exempla*, almost in the tone that Shakespeare in his earlier plays gave to this king's son, Henry VI. "God Almighty!" he exclaims, "There is some soul of goodness in things evil,/Would men observingly distil it out." Their bad neighbors, he says, make them get up early, which is a desirable practice, and they act as external consciences and preachers that admonish them to prepare well for their end.[132] "Thus may we gather honey from the weed," he concludes, "and make a moral of the devil himself." [133] He continues in this meditative mood through the rest of the scene,[134] although there are some aspects of his dealings with the three soldiers that remind us of the Hal of former days. His remarks on ceremony too are reminiscent of his musings on small beer in the

---

[130] H5 3.6.26–120. For the origin of this incident, see above, Chap. I at n. 104.

[131] H5 3.6.165–178. Cf. Vergil, above, Chap. IV, n. 25.

[132] It is perhaps not a coincidence that just before the battle, Montjoy comes in with a message from the constable explicitly (and disdainfully) admonishing the English to remind their followers of repentance before they are killed (4.3.83–88). For early accounts of the night before Agincourt, see above, Chap. I at nn. 106 and 118; other sources (besides the *Gesta* and Waurin) which mention that the English soldiers confessed their sins are 2Wals 94; 1Elmham 119; 1Capgrave 116; Fabyan 579; Hall 65; 1–2Hol 3.78. Hall and Holinshed add that they also received the sacrament (of the Eucharist).

[133] H5 4.1.3–12.

[134] His religious demeanor is given external support by the salutation of Sir Thomas Erpingham: "The Lord in heaven bless thee, noble Harry!" (v. 33).

previous play.[135] It is noteworthy that he makes no allowance here for the divine aspect of the state of kingship; it is all a matter of ceremony, including even the sacred balm.

When Henry asserts that the king's cause in waging the war is just and honorable, Williams points out that they do not really know whether it is or not. Bates however maintains that as far as they are concerned, it is enough that they are obedient to the king; and even if his cause is wrong, they do no wrong in obeying. Williams answers:

But if the cause be not good, the king himself hath a heavy reckoning to make, when all those legs and arms and heads, chopped off in a battle, shall join together at the latter day and cry all, "We died at such a place"; some swearing, some crying for a surgeon, some upon their wives left poor behind them, some upon the debts they owe, some upon their children rawly left. I am afeard there are few die well that die in a battle; for how can they charitably dispose of anything, when blood is their argument? Now, if these men do not die well, it will be a black matter for the king that led them to it; who to disobey were against all proportion of subjection.[136]

It does not take much reflection to realize that Williams is simply repeating the very same kind of argument that Henry himself had used with great insistence in his dealings with the Archbishop of Canterbury and the French — namely, that whoever starts a war for an unjust cause is responsible for all the death and suffering it results in. But strangely enough. Henry completely ignores this major premise of Williams' argument and attacks only his minor; or rather he substitutes a major of his own, and responds as if Williams had said that even if the king's cause were just, he would still be responsible for the bad deaths of those who fought under him. This is not true, Henry says; the king is not bound to answer for the "particular endings" of his soldiers, any more than the father for his son or the master for his servant. For they do not intend their death when they engage their services. "Besides," he continues, "there is no king, be his cause never so spotless, if it come to the arbitrament of swords, can try it out with all unspotted soldiers." He proceeds to name a few of the crimes they may have committed, and observes:

[135] H5 4.1. 105ff., 255–310; 2H4 2.2.1ff.
[136] H5 4.1.134–153.

Now, if these men have defeated the law and outrun native punishment, though they can outstrip men, they have no wings to fly from God. War is his beadle, war is his vengeance; so that here men are punished for before-breach of the king's laws in now the king's quarrel.[137] Where they feared the death, they have borne life away; and where they would be safe, they perish. Then if they die unprovided, no more is the king guilty of their damnation than he was before guilty of those impieties for the which they are now visited. Every subject's duty is the king's; but every subject's soul is his own. Therefore should every soldier in the wars do as every sick man in his bed, wash every mote out of his conscience; and dying so, death is to him advantage; or not dying, the time was blessedly lost wherein such preparation was gained; and in him that escapes, it were not sin to think that, making God so free an offer, he let him outlive that day to see his greatness and to teach others how they should prepare.[138]

It would seem that Henry means that when a man washes every mote out of his consciece, God sometimes not merely postpones punishment, but absolves him of the punishment that was due, so that even death in this instance would not be a punishment but an advantage. In other words, Shakespeare seems to be drawing on the very common religious notion that sins can be forgiven, and that punishment can be averted by heartfelt repentance, prayerful reparation, and the satifaction for sin that comes from devotion and deeds of charity and self-sacrifice. As we have seen, historiographers of the exemplary school did not like to admit that there were some sins that were not punished by an observable catastrophe; it did not make good history to recount such instances, because they were not felt to provide an adequate deterrent to sin.

Shakespeare resorts to similar notions of repentance and hope of forgiveness in the prayer he has Henry make after his soliloquy on the responsibilities and concerns of kingship:

[137] As we have seen, Henry envisions himself as the scourge of God against the French for their sins in the Translator of Livius' history, and this attitude can be inferred from many other contemporary accounts. But here Shakespeare has Henry assume a more modest role.

[138] H5 4.1.154–196. Williams has no problem in agreeing with Henry's point, and he says that it is certain that for every man who dies badly, the evil is on his own head, and that the king is not bound to answer for it (vv. 197–198). In other words, he speaks as if Henry has completely answered his argument, and we are perhaps to assume that the objection which Henry answered was implicit in Williams' mind at the close of his speech (v. 153).

> O God of battles! steel my soldiers' hearts.
> Possess them not with fear. Take from them now
> The sense of reckoning, if th' opposed numbers
> Pluck their hearts from them. Not today, O Lord,
> Oh, not today, think not upon the fault
> My father made in compassing the crown!
> I Richard's body have interred new,
> And on it have bestowed more contrite tears
> Than from it issued forced drops of blood.
> Five hundred poor I have in yearly pay,
> Who twice a day their withered hands hold up
> Toward heaven, to pardon blood; and I have built
> Two chantries, where the sad and solemn priests
> Sing still for Richard's soul. More will I do;
> Though all that I can do is nothing worth,
> Since that my penitence comes after all,
> Imploring pardon.[139]

Shakespeare is drawing on Fabyan here, who repeated the *Brut's* account of the penance imposed by the pope upon Henry IV for Richard's death, which was fulfilled by Henry V, and who construed the religious houses built by Henry V as part of the penance to be performed for Richard.[140] In the sources, it is clear that Henry V intended to help effect the release from purgatory of his father's soul as well as Richard's, but this is not so clear in Shakespeare. Henry does pray for the repose of Richard's soul; but in speaking of prayers for the pardon of blood, he would seem to have in mind only the averting of punishment from himself as the heir of the crown that was obtained by the sin of his father. When he asks God not to remember it today, he is saying implicitly that if he is to be punished, he desires the punishment to be postponed. But when he goes on to speak of what he is doing to obtain pardon for blood, and when he promises to do more in the future, it is evident that he is thinking in terms not of postponed punishment, but of remission of the temporal punishment assessed for the sin.

There is no question here of detaining the property of another; as we have seen, the theme of an alternate heir to the crown was dropped long ago. The only question of reparation or justice on the human level involved here is the duty of repairing the wrong done to Richard; and this duty is performed by offering prayers for his soul.

[139] H5 4.1.306–322.
[140] See above, 47.

Henry's final remark is ambiguous; he says that nothing he can do can merit forgiveness, since everything he does by way of penance and penitence comes "after all." What he means by "all" is difficult to say. All penitence necessarily comes after the sin repented for has been committed. He may mean therefore that his penitence comes after both the sin and the sinner, since the sin he repents for was not committed in his own person. Yet this does not clarify matters; for though he obviously inherited the obligation to right as far as possible the wrong done to Richard, it is difficult to see how he could inherit any guilt in the matter, once the notion of a deprived lineage is put aside, unless he is simply working on the biblical notion of the sins of the father being visited upon the children. Of course, the mere fact that he was enjoying the fruit of his father's sin would perhaps be sufficient to cause him uneasiness in the matter. But even so, it is not clear why it should be efficacious for Henry IV to beg for pardon and not efficacious for his son to counteract the effects of the sin upon himself. However, this may not be Henry's meaning at all; he may simply be saying that no penitence is of any worth in itself and that all forgiveness is in the gift of God.

At any rate it is obvious that Henry hopes for pardon, even though he is not certain of obtaining it. To paraphrase the sentiments he expressed to Williams, he is washing every mote out of his conscience; he has no outstanding sins of his own to repent for, but he recalls that of his father (murder was among the sins he named to Williams as those for which men often escape human punishment); and since he will in fact escape death and come out victorious, it would not be sinful for him (or us) to think that, "making God so free an offer, he let him outlive that day to see his greatness and to teach others how they should prepare." There is no indication, in other words, either in this prayer or in the events that follow, of any foreboding of future disaster, or of any notion that God is withholding punishment until the time is ripe.[141]

Before his account of the battle of Agincourt, Holinshed reports the words of Henry to his captains, by combining the version of the Chaplain's *Gesta* (as found there or in Elmham's *Liber metricus* or the Pseudo-Elmham account) and that of Tito Livio; he recounts that Henry answered the wish of one of his

---

[141] Zdeněk Stříbrný, "*Henry V* and History," *Shakespeare in a Changing World*, ed. Arnold Kettle (London 1964) 101, says that "the sin which has tormented Henry IV is exorcised, not by time or argument, but by his son's victory over the French at Agincourt."

men for more soldiers by saying he himself did not want a single man more. For if their side won with their small number they would attribute the honor to God and not be tempted to ascribe it to their own strength; and if they lost, it would be less damage to England.[142]

Shakespeare however has Henry draw precisely the opposite conclusion with regard to the eventuality of victory. He says it will contribute all the more to their own honor, of which he is the most covetous man alive.[143] In its stress upon personal glory, Henry's speech most closely resembles the tone of Vergil-Hall.[144] But Shakespeare far outdoes Hall in oratorical display, and once again, as in the speech before Harfleur, he creates a picture of Henry hardly in accord with the character he is given in the rest of the play — even when one allows for the consideration that the king was seeking to inspire his followers to fight well.[145]

Henry appealed to a similar motive before in addressing his men, but coupled it with the assurance of God's support:

> Now, lords, for France; the enterprise whereof
> Shall be to you, as us, like glorious.
> We doubt not of a fair and lucky war,
> Since God so graciously hath brought to light
> This dangerous treason lurking in our way
> To hinder our beginnings.[146]

And in fact the supernatural perspective is restored to the present scene at the end of the speech on honor, as Henry prays God to be with them all, and twice refers the outcome to the good pleasure of God.[147] And after the battle he expressly for-

---

[142] 1–2Hol 3.79–80.

[143] H5 4.3.16–77.

[144] See above, Chap IV, n. 25.

[145] Miss Campbell (Shakespeare's "Histories" [San Marino 1947] 280) notes that in the speech before Agincourt, Henry takes the name of God in vain (he swears by God's will and God's peace). This is perhaps another indication that Henry is speaking out of character here, although it may also indicate that Shakespeare did not consider the practice of swearing as particularly reprehensible (it is however, one of the features of a bad death mentioned by Williams). In this he would be sharing a tendency that eventually became universal and resulted in rendering the practice of idle swearing an obsolete sin. Furthermore, we may recall that in the Chaplain's Gesta, the ultimate source of this incident (and perhaps an accurate account of Henry's words), Henry is represented as enforcing his sentiment with an oath, though granted it is an eminently pious oath: " 'Stulte,' inquit, 'loqueris, quia per Deum caeli, cujus annixus sum gratiae, et in quo est mihi spes firma victoriae, nollem habere etsi possem plures per unum quam habeo' " (p. 47).

[146] H5 2.2.182–187.

[147] H5 4.3.78–132.

bids, on pain of death, the kind of self-congratulation he described in vivid terms before the fighting as the chief reward to be gained from a victory.[148]

When Montjoy informs him the day is his, Henry exclaims, "Praised be God, and not our strength, for it!" [149] This prayerful outburst is a manifestation of the reverent bent of his mind in actual situations where glory could easily be claimed, and is an indication that it is not merely the miraculous aspect of the battle, brought out in the next scene, which prompts him to deny all glory to their human prowess. He later reads over the list of the dead, and it is interesting to note that while Shakespeare accepts the enormous number of 10,000 French dead reported by the sources, he also accepts the smallest possible number of slain Englishmen. Polydore Vergil had said with some irony that if we can believe those who write miracles, only a hundred English died. Hall kept the ironical remark but quartered the miraculous figure, to tally with the most common report of the English chronicles.[150] In taking this figure as the authentic one, therefore, Shakespeare believes those who write miracles and has Henry for all practical purposes treat the victory as a miracle; for in his mind, apparently, not all miracles had ceased, in spite of what his archbishop might think.[151]

After he sees the report of the casualties, Henry cries out:

> O God, thy arm was here;
> And not to us, but to thy arm alone,
> Ascribe we all! When, without stratagem,
> But in plain shock and even play of battle,
> Was ever known so great and little loss
> On one part and on the other? Take it, God,
> For it is none but thine! . . .
> Come, go we in procession to the village;
> And be it death proclaimed through our host
> To boast of this or take that praise from God
> Which is his only.

[148] H5 4.8.119–121.
[149] H5 4.7.90.
[150] The ranking victim on the English side was the valiant Duke of York, who requested to lead the charge (4.3.129–130; 6.3–27; 8.108). This Duke of York was the Aumerle of *Richard II* and the elder brother of the Earl of Cambridge, who was executed by Henry before the invasion of Normandy. On York's death here at Agincourt, his right passed to Cambridge's son Richard, who was the Duke of York that sought to oust Henry VI from the throne. But Shakespeare nowhere indicates his awareness of these relationships.
[151] The Archbishop of Canterbury's remark is cited above, n. 115.

244 / The Views of the Elizabethan Poets

He allows Fluellen to report the casualties only on condition that he acknowledge that God fought for them. Fluellen agrees: "Yes, my conscience, he did us great good." [152]

Even Hall was convinced that this victory was the work of God (though he accepted a more credible number of casualties),[153] and it is the prayers of thanks recorded by Hall that Shakespeare has Henry order to be sung — namely, the *Te Deum* and the Psalm *In exitu Israel,* or at least the "Non nobis" verse of the latter.[154] Henry's humble attitude is reiterated by the Chorus in the Prologue to the fifth act, where he says that Henry forbade his lords to have his dented helmet and bent sword borne before him,

> Being free from vainness and self-glorious pride,
> Giving full trophy, signal, and ostent
> Quite from himself to God.[155]

In the scene in which Henry courts Katherine, he tells her that she will be a good "soldier-breeder." "Shalt not thou and I," he says, "between Saint Denis and Saint George, compound a boy, half French, half English, that shall go to Constantinople and take the Turk by the beard?" [156] Quite obviously, Shakespeare at this point is not thinking of poor Henry VI and his fate, nor is he doing so when he has Henry make a jocular allusion to Henry IV's rise to power: "Now beshrew my father's ambition! he was thinking of civil wars when he got me; therefore was I created with a stubborn outside, with an aspect of iron, that, when I come to woo ladies, I fright them." [157]

The remarks of King Charles and Queen Isabel also manifest that no prophecy of Henry VI's misfortunes is in Shakespeare's mind, unless we are to postulate a very unlikely kind of irony in the scene. Charles bids Henry and Katherine to raise up issue to him, so that these kingdoms may always live in peace; and Isabel says:

[152] H5 4.8.85–126. Cf. the contemporary report that God and St. George fought for the English.

[153] Above, Chap. V at n. 34.

[154] H5 4.8.127–128; Hall 70; 1–2Hol 3.82. Hall is the first to name these prayers here, but he may have been drawing on a lost source.

[155] H5 5.pro.17–22. Cf. the Chaplain's account, treated in Chap. I; see also TL Trans 65; PsElmham 72; 1–2Hol 3.84.

[156] This remark offers an interesting parallel to the report of the *Brut,* Monstrelet, etc., that Henry V on his deathbed said he intended to go on a crusade when he finished pacifying France.

[157] H5 5.2.219–245.

God, the best maker of all marriages,
Combine your hearts in one, your realms in one!
As man and wife, being two, are one in love,
So be there 'twixt your kingdoms such a spousal,
That never may ill office, or fell jealousy,
Which troubles oft the bed of blessed marriage,
Thrust in between the paction of these kingdoms,
To make divorce of their incorporate league;
That English may as French, French Englishmen,
Receive each other. God speak this Amen!

All present answer amen to each of these appeals. And Henry says that he and Katherine and all the lords will bind themselves together by oath. "And," he adds, "may our oaths well kept and prosperous be!"[158]

In the sonnet that closes the play, the Chorus says:

Small time, but in that small most greatly lived
    This star of England. Fortune made his sword,
By which the world's best garden he achieved,
    And of it left his son imperial lord.
Henry the Sixth, in infant bands crowned King
    Of France and England, did this king succeed;
Whose state so many had the managing,
    That they lost France and made his England bleed;
Which oft our stage hath shown; and, for their sake,
In your fair minds let this acceptance take.[159]

In this preview of the reign of Henry VI and summary of the three plays he composed on the subject, Shakespeare makes his final statement on the civil wars of England in the previous century, speaking now in the closest approximation to his own voice that he has done in any of the eight plays before. He envisages the conflicts that arose within England after Henry V's glorious reign as a new situation with causes of its own; he regards the matter as an example of "too many cooks spoiling the broth." And, what is significant for our present purposes, he does not give the least indication that it resulted from a plague of divine retribution that finally alighted on the house of Lancaster. Shakespeare withdraws from the battles of the fifteenth century with the Lancaster myth in full possession of the field.

[158] H5 5.2.376–402.
[159] H5 Epilogue, vv. 5–14.

I Henry VI

We have seen Shakespeare's reconstruction of the earlier part of our period, and his concluding synopsis of the plays he had written many years before on the events that followed the death of Henry V. It is now time to examine these plays themselves in order to ascertain the ways in which he employed providential themes at the beginning of his historiographical career.

The first play in the series begins with Henry V's burial, a scene of great mourning and despair. Bedford (an older Lord John of Lancaster) makes a literary apostrophe to the astronomical heavens, where he places the blame for Henry's untimely death. Exeter disagrees with this interpretation of the cause of their misfortune, and thinks it more likely that the "subtle-witted French/Conjurors and sorcerers" brought about his death with their magic verses.[160]

It was common during this period to fear the effects of witchcraft against the life or well-being of the king. The chronicles report supposed plots of this sort against every king from Edward III to Richard III, including Henry V.[161]

But the reference to sorcery just quoted can hardly be taken as anything more than another rhetorical outburst of grief and disappointment. No further use is made of the idea in the play, and while one could make a case for its thematic reference to the sorcery of Joan of Arc,[162] it is hard to believe that there is a diabolical understructure (or providential superstructure) in this play connecting the death of Henry V with the havoc wrought by Joan.

It is true that it was a common belief of the time that all efficacious sorcery had a diabolical explanation, and that all demonic activity as well as every other kind of activity was under the control of Providence. But it is hardly true that everyone was always conscious, in every particular event, of the ultimate unities of purpose postulated in the unseen forces that ruled the world, even though upon reflection or interrogation a given author might easily have been led to assert such relationships. It is always dangerous to assume the active presence of all-pervading notions of this sort when actual references are lacking. The ordinary way of discussing devils as well as witches in

---

[160] 1H6 1.1.2–27.
[161] See above, Chap. V, n. 80.
[162] Tillyard attempts to make such a case (*Shakespeare's History Plays* 163–169).

medieval and Renaissance times was to describe them as independent agents, and to consider them as no more explicitly under God's providence than other kinds of malefactors.

The sorcery of Joan may have the same motive as that implied by Exeter for his hypothetical French conjurors, namely, the desire to rid France of the English. But if Exeter's supposition is taken seriously, then the French must be considered successful in their attempt, whereas Joan's opposition to the English serves a completely different function in the play; it is simply utilized as a foil to glorify the virtue and prowess of the English in their eventual victory, in which they overcome even the forces of hell with the greatest intrepidity.[163] This function is made clear in the last act, where Joan is forced to admit that the time has come for France to let her head fall into England's lap. Her own ancient incantations are too weak, "and hell too strong for me to buckle with." [164] That is, she cannot force the evil spirits to her power any more, and the implication is that the goodness of the English cause necessitated its eventual triumph over her, and that in fact it was brought about with divine aid, an opinion recorded by the chronicles.[165]

At the siege of Rouen, Talbot asked: "Heavens, can you suffer hell so to prevail?" [166] And later he affirms that their own position is foursquare on the side of God, and vice versa:

Well, let them practice and converse with spirits.
God is our fortress, in whose conquering name
Let us resolve to scale their flinty bulwarks.[167]

[163]The play is hardly successful from this point of view, of course, since Joan herself is the most attractive character in these scenes. Her wit and feigned piety remind us somewhat of Richard III, but she hardly strikes us as exemplifying the same kind of essential evil that Richard represents, in spite of her degradation in her final appearance. Next to her Talbot is a blundering oaf, a railing *miles gloriosus* who furiously attributes her successes to sorcery, whereas the audience, who has witnessed her in operation, knows that she has simply outfoxed him by superior military strategy. It does seem, however, that we are to think Talbot somewhat bewitched when he is unable to defeat Joan in single combat before Orleans, in 1.5.1–26, though Talbot himself attributes the general rout of the English to fear of the witch, and not to the power of her witchcraft.

[164] 1H6 5.3.24–29.

[165] Brut 439; CLgreat 155. Shakespeare follows the English sources, which were unfavorable to Joan, especially Hall (148–159) and the second edition of Holinshed, where "W.P." refutes her apologists at great length (3.163–172). Hall seems to think he clinches the case against Joan by reproducing the letter he found in Monstrelet written by the King of England to the Duke of Burgundy, as if to say that if the king described it in this way it must be true. However, he does not advert to the fact that the king was only about nine years old at the time.

[166] 1H6 1.5.9.

[167] 1H6 2.1.25–27.

Accordingly, he attributes his victories to divine aid.[168] When, therefore, Joan says that she is assigned "to be the English scourge," [169] she no doubt intends to say she is assigned to this office by God, but there is no reason for us to think she is intended to be considered by the audience as a scourge sent by God; if she has been assigned by a supernatural power, it is the power of hell in opposition to the cause of godliness. This was the opinion of the chronicles,[170] and it is quite obviously the position of the playwright. There is not the slightest indication that England is considered by anyone in the play as deserving of God's punishment, and there is no link in Shakespeare, or in any of the historiographers before or after him, between the English fortunes in connection with Joan of Arc and the Lancastrian overthrow of Richard II or any other specified crime committed by an Englishman. Fabyan is the only chronicler to place Joan's activity within a providential framework, but he does so in a manner that is in no way prejudicial to the English. After rehearsing the French allegations of her divine mission, he says: "But Almighty God, which for a season suffereth such sorcery and devilish ways to prosper and reign, to the correction of sinners, hastily to show his power, and that good men should not fall into any error, he showeth the clearness of such mystical things, and so he did in this." [171]

In the play, it is true that Talbot is eventually defeated and slain, but this catastrophe is in no way ascribed to Joan or her hellish support, but is blamed entirely upon the discord among the English leaders, as Sir William Lucy emphasizes in two scenes of Act IV.[172] It is precisely this kind of strife and emulation that Shakespeare names in the Epilogue of *Henry V* as the cause of the loss of France and as the basis of England's internal troubles in the reign of Henry VI; and he begins his dramatization of the dissension among Henry's governors in the very first scene of *I Henry VI*, specifically the ill feeling between

---

[168] 1H6 3.2.117; 3.4.12.

[169] 1H6 1.2.129. In 1.6.12–29, the French explicitly claim divine assistance in their victory at Orleans.

[170] As Hall puts it, she was surely not sent from God but from the devil (p. 157). And W.P. says: "But what purity or regard of devotion or conscience is in these writers, trow ye, who make no consideration of her heinous enormities, or else any difference between one stirred up by mercy divine, or natural love, and a damnable sorcerer suborned by Satan?" (2Hol 3.172). Cf. also Giles 3.11.

[171] Fabyan 641–642.

[172] 1H6 4.3.47–53; 4.13–46.

Humphrey of Gloucester and the Bishop of Winchester. Winchester attributes Henry V's victories to the prayers of the Church, and Gloucester counters by attributing his early end to the churchmen's prayers, who prayed against him because they were not able to have their way with him.[173] Shakespeare thereby brings forth in this opening scene a third suprahuman reason for Henry's death which is scarcely to be taken any more seriously than the first two (namely, contrary stars and French sorcery).

Another cause of internal division is eventually brought to the fore; namely, York's claim to the throne. This claim is explained to York (that is, Richard Plantagenet, York-to-be) by his uncle, Edmund Mortimer, who is the merged sixteenth-century characterization of two historical Edmund Mortimers, namely, Sir Edmund, who was involved in the revolt of Glendower and the Percys, and his nephew, the Earl of March, who was indeed the uncle of Richard, Duke of York. The confusion between the two apparently originated with Hall.[174]

Edmund first tells himself in soliloquy that before Henry Monmouth began to reign, he was "great in arms," but ever since his accession he has been loathsomely imprisoned,[175] and his nephew Richard Plantagenet has been kept from honor and inheritance.[176] When Plantagenet joins him, Edmund tells him that the cause of his own imprisonment was also the "cursed instrument" of the death of Plantagenet's father, the Earl of Cambridge. In giving a history of the realm from the time of Richard II's deposition, he says that the Percys considered Henry IV's usurpation a great injustice, and they worked for his own advancement to the throne, since he was the true heir to the crown when King Richard was done away with. And in this effort they lost their lives and he his liberty. Long after this, in Henry V's time, Cambridge, Richard's father, took pity on

---

[173] 1H6 1.1.35–36.
[174] See above, Chap. V, n. 5.
[175] In fact, Sir Edmund died while still detained by Glendower, whereas Edmund, Earl of March, was held in custody from childhood until Henry V's accession to the throne, whereupon he was released, restored to his earldom, and honorably employed in the service of his country (and according to the early sources, it was he who revealed Cambridge's plot to Henry). On Henry's death in 1422, he became a member of the council of regency. It may be, however, that by Henry Monmouth is meant Henry Bolingbroke, for in his recital to his nephew, Mortimer says he lost his freedom after the defeat of the Percys (2.5.81). But Henry V is clearly said to have been born at Monmouth in 1H6 3.1.195–198.
[176] 1H6 2.5.23–27.

Mortimer and levied an army to release him and install him as king. But he fell like the others. Thus the Mortimers, in whom the title rested, were suppressed.[177]

As we have seen, Shakespeare himself suppressed the Mortimers by leaving out all mention of them when he came to dramatize the Cambridge plot in *Henry V* from a very Lancastrian point of view. The present play's distorted account of the doings of Henry IV and Henry V is typical of the Yorkist summaries of the Lancastrian regimes, and it is given great authority here by the circumstances of the scene, for there is no indication that Mortimer is telling anything but the truth; and, therefore, for the purposes of the play, it is the truth; it is precisely the way things happened, and Plantagenet is justified, in view of this, in saying that his father's execution was "nothing less than bloody tyranny." [178]

Edmund goes on to point out to his nephew that he is his heir (a fact that Plantagenet seems to have been ignorant of until now, just as Hotspur will later be portrayed as unaware of Mortimer's title).[179] He urges him to vindicate his right to the throne, but recommends caution. He then dies, and Plantagenet blames the extinction of the Mortimers on "ambition of the meaner sort," [180] meaning by this, of course, the ambition of the Henrys.

In the Parliament scene that follows, Warwick verifies the preceding historical account given by Mortimer when he says without contradiction that by Plantagenet's restoration to his inheritance of the Duchy of York, his father's wrongs will be compensated for.[181] York then makes his oath of loyalty to Henry:

> Thy humble servant vows obedience
> And humble service till the point of death.

And he repeats it in different words:

> And so thrive Richard as thy foes may fall!
> And as my duty springs, so perish they
> That grudge one thought against your Majesty![182]

[177] 1H6 2.5.55–92. This account seems to be derived from Holinshed (1–2Hol 3.71–72), since Hall mentions nothing about Cambridge's levying of an army.
[178] 1H6 2.5.99–100. This expression matches the harsh characterization of Henry V by York in the *Mirror for Magistrates*.
[179] Above at n. 53.
[180] 1H6 2.5.94–123.
[181] 1H6 3.1.160–161.
[182] 1H6 3.1.167–176.

York comes close to deliberately perjuring himself here, in the eyes of the audience; for though he did not directly assent to the devious policy urged by his uncle Mortimer in going after the crown, it is natural to assume that he approved of it and put it into operation, and that he accordingly grudged at least "one thought" against Henry's majesty.

If therefore Henry IV and Henry V are not characterized as having been upright in their treatment of Richard II and the Mortimers, York himself does not possess the moral credentials that would win automatic providential support for his right in the mind of the audience. Exeter closes this scene with a soliloquy on the dissension between Winchester and Gloucester, and his analysis may also be meant to include the discord between York and Somerset, since Somerset voices a bitter aside against York just before this.[183] Exeter feels that this "base and envious discord" will spread like rot in a diseased body;

> And now I fear that fatal prophecy
> Which in the time of Henry named the Fifth
> Was in the mouth of every sucking babe,
> That Henry born at Monmouth should win all,
> And Henry born at Windsor should lose all.
> Which is so plain that Exeter doth wish
> His days may finish ere that hapless time.[184]

Thus Shakespeare used this Vergil-Hall-Holinshed report of Henry V's foreboding[185] in the early play on Henry VI, but abandoned it when he came to portray Henry V himself. Exeter has another soliloquy following a renewal of the quarrel between the York-Somerset factions; he says that no one can witness this discord without concluding that it presages some evil event;

> 'Tis much when scepters are in children's hands;
> But more when envy breeds unkind division.
> There comes the ruin, there begins confusion.[186]

Exeter is by no means implying that a *Vae terrae* curse lies on the land, but is merely pointing out that there is trouble enough when a child reigns, but far more when envy causes division.[187]

---

[183] 1H6 3.1.178.
[184] 1H6 3.1.187–201.
[185] Above, Chap. V at n. 37.
[186] 1H6 4.1.182–194.
[187] Cf. the attribution of the *Vae terrae* to Henry VI as a natural fact, not as

This is more or less the viewpoint of the Epilogue to *Henry V*,[188] and we need not think that Exeter is endowed with some kind of divine prophetic power when he can presage disaster from what he observes.

The last act of the play, dealing with the marriage negotiations of Henry VI, brings out both the piety and the naïveté of the young king. He is happy to receive the letters from the pope, the emperor, and the Earl of Armagnac urging peace, for it always seemed impious and unnatural to him to have these bloody quarrels "among professors of one faith";[189] and he agrees to Gloucester's choice of the earl's daughter for his bride by saying he will be completely satisfied with any choice that tends to God's glory and his country's good.[190]

In the final scene, in which Suffolk urges Henry to marry Margaret instead, Gloucester refuses to consent to it — to do so would be to "flatter sin." Suffolk says that the king's oath to marry the Armagnac girl can be broken without offense; and in spite of Gloucester's refutation of his reasoning, Henry agrees to have Margaret brought and crowned his "faithful and anointed queen." And the play ends with Suffolk's expression of his intention to rule the queen, the king, and the realm.[191]

Hence the *First Part of Henry the Sixth* ends its tale of strife and division with the promise of much more of the same to come, but without implicating to any discernible extent the operation of divine providence. Nor has there been much occasion to see God's workings during the course of the play, except on behalf of the English in their war against the French.

The English chronicles from Fabyan onward put forth the hypothesis that God was displeased with Henry's marriage to Margaret, and for this reason permitted the various disasters to follow.[192] But God's role is not alluded to in Shakespeare's presentation of the matter, and though Henry would appear to be objectively wrong in breaking his oath, subjectively he is portrayed as gullible rather than as willfully consenting to wrong.

---

a curse, in Ferrers' tragedy of Somerset in the 1571 *Mirror for Magistrates* (Mirror 391). For earlier instances of citing this scriptural proverb in reference to Henry VI, see above, Chap. II at nn. 2, 45; cf. York's speech in Hall. Vergil reported that it was quoted against Richard II (1PV 402); More had it applied to Edward V, and Shakespeare will do the same in *Richard III*.

[188] Above at n. 159.

[189] Cf. the reasons given for Henry IV's projected crusade in Vergil-Hall-Holinshed.

[190] 1H6 5.1.11–27.

[191] 1H6 5.5.1–108.

[192] See above, Chap. V at n. 43.

(We saw in the *Mirror for Magistrates*, however, that Henry believed himself punished in spite of his good intentions.)[193] Finally we may note that there is no adequate reason to support the view of Tillyard (and of Cairncross in the Arden edition) in regarding Margaret as the diabolical successor of Joan in the saga of England's divine punishment. In the next play, Gloucester objects to the marriage to Margaret not because of any breach of contract or offense against God, but because it involves the loss of Anjou and Maine.[194]

II Henry VI

The *Second Part of Henry the Sixth* begins with Henry's reception of his queen into England. He beseeches God to make him sufficiently grateful for her.[195] But we find out in good enough time that Margaret is disillusioned about Henry and considers him more suited to be pope than king.[196] Margaret unknowingly echoes the sentiments of York, who reveals his ambitions and his devices for achieving them in a soliloquy in the first scene:

> Nor shall proud Lancaster usurp my right,
> Nor hold the scepter in his childish fist,
> Nor wear the diadem upon his head,
> Whose churchlike humors fits not for a crown.[197]

York is basically an unrighteous and hypocritical character in this play. His plan consists in encouraging the rift between Gloucester and the other peers, none of whom have any inkling of York's goal. Even Gloucester himself, who realizes the force of the opposition against him, foresees at this point no more disaster ahead than the losses abroad — "Say, when I am gone," he tells them, "I prophesied France will be lost ere long." [198] The Cardinal of Winchester attributes Gloucester's dislike of Henry's marriage with Margaret to the fact that Gloucester himself is heir apparent to the throne, and does not want Henry to beget another heir.[199]

---

[193] Above, Chap. VII at n. 38.
[194] 2H6 1.1.98–112.
[195] 2H6 1.1.19–20.
[196] 2H6 1.3.56–67.
[197] 2H6 1.1.244–247.
[198] 2H6 1.1.145–146.
[199] 2H6 1.1.150–155.

Gloucester, of course, is completely innocent of any such motives, as he makes clear to his duchess, Eleanor Cobham. But Eleanor's ambition makes up for her husband's lack of it. When he tells her his troublesome dream, in which the cardinal broke his staff of office and gave the pieces to Suffolk and Somerset, he says that only God knows what it presages; but he is clearly apprehensive of its obvious drift. His wife, however, blandly interprets it in his favor, and counters his fears with her own fair-boding dream, in which she saw herself crowned by Henry and Margaret.[200]

In spite of Gloucester's rebuke, Eleanor is determined not to be slack in playing her part in "Fortune's pageant," and Hume encourages her by telling her that she will become queen "by the grace of God and Hume's advice." He says that his associates will show her "a spirit raised from depth of underground" that will answer her questions; but later he tells himself that he has been hired by Suffolk and the cardinal to "buzz these conjurations in her brain." [201]

This confession on Hume's part raises some question about the authenticity of the spirit that appears in the conjuration scene and about the preternatural authority of the oracles given concerning Henry, Suffolk, and Somerset. Perhaps all that can be said is that in the scene itself, the text as we have it, including the stage directions, presents the spirit as a real denizen of the underworld, though hardly characterized in terms of a traditional devil or damned soul. The scene was perhaps presented in this way chiefly for its spectacular dramatic effect. And yet the fact remains that the oracles given are eventually fulfilled. But the physics or metaphysics of this foreknowledge and fulfillment is not worked out in the play. As far as theological doctrine is concerned, it was universally accepted by Christians in Shakespeare's day that only God had certain knowledge of the future, and that evil spirits could only conjecture future events from already existing causes. But we must no doubt admit that this doctrine was often contradicted in practice, and that men ascribed more knowledge to spirits than theologians could justify.

---

[200] 2H6 1.2.19–40. See Campbell, Shakespeare's "Histories" 109–110, who points out that Shakespeare is following Ferrers in the Mirror for Magistrates in presenting an unhistorical clash between Eleanor and Margaret (historically, Eleanor was sentenced some years before Margaret's arrival in England).

[201] 2H6 1.2.66–99. Suffolk tells Margaret in the next scene that he has a plan to get rid of Eleanor (1.3.91–94).

When Richard (Richard III-to-be) kills Somerset in the first battle of St. Albans, he tells him to lie where he falls,

> For underneath an alehouse' paltry sign,
> The Castle in St. Albans, Somerset
> Hath made the wizard famous in his death.[202]

This is clearly an allusion to the spirit's warning to Somerset to avoid castles, with the explanation that he would be safer on the sandy plains than "where castles mounted stand." [203] But Richard refers the prophecy to the wizard and not to the spirit, and he obviously does not take its fulfillment seriously himself.

Hall repeated the prophecy about Somerset that is found in the fifteenth-century Davies' Chronicle, and it is interesting to note that this chronicle has a prophecy about Suffolk that Hall does not take over. The episode involves the same kind of ambiguity that the Somerset oracle did — Suffolk was told by an astrologer that he would die a shameful death, and that he should avoid the Tower. His friends therefore succeeded in getting him released from the Tower; but on his way to exile his ship was intercepted by another ship, called "Nicholas of the Tower." He was then given a day and a half to prepare himself for God, and thereupon an Irish knave cut off his head, in spite of his safe-conduct.[204] In the conjuration scene of *II Henry VI*, the spirit says that Suffolk will die by water. And when Suffolk learns that his captor's name is Wa(l)ter Whitmore, he says:

> Thy name affrights me, in whose sound is death.
> A cunning man did calculate my birth
> And told me that by water I should die:
> Yet let not this make thee be bloody-minded;
> Thy name is Gualtier, being rightly sounded.[205]

Suffolk's description of the origin of the prophecy concerning himself adds weight to the interpretation that the whole conjuration scene was fabricated, and that Suffolk supplied the prophecies; these were the conjurations he hired Hume to buzz in the duchess's ear, and he was drawing upon predictions already current.

[202] 2H6 5.2.66–69
[203] 2H6 1.4.38–40.
[204] Hall 233, Davies 69, 72.
[205] 2H6 4.1.33–37. The ambiguity of these prophecies in the light of their fulfillment resembles that of the prophecy that Henry IV would die in Jerusalem, which Adam of Usk says was based on Henry's horoscope.

We have not yet discussed the prophecy about Henry; it runs as follows:

> The duke yet lives that Henry shall depose;
> But him outlive, and die a violent death.

When York reads this "devil's writ," as he calls it, he points out that it is simply the kind of ambiguous answer that Apollo gave to Pyrrhus[206] — it could mean either that Gloucester would depose Henry (as the duchess was obviously intended to read it), or that Henry would depose Gloucester from his protectorship (as Suffolk intended it to happen). It is not so clear how the second line could be meant to apply to Gloucester (as subject); it does fit Henry, of course (in the event), but it is not the sort of thing that Suffolk would either intend to happen or invent for Eleanor's consolation.

The chronicle accounts of the sorcery charges against Eleanor disagree or are unclear as to whether or not she was practicing against the king's life as well as attempting to ascertain his future.[207] Shakespeare does not include the attempt against Henry's life, but restricts the operation to the divination of what is to come; however, the duchess is accused later of practicing dangerously against Henry's state.[208]

Word is brought of Eleanor's arrest when Henry and his lords are at their falconry. They have witnessed a supposed miracle, and Henry praises God for it; but when Gloucester exposes the fraud, Henry says: "O God, seest thou this and bearest so long?"[209] When hearing of the sorcery affair, he says he will weigh the case in the scales of Justice, "whose beam stands sure, whose rightful cause prevails."[210] Shakespeare surely intends dramatic irony in Henry's naive use of this apothegmatic sentiment, on one level, at least. It is true that Eleanor had bad intentions; as Henry tells her and her associates:

> In sight of God and us your guilt is great.
> Receive the sentence of the law for sins
> Such as by God's book are adjudged to death.[211]

[206] 2H6 1.4.60–65.
[207] There is a reflection of this situation in the two Gloucester tragedies in the *Mirror for Magistrates*. Hall (202) seems to indicate that the action brought against Eleanor was largely trumped up by Gloucester's unscrupulous enemies. For the references to the earlier chronicles, see above, Chap. V, n. 80.
[208] 2H6 2.1.171.
[209] 2H6 2.1.66–153.
[210] 2H6 2.1.204–205.
[211] 2H6 2.3.2–4. Cf. Exodus 22.18: "Thou shalt not suffer a witch to live."

But the fact remains that she is the victim of a plot, and the plotters are not convicted. However, in another sense Henry is right, for justice does demonstrably prevail, at least against the chief villains, Suffolk and the cardinal, when they meet sudden death.

It is abundantly evident that Henry relies completely upon the dispositions of Providence for himself and his people. He is confident not only of God's concurrence in the correction of the sorcerers; but later in the same scene, after having witnessed the trial by combat between Horner the armorer and his man Peter Thump, he says of the outcome that he perceives Horner's guilt by his death, and that God in his justice has revealed the truth and innocence of the servant.[212]

We continue to see evidences of Henry's faith in God's government of him. When he reluctantly takes the staff of office from Gloucester, he says that "God will be my hope,/My stay, my guide, and lantern to my feet." [213] When he hears that France is lost, he says: "Cold news, Lord Somerset; but God's will be done!" [214] He accepts God's will without knowing his reason for it. But usually in the course of troubles, his attitude is more one of confidence than of resignation. In the Cade rebellion, for instance, he tells Margaret that God, their hope, will come to their aid;[215] and he implicitly acknowledges God's aid in putting down the rising when he praises God for it.[216]

Henry does not see his uncle Gloucester's troubles as providentially based but rather speaks in terms of a lowering star that envies him and incites the queen and other nobles to plot against his innocent life.[217] The cardinal explains Gloucester's sudden death as God's judgment upon him, and verifies his explanation by citing a dream he had in which Gloucester was not able to speak a word (in his own defense at the scheduled hearing, presumably).[218] Henry, however, will not be put off, though he does ask God to stop the course of his thoughts and to forgive him if he is mistaken. Warwick verifies Gloucester's violent death, and Salisbury comes in with the demand of the commons that Suffolk be exiled or executed. Henry says that

[212] 2H6 2.3.104–106.

[213] 2H6 2.3.24–25.

[214] 2H6 3.1.86.

[215] 2H6 4.4.55.

[216] 2H6 4.9.13–14; 5.1.68.

[217] 2H6 3.1.206–208.

[218] 2H6 3.2.31–32.

this was his intention, and he swears by the majesty of God, whose "far unworthy deputy" he is, that Suffolk must leave the kingdom within three days on pain of death.[219]

Suffolk's death is not expressly portrayed as the effect of God's justice for his murder of Gloucester — though the latter is one of the first charges that the lieutenant alleges against him.[220] But it does not seem overly presumptuous to suppose that providential concurrence may be intended, in view of the strong statement of this opinion in Vergil-Hall-Holinshed;[221] furthermore, the scene is juxtaposed to the deathbed scene of the cardinal, where the punishing hand of God is more evident. This latter episode, Shakespeare's own invention, shows Henry's religious spirit to its best effect, as he perceives the evil character of the cardinal's life and prays God to forgive him. He urges him in vain to give some sign of his hope of salvation, and he tells Warwick to suspend judgment upon him, "for we are sinners all." [222]

Earlier in the play, in detailing to the Nevil lords, Warwick and Salisbury, his plans to take over the realm, York speaks of the effort that is being made against Gloucester; and, "if York can prophesy," in seeking the death of "that virtuous prince, the good Duke Humphrey," his enemies will bring about their own deaths. The Nevils at this time join him in his campaign to be crowned and to stain his sword in the "heartblood of the house of Lancaster." [223] For York has explained to them his claim to the throne, recalling how Henry Bolingbroke seized the throne, deposed the legitimate king, and sent him to Pomfret, where, as they knew, "harmless Richard was murdered traitorously." He then runs through his own pedigree. Concerning Edmund Mortimer, Salisbury interjects a comment:

> This Edmund, in the reign of Bolingbroke,
> As I have read, laid claim unto the crown;
> And, but for Owen Glendower, had been king,
> Who kept him in captivity till he died.

The antecedent of "who" in the last line would seem to be Glendower and not Bolingbroke, and therefore Shakespeare ap-

---

[219] 2H6 3.2.136–288.
[220] 2H6 4.1.76–82.
[221] Above, Chap. VI, n. 39.
[222] 2H6 3.3.1–33.
[223] 2H6 2.2.63–76.

parently has in mind only the fate of Sir Edmund Mortimer, the ally of the Percys, and not the Earl of March whom Cambridge conspired to put on the throne.[224] York continues the genealogy and completely ignores the plot of his father, the Earl of Cambridge.[225] Thus we have a different Yorkist review of history from that found in *I Henry VI*.[226]

In spite of York's apparent right to the crown by blood, we continue to receive an impression of the unholy nature of his pursuit. In his soliloquy before departing to Ireland, he compares himself to a spider and a snake, and he describes his plan to start a rebellion by having Jack Cade pose as John Mortimer, true heir to the throne. "This devil here," he says, "shall be my substitute," and he believes that he can profit by the sequel, no matter what it is.[227]

In the soliloquy he makes on his return from Ireland, he says:

Ah! *sancta majestas,* who would not buy thee dear?
Let them obey that knows not how to rule;
This hand was made to handle nought but gold.[228]

His attitude here does not strike us as being one of respect for the divine dignity of kingship so much as a virtual idolatry of power for its own sake. But there is implicit in his words the notion that he was ordained to be a king, and this theme receives further development in the scene. He says in a testy aside that he is far better born than Henry, "more like a king, more kingly in my thoughts." [229] And after accusing Henry of breaking faith with him over Somerset, he tells him he is not a king, and not fit for rule —

That head of thine doth not become a crown,
Thy hand is made to grasp a palmer's staff
And not to grace an awful princely scepter.

[224] Salisbury's account of Edmund Mortimer's death resembles that of Walsingham's *Historia anglicana,* where it is said that Mortimer died while still in Glendower's power (3Wals 2.253). But cf. also Hall 28. If, however, it is Bolingbroke whom Salisbury means to designate as keeping Mortimer in prison, then perhaps this account could be reconciled with that of *I Henry VI* if we include all three Lancastrian Henrys as Mortimer's captors. Wilson and Cairncross in their editions of this play suggest that Shakespeare confused Mortimer's fate with that of another son-in-law of Glendower's, Lord Gray of Ruthvin, described in Hall 23.
[225] 2H6 2.2.1–52.
[226] See above at n. 174.
[227] 2H6 3.1.331–383.
[228] 2H6 5.1.5–7.
[229] 2H6 5.1.28–29.

But he maintains that his own head and hand are extraordinarily fit for kingship, and he ends by saying:

> Give place! By Heaven, thou shalt rule not more
> O'er him whom Heaven created for thy ruler.[230]

There follows a very significant exchange between Henry and Salisbury. When Warwick and Salisbury do not kneel to him, Henry cries out, "Oh, where is faith? Oh, where is loyalty?" and attempts to shame Salisbury into allegiance. Salisbury answers that he believes in his conscience that York is the lawful heir to England. Henry points out that he has sworn allegiance to him: "Canst thou dispense with Heaven for such an oath?" Salisbury responds:

> It is great sin to swear unto a sin,
> But greater sin to keep a sinful oath.
> Who can be bound by any solemn vow
> To do a murderous deed, to rob a man,
> To force a spotless virgin's chastity,
> To reave the orphan of his patrimony,
> To wring the widow from her customed right,
> And have no other reason for this wrong
> But that he was bound by a solemn oath?

The queen supplies the Lancastrian refutation to this argument: "A subtle traitor needs no sophister." [231]

Salisbury is justified in his position, absolutely speaking, but it is probable that Henry is meant to appear here as the upholder of right; Salisbury's principles hardly cover the sort of falsified allegiance York has practiced in the past and urged on the Nevils. Earlier in this scene, York tells himself he must dissemble, and he promises all he possesses as pledges of his fealty and love on condition that Somerset is removed; but he intends all the while to continue seeking the crown on any condition.[232] York then comes to Henry and presents himself to him "in all submission and humility," saying that he intended to use his

---

[230] 2H6 5.1.91–105. Cf. Hardyng's explicitly providential interpretation of Henry's inability and York's ability.

[231] 2H6 5.1.161–191.

[232] 2H6 5.1.13–53; cf. 2.2.64–82.

forces against the traitor Somerset and "that monstrous rebel Cade." It is at this point that Iden brings in Cade's head, and Henry exclaims: "Great God, how just are thou!" [233] Hence, as was noted above, we see that Henry attributes to God the suppression of the rebel raised by York.

As York prepares to fight, he says he is resolved for death or dignity, and Clifford answers him: "The first I warrant thee, if dreams prove true"; and he tells Warwick he is determined to weather a more violent storm than any he can conjure up that day.[234] These predictions and the ones that follow are probably not to be taken as anything more than pre-battle bluster. But we may observe that though York wins this battle, he will meet death before he achieves the dignity he seeks; in a sense, therefore, the dreams Clifford alludes to are verified, as was the dream of Humphrey of Gloucester. Even Cardinal Beaufort's dream could be considered as coming true (though of course its fulfillment was brought about by the cardinal himself); and therefore only Eleanor Cobham's dream in this play is completely lacking in verification.

When the battle turns against the Lancastrians, the queen urges Henry to flee, but Henry answers: "Can we outrun the Heavens?" [235] This expression would seem to indicate on his part a belief that it is the will of God that they lose. He gives no reason for this belief, however, and there is nothing in the play to indicate that he feels he has injured York in any way, or that he or his family is deserving of divine punishment. His statement would appear rather to conform to his previous expressions of resignation to God's wishes.[236]

However, if one were to judge merely from the circumstances of defeat and victory, this battle might seem to give the impression that the York cause is more favored by God than that of Lancaster, at least at this point. Salisbury adds to this impression in the final scene when he attributes to God his three rescues by Richard.[237] But it is doubtful that this impression is meant to overcome the effect of Henry as a man of God and upholder of right in the play, and as the most likely recipient of providential benefits.

---

[233] 2H6 5.1.58–68.
[234] 2H6 5.1.194–199.
[235] 2H6 5.2.73.
[236] Above at nn. 213–214.
[237] 2H6 5.3.16–19.

III Henry VI

The *Third Part of Henry the Sixth* begins with the celebrated Parliament session in which the crown was entailed to York and his heirs. If one recalls the unprecedented stress that York placed on providential justice in the speech of Hall's account, and even in the shortened version of Grafton-Holinshed,[238] Shakespeare's failure to make use of the theme would almost seem to amount to an outright rejection of it. We noticed a similar neglect of this theme when York's self-justification was taken up in the *Mirror for Magistrates*.[239]

York and his allies appeal to no force other than their own in overcoming their enemies. When Henry enters, he denounces York as a "sturdy rebel," and reminds Clifford and Northumberland that they vowed to be revenged on him for the death of their fathers. Northumberland answers: "If I be not, Heavens be revenged on me!"[240] By the end of the act so much revenge will have fallen on York that Northumberland will almost be forced to weep for him.

There follows a dispute concerning the true heir to the throne. And if Shakespeare does not make use of the York myth in its aspect of providential vengeance against the house of Lancaster and divine support for its own cause, he does at least make the Yorkist claim so clear that it elicits a silent doubt on Henry's part as to the validity of his own right — "I know not what to say; my title's weak."[241] This is the first time that a Lancastrian admission of this sort has been conjectured in the historical treatments of this period.

Henry first argued that Henry IV got the crown by conquest; York answered that it was by rebelling against his king.[242] Now

---

[238] See above, Chap. V, nn. 45–47.
[239] Above, Chap. VII at n. 22.
[240] 3H6 1.1.50–57.
[241] 3H6 1.1.134.
[242] In claiming that his title was better than York's, Henry held up his own father, Henry V, who won France, in contrast to York's father, who was only Duke of York, and his grandfather, who was Roger Mortimer, Earl of March (vv. 104–109). This is not quite accurate. York's maternal grandfather, to be sure, was, as Henry says, Roger Mortimer; but it was York's grandfather and uncle (Aumerle) who were Dukes of York. When Aumerle died at Agincourt, York's father, Cambridge, Aumerle's younger brother, would have succeeded to the dukedom had he not been executed shortly before. As it was, his blood was considered attainted, and the dukedom did not fall on York until later, as we saw in *I Henry VI* (above, 250). Once again, here in *III Henry VI*, as in *II Henry VI* and *Henry V*, Shakespeare is silent concerning Cambridge's role in the fortunes of the line of March-York.

Henry alleges that Richard resigned his crown to his grandfather, and York replies that he rose against him and forced him to resign. And then Exeter, hitherto Henry's supporter, points out that he could not have resigned it legitimately to any but the nearest heir; and therefore in his own conscience he is forced to acknowledge York as the lawful king.[243]

Clifford vows to fight for Henry whether his title is right or wrong, and he wishes the ground to swallow him if he ever kneels to his father's slayer. Henry is encouraged by this support, but he is not so defiant as he was at first, especially when Warwick calls in his men and threatens to write York's title over the throne in Henry's "usurping blood." He therefore suggests a compromise, which is accepted by York.[244]

Henry laments that this agreement will require him to disinherit his son; but he proceeds nevertheless, and wills the crown to York on condition that he take an oath to put an end to the civil war and never to agitate against his rule. York willingly takes the oath and affirms that he will carry it out.[245]

It should be noted that Henry nowhere expresses any feelings of guilt or remorse for retaining the crown with his weak title, nor does he view his troubles as deserved in any way or as caused by God's avenging justice. He excuses his action to Margaret by saying that York and Warwick forced him to it. And in soliloquy he says:

> Revenged may she be on that hateful duke,
> Whose haughty spirit, winged with desire,
> Will cost my crown, and like an empty eagle
> Tire on the flesh of me and of my son! [246]

It is quite obvious then that Henry believes York will not keep his oath but will depose and kill him and his son.

There are curses uttered in this scene that seem designed to tally with the future events as they fall out; that is, the curses are dramatized as taking effect. Northumberland says to Henry:

> Be thou a prey unto the house of York,
> And die in bands for this unmanly deed!

[243] 3H6 1.1.132–150.
[244] 3H6 1.1.163–175; cf. vv. 124–130.
[245] 3H6 1.1.191–201.
[246] 3H6 1.1.228–269.

And Clifford adds:

> In dreadful war mayst thou be overcome,
> Or live in peace abandoned and despised.[247]

If, therefore, we are to see anything providential in the fulfillment of these curses (and this is by no means certain), the sin of Henry that is singled out for punishment is his cowardly disinheritance of his son.

Exeter too utters an imprecation that might seem intended for dramatic fulfillment. He is referring to the reconciliation between York and Lancaster, and says: "Accursed be he that seeks to make them foes!" [248] His words could be applied to Margaret, of course, but they are more applicable to York's sons and Montague, for in the next scene they persuade York to ignore his vow and proceed against Henry without provocation.

York himself is reluctant to break his vow, until Richard tells him it was invalid in the first place, since Henry had no authority to act as a magistrate over him; he also stresses what is perhaps meant to be a weightier consideration for York, namely, the joys of kingship, for one year of which Edward professes himself willing to break a thousand oaths.[249]

It is not likely that an audience in Shakespeare's time or later would accept Richard's sophism concerning the validity of oaths, which are always sworn directly to God, no matter for whose benefit. Therefore, when York says he will be king or die and does die shortly after, he would seem at least a likely candidate for inclusion under Exeter's curse. It was, we recall, Holinshed's final judgment that York and his line were divinely punished for his violation of the oath he swore to let Henry live out his reign.[250]

In dramatizing the death of York, Shakespeare uses the account of Whethamstede-Holinshed, according to which York was captured alive and taunted in a mock coronation ceremony. Margaret says to him:

> But how is it that great Plantagenet
> Is crowned so soon, and broke his solemn oath?

---

[247] 3H6 1.1.185–188.
[248] 3H6 1.1.205.
[249] 3H6 1.2.9–35.
[250] It is rather ironic when York sends word to Warwick to "trust not simple Henry nor his oaths" (1.2.56–59).

As I bethink me, you should not be king
Till our King Henry had shook hands with Death.
And will you pale your head in Henry's glory,
And rob his temples of the diadem
Now in his life, against your holy oath?
Oh, 'tis a fault too too unpardonable! [251]

If we are not to assume that Margaret is being completely ironic but is accusing York of really breaking his oath, then we must also assume that she somehow has knowledge of his decision to go after the crown immediately. Of course, there would be even more irony in the scene if she is meant to accuse him in bitter jest of a crime which, unknown to her, he fully intended and was in the process of committing.

However, York by no means admits any guilt on his part. He attributes his fall to Fortune, not God. When he is first captured, he is scornful and defiant:

My ashes, as the phoenix, may bring forth
A bird that will revenge upon you all;
And in that hope I throw mine eyes to heaven,
Scorning whatever you can afflict me with. [252]

The queen accepts this challenge and succeeds in breaking down his scorn, but his hope of being revenged persists, and so does his gaze toward heaven. He says of his tears that each drop cries out for vengeance against Clifford and Margaret, and he tells Margaret to take his curse along with the crown (he seems to specify the curse by wishing on her the same kind of cruel torment that she is inflicting upon him). He then bids Clifford to take him from the world: "My soul to heaven, my blood upon your heads!" His final words repeat the hope he has of salvation:

Open thy gate of mercy, gracious God!
My soul flies through these wounds to seek out thee. [253]

If we are meant to view the queen's subsequent misfortunes, especially the murder of her son, as somehow influenced by York's curse, we must keep in mind that the crime designated by York for revenge is not her defense of the house of Lancaster,

---

[251] 3H6 1.4.99–106.
[252] 3H6 1.4.35–38, 115.
[253] 3H6 1.4.148–178.

but her cruelty here at Wakefield, especially her assent to the slaughter of Rutland, York's young son.

The queen's victory at the second battle of St. Albans is won offstage, and we have dramatized for us only the reactions to it in Edward's camp at Mortimer's Cross. The scene here opens with the prodigy of the triple sun that was recorded by Hall from Davies Chronicle or one of the London Chronicles.[254] Both Edward and Richard see it, and Richard says that "the heaven figures some event" by it. Edward believes it signifies the glory that the three Plantagenet brothers will win together. Obviously Edward is wrong in this surmise, if we are meant to think in long-range terms. Richard offers no explanation of his own, but simply makes a jesting remark on Edward's amorous tendencies.[255]

Then news of the disasters of Wakefield and St. Albans is brought. Of the latter, Warwick reports that he encouraged his men by pointing out the justice of their cause, but they were routed nevertheless. He tells Edward that Henry swore consent to his succession, but that now he and the rest have gone to London to render his oath void.[256]

In the next scene, at York, Henry is asked by Margaret if the sight of York's head does not "cheer your heart," and Henry responds:

Ay, as the rocks cheer them that fear their wreck.
To see this sight, it irks my very soul.
Withhold revenge, dear God! 'tis not my fault,
Nor wittingly have I infringed my vow.[257]

Henry's attitude is in strange contradiction to the one he evinced at the end of the first scene, immediately after making his vow, where, as we saw, he wished Margaret to be revenged on York, and showed himself convinced of York's intention to violate the agreement and seize the crown while he still held it. And we also saw that York did break his oath by entering into battle with precisely this intention. But now Henry believes that Margaret's revenge upon York constituted a violation of his own oath, though one effected without his knowledge or consent. It is obvious therefore that Henry (or Shakespeare) speaks without

[254] Above, Chap. V, n. 63.
[255] 3H6 2.1.25–42.
[256] 3H6 2.1.133–176.
[257] 3H6 2.2.2–8.

adverting to the determination of York and his sons to disregard the oath that was the condition of Henry's oath, and in this scene the agreement is regarded as still in force.

Clifford tries to dissuade Henry from his stand by appealing to the duties he has to his son. But Henry answers:

> Full well hath Clifford played the orator,
> Inferring arguments of mighty force.
> But, Clifford, tell me, didst thou never hear
> That things ill-got had ever bad success?
> And happy always was it for that son
> Whose father for his hoarding went to hell?
> I'll leave my son my virtuous deeds behind,
> And would my father had left me no more!
> For all the rest is held at such a rate
> As brings a thousandfold more care to keep
> Than in possession any jot of pleasure.
> Ah, cousin York! would thy best friends did know
> How it doth grieve me that thy head is here! [258]

We have seen that Hardyng and other Yorkist writers used a variant of the proverb concerning ill-gotten gains to encourage or explain Henry VI's overthrow by reason of his grandfather's usurpation of the throne, and Hall has York speak to this same effect in his speech in Parliament.[259] But Henry is not speaking in these terms here; his meaning is that his son would inherit a kingdom obtained through the violation of an oath. Nor is it at all likely that in the lines that follow Henry is suggesting that the kingdoms he inherited from his father were ill-gotten. For the context clearly shows that he is simply speaking in generic terms concerning all the troubles his possessions have cost him, without specifying any cause for the troubles beyond his proprietorship. It could hardly be maintained that Shakespeare is giving an ironic expression to the Yorkist theme of hereditary punishment on the house of Lancaster, unless some other unequivocal statement of it could be adduced. As we have seen, Shakespeare disregarded York's formulation of it in Hall's account.

Henry knights his son at Margaret's bidding, and instructs him to draw his sword "in right." Prince Edward answers that "by your kingly leave," he will draw it as heir apparent to the

---

[258] 3H6 2.2.9-55.
[259] Above, Chap. II at n. 12.

crown; and thus he signifies his disagreement with Henry's evaluation of what is right.[260]

Edward then appears with his forces; he addresses Henry as "perjured," and in answer to Margaret he says:

> I am his king, and he should bow his knee.
> I was adopted heir by his consent;
> Since when, his oath is broke; for, as I hear,
> You, that are king though he do wear the crown,
> Have caused him, by new act of Parliament,
> To blot out me, and put his own son in.[261]

Shakespeare here follows the chronicles to the extent of having Edward claim the kingship on the grounds that Henry violated his oath by joining Margaret after the battle of St. Albans;[262] but within the context of the play his cause can scarcely seem righteous, since he urged York to violate his oath (thereby rendering the act of entailment void) before Henry's alleged violation. But since neither Henry nor Edward are refuted in their assumption that the Parliament agreement was broken only on the Lancastrian side, it seems that we are to accept this as Shakespeare's own view of the situation for the present scene, even though it contradicts the events and attitudes of other scenes before and after it.

Henry demands to speak — "I am a king, and privileged to speak";[263] perhaps we are to take this declaration as an indication that he does not believe he has forfeited his crown, in spite of the broken oath. However, we do not hear what he has to say, for Margaret and Clifford will not allow him to speak his mind.

Queen Margaret's observation on Richard's deformity (he is "marked by the Destinies to be avoided") educed tirades against her by the three York brothers. Edward concludes his by saying that it was Henry's marriage to her that caused all his losses in France and all his troubles in England;

> For what hath broached this tumult but thy pride?
> Hadst thou been meek, our title still had slept;

---

[260] 3H6 2.2.58–65.
[261] 3H6 2.2.81–91.
[262] Hall 253; 1–2Hol 3.272.
[263] 3H6 2.2.117.

> And we, in pity of the gentle king,
> Had slipped our claim until another age.[264]

In having Edward attribute the decline of Henry's fortunes at home and abroad to his marriage, Shakespeare may be drawing on the view of Fabyan-Hall-Holinshed, although he omits the providential dimension given to it in the chronicles.[265]

However, it can scarcely be thought that Edward is sincere at this point; or, if he is, he has undergone an unnoticed reform, or else his present attitude is another example of the way in which this scene contradicts the themes of the rest of the play. For, not to mention the fact that York plotted to gain the crown independently of any provocation by Margaret in the first two parts of *Henry VI*, neither Edward nor any of the Yorkists have evinced pity for the "gentle king" in the present play before this scene.

In the battle of Towton that follows, Edward kneels and makes his appeal to God:

> I throw my hands, mine eyes, my heart to thee,
> Thou setter up and plucker down of kings,
> Beseeching thee, if with thy will it stands
> That to my foes this body must be prey,
> Yet that thy brazen gates of heaven may ope
> And give sweet passage to my sinful soul! [266]

In his prayer Edward does not conceive of God as deciding the outcome of the battle on the basis of the rightness or wrongness of his cause. His confession of sinfulness should not be taken as referring to his effort to attain the crown or to win this battle, since he considers his determination to continue fighting to the death as compatible with his admission to heaven. When he finally wins, it is noteworthy that he does not attribute his triumph to God, but says that "good fortune" bids them pause "and smooth the frowns of war with peaceful looks." [267]

In the reflections of Henry VI during the battle, he parallels Edward's by giving utterance to a similar but even more intense dependence on the will of God, regardless of the question of right involved in the struggle. He says: "To whom God will, there be

[264] 3H6 2.2.135–162.
[265] See the discussion of the last scene of *I Henry VI*, above.
[266] 3H6 2.3.36–41.
[267] 3H6 2.6.31–32.

the victory!" And before his meditation on the pastoral life, he says:

> Would I were dead! if God's good will were so;
> For what is in this world but grief and woe?

And after witnessing scenes of interfamilial slaughter, he says:

> O that my death would stay these ruthful deeds!
> O pity, pity, gentle Heaven, pity! [268]

At the beginning of the third act, we are given Henry's further views on his kingship. He has stolen back into England and sadly tells himself that the land is no longer his; the scepter has been taken from him, and the balm with which he was anointed has been washed off.[269] Then he is seized by the keepers of the forest in the name of King Edward, to whom they have sworn allegiance. Henry asks them: "But did you never swear and break an oath?" — and we might be reminded of Henry's belief in the previous act that he had unknowingly violated the oath he took in Parliament. But it is evident that he himself is not thinking in those terms, for he attempts to convince the keepers of their own previous infidelity:

> I was anointed king at nine months old;
> My father and my grandfather were kings,
> And you were sworn true subjects unto me;
> And tell me, then, have you not broke your oaths?

They deny it, and say they were his subjects only while he was king. Henry points out that he is still alive, thus affirming his belief that he is still their lawful king. He tells them they take their oaths without knowing what they swear to, and, like all commoners, shift with the wind. He adds:

> But do not break your oath; for of that sin
> My mild entreaty shall not make you guilty.
> Go where you will, the king shall be commanded;
> And be you kings, command, and I'll obey.

But he remarks that they would be true subjects to him once more if he were again on the throne. The keepers charge him

[268] 3H6 2.5.15–96.
[269] 3H6 3.1.15–17.

in God's name to go with them, and he replies, "In God's name, lead; your king's name be obeyed," that is, even though they attribute it to a usurper;

> And what God will, that let your king perform;
> And what He will, I humbly yield unto.[270]

Once again Henry submits himself to the will of God; however, he does not view the trials he undergoes as punishments sent by God, but as wrongs done to him by men, for he clearly asserts his belief in the rightness of his claim to the throne. He has therefore returned to the unshaken view he held before the debate in Parliament in the first scene of the play.

In the scene in the French court, which Henry envisioned as going against Margaret,[271] there is a further illustration of the clash between the Lancaster and York myths on a theoretical and providential level; but the decisions on the practical level are reached on the basis of expediency and personal enmity. Margaret warns Lewis against a marriage alliance with the tyrant Edward, for fear of bringing danger and dishonor on himself;

> For though usurpers sway the rule a while,
> Yet Heavens are just and time suppresseth wrongs.

She prays "Heavens" to prevent Lewis from being bewitched by Warwick's words; but Lewis does not need bewitching, and he justifies himself to Margaret by an implicit appeal to Providence:

> But if your title to the crown be weak,
> As may appear by Edward's good success,
> Then 'tis but reason that I be released
> From giving aid which late I promised.[272]

The sudden reversal of Warwick and Lewis, however, when news of Edward's marriage is brought, does not speak well for their integrity as spokesmen for the right.

Objectively speaking, it would seem that Shakespeare presents the Yorkist title to the throne as having greater validity than that of Lancaster, in spite of the upright Henry's present conviction to the contrary. But this is not to say that Shakespeare intends us

---

[270] 3H6 3.1.69–101.
[271] 3H6 3.1.28–54.
[272] 3H6 3.3.65–148.

to agree with some providential judgment as that implied by
King Lewis, which would regard Edward's recent successes as
a divine authorization of his right. We must remember that the
scene in the French court is immediately preceded by Richard
of Gloucester's intimation of the deadly fortune he has in store
for the members of his family that stand between him and the
throne.[273] And we must also remember that Edward is about to
be ousted from his throne.[274] It seems best, therefore, to regard
opinions concerning the providential outcome of solitary events
as characterizing only the sentiments of the speakers at the time
in which they speak them, and not Shakespeare's own view.

Edward is captured by Warwick, and he attributes it to "mis-
chance," Fortune's malice, and the Fates.[275] Similarly, Henry
blames his troubles on "Fortune's spite" and "my thwarting
stars," although he ascribes his restoration to the work of God
and the help of his friends, especially Warwick, as he tells him:

> But, Warwick, after God, thou settest me free,
> And chiefly therefore I thank God and thee.
> He was the author, thou the instrument.[276]

We have noticed before the tendency to ascribe misfortunes to
Fortune, and fortunate events to God.[277]

Henry's confidence in God's support through Warwick's in-
strumentality is destined to be reversed, tacitly at least. But it is
at this point that Shakespeare has Henry make his prophecy
concerning Richmond, in which his confidence is hypothetical
but more justified, as it turns out. He sees the young earl with
Somerset, and says:

> Come hither, England's hope. If secret powers
> Suggest but truth to my divining thoughts,
> This pretty lad will prove our country's bliss.
> His looks are full of peaceful majesty,
> His head by nature framed to wear a crown,
> His hand to wield a scepter, and himself

[273] 3H6 3.2.124–195.
[274] In the next scene, Hastings tells Edward to ignore the threat from France—
> Let us be backed with God and with the seas
> Which he hath given for fence impregnable,
> And with their helps only defend ourselves.
> In them and in ourselves our safety lies. (4.1.43–46)
[275] 3H6 4.3.43–59.
[276] 3H6 4.6.1–22.
[277] See n. 17 above.

Likely in time to bless a regal throne.
Make much of him, my lords, for this is he
Must help you more than you are hurt by me.[278]

Shakespeare does not have Henry refer to God's ordination (as in the Hall-Holinshed commentary),[279] and he has him draw on natural characteristics which show him likely to become a king "in time." However, Henry also alludes to the possibility that secret powers are prompting him to prophesy as he does, and perhaps some kind of providential ordering is implied. His words also tell us that his hopes for his own success are not really very high.

In dramatizing Edward's recovery of the city of York, Shakespeare did not choose to utilize the strong opinion of Vergil-Hall and Holinshed-Fleming that he committed an act of willful perjury that perhaps was divinely punished in the destruction of his children.[280] Shakespeare does not specify it as perjury, for Edward takes no oath; and he is not clearly characterized as intending to break his promise in advance, although in the final analysis it seems likely that he meant to claim his kingship eventually, especially if we remember his statement in the first act that for a kingdom any oath may be broken, and that he would break a thousand oaths to reign one year.[281]

In the scene of Clarence's reconciliation with Edward, Clarence anticipates Warwick's charge of perjury against him and says:

Perhaps thou wilt object my holy oath.
To keep that oath were more impiety
Than Jephthah's when he sacrificed his daughter.
I am so sorry for my trespass made
That, to deserve well at my brother's hands,
I here proclaim myself thy mortal foe,

and he determines to punish Warwick for leading him astray.[282] This is the same argument that Salisbury, Warwick's father, used against Henry in the last act of the previous play.[283] And just as Margaret called Salisbury a subtle traitor then, so Warwick now cries after Clarence: "Oh, passing traitor, perjured and un-

[278] 3H6 4.6.65–76.
[279] Above, Chap. V at n. 91; Chap. VI at n. 59.
[280] See above, Chap. I at n. 59; Chap. VI at n. 67.
[281] 3H6 4.7.1–78; cf. 1.2.16–17.
[282] 3H6 5.1.89–97.
[283] Above at n. 231.

just!" [284] But it is difficult to say whether Shakespeare considers Clarence as justified or not. Later, when Margaret begs Clarence to kill her after her son's death, and he swears he will not, she says:

> Ay, but thou usest to forswear thyself;
> 'Twas sin before, but now 'tis charity.[285]

In the next play, as we shall see, Margaret's opinion of Clarence's action is shared by everyone, including Clarence himself.[286]

The last battle scene of *III Henry VI* is that of Tewkesbury. Both Edward and Margaret express their reliance upon divine assistance,[287] but it is Edward who wins. After the battle, as in Holinshed, Edward promises to preserve Prince Edward's life if he is captured.[288] But when he becomes enraged at the boy's answers, he does not strike him but stabs him himself, as do Richard and Clarence. Edward manifests an immediate awareness that he allowed his passions to get the better of his judgment, for he prevents Richard from killing Margaret by saying: "Hold, Richard, hold; for we have done too much." Margaret cries out against her son's murderers:

> You have no children, butchers! if you had,
> The thought of them would have stirred up remorse;
> But if you ever chance to have a child,
> Look in his youth to have him so cut off
> As, deathsmen, you have rid this sweet young prince! [289]

This passage is perhaps meant to correspond to the statement of Vergil-Hall-Holinshed that some of the murderers were later punished by God for their deed.[290] Historically speaking, Margaret's wish could be said to have been fulfilled in all three brothers, for all had children who died untimely deaths. But though Richard is the only one who saw his own child die,[291] Shakespeare does not use this motif in *Richard III,* and he

---

[284] 3H6 5.1.106.

[285] 3H6 5.5.75–76. Prince Edward also refers to him as "perjured George" (v. 34), and Clarence stabs him "for twitting me with perjury" (v. 40).

[286] As was pointed out above, Clarence is considered guilty and eventually punished by God in Vergil-Hall.

[287] 3H6 5.4.68–69, 81–82.

[288] 3H6 5.5.9–10.

[289] 3H6 5.5.38–67.

[290] See above, Chap. V at n. 55; Chap. VI at n. 66.

[291] Cf. above, Chap. III at n. 6.

probably has in mind here only the murder of Edward's two sons.

When Richard confronts Henry in the Tower, Henry recalls the portentous circumstances of Richard's birth, and prophesies that many thousands will lament the day he was born.[292]

But Richard interrupts him:

> I'll hear no more; die, prophet, in thy speech.
> For this, among the rest, was I ordained.[293]

Henry answers:

> Ay, and for much more slaughter after this.
> Oh, God forgive my sins, and pardon thee!

Richard in mock surprise wonders that "the aspiring blood of Lancaster" sinks into the ground instead of rising into the air. He wishes the same end for all who desire the downfall of their house, and strikes him again, saying:

> Down, down to hell; and say I sent thee thither,
> I, that have neither pity, love, nor fear.[294]

There is no indication here that either Richard or Henry is speaking in terms of hereditary guilt, nor should Henry be taken to be referring to any specific sins of his own; he is simply making a humble confession of sinfulness in general, for which he begs (and expects) pardon from God.

And Richard can hardly be taken to express God's predestining intentions when he speaks of himself as ordained to kill Henry. His evil is his own doing, not God's; for as he says of himself, after confirming Henry's report of the "irregularities" of his birth:

> Then, since the Heavens have shaped my body so,
> Let Hell make crooked my mind to answer it.

And though he acts in the guise of the defender of the house of York when he kills Henry and speaks of coming into the world

---

[292] 3H6 5.6.11–56.
[293] Cf. Margaret's words to Richard: "Ay, thou wast born to be a plague to men" (5.5.28). And Richard says of himself in the last scene:

> This shoulder was ordained so thick to heave;
> And heave it shall some weight, or break my back. (5.7.23–24)

[294] 3H6 5.6.57–68.

feet-first to make haste "and seek their ruin that usurped our right," he foreswears his kinship with his family later on: "I have no brother, I am like no brother." [295]

When King Edward sums up the action in the last scene by saying that they have all suffered in order to let his young son reign in peace and reap the fruit of their labors, Richard asides a promise to "blast his harvest"; and when Richard gives the prince a "loving kiss," he says that this is the way that Judas kissed his master "and cried 'All hail!' whenas he meant all harm." Edward's final farewell to "sour annoy," then, is highly ironic, as in his hope for their lasting joy.[296]

The last two parts of *Henry VI* show a good deal of unity, more, in fact than *III Henry VI* does in itself, for the latter play contains a second act that is largely inconsistent with the rest of the play, especially in Henry's attitudes concerning his right to the crown (these in fact undergo change in other parts of the play as well). It may be said of the three parts as a whole, however, that while much appropriate use is made of the Lancaster, York, and Tudor myths by the partisans of the different sides, the plays cannot be said to illustrate as themes either the providential punishment of the house of Lancaster or the divine approval of the house of York. But there are many individual allusions to God's operations for separate events; and perhaps Henry VI's frequent acts of conformity to God's will could be construed as a reflection of the chronicle comments on the fatal decline of Lancastrian fortunes, which is ascribed by Hall to the will of God, but for unknown or unspecified reasons.[297]

Richard III

Richard III, the last play of Shakespeare's connected series on fifteenth-century English history and the concluding member of his early tetralogy, contains an immense number of references to the events of the previous play, *III Henry VI.* They consist chiefly of continuations of actions begun in the earlier play, especially Richard's play for power, and of recollections of old injuries, adduced in connection with retaliatory motifs.

Richard begins with another discourse on his deformity, and this time it is "dissembling Nature" that is blamed for his con-

[295] 3H6 5.6.64–80.
[296] 3H6 5.7.1–46.
[297] See above, especially Chap. V at n. 64.

dition. He dwells again on his unfitness for amatory occupations; and since he cannot be a lover, he is "determined" to be a villain — referring, of course, to his own determination and not to that of destiny or Providence.[298] Margaret, however, does profess to see him determined in this latter sense, as she makes clear:

> Thou elvish-marked, abortive, rooting hog!
> Thou that wast sealed in thy nativity
> The slave of nature and the son of hell! [299]

Richard also takes up again his plan of spreading prophecies about Clarence in order to frighten Edward into destroying him.[300] The story of the "G-prophecy" is first found in Rous's history, but Shakespeare would have read it in the Vergil-Hall-Holinshed account, where the claim of its fulfillment in Richard of Gloucester is attributed to the deceit of the devil.[301] This remark may have influenced Shakespeare to link Richard to the devil and diabolical operation with great insistence at this point in the play,[302] whereas such references are comparatively infrequent in *III Henry VI* and later in *Richard III*. Richard's surreptitious furthering of Clarence's untimely death is suggested in More, but it is most fully developed in Baldwin's tragedy of Clarence in the *Mirror for Magistrates,* where Richard personally supervises his execution.[303]

Richard has spread "drunken prophecies, libels, and dreams" about Clarence, and Clarence says that Edward "hearkens after prophecies and dreams." [304] But Clarence himself soon has a dream that is truly prophetic, at least in foretelling his death. In this it can be compared with Stanley's dream and with Richard's own dream before the battle of Bosworth, as well as with the dream of Humphrey of Gloucester in *II Henry VI.*

Clarence dreamed that his brother Gloucester "tempted" him to walk along the deck and pushed him overboard, seemingly

---

[298] R3 1.1.14–30.

[299] R3 1.3.228–230.

[300] R3 1.1.32–40; see 3H6 5.6.84–88.

[301] Vergil's "daemones" is rendered as "the devil" in Hall 326 and 1–2Hol 3.346.

[302] There are eight such references in the scene with Anne (1.2.34, 45, 50, 51, 67, 73, 90, 237), and four more in the following scene (1.3.118, 144, 293–294, 298).

[303] The phrase "new christened" is used both in Shakespeare and Baldwin (Mirror 233). The dramatic reference could be to Clarence's ironic baptism by immersion in the butt of wine, even though it is an expedient improvised by one of the murderers and not by Richard, according to Shakespeare's presentation.

[304] R3 1.1.33, 54.

by accident. His soul eventually found its way into a classical Hades; and whereas before he had been dreaming that he and Richard "cited up a thousand heavy times" that had befallen them during the wars of York and Lancaster, now he dreamed that Warwick and young Prince Edward were citing against him the heavy times he had caused them; both of them accused him of perjury, and Prince Edward alleged against him his part in the prince's murder at Tewkesbury. They called on the torments and tormentors of hell to punish him for these sins, and such a tumult ensued that he thought he was in hell even after he woke. After he finishes relating the dream, he says:

> Ah! keeper, keeper, I have done these things
> That now give evidence against my soul
> For Edward's sake; and see how he requites me!
> O God! if my deep prayers cannot appease thee,
> But thou wilt be avenged on my misdeeds,
> Yet execute thy wrath in me alone!
> Oh, spare my guiltless wife and my poor children!

This part of the scene ends with the keeper's significant prayer, "God give your Grace good rest!" [305]

It is noteworthy that Clarence denied being guilty of perjury in the last play and killed Prince Edward for accusing him of it. This violent deed may have been a reflex action caused by a guilty conscience (that is, perhaps we were meant to discredit Clarence's self-justification in *III Henry VI*); but there is no doubt about what sins his guilt is derived from in *Richard III*. He sinned not in forsaking Edward IV (as he maintained in *III Henry VI*) but in abandoning the Lancastrian cause and in killing the Lancastrian heir.

As for Clarence's appeal to God, we meet once more with the concept that God can be appeased by prayers of repentance. And if his request that his innocent wife and children be spared punishment has any larger meaning in the play, it would mean at least that Shakespeare has rejected the concept that Clarence's children were punished by God (the possibility of a providential punishment in their case may be hinted at by Vergil-Hall-Holinshed). For Richard takes only mild measures to keep Clarence's children out of the way, and there is no reference to their tragic end under Henry VII and Henry VIII.[306] If Clarence's dream is

[305] R3 1.4.1–75.
[306] Cf. oPV 211; 1PV 530; Hall 326–327, 1–2Hol 3.346. Miss Campbell seems to

to be regarded as somehow providential, as perhaps would be indicated from the fact that it foretells the manner of his death, we can regard it as not completely prophetic (that is, as not necessarily foretelling that Clarence would go to hell after dying), but as a divine warning for him to repent before it is too late. It is in this spirit that Clarence receives it, though he regards it solely as the effect of his bad conscience.

The fact that Clarence is violently slain in spite of his supplication does not automatically indicate that God has not been appeased by his "deep prayers," though, of course, this is a tenable view, and would accord with Shakespeare's sources.[307] Clarence and his intended murderers debate some of the problems involved in this question a little later, when he refutes their excuse of acting under the king's command by saying that "the great King of kings" has forbidden murder; he warns them to

> Take heed; for he holds vengeance in his hand,
> To hurl upon their heads that break his law.

Clarence has left himself vulnerable in using this *Mirror for Magistrates* didacticism, and his opponents are quick to strike; one of them says:

> And that same vengeance doth he hurl on thee
> For false forswearing and for murder too.
> Thou didst receive the sacrament to fight
> In quarrel of the house of Lancaster.

The other murderer adds that "like a traitor to the name of God" he broke that vow, and his treacherous sword cut open his sovereign's son, whom (the first murderer says) he had sworn to defend. How, they ask him, can he "urge God's dreadful law" to them when he has flagrantly violated it himself? Clarence answers:

---

assume too much when she says that Shakespeare's audience would readily remember the fate of Clarence's children and would conclude that God did take vengeance on them (*Shakespeare's "Histories"* 314). Even if one were to grant that the execution of Clarence's son and daughter would be recalled, it would not necessarily follow that they would be considered to have been divinely punished for Clarence's sins. Hall said it was either by destiny or by their own merits that it came about, and Holinshed adds an "as it were" to the destiny alternative.

[307] The chronicles regard Clarence as providentially punished in his cruel death both for his perjury and for his killing of Prince Edward.

> Alas! for whose sake did I that ill deed?
> For Edward, for my brother, for his sake.
> He sends you not to murder me for this,
> For in that sin he is as deep as I.
> If God will be avenged for the deed,
> Oh, know you yet, he doth it publicly.
> Take not the quarrel from his powerful arm;
> He needs no indirect or lawless course
> To cut off those that have offended him.

One of the murderers asks him:

> Who made thee then a bloody minister,
> When gallant-springing brave Plantagenet,
> That princely novice, was struck dead by thee?

Clarence can only answer: "My brother's love, the devil, and my rage." [308]

In this highly important interchange, we learn that not only Clarence but also implicitly the murderers and Edward IV himself consider Henry VI to have been their lawful sovereign. Moreover, in denying that the murderers are in any way instruments of God's justice, Clarence also denies that he was a providential instrument in striking down the heir of Lancaster. And though Clarence's argument is not entirely logic-proof (it is true that God does not need lawless courses, but it was universally held that he often made use of them, thereby drawing good out of evil),[309] yet perhaps it is meant to be convincing in the economy of the scene and in light of its place in the whole play. That is, it seems likely that we are not meant to regard Clarence's death as the result of divine justice. This interpretation would appear to gain strength from the intensity of the second murderer's repentance, who wishes, like Pilate, that he could wash his hands of "this most grievous murder." [310]

In discussing Shakespeare's plays, we have seen that there is great difficulty in knowing when to assign to the play as a whole or to Shakespeare himself the various themes and judgments put forward by the characters. But sometimes there are objective

[308] R3 1.4.198–229.
[309] Cf. Campbell, Shakespeare's "Histories" 313. Richard is referred to in the play not as God's instrument but as the "dreadful minister of hell" (1.2.46) and "hell's black intelligencer" (4.4.71). See the discussion on Joan of Arc in I Henry VI, above.
[310] R3 1.4.278–285.

occurrences that support the opinions of the characters. Thus, there is nothing more evident in *Richard III* than Richard's status as an evil man abundantly deserving of the punishment called down upon him by the other characters and of the disasters that actually befall him. But even all this in itself would not be decisive proof that Shakespeare in his own person is saying that the play illustrates the man's providential overthrow. However, in Richard's case there does occur an incident that deserves to be called a miracle or at least a divine sign of disapproval against him. When he approaches Anne and the dead body of Henry VI, Henry's wounds start bleeding afresh in accordance with the traditional belief concerning the ordeal of bier right, according to which the corpse of a murdered man would bleed if approached by his slayer.[311] Anne's description of the state of the corpse and her explanation of the phenomenon may be taken as an objective authorization of its supernatural character:

> Oh, gentlemen, see, see! dead Henry's wounds
> Open their congealed mouths and bleed afresh!
> Blush, blush, thou lump of foul deformity;
> For 'tis thy presence that exhales this blood
> From cold and empty veins, where no blood dwells.
> Thy deed, inhuman and unnatural,
> Provokes this deluge most unnatural.
> O God, which this blood madest, revenge his death! [312]

The final line just quoted brings us to the problem of the omnipresent curses of *Richard III*. Sometimes, as in this case, they are phrased as prayers to God, and at other times, they are demands or requests to apostrophized inanimate objects (as in the lines Anne speaks immediately following, addressing the earth); but more often they are simply third-person subjunctives — "let this happen, may that come about, would that," etc. In

---

[311] See Rossell Hope Robbins, *The Encyclopedia of Witchcraft and Demonology* (New York 1960), under "Bier Right." Shakespeare is drawing on the second edition of Holinshed, according to which Henry's body was seen to bleed when it was on display before burial, both at St. Paul's and at Blackfriars (2Hol 3.324).

[312] R3 1.2.55–62. The appearance of the ghosts of Richard's victims in the last act and their speaking to both Richard and Richmond might also be taken as an objective event indicating supernatural disapproval and approval. Supposing that this is so (and that it is not just a theatrical way of showing dreams), there still could be no certainty that they have come with a divine seal of approval, or as divine emissaries; for if Shakespeare's eschatology in general cannot be categorized according to ordinary theological concepts, it is especially true of his "ghostology." Cf. Robert H. West, *The Invisible World: A Study of Pneumatology in Elizabethan Drama* (Athens, Ga. 1939) 52.

most cases Shakespeare deliberately designs the curses to come true, and puts a great deal of emphasis upon the fittingness of the disasters that occur when considered from the viewpoint of retribution. Such uncanny accuracy has an air of the objectively supernatural about it. But whether the curses are meant to be effective, like the blessings and curses of Balaam in the Book of Numbers, or whether the fulfillments and correspondences should be regarded as providential retaliations or simply as instances of poetic justice or Senecan dramaturgy, are questions that cannot readily be answered with certainty. We can, however, analyze the sentiments of the characters in this regard, as we have done in the other plays, and attempt to draw some conclusions from this limited point of view.

Anne's curses upon Richard's future wife, which she later believes to be fulfilled in herself,[313] are largely peripheral to the central themes that we have been pursuing. But the curses of the next scene offer some significant material for our purposes. Richard's pious mouthings, some of which we have seen already, elaborate the theme of a hypocritical appeal to Providence that we found in More, which amounted to the creation of a counter-myth, a parody of the systems of divine support for governments that tended to evolve out of basically sincere religious and political beliefs.[314] Richard prays God to preserve the king, his brother, and he says that God has made it necessary for him to seek the aid of the queen and her allies in securing Clarence's release.[315]

In the course of his feigned defense of Clarence, Richard points out that Queen Elizabeth and her family were on the side of the house of Lancaster, whereas "poor Clarence" abandoned his father-in-law Warwick for Edward's sake and forswore himself in doing so — "which Jesu pardon!" (Margaret asides: "Which God revenge!"). We have here another acknowledgment of Clarence's guilt for perjury, not only by Margaret, but by Richard in his outwardly fervent mood. And we must note also Rivers' unchallenged remark that Henry was their sovereign king at the time of the second battle of St. Albans.[316] It is characteristic of the play, as of the sources for it, that it does not extend its historical references back beyond the time when Henry VI was lawful king of England. This is also true of the works of the court

---

[313] R3 1.2.26–28, 112–133; 4.1.71–85.
[314] Cf. the discussion of myths at the beginning of Chap. IV, above.
[315] R3 1.3.59, 76.
[316] R3 1.3.127–147.

poets of Henry VII who helped to establish the Tudor myth.[317]

Thus, when Margaret steps forward and says that they all owe her allegiance, and that the pleasures they "usurp" are hers, Richard answers that the curse his father York laid on her when she crowned him with paper and gave him a cloth "steeped in the faultless blood of pretty Rutland" has fallen upon her, "and God, not we, hath plagued thy bloody deed"; Queen Elizabeth, Hastings, Rivers, Dorset, and Buckingham all agree with this interpretation, and no mention is made of the Lancastrians as usurpers. In answering, Margaret follows the same train of thought, and accepts, though perhaps ironically, the possibility or even the likelihood of Richard's contention that her own sufferings were the result of God's response to York's curse; she says:

> Did York's dread curse prevail so much with Heaven
> That Henry's death, my lovely Edward's death,
> Their kingdom's loss, my woeful banishment,
> Should all but answer for that peevish brat?
> Can curses pierce the clouds and enter heaven?
> Why, then, give way, dull clouds, to my quick curses!
> Though not by war, by surfeit die your king,
> As ours by murder to make him a king!

She continues, detailing the fate which she wishes, and which eventually occurs, for the others, namely, Queen Elizabeth, Rivers, Hastings, and Richard.[318] Dorset is coupled with Rivers, but it is Vaughan and Grey who are to be his companions in death. Richard tells her he has turned the curse against herself by speaking her name before she can utter his. However, this trickery does not prevent her imprecation from being fulfilled in him. It has many of the overtones of the providential references to him in Vergil-Hall-Holinshed (and More-Hall-Holinshed):

> If Heaven have any grievous plague in store
> Exceeding those that I can wish upon thee,
> Oh, let them keep it till thy sins be ripe,
> And then hurl down their indignation
> On thee, the troubler of the poor world's peace!

---

[317] Holinshed's providential summary, which recalls the Lancastrian usurpation, is an exception. Shakespeare even omits the sources' reference to the connection of the Lancastrian claim to the duchy of Hereford when Buckingham claims it (4.2.91ff.; see above, Chap. IV, n. 86). For Rivers' apostrophe to Pomfret, the site of Richard II's murder, see below.

[318] R3 1.3.170–240.

> The worm of conscience will begnaw thy soul!
> Thy friends suspect for traitors while thou livest
> And take deep traitors for thy dearest friends!
> No sleep close up that deadly eye of thine
> Unless it be while some tormenting dream
> Affrights thee with a hell of ugly devils! [319]

This description of his dreams tallies better with the tradition of his dream before Bosworth Field, reported in the Croyland Continuation and Polydore Vergil, than the one Shakespeare gives him in Act V. But Queen Anne's description of his troubled sleep shows the fulfillment of both her curse upon herself and of Margaret's curse on Richard.[320]

It will not be necessary to detail all of Richard's pietistic statements; we may simply cite his own characterization of his policy in the Vice-like address he gives at the end of this scene:

> But then I sigh, and, with a piece of scripture,
> Tell them that God bids us do good for evil;
> And thus I clothe my naked villainy
> With odd old ends stolen forth of Holy Writ,
> And seem a saint when most I play the devil.[321]

He illustrates his skill in this kind of dissimulation once more in the deathbed scene of Edward IV, who believes that he has effected a reconciliation between his nobles. It is perhaps significant for our purposes that Edward expresses confidence of going to heaven after fulfilling his responsibility as a peacemaker. He has implicitly made his peace with God regarding any other sins he might have committed, including those constantly alleged against him in the play, deeds of blood in securing his crown and faults of sensual indulgence afterwards; and therefore he can say:

> I every day expect an embassage
> From my Redeemer to redeem me hence;
> And more in peace my soul shall part to heaven
> Since I have made my friends at peace on earth.[322]

[319] R3 1.3.217–227.
[320] R3 4.1.66–85.
[321] R3 1.3.334–338. In Legge's *Ricardus tertius* 2.1, Lovel tells Richard how effective such a campaign of feigned religiosity is, and Richard believes the people will be convinced he is a god from heaven. For Richard's role as a Vice, see Bernard Spivack, *Shakespeare and the Allegory of Evil* (New York 1958).
[322] R3 2.1.3–6.

The fervor of his remarks corresponds to that of the dying speeches given to him by More and Hall.[323] In Shakespeare he goes on to give a solemn warning of divine retribution:

Take heed you dally not before your king
Lest he that is the supreme King of kings
Confound your hidden falsehood and award
Either of you to be the other's end.

This admonition is addressed specifically to Hastings and Rivers, but Edward goes on to tell his queen, Dorset, and Buckingham that they are not exempt from it.[324] However, the queen and her party are probably meant to be sincere in their reconciliation, so that their fate can hardly be said to fulfill Edward's warning; and on the other hand, Hastings and Buckingham are not brought to their end by the queen's party. But Buckingham at this point calls down an appropriate punishment from God upon himself, which he later regards as fulfilled, along with Margaret's curse, thus agreeing with the chronicles concerning his fate.[325]

When Richard reveals Clarence's death, Edward becomes disturbed over the state of his soul. He says that his "brutish wrath" was responsible for his brother's execution, for it drove out the memory of all he had done for Edward in the past; and he ends by saying:

O God, I fear thy justice will take hold
On me and you, and mine and yours for this! [326]

Shakespeare may be recalling here part of the suggested explanation of Vergil-Hall for the destruction of Edward's children, namely, that in killing Clarence it was likely that Edward incurred God's great displeasure.[327] However, when the princes are mentioned specifically in the context of retaliation in *Richard III*, namely, in Margaret's curses and tirades, their death is wished for as a punishment not of Edward IV, but of Queen Elizabeth, so that she may bewail her children's death like herself.[328] The stress upon inherited punishment is thereby removed.

[323] Hall 339–341; More-Hall 344–345 [11–13].
[324] R3 2.1.12–20.
[325] R3 2.1.32–40; 5.1.12–29. See 1PV 546; Hall 395; 2Hol 417–418.
[326] R3 2.1.102–132.
[327] Above, Chap. V, n. 59.
[328] R3 1.3.199–209. This is also the tenor of Margaret's wish or curse uttered against the three York brothers in *III Henry VI*, above, 274; that is, she desires them to *witness* the deaths of their children.

After the event, Margaret instructs the souls of the two princes to inform their mother that "right for right/Hath dimmed your infant morn to aged night." And when Elizabeth asks God if he will "fly from such gentle lambs/And throw them in the entrails of the wolf," and asks when he has ever slept "when such a deed was done," Margaret answers: "When holy Harry died, and my sweet son"; and later she declares Edward IV, Clarence, Hastings, Rivers, Vaughan, and Grey as well as the princes to have died in requital for her son, and she looks forward to Richard's fitting end.[329]

A further reason can be adduced to disagree with Edward's self-incrimination and fear of divine punishment for Clarence's death; namely, the fact that he is not really guilty of this crime in Shakespeare's presentation. Aside from the consideration that he had acted in the first place only out of the fear and suspicion that Richard had engendered in him, he had also rescinded the order for his brother's execution.[330] Edward then is as mistaken about the deserving object of God's vengeance as Clarence's children are. Clarence's son says:

> The king mine uncle is to blame for it.
> God will revenge it, whom I will importune
> With earnest prayers all to that effect.

His daughter says she too will do so, but their grandmother, the Duchess of York, silences them:

> Peace, children, peace! the king doth love you well.
> Incapable and shallow innocents,
> You cannot guess who caused your father's death.[331]

Similarly, when Richard pretends to believe that the kindred of the queen are responsible for Clarence's death, and says to Buckingham and others, "God will revenge it," [332] we are not to believe that God will revenge the crime on anyone but Richard himself.[333]

The premonition of the people, reported by More, is given

---

[329] R3 4.4.15–78.
[330] R3 2.1.86.
[331] R3 2.2.13–19.
[332] R3 2.1.134–138.
[333] Miss Campbell, however, seems to think that the queen and the others are partially guilty for failing to plead for Clarence, and that God does punish them through Richard's malice (*Shakespeare's "Histories"* 315).

a whole scene in *Richard III,* much to the same effect as in More. One of the citizens says that men have misgivings of future troubles by a divine instinct, just as the water swells before a boisterous storm; God may prevent the trouble they now fear, though it is more than he expects or they deserve. But he leaves it all to God.[334] The citizen is not pointing out any sins that the people are guilty of when he says they do not deserve any better future. The same citizen applies the *Vae terrae* to the present time, and when the hopeful citizen compares the situation to Henry VI's youth (implying that the land was well governed at that time), the pessimistic citizen says that Henry had virtuous uncles to guide him, whereas now there is emulation between the paternal and maternal uncles; Gloucester is "full of danger," and the queen's sons and brothers are proud and haughty.[335]

Stanley's dream and the other signs unheeded by Hastings, together with his arrest and execution at the Tower, also follow More closely. Hastings tells himself that he could have prevented his fate if he had been alert; "Oh, now I need the priest that spake to me!" he says, and repents for triumphing over his enemies at Pomfret. He sees the curse of Margaret now lighting upon his head, and he prophesies a fearful time for England.[336]

When word is brought of the arrest of Rivers, Grey, and Vaughan, the Duchess of York says:

> Accursed and unquiet wrangling days,
> How many of you have mine eyes beheld!
> My husband lost his life to get the crown,
> And often up and down my sons were tossed
> For me to joy and weep their gain and loss;
> And being seated and domestic broils
> Clean over-blown, themselves, the conquerors,
> Make war upon themselves, brother to brother,
> Blood to blood, self against self. Oh, preposterous
> And frantic outrage, end thy damned spleen;
> Or let me die, to look on earth no more! [337]

[334] R3 2.3.32–45. More-Hall 358 [44]. More does not know whether the foreboding was caused by a natural instinct or by the report of someone who had information of what was going to happen.

[335] R3 2.3.11–30. Cf. Exeter's speech in *I Henry VI,* and other instances of the *Vae* cited above. In More, it is Buckingham who applies the proverb to the present time, after Edward IV's death.

[336] R3 3.4.83–107; More-Hall 360–362 [49–52]. More is unable to come to any definite conclusions about the meaning and nature of these signs. For the traditional background of Richard's charge of witchcraft practiced against him (3.4.61–74), see above, Chap. V, n. 80. For parallels in *Henry VI,* see above, 246, 256.

[337] R3 2.4.55–65.

The duchess's words here are reminiscent of the judgment of Vergil-Hall that the York brothers paid the penalty for murdering Henry VI by turning upon themselves and polluting their hands with their own blood.[338] Of the same tenor is Margaret's outburst later:

> O upright, just, and true-disposing God,
> How do I thank thee that this carnal cur
> Preys on the issue of his mother's body
> And makes her pew-fellow with others' moan! [339]

The scene in which Rivers and the others are executed is placed just before the one in which Hastings comes to his end, to indicate the closeness of their downfalls as well as the fulfillment of the curse of Margaret upon them. Grey includes himself and Vaughan as well as Rivers among those that Margaret cursed for standing by when her son was killed, and now he says it has fallen upon them as she specified. Rivers says she also cursed Richard, Buckingham, and Hastings, and he asks God to remember her prayer for them also;

> And for my sister and her princely sons,
> Be satisfied, dear God, with our true blood,
> Which, as thou knowest, unjustly must be spilt.[340]

Earlier in the scene Vaughan said that those who lived on (meaning Ratcliff, Richard, and the rest) would "cry woe" for the deed,[341] so that punishment is implied for them not only for the offenses enumerated by Margaret but also for this fresh crime. Rivers and his companions are innocent of whatever it is that Richard alleges against them as an excuse for executing them; but they seem to admit that they deserve this punishment for consenting to the death of Prince Edward, the son of Henry VI, and they hope that God will require no further blood to be paid by their family. (Of course, the fact that more of their blood is spilled, namely, that of the two young princes, does

[338] Above, Chap. V, n. 66.

[339] R3 4.4.55–58.

[340] R3 3.3.15–22. Izumi Momose, "The Temporal Awareness in *Richard III*," *Shakespeare Studies* (The Shakespeare Society of Japan) 3:65–69 (1964), finds it significant that Dorset, who was really the object of Margaret's curse (not Grey and Vaughan), is the only one in whom her curse is not fulfilled; it is his escape that initiates Richmond's action against Richard (4.2.47–49) and is "the moment of grace" foreshowing a brighter future.

[341] R3 3.3.7.

not necessarily mean that Shakespeare is saying that it was part of the punishment demanded by divine justice from the Woodville family.) Rivers ends by saying: "Farewell, until we meet again in heaven," thus assuming that the debt they owed God for the prince's death is atoned for by their deaths, as far as they themselves are concerned.[342]

Before Margaret's curse was alluded to, Rivers recalled the murder of Richard II and addressed the castle:

> O Pomfret, Pomfret! O thou bloody prison,
> Fatal and ominous to noble peers!
> Within the guilty closure of thy walls
> Richard the Second here was hacked to death;
> And, for more slander to thy dismal seat,
> We give to thee our guiltless blood to drink.[343]

If there is any causal connection implied here between the death of Richard II and that of Rivers, Grey, and Vaughan, it is that the castle itself is somehow responsible for both crimes, since it is called "fatal" and "ominous" to peers. But this is hardly what is meant, since their own deaths are said to add to its "slander"; it is rather the passive background of the crimes. There is not the least suggestion that their deaths are meant to expiate for Richard's death, or that they are in some way the victims of a curse that his death laid on the castle or on the land. The only curse that operates in the scene is the one based on their personal guilt in the death of Prince Edward. And it is hardly likely that Shakespeare is implying a more general curse, by making a subtle allusion to a familar commonplace that would be recognized by all his listeners; for, as we have seen, the notion of a divine vendetta deriving from Richard II's overthrow and death and extending through the reign of Richard III was so uncommon as to be found in none of the chronicle accounts or plays of the fifteenth and sixteenth centuries.

In dramatizing Buckingham's public appeal to Richard to take over the rule, Shakespeare draws on More's humorous description of Richard's hypocritical piety, to make the episode one of high comedy. As was mentioned before, Hall's version of More supplies the two bishops. Shakespeare does not dramatize Doctor Shaw's sermon on the text, "Spuria vitulamina non dabunt

[342] R3 3.3.25.
[343] R3 3.3.9–14.

radices altos," but perhaps Buckingham is reflecting this argument when he tells Richard to accept the dignity,

> If not to bless us and the land withal,
> Yet to draw forth your noble ancestry
> From the corruption of abusing times
> Unto a lineal true-derived course.[344]

Shakespeare omits the elaborate conversations between Buckingham and Morton, and alters the sources by having Queen Elizabeth only pretend her consent to an alliance with Richard, after which Stanley sends word to Richmond of her agreement to have her daughter marry him.[345]

When Richard hears that Richmond is on his way to England and asks Stanley about him, he becomes enraged at Stanley's answer that he comes to claim the crown, and he says:

> Is the king dead? the empire unpossessed?
> What heir of York is there alive but we?
> And who is England's king but great York's heir? [346]

This is the closest that Shakespeare comes in *Richard III* to presenting the dynastic claims of the houses of York and Lancaster, and Richard's question regarding York's sole right is never answered.

Richmond's right is reinforced instead by Richard's earlier recollection of Henry's prophecy:

> I do remember me, Henry the Sixth
> Did prophesy that Richmond should be king,
> When Richmond was a little peevish boy.
> A king, perhaps, perhaps . . .

but Richard dismisses any serious acknowledgment of prophetic power in Henry by saying,

---

[344] R3 3.7.195–200. See above, Chap. VI, n. 74.

[345] Tillyard prefers to think Elizabeth really did consent to Richard's plan (*Shakespeare's History Plays* 214); this, however, would mean that she changed her mind again offstage.

[346] R3 4.4.463–473. Cf. Hall's version of More; after Richard slays Henry VI, he says: "Now is there no heir male of King Edward the Third but we of the house of York" (p. 343 [81]).

How chance the prophet could not at that time
Have told me, I being by, that I should kill him? [347]

However, he goes on to muse about the prophecy that John Hooker supplied to Abraham Fleming for the second edition of Holinshed:

Richmond! When last I was at Exeter,
The mayor in courtesy showed me the castle
And called it Rougemont; at which name I started,
Because a bard of Ireland told me once
I should not live long after I saw Richmond.[348]

Concerning Richard III's providential overthrow, as we noted before, there is such a congruence of opinions, not only those of the characters of the play but also those of the chronicles, that it would no doubt be safe to suppose that Shakespeare meant him to be dramatized objectively as coming under the scourge of divine justice.

Richard's mother tells him that she will see him no more, for either he will die "by God's just ordinance" before he returns victorious from this war, or she will die of grief, and therefore she leaves with him her "most grievous curse," hoping that it will tire him in battle, and that her prayers will fight on the opposing side; and she wishes the souls of Edward's children to whisper to the spirits of his enemies, "and promise them success and victory." [349] These words are no doubt meant to be a preview of Richard's and Richmond's dream that night, as is his own curse upon himself which he invokes when trying to win over Elizabeth:

As I intend to prosper and repent,
So thrive I in my dangerous affairs
Of hostile arms! Myself myself confound!
Heaven and Fortune bar me happy hours!
Day, yield me not thy light, nor, night, thy rest!
Be opposite all planets of good luck
To my proceeding, if, with dear heart's love,

---

[347] We have noted above (n. 83) that Shakespeare changes the circumstances of the prophecy in this play from those under which it occurred in *III Henry VI.*
[348] R3 4.2.98–110.
[349] R3 4.4.183–193.

> Immaculate devotion, holy thoughts,
> I tender not thy beauteous princely daughter! [350]

If there has been any suggestion that the victims of Richard's bloodthirsty cruelty were in any way suffering the pains of divine justice earlier in the play, it is effectively overruled (except perhaps for those who admitted that they were being justly punished for some previous crime) by the appearance of their ghosts in the dream scene, and their denunciation of Richard and support of Richmond. It would seem likely that their injunction to Richard, that he "despair and die," is meant to be fulfilled in the action that follows; at least, some of his expressions could be taken as indicative of despair in the theological sense. When he wakes, he first inadvertently prays, "Have mercy, Jesu!" and then takes it back — "Soft, I did but dream"; he proceeds to account for the whole experience as the effect of his conscience, as does the Vergil-Hall-Holinshed account.[351] And in the psychomachy that follows, he admits his guilt but never takes another thought for forgiveness. He says, in fact, "I shall despair." Later, he tells his men:

> March on, join bravely, let us to't pell-mell;
> If not to heaven, then hand in hand to hell.[352]

And though, like Richmond, he calls on St. George, he characterizes the saint as their "ancient word of courage" that is to inspire them "with the spleen of fiery dragons," which is hardly in St. George's line.[353]

Richmond on the other hand is consistently placed on the side of heaven and the angels. He and his men go forward "in God's name" (bis) against that "foul swine" and "guilty homicide" Richard.[354] The night before the battle, Stanley imparts to Richmond his mother's blessings and says that she prays con-

---

[350] R3 4.4.397–405. Cf. Margaret's curse on Richard in Act I, scene 3.

[351] For Vergil, see above, Chap. IV at n. 65; repeated in Hall 414 and 1–2Hol 3.438.

[352] R3 5.3.312–313.

[353] R3 5.3.349–350. At the beginning of the third scene, Shakespeare has Richard say:

> Besides, the king's name is a tower of strength
> Which they upon the adverse faction want. (5.3.12–13)

This sentiment is reminiscent of the speech Hall gave Richard at this time. Shakespeare later gave sentiments to Richard II that even more closely parallel this speech.

[354] R3 5.2.1–22.

tinually for his good; and Richmond himself utters a fervent
prayer to God:

> O thou whose captain I account myself,
> Look on my forces with a gracious eye!
> Put in their hands thy bruising irons of wrath
> That they may crush down with a heavy fall
> The usurping helmets of our adversaries!
> Make us thy ministers of chastisement
> That we may praise thee in the victory!
> To thee I do commend my watchful soul
> Ere I let fall the windows of mine eyes.
> Sleeping and waking, Oh, defend me still! [355]

Because Henry prays to be God's minister of chastisement and
does win and thanks God for the victory, it must no doubt be
assumed that Shakespeare means him to be objectively viewed
as supported by divine authority. His action against Richard can
be justified on the principles of contemporary political theory;
for Henry was not rebelling against a tyrant but was putting down
a tyrannous usurper, which, as we have seen, the *Mirror for
Magistrates* allowed.[356] Thus, as Henry tells his men,

> God and our good cause fight upon our side;
> The prayers of holy saints and wronged souls,
> Like high-reared bulwarks, stand before our faces.
> Richard except, those whom we fight against
> Had rather have us win than him they follow.
> For what is he they follow? Truly, gentlemen,
> A bloody tyrant and a homicide;
> One raised in blood, and one in blood established;
> One that made means to come by what he hath
> And slaughtered those that were the means to help him;
> A base foul stone, made precious by the foil
> Of England's chair, where he is falsely set;
> One that hath ever been God's enemy.
> Then, if you fight against God's enemy,
> God will in justice ward you as his soldiers.[357]

Shakespeare does not have Richmond phrase his right so baldly
as the Hall-Holinshed account does, in which he says that Richard

---

[355] R3 5.3.83–117.
[356] Cf. Tillyard, *Shakespeare's History Plays* 89–90, 212.
[357] R3 5.3.240–254.

wrongfully keeps him from the crown.[358] But the crown is planted on his head just as firmly here as in the sources. When the victory is won, and Henry says,

> God and your arms be praised, victorious friends;
> The day is ours, the bloody dog is dead,

Stanley takes up the crown, and declares:

> Lo, here, these long-usurped royalties
> From the dead temples of this bloody wretch
> Have I plucked off to grace thy brows withal.
> Wear it, enjoy it, and make much of it.

Richmond's way of accepting it is to say: "Great God of heaven, say amen to all!" Hereupon he begins to use the royal plural; after instructing the dead to be buried and pardons proclaimed to those "that in submission will return to us," he says:

> And then, as we have taken the sacrament,
> We will unite the white rose and the red.
> Smile Heaven upon this fair conjunction,
> That long have frowned upon their enmity!
> What traitor hears me, and says not amen?
> England hath long been mad and scarred herself;
> The brother blindly shed the brother's blood,
> The father rashly slaughtered his own son,
> The son, compelled, been butcher to the sire.
> All this divided York and Lancaster,
> Divided in their dire division,
> Oh, now let Richmond and Elizabeth,
> The true succeeders of each royal house,
> By God's fair ordinance conjoin together!
> And let their heirs, God, if thy will be so,
> Enrich the time to come with smooth-faced Peace,
> With smiling Plenty and fair prosperous days!
> Abate the edge of traitors, gracious Lord,
> That would reduce these bloody days again
> And make poor England weep in streams of blood!
> Let them not live to taste this land's increase
> That would with treason wound this fair land's peace!
> Now civil wounds are stopped, Peace lives again;
> That she may long live here, God say amen! [359]

[358] Above, Chap. V at n. 94.
[359] R3 5.5.1–41.

There is some question as to what Stanley means by "long-usurped" when referring to the crown. He could mean either the comparatively short time it was possessed by Richard or the longer time it was possessed by the house of York, thus implying that Lancaster had the true right to the throne. At any rate, once more we see that history in *Richard III* does not extend back beyond the time of the Wars of the Roses, which, of course, began in the time of Henry VI. Richmond is summing up Shakespeare's early tetralogy here without including the earlier period covered by the series he was still to write. The frown of Heaven could be conceived of as God's active plaguing of the participants in the wars and as somehow a cause of the wars; but more probably it refers to the divine displeasure at the evil that men were committing. However, the smile of Heaven most likely includes not only God's pleasure but his blessing and favor as well.

From a providential point of view, what we have in *Richard III* is the Tudor myth more or less as it existed before the time of Polydore Vergil. It includes the recognition of Henry VI as the lawful king, the atrocious cruelty of the York brothers in killing Henry and his son, and the punishment that befell them because of this, especially as manifested in the divinely authorized and supported campaign of Henry Tudor, whose coming reign of reconciliation was foretold by the saintly Henry VI. All that is missing is the Welsh lineage and the prophecy of Cadwallader; Henry here bases his claim solely on the grounds of his Lancastrian right,[360] and he joins himself to the Yorkist heiress as a means of reconciling the claims of that house and putting an end to the war. There is no indication in this play or in the whole of this tetralogy that Henry VI or his family was divinely punished because of the sins of his grandfather, Henry IV. In Shakespeare's mind, Henry IV was involved in a more remote set of difficulties which would call for a separate treatment, in which there would be only vague and indefinite references to the period of history beginning with the reign of Henry VI and ending with the accession of the first Tudor monarch.

[360] Later Shakespeare was to stress the Welsh qualities of the Lancastrian Henry V (H5 4.7.101–121). And we may recall that the prophecy of the eventual Welsh recovery of England was applied to Henry V long before being applied to Henry VII.

X

Conclusion

In previous analyses of the historical treatments of fifteenth-century England (it is particularly Professor Tillyard's that is in question here), a number of themes have been studied simultaneously, and used to supplement each other in formulating the basic patterns of thought involved in these writings. The political and providential aspects of discord and unity have been especially stressed. But a certain amount of distortion has resulted from the failure to consider each element in its own right, and too often lacunae in the pattern postulated for both themes are filled by inferences illegitimately drawn from one theme alone.[1]

Specifically, the political theme of discord beginning with the usurpation of Henry IV and ending with the marriage of Henry VII and Elizabeth of York (or with the reign of their offspring, Henry VIII), which is formulated most clearly in Hall's preface, has been taken as the primary analogue of an over-all metahistorical pattern that involves not only the human element of sin and its effects, in terms of suffering and further sins in reaction to the suffering, but also the divine dimension of the providential rule of all created being. To correspond precisely to the political theme of Hall, the role of Providence in this period of history would have to be conceived of in terms of a divine curse laid upon the land and its people for the sins committed in deposing and killing Richard II, so that from this point of view all the disturbances and injustices that followed would be somehow regarded as God's punishment not only of the guilty persons but of the innocent as well, until he finally took pity upon the people and relented from his wrath by send-

---

[1] A similar analysis could be made for the themes of order and hierarchy in Tillyard's *Elizabethan World Picture.*

ing peace in the person and dynasty of Henry Tudor. And the fact that this theme was never expressed in this way has been taken to mean that everyone assumed the whole when referring to the parts, just as references to planets presupposed the rest of the cosmos, or just as tangible objects were considered by Plato to participate in and express the reality of the Ideas, but only in fragmentary and incomplete ways.

However, it would seem that the providential aspect of the Tudor myth as described by Mr. Tillyard is an ex post facto Platonic Form, made up of many fragments that were never fitted together into a mental pattern until they felt the force of his own synthesizing energy. This judgment is not meant to detract from the valuable insights that his undertaking has produced and inspired; and he himself indicated that many of the large vistas which he discovered and described could profit from a more minute attention to individual details.

In tracing the development of providential interpretations in the chronicles of the fifteenth century, we saw that myths or mystiques tended to develop along the political lines of the immediate present, enveloping favorite sons with an aura of personal integrity and divine support, and supplying appropriately evil motives and cosmically based troubles for the members of the opposition. Thus there developed a Lancastrian God who overshadowed for a long time the comparatively feeble efforts of the opposing divinity that favored Richard. But as time went on God developed decided Yorkist tendencies and reversed much of the work he had done as the protector of the house of Lancaster. But soon the God of Henry Tudor appeared on the scene, and the religion of later Lancastrianism was revived.

When Polydore Vergil came to England from Italy, it was the Tudor view of history that he found ready at hand, and it was this that he first incorporated into his comprehensive history. He accepted the representation of his patron as having been sent by God to put down usurpation and tyranny in the person of Richard III and to bring peace to England. But later, in preparing the early rough draft of his work for publication, he meditated upon the lessons that could be taught from the events of earlier years, and supplemented with new insights the occasional providential interpretations he had previously obtained from writings inspired by the numinous influences of Lancaster and York. However, Vergil's views of those early times were not politically motivated or grounded, and he attempted to arrive at the providential cause for certain events on the basis of absolute justice, whereby sin is punished and virtue tested and rewarded.

And because of the nature of the circumstances concerning the Lancastrian usurpation and the failure of its dynasty three generations later, he seemed to accept as a real possibility that the reason for its failure was the working of divine justice, which deprived that family of the realm and restored it to its proper owner. But he also maintained that the troubles that happened to the saintly heir of the Lancasters, Henry VI, were providentially beneficial to him, and that he found at least as much favor with God as did his glorious father, Henry V.

Vergil also reflected upon the sins committed by Edward IV in securing the crown and maintaining it, and since he died an apparently natural death, whereas his two sons were cruelly murdered, Vergil invoked the early biblical notion of the sins of the father being visited upon the children, and considered it likely that the death of his sons constituted a divine punishment upon Edward; however, Edward's brothers, Clarence and especially Richard, were punished for their sins in their own persons. At the same time, the divine element in Henry Tudor's accession was noticeably lessened, perhaps because Vergil felt that the peace it brought in the person of his son was not developing in directions entirely pleasing to God.

Edward Hall inherited Vergil's providential interpretations and adopted most of them without much critical evaluation, and also accepted, in an equally uncritical way, many similar and dissimilar interpretations from other sources. As a result he often upset the already precarious balance of reason and justice in Vergil's account of God's workings. Holinshed made a new synthesis of previous ideas concerning providential retribution in this century, one in some ways more satisfactory than Vergil's. But once again his balance was upset by the clumsy additions of Abraham Fleming .

In all these accounts it is the guilty persons who suffer divine punishment. But in some rare cases, the punishment falls upon their children or grandchildren; the punishment as such, however, never extends beyond the immediate family circle.

However, the crude morality of inherited guilt and punishment is rather difficult to reconcile with God's justice and mercy, and the concept was almost completely ignored by the authors of the *Mirror for Magistrates* and used only sparingly and with reluctance by Daniel. In Shakespeare hereditary providential punishment seems to be predicted once by Richard II, and feared by Henry V in his own person and by Henry IV and Clarence in the persons of their children. But it is never dramatized as taking effect, except perhaps in the mind of Queen Margaret, who sees the innocent as well as the guilty members of the York faction as falling under God's scourge in payment for her losses.

This is a highly oversimplified account of the divine elements in fifteenth- and sixteenth-century English historiography, but it is hoped that most of the necessary qualifications have been made in the preceding chapters.

We may add that if the concept of God's punishment extending beyond the sinner to his innocent children was difficult to accept, the concept of divine wrath extending for generations over a whole people for a crime committed in the remote past presupposes the kind of avenging God completely foreign to the piety of the historiographers of medieval and Renaissance England.

As for the practice of writing from a providential point of view, which was strongly influenced, especially in the sixteenth century, by the didactic concept of historiography, it eventually gave way to the conscientious fact-finding and documentary approach represented by a man like John Stow, and to an analysis of causes on the natural level. Providential interpretations, since they involved the acceptance or formulation of absolutely unverifiable conjectures as to the divine reasoning that would account for individual events in the course of the providential rule of the universe, were set aside as mere idle speculation. This kind of realistic evaluation was clearly made by Edward Hall in some of his independent moments, though he was sometimes maneuvered into this position by his detestation of old religious abuses. But more often than not, he followed the example, and used the examples, of the histories before him in sounding out the mind of God. And Sir Walter Raleigh was still to bring the practice to its ultimate incoherence.

Raleigh covers our period of English history as part of his demonstration in the preface to his *History of the World* that the ways of God in punishing sin are unchanging, and he incorporates some of the providential judgments we have seen in the chronicles. Thus, for instance, he says that Richard II was punished for his misrule; Henry IV was punished for his sins not only while he was still alive but also after his death, in the deprivation of his grandson, Henry VI; Richard of York was struck down for his breach of oath; and Henry VII, acting no doubt as "the immediate instrument of God's justice," cut off the cruel Richard III. However, he incorporates these events into a larger continuous stretch of history extending from Edward II to James I, in which Edward III was punished in his grandson Richard II, and Henry VII and Henry VIII were punished in the extinction of their line, and the union of England and Scotland was an even greater gift of God than the union of York and Lancaster.[2]

Unlike most of the chroniclers before him, Raleigh explains in some detail his concept of the workings of God's justice in the world, and it is important to note that the exemplary conception of history (and not just of historiography) took such a hold upon his mind that he believed in effect that every sin must be punished by some external calamity in this world; and though he includes in his world-view the doctrines of heaven and hell as the ultimate destinations of men, yet it never occurs to him, in the context, at least, to consider hell as compensating for deserved punishment not received in the lifetime of a guilty individual. Instead, he sees God as punishing the guilty man after his death by inflicting disasters on his children or grandchildren. We have seen that Raleigh had abundant precedent for this kind of providential view, not only in the English chronicles but also in the historical books of the Old Testament, from which he derived his chief inspiration. But he goes on in his preface to defend the concept of a kind of half-life for souls between the time of death and the general resurrection, and to affirm that departed souls have no joy nor sorrow over the successes or failures of their posterity.[3]

Therefore it is quite evident that a man could not be considered punished for his sins in any just or reasonable way by having plagues descend upon his posterity after his death. In fact it seems that Raleigh had some misgivings on this score before when speaking of Henry IV, of whom he says: "He saw (if souls immortal see and discern any things after the body's death) his grandchild Henry the Sixth, and his son the prince, suddenly, and without mercy, murdered." But he repressed this doubt and proceeded to make similar judgments, and did not

---

[2] Raleigh, Preface viii-xx.

[3] Preface xxxiv-xxxv. This old eschatological notion was condemned in the Forty-two Articles under Edward VI, but not mentioned in the Thirty-nine Articles that superceded them. On Raleigh's religious ideas in general, see Pierre Lefranc, *Sir Walter Raleigh Écrivain* (Quebec 1968).

notice the contradiction to his system involved in his later explicit denial of worldly knowledge and emotions to departed souls.

Raleigh's interest, therefore, consists chiefly in setting up tableaus of instruction concerning God's justice for the edification of the viewers, rather than in justifying God's distribution of punishment with regard to guilt. However, wherever possible, he does specify personal guilt in those punished for their ancestors, as in Richard II, and even in Henry VI. The latter, he says, though "generally esteemed for a gentle and innocent prince," drew great disasters on himself and his kingdom by breaking his marriage contract and by permitting the death of his uncle, Humphrey of Gloucester.[4] But is it evident from his further remarks that he is uneasy about Henry's fate and considers it more a matter for pity than an example of God's justice. And it is noteworthy that he cannot point out any fault in Henry's son, Prince Edward, and that he avoids attributing directly to God the punishment received by Edward IV in the cruel deaths of his two innocent sons.

Raleigh further exposes the naïveté of his method (which involves not only the presumption that some visible calamity must eventually follow upon the commission of a sin but also the presumption that external calamities are an indication that some grievous sin has gone before) by admitting later the very obvious fact that worldly success or worldly adversity can never serve as a valid criterion of God's favor or disfavor, and also by his strong insistence upon God's practice of sending suffering and death to those whom he favors.[5]

Raleigh's remarks concerning the murder of Edward II and the fate of Edward III's descendants[6] might seem to indicate that he has some kind of curse in mind whereby God wiped out not

[4] Cf. the *Mirror for Magistrates*, above, Chap. VII at n. 40.
[5] Preface xxxiv; *History* 2.22.3 (IV 627).
[6] He says that Edward II's death caused many deaths in the times to follow. He shows that Edward III manifested his approval of the deed and was therefore punished for it: "This cruelty the secret and unsearchable judgment of God revenged on the grandchild of Edward the Third: and so it fell out, even to the last of that line, that in the second or third descent they were all buried under the ruins of those buildings, of which the mortar had been tempered with innocent blood" (Preface ix). It is not clear how far down Raleigh intended to trace Edward III's descendants in this sentence, that is, whether or not he really intended God to be viewed as punishing even the children of Henry VIII for Edward III's sins. But he does say later: "And as it pleased him to punish the usurpation and unnatural cruelty of Henry the First and of our third Edward in their children for many generations; so dealt he with the sons of Louis Debonaire, the son of Charles the Great, or Charlemagne" (Preface xx).

only Edward III's grandson Richard II, but also his descendants in succeeding generations, all the way down to the children of Henry VIII. If so, it would resemble in its extent the effect of the darnel seed sown by the devil, as reported in Ferrers' tragedy of Gloucester in the *Mirror for Magistrates*; this diabolical (rather than divine) curse resulted in the destruction of all the male descendants of Henry II.[7] However, even if Raleigh did conceive of Edward III's sins as being punished by God for numerous generations, this providential curse would differ essentially from the usual description that Tillyard gives to his supposedly all-pervading conception, not only in its far greater extent in time, but also in its being restricted to the lineal descendants of the offender. In Tillyard's scheme, the Yorkists must logically be visualized as being punished not for sins committed by one of their ancestors, but for sins committed against their ancestors.

However, in Raleigh's specific accounts of the figures of English history who followed Edward III, as well as in his accounts of God's punishments elsewhere in his preface and in the *History of the World,* he does not picture these punishments as extending beyond the children or grandchildren of the offenders (except in the case of Prince Edward, Henry IV's great-grandson).

After this review of Raleigh's thoughts upon Providence, we may most appropriately deal with the analysis of Miss Campbell, who, though she is more realistic than Tillyard in recognizing that the period from Richard II to Richard III is viewed by the chronicles as consisting of not one but two providential cycles (encompassing the rise and fall of the houses of Lancaster and York, respectively), yet takes Raleigh's account as her principal model and reads concepts into earlier chronicles which are not to be found there.[8]

She expresses the pattern thus: "An usurper seizes the throne; God avenges his sin upon the third heir through the agency of another usurper, whose sin is again avenged upon the third heir." This schema is based on an overreading of Raleigh. In the first place, he does not have any specific pattern for the fall

[7] Mirror 447–450. As Raleigh states it: "It is certain that after the murder of that king [Edward II], the issue of blood then made, though it had some times of stay and stopping, did again break out; and that so often, and in such abundance, as all our princes of the masculine race (very few excepted) died of the same disease" (Preface ix).
[8] See her *Shakespeare's "Histories"* 84, 122–125.

of God's punishment; it happens when it happens, either in the offender or in his children or grandchildren, and sometimes both in the offender and in his descendants. In the case of Henry VII, it happened in his grandchildren; in the case of Henry VIII, it happened in his children (that is, the same punishment in Edward VI, Mary, and Elizabeth, namely, their lack of heirs, does service for the sins of both the father and the grandfather). Furthermore, though Raleigh does note the similarity in Edward III, Henry IV, and Henry VII, in their being punished in their grandchildren, he does not give the least hint that this is a pattern that is found elsewhere in English history, and certainly he does not state anything of the kind with regard to Edward IV and Richard III, whereby Richard is regarded as the third Yorkist heir from Edward. Nor is this interpretation to be found in any of the previous chroniclers we have studied. Raleigh makes it clear that Edward IV was punished in the deaths of his sons, but we can hardly assume that he thought him further punished in the death of Richard III, who murdered his heirs. Moreover, it is not clear that Raleigh regards either Edward IV or Henry VII as usurpers; it is more probable that he considered them the legitimate heirs.

Further, the attribution of Richard II's fall to God's punishment of Edward III is far from being a common interpretation, and it seems to have been suggested before Raleigh only in the reflections Richard II makes on his fate in Hayward's *Life of Henry IV* (1599) and in John Davies of Hereford's *Microcosmos* (1603).[9] As for Miss Campbell's statement that "Ralegh, like many another writer, thus found in the fact that Henry VII's grandchild, Elizabeth, was the last heir in the direct line new proof that history repeats itself in this recurrent cyclical pattern," [10] she does not cite another writer with this view, and therefore it would seem that we must for the present continue to regard it as a *hapax legomenon*, found only in Raleigh, and there in only a very limited form.

Shakespeare's great contribution was to unsynthesize the syntheses of his contemporaries and to unmoralize their moralizations. His genius for sounding the realities of human passion and action, which are the components and raw materials of historical reflections, enabled him to sort out the partisan layers that had been combined in rather ill-digested lumps in Hall and

[9] Hayward 133; Davies of Hereford 55.
[10] Campbell, *Shakespeare's "Histories"* 123.

Holinshed and to distribute them to appropriate spokesmen. Thus the sentiments of the Lancaster myth are spoken by Lancastrians, and opposing views are voiced by anti-Lancastrians and Yorkists. And the Tudor myth finds its fullest statement in the mouth of Henry Tudor. In this way Shakespeare often reproduces by instinct the viewpoints of fifteenth-century documents which for the most part were either completely unavailable to him or present only in their assimilated forms in the large compilations which he drew upon.

This characterization of Shakespeare's histories is not completely verified throughout, of course, since he often accepts the moral portraitures of the chronicles which were originally produced by political bias, and has his characters commit or confess to the crimes which their enemies falsely accused them of.

There were, obviously, elements of dramatization in all the sources before Shakespeare, in the contemporary as well as in the sixteenth-century histories; and Vergil, More, Redmayne, Hall, and Daniel (and also, in a sense, the authors of the *Mirror for Magistrates*) added to the given historical scenes by composing their own orations in the spirit of the various historical characters that they portrayed. But in these authors the sentiments of the characters are usually weighed in the balance of a pedagogical absolute morality in order that suitable lessons might be extracted for public consumption.

Shakespeare, however, as a playwright, completely dramatized the characters, and so eliminated all the purportedly objective providential judgments made by the histories upon historical characters, the kind of reflection which would be valid or pertinent only if made by God himself. All such judgments were placed where they belonged and where many of them originated — in the mouths of the characters themselves. Here these judgments, which reflect belief in God's providential control of all things and all events, are expressed in terms of petitions and aspirations to God (which may or may not be answered), of prayers of thanksgiving to God for some favor (though the reason ascribed to him may not have entered into his motives at all), and of providential attributions that are obviously based on personal viewpoints.

And though this kind of characterization involves making moral judgments on the motives of the characters for their own actions, it eliminates simplistic evaluations of complex moral situations, and leaves the question open as to how God would distribute praise and blame and sanctions for good and evil in these instances. There are, certainly, exceptional cases, like those of Henry V and Richard III, where Shakespeare seems to reinforce his play as a whole with the unanimous expression of divine approval or disfavor towards individuals. But even in these cases Shakespeare's opinion is not ventured as his own.

Shakespeare's individual characterizations of men and their moral attitudes change from play to play, which indicates that he is not concerned with the absolute fixing of praise and blame in the historical characters; but he does ordinarily take pains to achieve a general consistency within each play or each scene. That is, Shakespeare was primarily a dramatist and not a historian — though many of his changes in characterization must be blamed upon the faulty inconsistencies of the historians and moralists before him. For this reason, the moral conflicts of each play must be taken on the terms of the play and not supplemented from the other plays, or from his sources, or from general principles, without extreme caution. Each play creates its own moral ethos and mythos, and though the details may vary from those established in other plays concerning the same characters and events, still each view can serve as a valid hypothesis to demonstrate the springs of human and cosmic action from a world of bygone events whose inner causes are essentially lost and irretrievable.

Appendices

Bibliography

Index

Extracts from the early (Lancastrian) version
of John Hardyng's "Chronicle,"
British Museum MS. Lansdowne 204.

1   **The death and burial of Richard II, fol. 204**

*How this same Kyng Richard died at Pountfrayt; caryed and
biryed atte Freres of Langley by commaundment of the Kynge
Henry*
   O speculum mundi, quod debet in aure refundi,
   Ex quo prouisum sapiens acuat sibi visum;
   Cum male viuentes Deus odit in orbe regentes,
   Est qui peccator non esse potest dominator;
   Ricardo teste, finis probat hoc manifeste.
   Sic diffinita fecit regia sors stabilita;
   Regis vt est vita cronica stabit ita.
      *Vt patet in metris dicti Iohannis Gower in cronica sua tem-
      pore Ricardi Regis predicti.*

Sone after so the Kynge Rycharde was dede
And brought to Poules with grete solempnyte;
Men sayde he was forhungred and lapte in lede.
Bot thar his messe was done and dyrige;
In herse Rial his corse lay thare, I se,
And aftir masse to Westmynstir was ledde,
Whare placebo and dirige he hedde,

Wyth messe on morne in alkyn riall wyse,
With clothes of golde offred at bothe the place.
And sone anone right at the kynges devyse
Vnto Langley fro thens thay dyd arase
His corse, whiche in the Freres thay dyd vnlace
And byried thar with riall exequyse,
As Freres myght do with all devyne seruyse.

2 Death of Henry IV and accession of Henry V, foll. 209–210

*How the kynge lay in sekenes that he dyed of at Westminster in
the Abbay with grete thankynges and lovynges makyng to God
almyghty*

In this mene while the kynge with grete sekenesse
Enfeblisshynge of body more and more,
The deth than toke the nynetene day doutlesse
Of Marche in his fourtene yere, distressed sore
By soonde of God—whom he gan thonke therfore
With contrite herte and humble yolden chere,
And of his grace and mercy dyd requere.

"O Lorde," he sayde, "O God omnipotent,
Now se I wele thy godhed lykethe me,
That suffred neuere my fose haue thair intent
Of my persone in myne aduersyte,
Bot euermore, Lorde, of thy benyngnyte
Thou haste me kepte from thair malyvolence,
Me chastysynge oonly by thy sentence.

"O Lorde, I thonke the now with all myne herte,
With all my Soule, and all my Spiritʒ clere;
This wormes mete, this carion foule vnquerte,
That some tyme thought in worlde it had no pere,
This face so foule that leprouse doth appere,
That here afore I haue hadde suche a pryde
To portray ofte in mony place full wyde,

"Of whiche right now the porest of this londe
Sauf oonly of thair owne benygnyte
Wolde lothe to loke vpon, I vndyrstonde,
Of whiche, gode Lorde, that thou so vysyte me,
A thousonde tymes, the Lorde in Trynyte,
With all myne herte I thonke and now commende
Into thi hondes my soule withouten ende."

And so he dyed in fayth and hole creaunce;
At Caunterbery beried with hiegh reuerence,
As kynge shulde be, with alkyn Cyrcumstaunce,
Accordynge with his hiegh magnyficence
Byside the prynce Edwarde with grete expense.
Of Criste was than a thousonde yere full oute,
Foure hundre eke and threttene, oute of doute.

Conceyte of the maker touchant this gode Kynge Henry Fourth

O verry God, what tourment had this kynge,
To remembre in brief and shorte intent,
Some in his sarke venym so dyd hym brynge,

And some in mete and drynke grete poysonment,
Some in his hose by grete Imagynement,
Some in bedstraw irnes doun dyd putte and threste,
To steke hym on whare he shulde slepe or reste.

Some made for hym also enchauntement
To waste hym oute and vtterly distroye,
And some gafe hym batayle felonousment
In feelde within his Reme hym forto noye;
And on thaym self the Sorow and the noye
Ay fell at ende, that honged were and hede
As Traytours awght to bene in euery stede.

THE VIJ BOOK
Primum Capitulum
Henry the Fyfte, Kynge of Englonde and Fraunce and Lorde of Irelonde, Duke of Normandye, Guyen, and of Aungeoy.
Nota quod Cronica istius Regis Henrici patet in quadam Cronica Magistri Norham doctoris Theologie, et secundum quod compilator huius libri vidit et audiuit.

Henry, his sonne that Prynce of Wales was than,
On Seynt Cuthbert Day than next folowynge
In Marce was crounde, as I remembre can,
And als ennoynte at Westmynster for kynge,
Of whom the Reme was glad withoute lesynge,
Obeyand hym in alkyns ordynaunce,
As subgytʒ owe to Ryall gouernaunce.

[Three stanzas on John Oldcastle follow, much as in 2Hard 371–372, with the marginal heading: *How the kynge fortifyed the Cherche to done execucion of the Lord Cobham and hys Lollers and Errytykes for errysyes.*]
How Kynge Henry the Fyfte Fyrste gafe licence to all men to offre to the Archebisshop Richard Scrope and worship hym

The kynge than sette vpon all rightwysnesse
Of morall wytte and all benygnyte.
All openly he ordeynde in expresse
That all men myght with oute diffyculte
The Archebisshop of Yorke vysyte and se,
That Rychard Scrope so hight, full graciouse,
For whom God shewed myracles plentyuouse.

How he toke vp Kynge Richard at Langley and entowmbid hym Rialy at Westminster with Quene Anne, as was his own will whiles he was on lyfe

Kynge Rycharde als, at Langley leyde in erthe
Agayne his wyll and all his ordynaunce
By comaundement of Kynge Henry the Ferthe

For folke of hym shulde haue no remembraunce,
The kynge toke vp with riall ordynaunce
And toumbed fayre byside his wife, Quene Anne,
With all honoure that myght be done by manne.

3 Henry V's first French campaign, foll. 210v–211

*How Kynge Henry hedid the Erle of Cambrige, The Lorde
Scrope, and Sir Thomas Gray of Werke, and went to Normandy
and wanne Harflete, and commynge homewarde he stroke than
The batayll of Agyncourt*

At Lammesse after the kynge to Normandy
At Hampton was with all his hoste to sayle,
Whare than the Erle of Cambrige certanly,
The Lorde Scrope als, Sir Thomas Gray, no fayle,
The kynges deth had caste for thair avayle;
Of whiche the kynge was ware and toke all thre
And heded hem at Hampton by decre;

And helde hys way to Harflete than anone
And wanne it so and made thereof Captayne
His Eme the Duke of Excester allone;
Ande homwarde went by Calays so agayne.
At Agyncourte the Frenssh hym mette sertayne,
And with hym faught with hoste innomerable,
Whare thay were take and wonne withouten fable.

The Duke was take that day of Orlience,
The Duke also of Burboyne certaynly,
The Erle Wendome that was of grete credence,
And Sir Arthur of Bretayn sykyrly,
The Dukes brother of Bretayn verryly,
With many mo of other prisoners
That taken wer as sayne Cronyclers.

The Dukes thre of Bare and Alaunson
And of Loreyne were in that batayle slayn,
And for thaire lyfes thay payde no more raunson,
Who to thayre wyfes so more cam nought agayne,
Bot on that grounde thar dyed thay certayn.
Fourty thousonde thar layde thair lyfes to wedde;
For thair raunson me thought thay had wele spedde.

On oure syde was of Yorke Duke Edward Slayne,
A myghty lorde and Full of Sapience,
And few elles mo of Englisshe men certayne,
As I consayue that were of Reuerence;
That was bot grace of Goddes omnipotence,

For Englisshe men nyne thousond noght excede
That faught agayne an hundre thousonde in dede.

Nota the date of the Batayll of Agencourte, whan it was
[The above rubric continues with a Latin account of the French
nobles taken or slain.]

On Seynt Crispyne and Crispynyan Day
This batayle sore certanly was smyten
At Agyncourte, as thay withsette his way,
For whiche the kynge gan fight as wele was wyten
With thaym anone, whare were slayne vnsmyten
Thousondes smored thurgh thayre multitude,
That wolde haue fledde fro his excelsitude.

4 The death of Henry V, foll. 215v-216

*How the kynge fell seke, made his devyse, and dyed at Boys Vyn-
cent, leuynge the Kynge and Quene of Fraunce, the Lord Crom-
well thaire Gouernour and keper*

Genyus, god of all humayne nature,
No thynge myght stretche his lyfe forto solace,
So all repose by cruell coniecture
The threde of lyfe in mydde dyd breke and Race,
Whiche Lathesis had sponne, and gan out lace
Parcas Systres, amonge whom suche envye
Es, what oon spynth the tother breketh in hy.

So than the deth anone hym dyd assayle
With peynes stronge that he ne myght endure
Ne farrer fle, his body to prevayle,
Bot oonly to the Erthe and Sepulture,
Whiche is the kynde of all flesshy fygure
And kyndely place agayne forto retorne
Whan that the soule with God shall euer soiorne.

Afore his deth he had his sacrementes
In all hole fayth and Cristen hole creance,
And of his londes made sure establismentes
To bene gouernde after his ordynaunce,
To tyme his sonne had age and gouernaunce
To reule thaym all by wysdome and manhede;
Whose age so than thre quarters noght excede;

Of whom he made his keper and Custode
Of Excestre the Duke Beauford, men kende,
To gouerne hym in alkyns worthihode,
As to suche prynce of reson shuld appende,
Tyll that his age to gouerne couth pretende

His Remes two of Englond and of Fraunce
And other londes that ow hym obeysshance.

The Duke also his brother of Bedforde
He made Regent of Fraunce and Normandy,
The Muntagu manly of dede and worde
That Erle was than called of Salesbyry,
The Erle also of Suffolke full manly,
With lordes fele to his estate attende
In all that myght to gode reule ought extende.

Of Auguste than the laste day so byfell,
This noble prynce regnynge in his tenth yere,
His soule, I trow, thurgh peynes smert and fell
That slew his corse went to the blysse full clere,
As by his werkes it doth right wele appere,
That loued euere in Cristen fayth and lawe,
Kepynge the pese in all his londes thurgh awe.

So dyed he than in Fraunce at Boys Vyncent,
Whare he had in his reule and gouernance
Syr Charles, Kynge of Fraunce, in gode intent,
And Isabell the Quene, to that fynance,
Thayr hiegh estates to kepe in all surance
Tyll deth thaym toke, that after dyed anone
For thought they had fro he was fro thaym gone.

*How the quene, the Kyng of Scottes, the Duke off Excestre, with
other lordes broght home the kynges bones to London*

The Quene so than of Englond, Kateryne,
With knyghtes feel and Squyers of gode names,
With ladyse fayre and maydyns femynyne,
The Kynge also of Scottes that hight Sir Iames,
Thomas Bewforde, that bare that tyme grete fames,
That Duke was than of Excester of myght,
This kynges bones to Englond brought than right.

Wyth worship grete and holy exequyse
Ay whare thay lay grete Almonse and expense
Thay gafe eche day in gode and deuoute wyse,
And beried hym with moste hiegh reuerence
At Westmynster, whare by his provydence
Laste beynge thare devysed his sepulture
Lyke Edwarde Fyrste withouten depycture.

[For the rest of Hardyng's praise of Henry V and his admonition to
Henry VI, see Kingsford, 1Hard 744–746.]

Dedicatory epistle for Pietro Carmeliano's versified life
of St. Catherine of Alexandria (*Beatae Katerine
Egyptiae, Christi Sponsae, uita*),
Bodleian MS. Laud Misc. 501, foll. 1v-2v.

Magnifico atque excellenti uiro Domino Roberto Bracunbure,
turris London. rectori meritissimo, Petrus Carmelianus
Salutem plurimam Dicit.

Solent omnes, uir insignis, qui opus aliquod nuperrime ediderint,
alicui principi et doctrinas et doctos uiros excolenti illud dedicare.
Quocirca et ego illorum uestigia imitatus, cum paulo antea Libellum
de beatae Katerinae Aegyptiae, Christi Sponsae, uita composuissem,
Serenissimo regi nostro Ricardo tercio illum consacraui. Neminem
enim eo digniorem principem inueni cui libellus meus dedicaretur.
Sed ne uideamur absque ratione Maiestatem suam extollere, tu ipse,
uir sapientissime, mihi ipsi testis eris an uera uel uana feram. Si
religionem inprimis spectamus, quem nam aetas nostra principem
magis religiosum habet? Si iusticiam, quem sibi in toto terrarum orbe
praeponendum putabimus? Si et pacis seruandae et gerendorum
bellorum prudentiam intueramur quem sibi unquam parem adiudi-
cabimus? Si uero animi tum sapientiam tum magnitudinem simul
et modestiam inspexerimus, cui regem nostrum Ricardum post-
ponemus? Quis sane christianus imperator aut princeps in bene-
meritos magis liberalis munificusque comprobari potest? Nemo, sane,
nemo. Cui magis furta, latrocinia, stupra, adulteria, homicidia,
fenus, heresisque et alia nephandissima scelera exosa sunt quam
sibi? Nemini, plane. Opusculum igitur meum non ab re suae Su-
blimitati ascripsi atque presentaui.

Caeterum cum non ignorarem Magnificentiam tuam maximae
auctoritatis apud suam Celsitudinem esse, atque mihi pro sua
benignitate plurimum afficere, uisum fuit mihi ut eiusdem opusculi
nostri exemplum tibi unum hoc Christi natali transmitterem, te
quoque rogatum facerem ut Serenissimo regi me notum ac com-
mendatum faceres. Scripsi itaque manu propria hoc exemplum, quod

in diuturnam mei tibi deditissimi memoriam seruares. Qui si in posterum quicquam operis fabricauero te profecto studiorum meorum et laborum participem faciam.

Reliquum est, Vir egregie, ut me inopiamque meam commendatam habere digneris, uelis quoque meus esse Maecenas, hoc est, protector. Nisi equidem tales uiri sicuti es mihi opem ferant, ab omni prorsus spe destitutum mē esse perspicio. Qui si aliquando maiestati regiae me cognitum feceris, spero illud fore ut perpetuo gaudeas te mihi opitulatum esse.

At ne longior sim, finem epistolae faciam, et Summum mundi Opificem precabor ut te et consortem tuam nobilissimam liberosque felices seruet et incolumes.

Vale, Decus meum.

Parua solent magnis semper dare munera parui;
Paruus ego magno do tibi parua uiro.
[Illumination of St. Catherine holding sword and wheel]
Sponsa Dei Katerina, Deum mihi redde benignum,
Et crebras pro me, te rogo, funde preces.

Petri Carmeliani Brixiensis poetæ Suasoria
Æneæ ad anglium pro sublatis bellis ciuilibus et Arthuro principe nato epistola.

Nglia post tātas clades rātasq̃ ruinas
Et tot cognata prælia facta manu
Stirpis et innumeras gentis utriq̃ neces
Te superum rector tandem profpexit ab alto
Cum faces esset tam miseranda tibi
Vndiq̃ ciuili cum sanguine terra maderet.
Inq̃ tuis populis Luctus ubiq̃ foret
Cum genitrix natum natus flereq̃ parētes
Et fratrem frater, nupta pudica uirus;
Filius et patrem fratrem,quandoq̃ necaret
Frater furens iret in omnē nefas

Pietro Carmeliano, Epistle to England urging her
to rejoice over the end of the civil wars and the birth
of Prince Arthur, British Museum Additional MS. 33736

[The first page of text is faced by the illumination shown here.
Two angels support the combined arms of England and France,
surrounded by red and white roses, with Henry VII's silver greyhound below; his red dragon (the badge of Wales) is looking on
from the opposite page. See above, Chap. III, n. 63.]

[fol. 2]
*Petri Carmeliani Brixiensis poetae Suasoria Laeticiae ad Angliam
pro sublatis bellis ciuilibus et Arthuro principe nato epistola*

Anglia, post tantas clades tantasque ruinas
   Et tot cognata praelia facta manu,
Post odium antiquum geminae de sanguine regum
   Stirpis et innumeras gentis utrinque neces,
Te superum Rector tandem prospexit ab alto,
   Cum facies esset tam miseranda tibi,
Vndique ciuili cum sanguine terra maderet,
   Inque tuis populis Luctus ubique foret;
Cum genitrix natum, natus fleretque parentem,
   Et fratrem frater, nupta pudica uirum;
Filius et patrem, fratrem quandoque necaret
   Frater, et ira furens iret in omne nefas;
[fol. 2v]
Cumque Duces etiam, proceres simul atque iacerent,
   Et foret extinctus nobilitatis honos.
Hic, ubi conspexit tot fortia corpora passim
   Strata solo, et passim feruere bella magis,
Protinus auertit uultus oculosque retorsit,
   Iam fera non patiens facta uidere Deus.
"Sit modus his," dixit, "bellis tantoque furori.

Romanos satis est exuperasse Duces;
Non gener atque Socer, quamuis ea bella fuerunt
   Maxima, non Marius, non quoque Sylla ferox
Hauserunt tantum romani sanguinis unquam,
   Imperium Licet his, uis quoque maior erat."
His dictis, diuos caelesti in sede Locatos
   Conuocat, atque sedens talia uerba refert.

Oratio Summi opificis Dei ad caetum sanctorum

[fol. 3]
[*Laus Angliae*]
"Anglia, terrarum regio Pulcherrima mundi,
   Terra potens armis atque opulenta, ferax,
Quae reliquas orbis partes contemnere possit,
   Et cui conferri patria nulla potest,
In partes diuisa duas, de principe semper
   Certat, et in nullo tempore Marte uacat.
Sunt geminae soboles regum de sanguine ductae,
   Regiaque ex titulis utraque sceptra petit.
Hanc populi pars una fouet, pars altera at illam,
   Atque fauet dominis bellica turba suis;
Vna domum sequitur cui dat Lancastria nomen,
   Cui regnum Brutus principiumque dedit;
Altera progeniem fouet et tutatur in armis
   Eboracensem, fortia bella mouens.
Sic semper gladios inter uersatur et enses
   Anglia, terra ferox, indomitumque genus,
[fol. 3v]
Paulatimque suos proceres dominosque trucidat,
   Frondibus et populus densior ipse cadit.
Ac nisi forsan opem sibi det mea maxima cura,
   Orba uiris paruo tempore tellus erit.
Hos ego non patiar populos occumbere prorsus,
   Ne pereant pariter debita sacra mihi.
Mens mea Longaeuam cogitat componere pacem.
   Dicite quo melius pax queat esse modo.
Haec causa est cur uos ad me, sacra turba, uocaui,
   Diceret ut mentem quilibet ordo suam."

Responsio Sanctorum ad Deum

Dixerat. Alma cohors sic protinus incipit: "Atqui
   Non opus est nobis, omnipotens Genitor;
Singula namque uides, per te tu singula nosti,
   Nilque latet numen praeterit aut ue tuum.
Si qua tamen tibi cura manet consulere quenquam
[fol. 4]
   Nostrum, consilijs atque adhibere tuis,
Henricus poterit Sextus tibi cuncta referre,
   Anglica qui quondam regia sceptra tulit,
Qui patriam nouit, populos populique furores,

Continuam geminae dissidiamque domus,
  Qui fuit illarum princeps, deductus ab una,
    Hostili cecidit quique deinde manu.
Is melius poterit quam nos ea bella britanna
    Quo tolli possint dicere nempe modo."
Finierant. Placuere Deo sanctissima uerba,
  Spectat et Henricum, mox iubet atque loqui.

Oratio Diui Henrici Sexti ad Deum

Ille refert: "O summe Pater que hominum que deorum,
    Qui caelum et terras et freta uasta regis,
Postquam me caeli dignatus honore fuisti,
    Gloria mortalis uanaque uisa mihi est;
[fol. 4v]
Contempsi terras pariter terrenaque regna
    Et male gesta mea lubrica sceptra manu.
At quia pax sancta est, patriaeque imponere pacem
    Est tibi cura meae, tollereque arma paras,
Vera feram: patriae et generis sanctissima tangit
    Me pietas; grata est et tua cura mihi.
Ast igitur dicam, quamuis, Deus, omnia nosti,
    Qua queat hic tolli bellicus arte furor.
Est opus ut geminae proles iungantur in unam,
    Fiat et ex geminis aedibus una domus.
Ardua res quondam, facilis sed tempore in isto est,
    Commoditas maior nec fuit ulla prius.
Extinctus Quartus regum fortissimus ille est
    Qui mihi de manibus abstulit imperium;
Hic moriens, fratri natos commisit utrosque;
    Hos male commissos perdidit ille ferox.
[fol. 5]
Atque ubi de medio dominos geminosque nepotes
    Sustulit, assumpsit non sua regna sibi.
Is est qui gladio sceleratus in ilia misso
    Me quoque confodit, promptus ad omne nefas.
Sed mea ne uidear recitando damna dolere,
    Quo fueram ueniam, propositumque sequar:
Nulla ex Eduardo superest iam mascula proles
    Quae populis possit imperitare suis;
Filia prima manet natu, pulcherrima uirgo,
    Nubilis Elisabet, bis duo lustra tenens,
Quae docta et sapiens plus quam sua tempora poscunt
    Fratribus extinctis ius genitoris habet.
Hic status unius stirpis de sanguine regum;
    Accipias igitur quis status alterius.
Dum captum celsa me Quartus in arce teneret
    Et manibus ferret regia sceptra suis,
[fol. 5v]
Expulsus pridem Eduardus meus, unica proles,
    Armatus redijt iura paterna petens.

Sed male pugnauit — sibi nam sua fata negabant
   Regna dari. Captus, caesus ab hoste fuit.
Mox ego confossus, soboles ut nostra periret
   Prorsus, et extinctum ius genus atque foret.
Sed tibi cura meum fuit asseruare nepotem
   Henricum, Quarti dum fugeret gladios.
Hic puer existens placidus, richmundia proles,
   Ad Gallos fugiens turgida uela dedit,
Sed sua cum medium pelagi ratis ipsa secaret,
   Pyratis casu fit noua praeda maris;
Adque Ducem fertur (fuerant sic fata) Britannum
   Captiuus ueniens carceribusque datur.
Sic tibi tum placuit puerum obiectare periclis,
   Casibus et uarijs exagitare, Pater,
[fol. 6]
Fortius ut iuuenis tolerare pericula posset,
   Vinceret et durus fortia cuncta Labor.
Hic heres regni restat de sanguine nostro:
   Magnanimus, praestans, nobilis, atque decens,
Integer, ac fortis, iustus, patiensque Laborum,
   Clemens, facundus, munificusque, pius.
Si tibi, summe Pater, cura est imponere pacem
   Anglis quae nullo sit moritura die,
Henricum tandem de carcere solue nepotem,
   Et iube ut armatus debita iura petat
Ac patrium repetat regnum, saeuumque tyrannum
   Expellat, patriam restituatque suam.
Eduardi accipiat Quarti pro coniuge natam
   Elisabet, titulum quae genitoris habet;
Sic solus gemino fiet de sanguine sanguis,
   Vna domus posthaec imperiumque petet."

[fol. 6v]

Finis Orationis Diui Henrici Sexti et illius approbatio

Finierat Sextus. Placuerunt uerba Tonanti,
   Atque ait: "Una mihi mens manet atque tibi;
Dicta puta quaecumque mones; curabimus, inquam,
   Vt faciant rebus haec tua dicta fidem.
Adde quod efficiam sceleratus ut ille tyrannus
   In te sacrilega qui tulit arma manu
Henrico meritas soluat pro crimine poenas,
   Manibus exsoluat inferiasque tuis."

Executio Diuinae sententiae

Nec mora, captiuus de carcere soluitur heros,
   Atque iter ad Gallos gallicaque arua facit.
Huc ubi peruenit comitatus milite paruo,
   In Karoli amplexum principis ille uolat,
Auxiliumque petit quo ius proauitaque regna

Vendicet, in patriam nauiget atque suam.
At Karolus, cum sit consanguinitate propinqus,
[fol. 7]
  Gaudeat et tali principe, spondet opem.
Non minus Henricum grauitas, generosaque uerba,
  Et uirtus, species, nobilitasque iuuant.
Interea proceres, damnantes facta tyranni,
  Henrico cupiunt regia sceptra dari.
Henrici gaudent audito nomine multi,
  Atque iter ad Gallos plurima turba capit.
Ianque patet Classis; puppim iam Septimus intrat,
  Et dextro primum cum pede carpit iter.
Ianque uiris naues epulisque implentur et armis,
  Ianque Deus misso fulmine signa facit.
Iam sparsa e summo dependent Carbasa malo,
  Iamque Nothus properans candida uela ferit.
[Portus Milford]
Sulcat aquas Classis, paruoque in tempore portum
  Intrat quem Milford incola turba uocat.
Protinus ecce sonant immensa tonitrua caelo
[fol. 7v]
  Signaque uictricis dant manifesta manus.

[Oratio Serenissimi Henrici Septimi ad natalem patriam in reditu
ab exilio]

Vt uidet Henricus portum tetigisse carinas
  Et natale solum Conspicit ante oculos,
Vix tenuit Lachrymas, patriae correptus amore,
  Et caput inclinans, "Anglia," dixit, "Aue!
Ad te post longos redeo multosque labores,
  Insons exilium per tria Lustra ferens.
Me, precor, alma parens, animo me sume benigno,
  Et faueas titulis, saepe uocata, meis.
Sum tua progenies, tuus et generosus alumnus;
  Regia sceptra peto debita iure mihi.
Non te commoueant quae tot portauimus arma —
  Insidias nullas nullaque damna time.
Albus aper tantum gladijs iugulabitur istis,
  Reddat ut inuitus quae male sceptra tenet."
[Finis orationis]
His dictis, puppim linquens terram pede pressit,
[fol. 8]
  Osculaque infigit cum pietate solo.
Hinc belli socios proceres atque arma recenset,
  Pro meritis spondens praemia cuique suis.
Parua mora est; gelidas cursu superauerat alpes
  Seque suos reficit potibus atque cibis.
Fama uolans dirum subito ut peruenit ad hostem,
  Conuocat armatos bellicaque arma parat.
Arma parat frustra — quis enim se uincere sanctos

Posse putet bello, consilium ue Dei?
Crimina praeterea tot tot commiserat ut mens
  Peccati et sceleris conscia uicta foret.
Ast animum simulat, fugiens ne crimina prodat
  Seque simul tacitus indicet esse reum.
Obuius ergo parat certamina maxima, quamuis
  Praelia non animus sed pudor ipse facit.
Vt breuibus dicam (neque enim mens dicere cuncta est,
[fol. 8v]
  Nec sumpsi ut bellum scriberet istud opus),
Septimus Henricus postquam peruenit ad hostem
  Atque inimica sibi cernere signa potest,
Vicinum subito fertur galeatus in hostem,
  Et patrui poenas sumit ab hoste sui.

[*Mors tyranni*]

Ianque aper extinctus sceleratus et ille tyrannus,
  Et iacet in sicca sanguinolentus humo.
Iam regni proceres, populi Iuuenesque senesque
  Exultant, gaudet femina uirque, puer;
Vndique concurrunt gentes ut cernere possint
  Qui nuper uenit principis ora sui.
Quotquot conspiciunt, "Tanta est praestantia formae,
  Non hominis," dicunt, "est, sed imago dei!"
Confestimque uocant regem regem que salutant,
  Nec possunt oculos exsaciare suos.
Non sic spectantes retinebant ora Medusae,
[fol. 9]
Si tamen ut fertur fabula uera fuit,
[*Comparationes*]
Non rutilis tantum radijs corruscat Apollo
  Exutus nebulis, sit deus ipse licet.
Henricum toto despectant sidera caelo,
  Gaudet et aduentu sol quoque luna suo;
Non pluuias illo quis cernere tempore posset;
  Seruabat clarum candida Luna diem.

[*Parliamentum: Declaratur Henricus septimus rex Angliae*]

Conueniunt proceres regni dominique potentes,
  Henricum regem constituuntque suum,
Huncque rogant Quarti natam pro coniuge ducat
  Elisabet, titulos colliget atque duos,
Vt sileant tandem tot tot ciuilia bella
  Et redeat regno Pax opulenta suo.

[*Nuptiae fiunt*]

Annuit ille pijs precibus regnoque petenti
  Praeponens uotis publica uota suis.
Nam potuit soceros quos uellet in orbe parare,

[fol. 9v]

Dotis et immensum pondus habere simul.
Sed satis est diues Rex quem sibi subdita regna
    Obseruant, metuunt, concelebrantque, colunt.
Prospicit oblatam dominam uisamque pererrat
    Luminibus totam, foederaque icta probat.

[*Comparationes*]

Talis erat facies qualem finxere Dianam
    Venantem uates dum sua lustra petit.
Quae Cassandra sibi uel quae Lucretia uel quae
    Penelopae similis aut Galathea fuit?
Quamuis ille prius speciem formamque futurae
    Coniugis audierat, pictaque mente foret,
Ante oculos tamen illa suos magis urget amantem,
    Vicinoque magis fomite crescit amor.
Nec minus ipsa suum spectans dominumque maritum
    Ardet amore sui regia uirgo uiri.
Ambobus pariter sunt uincla iugalia curae,

[fol. 10]

    Et damnant taciti tempora Longa nimis.

[*Dispensatio ab Innocentio octauo Summo pontifice facta*]

Obstabat tantum sacrae reuerentia Legis,
    Nam fuerat quarto iunctus uterque gradu;
Romanus princeps Christi summusque sacerdos
    Dat ueniam, celebrant foedera sancta thori.

[*Natiuitas principis Arthuri*]

Moxque tumet uenter; renouat sua cornua Phoebae,
    Atque implet nouies; nascitur ecce puer.
Nascitur ecce puer quo non generosior alter
    Seu matrem quaeras seu magis ipse patrem.
Nascitur ecce puer gemino de sanguine regum,
    Firma salus regni perpetuumque decus.

*Exortatio Laeticiae ad Angliam pro nato principe et rege ac
Regina nobilissimis*

Ad te iam redeo, regio celeberrima mundi,
    Anglia, terra potens, insula diues opum;
Deponas faciem tristem Longasque querelas,
    Signaque Laeticiae post mala tanta moue.

[fol. 10v]

Nascitur ecce puer per quem Pax sancta resurgit,
    Ciuilisque cadit tempus in omne furor.
Arthurus redijt per saecula tanta sepultus,
    Qui regum mundi prima Corona fuit.
Ille licet corpus terris et membra dedisset
    Viuebat toto semper in orbe tamen.

Arthurum quisquis praedixerat esse secundo
   Venturum uates maximus ille fuit.
Arthuri nomen terras penetrauit in omnes;
   Perpetuum faciunt fortia facta uirum.
Aurea iam redeunt cum principe Saecula tanto,
   Quaeque diu Latuit iam dea uirgo redit.
Bellica iam tandem redijt cum principe uirtus,
   Antiqumque decus, Anglia pulchra, tuum.
Vt primum Arthurus iuueniles sumpserit annos,
   Atque humeris poterit arma tenere suis,
Sub iuga uicinos hostes multosque remotos
[fol. 11]
   Mittet, et imperium proferet ille suum.
Gesta patris uincet, proauos superabit et omnes;
   Arthuri et ueteris gloria cedet ei.
Indue Purpureas pro nato principe uestes,
   Anglia; cesset opus, sit tibi festa dies;
Thura Deo et Laudes pro tanto munere redde;
   Cantibus et uarijs debita sacra face.
"Salue, festa dies," dicas, "qua pristina regni
   Gloria paxque redit, cessat et omne nefas;
Salue, festa dies, per quam ciuilia bella
   Tolluntur, Concors totaque terra manet."
Anglia, sume iocos, placidasque resume choreas;
   Sume dapes largas; dulcia uina bibe.
In triuijs pueri saltantes carmina cantent,
   Et feriant tenera tergora dura manu.
Femina, uirque, Senex, Iuuenis, puer, atque puella
[fol. 11v]
   Adsit, natalem concelebretque diem.

[*Conclusio operis*]

Sed Longo nimium ne te sermone fatigem,
   Anglia, cognoscas maxima dona Dei.
Rex, Regina, Puer uno tibi contigit anno,
   Quos quicunque uidet dixerit esse deos.
Funde preces igitur Christo Dominoque potenti;
   Principibus donet saecula Longa tuis.
Sic quoque tu uiues faelix, Ducesque triumphos,
   Viuet et aeternum Fama decusque tuum.

                    Finis

Canceled portion of Polydore Vergil's *Anglica historia*
dealing with the death of the Duke of Clarence,
Vatican Library cod. urbin. lat. 498, fol. 210v.

Cum illud potius accidisse credendum sit, quod Deus, iratus aut ob
periurium Edwardi quod Eboraci fecerat, ut superius monstratum est,
aut ob caedem tot principum, qui inter factiones perierant, uel
denique ob necem Henrici sexti principisque Edwardi eius filij, ita
fieri permisit ut frater fratrem ac patruus nepotes, uti in uita ipsius
Ricardi infra dicetur, crudeli morte e medio tolleret; quo demum
nobilissima domus Eboracensis proprio maculata sanguine regnare,
prout breui mox factum est, desineret. Alij uero aliam ferunt caedis
causam [*the following is more heavily canceled*] quae huiusmodi
est: Rex Edwardus, pacato iam regno, cum nullos haberet hostes quos
uinceret, solebat ut curis bellicis liberatus quandoque secum longa
cogitatione reuoluere quanta ob adipiscendum regnum uitae dis-
crimina adiuisset; et inter haec saepius animo subibat proditio
fratris in se; ex quo fiebat ut eum minus amaret, idque aliquando
per aspectum non laetum ipsi Duci significabat, atque alijs, quos
magis familiares maiorique in honore habebat, uerbis iracundis
declarabat. Cum ita saepius

[The account stops abruptly at the end of the folio. On fol. 211, Vergil
starts afresh by recounting the opinion of those who thought that the
trouble started when Edward interfered with Clarence's plans to
marry the daughter of the Duke of Burgundy; this report is carried
over into the printed versions.]

Bibliography

The following list includes the chronicles and literary historical works of the fifteenth and sixteenth centuries which are dealt with in this investigation. Shortened references are given in parentheses, except when consisting of the first word in the entry.

(RS = Rolls Series; EETS = Early English Text Society; CS = Camden Society.)

Agincourt. See *The Battle of Agincourt.*

André, Bernard. *Historia regis Henrici septimi.* Ed. James Gairdner, in *Memorials of King Henry the Seventh.* RS 10 (London 1858). Written ca. 1500–1502. Favorable to Lancastrians and Henry VII (against Yorkists).

Arrival of Edward IV. *History of the Arrival of Edward IV in England and the Final Recovery of His Kingdoms from Henry VI, A.D. 1471.* Ed. John Bruce. CS 1.1 (London 1838). Favors Edward IV against the Lancastrians. Used by Stow. Also used in a history by W. Fleetwood, which in turn was used by Holinshed.

Audelay, John. *A Recollection of Henry V.* Ed. R. H. Robbins, in *Historical Poems of the Fourteenth and Fifteenth Centuries* (New York 1959) 108–110. Written in 1429. Honors Henry V and Henry VI.

Baldwin, William, et al. (Mirror). *The Mirror for Magistrates.* Ed. Lily B. Campbell. Cambridge 1938. Includes the editions of 1559–1587.

The Battle of Agincourt (1–2Agincourt). Laudatory poem on Henry V's French campaigns; in two versions: (1) attributed to John Lydgate, printed by Nicolas and Tyrrell in CLn 214–233; (2) given in W. C. Hazlitt, *Remains of the Early Popular Poetry of England* (London 1866) 88–108. Cf. also the versions printed by Hearne in PsElmham 359–375, and by R. H. Robbins, *Historical Poems of the Fourteenth and Fifteenth Centuries* (New York 1959) 91–92.

Berners, Lord (Sir John Bourchier). *The Chronicle of Froissart.* Ed. William P. Ker. Vol. 6. London 1903. Translated 1523–1525. Used by Shakespeare. See Froissart.

Blakman, John. *Collectarium mansuetudinum et bonorum morum regis Henrici VI.* Ed. and trans. M. R. James, *Henry the Sixth.* Cambridge 1919. First printed in 1510. Contemporary reports laudatory of Henry VI. Possibly used by Vergil; used by Fleming via Stow in 2Hol.

The Brut or the Chronicles of England. Ed. Friedrich W. D. Brie. Vol. 2 (EETS 136). London 1908. The various MSS differ in their emphases, but are usually in favor of the reigning monarch. MS. G (1419–1461) is the latest and most important, especially for its Yorkist tendencies and its use by Caxton in his edition (1Caxton).

——— (Brut k). Variants of the *Brut* published by Kingsford, *English Historical Literature in the Fifteenth Century* (Oxford 1913) 299–337. The Latin *Brut* for the reign of Henry V (323–337) seems to have been used by Tito Livio.

——— Davies' Chronicles (q.v.).

Capgrave, John (1Capgrave). *Liber de illustribus Henricis.* Ed. Francis C. Hingeston. RS 7 (London 1858). The portion on the three Lancastrians (Henry IV, Henry V, and Henry VI) was written ca. 1422–1447 and is very favorable to them.

——— (2Capgrave). *The Chronicle of England.* Ed. Francis C. Hingeston. RS 1 (London 1858). Written ca. 1462–63. Wholly in favor of Edward IV, but with some Lancastrian sentiments taken over from 1–2Wals.

Carmeliano, Pietro. *Beatae Katerinae aegyptiae, Christi sponsae, vita.* Bod. MS. Laud misc. 501. The dedicatory epistle (Appendix B above), written ca. 1483–84, is laudatory of Richard III.

——— *Suasoria laetitiae ad Angliam pro sublatis bellis civilibus et Arthuro principe nato epistola.* B.M. Add. MS. 33.736 (Appendix C above). Written ca. 1486. Favors Henry VI and Henry VII against the Yorkists.

Caxton, William (1Caxton). *The Chronicles of England.* Edition of the *Brut,* first printed in 1480. References will be to Brie's edition of the *Brut.*

——— (2Caxton). "The Eighth Book of the Polychronicon from Caxton" in *Polychronicon Ranulphi Higden.* Ed. Joseph Rawson Lumby. RS 41.8 (London 1882) 522–587. Caxton's continuation of Trevisa, extending from 1377 to 1461, more or less following MSS. C and G of Brie's edition of the *Brut,* but with additions, notably from the *Traïson.* First printed in 1482. References common to 1–2Caxton will be to 2Caxton.

Chaplain's Account. See Gesta.

Chronicque de la traïson et mort de Richart deux roy Dengleterre (Traïson). Ed. and trans. Benjamin Williams. English Historical Society. London 1846. Covers 1397–1400; written by a partisan of Richard II, attacking Henry IV. Used by Caxton, Fabyan, Stow, Holinshed, and probably by Hall.

Chronicles of London (CL). See the various editions following. Their interpretations vary according to the times in which they were written, and usually favor the ruling regime.

—— (CLf). *Six Town Chronicles of England*. Ed. Ralph Flenley. Oxford 1911.

—— (CLgaird). A Chronicle of London in *Three Fifteenth-century Chronicles*. Ed. James Gairdner. CS 2.28 (London 1880). Ends in the fourth year of the reign of Edward IV. Yorkist tendencies.

—— (CLgreat). *The Great Chronicle of London*. Ed. A. H. Thomas and I. D. Thornley. London 1938. Goes to 1512 and reflects varying points of view. Used by Fabyan (and probably compiled by him), Hall (in another version), and Stow.

—— (CLgreg). Gregory's Chronicle. Ed. James Gairdner, in *The Historical Collections of a Citizen of London in the Fifteenth Century*. CS 2.17 (London 1876) 57–239.

—— (CLk). *Chronicles of London*. Ed. Charles L. Kingsford. Oxford 1905.

—— (CLn). *A Chronicle of London, from 1089 to 1483*. [Ed. Sir Nicholas Harris Nicolas and Edward Tyrrell.] London 1827.

Les cronicques de Normendie, 1223–1453 (CdeNorm). Ed. A. Hellot. Rouen 1881. Varying allegiances.

Comines, Philip de. *The Memoirs of Philip de Comines*. Ed. Andrew R. Scoble. 2 vols. London 1906. For the French, see the edition of Joseph Calmette. 3 vols. Paris 1924–25. Covers 1464 to 1498; written ca. 1489–1498. In general favors Lancaster and Tudor against York. Used by Hall.

Créton, Jean. *Histoire du roy d'Angleterre Richard*. Ed. and trans. John Webb, *Archaeologia* 20 (1824) 1–423. Covers 1399–1400. Written ca. 1400. Highly favorable to Richard II.

Croyland Chronicle Continuations (Croy). *Ingulph's Chronicle of the Abbey of Croyland, with the Continuations by Peter of Blois and Anonymous Writers*. Trans. Henry T. Riley. London 1854. The Latin text is in Vol. I of *Rerum anglicarum scriptores veterum*. [Ed. William Fulman at the request of John Fell.] Oxford 1684. The second continuation, by the Prior of Croyland, covers 1388–1469 (written in 1469), and is generally Yorkist. The third continuation, in large part seemingly by Bishop John Russell, covers ca. 1469–1486 (written 1486) and varies in allegiance (Lancaster, York, and Tudor). The fourth continuation is fragmentary. Perhaps used by PV.

Daniel, Samuel (0–3Dan). *The Civil Wars*. Ed. Laurence Michel. New Haven 1958. References are to book and stanza of the third edition of 1609 (3Dan), except for the prefaces, where page numbers are cited. Unless otherwise noted, the variants used are those of the first edition of 1595 (1Dan), which Shakespeare seems to have used. (0Dan = MS; 2Dan = second edition of 1601).

Davies' Chronicle (Davies). *An English Chronicle of the Reigns of Richard II, Henry IV, Henry V, and Henry VI*. Ed. John Silvester Davies. CS 1.64 (London 1856). Written before 1471. The chronicle is a continuation of the *Brut;* it draws on the *Eulogium* for the reigns of Richard II and Henry IV. Used by Stow and perhaps by Hall. Yorkist in tone.

Davies of Hereford, John. *Microcosmos.* Ed. A. B. Grosart, *Complete Works* (London 1878) 1.23–88. Written in 1603. Critical of most pre-Tudor kings except Henry V.

Deschamps, Eustace. *Ballade de Eustace Deschamps, dit Morel, de la mort du roy Richart Dangleterre.* Ed. Benjamin Williams, Traïson lxxiv n. 3. Protest against Henry IV for killing Richard II.

Dieulacres Chronicle. *Chronicle of Dieulacres Abbey, 1381–1403.* Ed. M. V. Clarke and V. H. Galbraith, in "The Deposition of Richard II," *Bulletin of the John Rylands Library* 14:125–181 (1930). An English Cistercian chronicle by two authors. Author A (1387–1400) is a strong partisan of Richard II, whereas author B (continuation to 1403) strongly favors Henry IV.

Elmham, Thomas (1Elmham). *Liber metricus de Henrico quinto.* Ed. C. A. Cole, in *Memorials of Henry the Fifth.* RS 11 (London 1858). Draws on the Chaplain's *Gesta* (see Galbraith, 2Wals xxiii n. 2). Praises Henry V.

—— (2Elmham). *On the Death of Henry IV.* Ed. Thomas Wright, *Political Poems and Songs.* RS 14.2 (London 1861) 118–123. Written ca. 1420. Gives advice to Henry V, with a favorable view of Henry IV.

—— See Gesta and PsElmham.

Eulogium Continuation (Eul). *Eulogium (Historiarum sive temporis).* Ed. F. S. Haydon. RS 9.3 (London 1863). Covers 1361–1413. Lancastrian, but with Franciscan and clerical elements that can be read as anti-Lancastrian. Used by Davies' Chronicle.

Evesham's History. *Historia vitae et regni Richardi II Angliae regis, a monacho quodam de Evesham consignata.* Ed. Thomas Hearne. Oxford 1729. Goes to 1402. Lancastrian.

Fabyan, Robert. *The New Chronicles of England and France.* Ed. Sir Henry Ellis. London 1811. Fabyan died in 1513; this work was printed in 1516, 1533, 1542, and 1559 (the last two editions are Protestantized). His views are usually those of his sources, except when he opposes French views. Draws on Brut (Caxton), Traïson, CdeNorm, Gaguin, CLgreat (see CLgreat, introduction). Used by Hall, Mirror, 1–2Hol, and Shakespeare.

Fleming, Abraham. See Holinshed.

Froissart, John (Frois). *Chronicles of England, France,* etc. Trans. Thomas Johnes. Vol. 2. London 1868. (See also Berners.) Extends to 1400. In general favors Richard II. Used by Vergil, Daniel, Shakespeare, etc.

Gaguin, Robert. *Compendium Roberti Gaguini super Francorum gestis.* Paris 1501. Sparse; pro-French. Used by Fabyan, Vergil, Hall, Mirror.

Gesta (Chaplain's Account). *Henrici quinti Angliae regis gesta.* Ed. Benjamin Williams. English Historical Society. London 1850. Covers 1413–1416; laudatory account of Henry V, by one of his chaplains. (The continuation to 1432 is probably based on PsElmham.) Influenced 1Elmham (and is sometimes ascribed to Elmham; see Galbraith, 2Wals xxiii n. 2).

Gigli, Giovanni. *Epithalamium de nuptiis serenissimi et clementissimi principis et domini, domini Henrici, Dei gratia Angliae et Franciae regis, etc., eius nominis septimi, et serenissimae dominae Elisabet, eius uxoris, reginae.* B. M. Harl. MS. 336. Written in 1486. Excerpted by James Gairdner, André lviii–lx, along with two epigrams on the name of Arthur. Helped formulate the Tudor myth.

Giles' Chronicle. *Incerti scriptoris chronicon Angliae de regnis trium regum lancastrensium, Henrici IV, Henrici V, et Henrici VI.* Ed. John Allen Giles. London 1848. Analyzed by Clarke, Dieulacres 146–153. The section on Henry V is the Chaplain's *Gesta.* Unless otherwise specified, references are to the first section (on Henry IV), in which there is a guarded sympathy for Richard II; it was possibly compiled by a member of the Scrope family. Perhaps an indirect influence on Hall.

Gower, John. *Vox clamantis* and *Chronica tripertita.* Ed. G. C. Macaulay in *The Complete Works of John Gower,* vol. 4, *The Latin Works.* Oxford 1902. For a translation, see Eric W. Stockton, *The Major Latin Works of John Gower.* Seattle 1962. The *Chronica* was written after the death of Richard II in 1400 and forms the conclusion of the revised *Vox.* Attacks Richard II, praises Henry IV.

Grafton, Richard (1Grafton). Continuation to Hardyng (in Ellis' edition of 2Hard), printed in 1543. Consists for the most part of a variant of More's *Richard III* and a translation of Vergil (1PV).

———— (2Grafton). *Grafton's Chronicle. (A Chronicle at Large.)* [Ed. Sir Henry Ellis.] 2 vols. London 1809. Printed in 1569. The history for the fifteenth century is mostly an abridgment of Hall. Influenced Holinshed in his use of Hall.

Hall, Edward, *Hall's Chronicle.* [Ed. Sir Henry Ellis.] London 1809. Original title: "The Union of the Two Noble and Illustre Families of Lancaster and York, Being Long in Continual Dissension for the Crown of This Noble Realm, with All the Acts Done in Both the Times of the Princes, Both of the One Lineage and of the Other, Beginning at the Time of King Henry the Fourth, the First Author of This Division, and So Successively Proceeding to the Reign of the High and Prudent Prince King Henry the Eighth, the Undubitate Flower and Very Heir of Both the Said Lineages." Printed by Richard Grafton in 1548 and 1550 (the 1542 edition is a myth, according to the Pollards, *Bul. Inst. Hist. Research* 9–10 [1931–1933]).

Hardyng, John (oHard). *Chronicle,* British Museum MS. Lansdowne 204. Excerpted in Appendix A above. Lancastrian; written ca. 1446–1457 for Henry VI.

———— (1Hard). oHard as discussed and excerpted by Charles L.

Kingsford, "The First Version of Hardyng's *Chronicle,*" *Eng. Hist. Rev.* 27:462–482, 740–753 (1912).

—— (2Hard). *The Chronicle of John Hardyng.* Ed. Sir Henry Ellis. London 1812. First published by Grafton in 1543 (for the Grafton continuation, see 1Grafton). The Yorkist version of Hardyng's history, written for Richard of York and Edward IV, ca. 1458–1465. Many of the old Lancastrian interpretations were carried over.

Hayward, Sir John. *The First Part of the Life and Reign of King Henry IV.* London 1599. Has providential summary of the fifteenth century.

Holinshed, Raphael (1Hol). *The Last Volume of the Chronicles of England, Scotland, and Ireland,* etc. London 1577. References in common with the second edition of 1587, ed. Abraham Fleming et al. (2Hol), are to *Holinshed's Chronicles of England, Scotland, and Ireland.* [Ed. Sir Henry Ellis.] Vol. 2 (goes up through the reign of Richard II) and vol. 3. London 1807–08.

Kirkstall Chronicle. "Short Chronicle," ed. John Taylor, in *Kirkstall Abbey Chronicles,* Publications of the Thoresby Society 42 (Leeds 1952) 52–133. Covers 1355–1400; written ca. 1399–1400. At first sympathetic to Richard II, but ends by accepting Henry IV.

Legge, Thomas. *Ricardus tertius.* In *Shakespeare's Library* [ed. William Carew Hazlitt] (London 1875 5.131–220. Written 1579. Follows the More-Hall tradition.

Livio, Tito (TL). *Vita Henrici quinti, regis Angliae.* Ed. Thomas Hearne. Oxford 1716. Written ca. 1440; eulogizes Henry V. References common to Livio and the Translator of Livius are cited TLTrans.

—— (Trans). *The First English Life of King Henry the Fifth, Written in 1513 by an Anonymous Author, Known Commonly as The Translator of Livius.* Ed. Charles L. Kingsford. Oxford 1911. Translates Livio, draws on Monstrelet, 2Caxton, and the stories of the Earl of Ormond. Used by Holinshed.

Mancini, Dominic. *The Usurpation of Richard the Third.* (*De occupatione regni Angliae per Ricardum tertium libellus.*) Ed. and trans. C. A. J. Armstrong. London 1936. Written in 1483. Attacks Richard III.

A Mirror for Magistrates. See Baldwin.

Monstrelet, Enguerrand de (Mons). *The Chronicles of Enguerrand de Monstrelet.* Trans. Thomas Johnes. 2 vols. London 1867. Monstrelet's history covers 1400–1444. The continuation ("Mons"), made by various authors, extends to 1516. In general, anti-Lancastrian (pro-Richard II and pro-French). Used by Vergil and Hall.

More, Sir Thomas. *The History of King Richard III.* Ed. Richard S. Sylvester, *The Complete Works of St. Thomas More,* vol. 2, New Haven 1963. Written ca. 1514–1518, drawing on contemporary sources. Highly unfavorable to Richard III. One form of the English history was used by 1Grafton and Hall, another by 2Grafton and 1–2Hol.

Mum and the Sothsegger. Ed. Mabel Day and Robert Steele. EETS 199 (London 1936). Only the "Richard the Redeless" part is relevant here. Written before Richard II's formal deposition in 1399. Considers Bolingbroke's rebellion providential, and is both critical of and sympathetic to Richard II.

A Northern Chronicle, 1399–1430 (North). Ed. Charles L. Kingsford, in his *English Historical Literature in the Fifteenth Century* (Oxford 1913) 279–291. Lancastrian, except re Archbishop Scrope. Indentified with the Whalley Chronicle (see Clarke, Dieulacres 144) and with the Stanlow Chronicle (see Taylor, Kirkstall 12, 35–36).

Ocland, Christopher. *Anglorum praelia*. London 1580. Versified textbook. Covers 1327–1558. Used by Fleming in 2Hol.

Otterbourne, Thomas. *Chronica regum Angliae*. Ed. Thomas Hearne, *Duo rerum anglicarum scriptores veteres*, vol. 1, Oxford 1732. Based on 1–2Wals (see Galbraith, 2Wals xvi–xvii). Keeps many of Walsingham's Lancastrian interpretations.

Page, John. *The Siege of Rouen*. Ed. James Gairdner, in *The Historical Collections of a Citizen of London in the Fifteenth Century*. CS 2.17 (London 1876) 1–46. Eyewitness account, in praise of Henry V. Used by Hall. Appears in some versions of the *Brut*.

A Political Retrospect. Ed. Thomas Wright, in *Political Poems*. RS 14.2 (London 1861) 267–270. Also ed. R. H. Robbins, *Historical Poems of the Fourteenth and Fifteenth Centuries* (New York 1959) 222–226. Written ca. 1462–63. Favorable to Edward IV against Henry VI.

Polychronicon. See 2Caxton.

Polydore Vergil (PV). See Vergil.

Pseudo-Elmham (PsElmham). *Thomae de Elmham Vita et gesta Henrici quinti, Anglorum regis*. Ed. Thomas Hearne. Oxford 1727. Mistakenly ascribed to Elmham. Based upon Livio; written ca. 1450. Laudatory of Henry V. Probably used by Vergil.

Raleigh, Sir Walter. *The History of the World*. Works, vols. 2–7. Oxford 1829. First published, 1614. The Preface, with its providential survey of English history, is in vol. 2.

Recovery of Edward IV. *On the Recovery of the Throne by Edward IV*. Ed. Thomas Wright, *Political Poems and Songs*. RS 14.2 (London 1861) 271–282. Yorkist. Stanza refrain attributes everything to the will of God. Draws on Arrival of Edward IV.

Redmayne, Robert. *Henrici quinti, illustrissimi Anglorum regis, historia*. Ed. C. A. Cole, in *Memorials of Henry the Fifth*. RS 11 (London 1858). In praise of Henry V. Written ca. 1540. Used by Hall.

"Richard the Redeless." See *Mum and the Sothsegger*.

Rous, John (1Rous). *Pageant of the Birth, Life, and Death of Richard Beauchamp, Earl of Warwick, K. G.* Ed. Viscount Dillon and W. H. St. John Hope. London 1914. Composed after 1439. MS dates from ca. 1485–1490.

Rous, John (2Rous). Warwick Roll. (Incipit: "Thys rol was laburd & finishid by Master John Rows of Warrewyk.") Ed. William

Courthope. London 1845 [1859]. This is the unaltered version, composed ca. 1477–1485. Favorable to Richard III. (The version Rous altered after Richard III's fall is not edited, but the changes are noted in this edition.)

—— (3Rous). *Rossi Warwicensis Historia regum Angliae*. Ed. Thomas Hearne. Oxford 1716. Written ca. 1489–1491. Attacks Richard III, favors Henry VII.

A Southern Chronicle, 1399–1422 (South). In Kingsford, *English Historical Literature in the Fifteenth Century* (Oxford 1913) 275–278. Lancastrian.

Shakespeare, William (*Richard II, Henry IV*, part I, etc.). *The Complete Plays and Poems of William Shakespeare*. Ed. William Allen Neilson and Charles Jarvis Hill. Cambridge, Mass. 1942.

Stanlow Chronicle. See North.

Stow, John. *Summary of English Chronicles*. London 1565, etc. Used by Holinshed.

—— *Chronicles of England*. London 1580. Used by Abraham Fleming in 2Hol.

Strecche, John. *The Chronicle of John Strecche for the Reign of Henry V (1414–1422)*. Ed. Frank Taylor, *Bul. J. Rylands Lib.* 16:137–187 (1932). Contemporary history eulogizing Henry V.

Tito Livio (TL). See Livio.

Traïson. See *Chronicque de la traïson*.

Translator of Livius (Trans). See Livio.

Usk, Adam. *Chronicon Adae de Usk, A.D. 1377–1421*. Ed. and trans. Sir Edward Maunde Thompson. 2d ed. London 1904. Written ca. 1421. Favorable to Henry IV and Henry V (against Richard II).

Vergil, Polydore (oPV). MS of *Anglica historia*. Codices urbinates latini 497–498. Vatican Library. References are to Codex 498. Written 1512–13. See Hay, PVh xiii.

—— (1PV). *Anglica historia*. Basel 1534. The main revision of the MS was made ca. 1521–1524. This is the version used by Hall.

—— (2PV). *Anglica historia*. 2 vols. (continuous pagination). Ghent n.d. Reprint of the 2d edition of 1546.

—— (2PVt). Partial edition of a sixteenth-century translation of the 2d edition of 1546, ed. Sir Henry Ellis, 2 vols.: vol. 1, *Polydore Vergil's English History*, CS 1.36 (London 1846), covers the first eight books; vol. 2, *Three Books of Polydore Vergil's English History*, CS 1.29 (London 1844), covers the reigns of Henry VI, Edward IV, and Richard III (Bks. 23–25). References are to vol. 2 unless otherwise noted.

—— (3PV). Third edition, 1555. Differs little from 2PV, except that it adds a chapter on Henry VIII.

—— (PVh). *The Anglica Historia of Polydore Vergil, A.D. 1485–1537*. Ed. Denys Hay. CS 3.74 (London 1950). Covers the reigns of Henry VII and Henry VIII; ed. and trans. of MS, collated with the three editions.

Versus rhythmici de Henrico quinto (VersH5). Ed. C. A. Cole, in *Memorials of Henry the Fifth*. RS 11 (London 1858). In praise of

Henry V, written by a Benedictine member of his household, ca. 1414.

Walsingham, Thomas (oWals). *Chronicon Angliae.* Ed. Sir Edward Maunde Thompson. RS 64 (London 1874). Covers 1328–1388. Short History: 1328–1376; 1382–1388. Long History: 1376–1382; this latter section is the "scandalous chronicle" attacking John of Gaunt, which was modified in the version of 3Wals.

Walsingham, Thomas (1Wals). *Annales Ricardi secundi et Henrici quarti.* Ed. Henry T. Riley, in *Johannis de Trokelow,* etc. *Chronica monasterii S. Albani.* RS 28.3 (London 1866). Long Chronicle for 1392–1406. Lancastrian, except re Archbishop Scrope.

—— (2Wals). *The St. Albans Chronicle, 1406–20.* Ed. V. H. Galbraith. Oxford 1937. Long Chronicle for 1406–1420. Lancastrian in general.

—— (3Wals). *Historia anglicana.* Ed. Henry T. Riley. 2 vols. *Chronica monasterii S. Albani.* RS 28.1 (London 1863–64). (References are to vol. 2 unless otherwise noted.) The section covering 1377–1382 is the Long History, modified in favor of John of Gaunt from oWals. The portion covering 1382–1392 is the continuation of the Long History. The section on 1392–1422 is the Short History, as is the part covering 1343–1377. First printed by John Stow for Archbishop Parker in 1574. Attacks Richard II, favorable to Henry IV and Henry V. Seems to be the version used by Holinshed.

—— (4Wals). *Ypodigma Neustriae.* Ed. Henry T. Riley. *Chronica monasterii S. Albani.* RS 28.7 (London 1876). Another short history, extending to 1419, compiled ca. 1421. Lancastrian. Used by Fleming in 2Hol and perhaps also by Holinshed himself. Ed. under Archbishop Parker's supervision, 1574, 1576.

Warkworth, John. *A Chronicle of the First Thirteen Years of the Reign of King Edward the Fourth.* Ed. James Orchard Halliwell [-Phillipps]. CS 1.10 (London 1839). Covers 1461–1474. Lancastrian.

Waurin (or Wavrin), John de. *A Collection of the Chronicles and Ancient Histories of Great Britain, Now Called England.* 3 vols. RS 40.2 (London 1887) trans. Sir William Hardy and Edward L. C. P. Hardy, A.D. 1399–1422; 3 (London 1891) trans. Edward L. C. P. Hardy, A.D. 1422–1431. The last part of Waurin's history is untranslated; references are to the French edition: *Recueil des croniques et anchiennes istories de la Grant Bretaigne, a present nomme Engleterre.* Ed. Sir William Hardy and Edward L. C. P. Hardy. 5 vols. RS 39.4 (London 1884) A.D. 1431–1447, 5 (London 1891) A.D. 1447–1471. Burgundian chronicler; often coincides with Monstrelet. Manifests the Continental anti-Lancastrian tendencies, but is often pro-English against the French. Apparently not used by the English chroniclers.

Whalley Chronicle. See North.

Woodstock: a Moral History. Ed. A. P. Rossiter. London 1946. Dated ca. 1591–1595. Unfavorable to Richard II. Probably used by Shakespeare.

Whethamstede Register (Whet). *Registra quorundam abbatum monasterii S. Albani, qui saeculo decimo quinto floruere,* vol. 1, *Registrum abbatiae Johannis Whethamstede.* Ed. Henry T. Riley. *Chronica monasterii S. Albani.* RS 28.6 (London 1872). Covers the two battles of St. Albans (1455, 1461), and associated events. By a Yorkist redactor, who often allows the Lancastrian views of his sources to stand. Used by Holinshed.

Index

Adam, sin of, 2, 51

Agincourt, 33n

Agincourt, battle of (1415), 32–34, 35, 39, 44, 46n, 60, 91–92, 118, 146, 237–244, 262n

André, Bernard, 41, 71n, 72, 75–81, 87, 94n, 103, 130, 134n

Angels, 61, 207; Henry VII as angelic, 67, 80n, 134, 317

Anne (Nevil, wife of Richard III), 66, 68, 70, 101, 281–282, 284

Anointed king, *see* Kingship, sacred

Antichrist, 71

Armstrong, C. A. J., 65n, 70n

Arrival of Edward IV, 62n, 151, 152

Arthur (son of Henry VII), 72, 73, 74, 75–76, 104n, 158n

Arthur, King, 72, 73, 75, 86, 104n

Arundel, Thomas Fitzalan of (Archbishop of Canterbury), 13, 18, 20, 43, 111–112

Arundel, Thomas Fitzalan, Earl of, 12, 14, 139n

Audelay, John, 27

Augustine, Saint, 2–4

Aumerle, Edward, Duke of Aumale and York, 91, 112n, 206, 212, 243n, 262n

Bagot, Sir William, 12n

Baldwin, William, 163–179, 277. See also *Mirror for Magistrates*

Barbary, Richard II's horse, 205

Bardolf, Shakespearean comic character, 237

Barnet, battle of (1471), 127n, 151n, 176

Beaufort family, 72n

Beaufort, Edmund, *see* Somerset

Beaufort, Henry, *see* Winchester

Beaufort, John, *see* Somerset

Beaufort, Margaret, Countess of Richmond (mother of Henry VII), 72n, 106n, 133, 292–293

Bede, the Venerable, 19, 61n

Bedford, Duke of, *see* Lancaster, John

Berners, Sir John Bourchier, Lord, 17n, 18

Bible, 32–33, 34, 50, 79, 284, 301; Acts, 134n; Chronicles, 3; 1 Corinthians, 96n; Daniel, 71n; Deuteronomy, 1, 2, 31, 236n; Ecclesiastes, 38 (see *Vae Terrae*); Exodus, 1n, 96n, 256n; Genesis, 55n; Isaiah, 38n, 122; Job, 2, 62n; John, 2, 134n; 1 John, 55; Jonah, 55; Kings, 3, 118; Luke, 134n; Maccabees, 32; Matthew, 38n, 42n, 78n; Numbers, 1n, 40, 96n, 282; Psalms, 3, 33, 38, 52n, 53n, 57n, 62n, 153, 154, 158, 244; Revelation, 56n, 71n; Romans, 62n; Samuel, 3, 13 ("Vir dominabitur"), 63n; Wisdom, 130, 289–290

Bier right, 281

Blacksmith, tragedy of the, 168

Blakman, John, 63n, 95, 153

Blessed Virgin, *see* Mary

Bloomfield, Morton W., 16n

Boccaccio, Giovanni, 164

Bosworth Field, battle of (1485), 65, 66–67, 80, 90n, 102, 105, 134, 154, 207n, 277, 292–293

Brackenbury, Sir Robert, 74, 278

Brockbank, J. P., 147n

Brut, 16n, 18n, 23n, 24n, 25n, 27, 33n, 36n, 39n, 46–47, 53n, 94, 119n, 121, 131n, 240, 244n, 247n

Brute (Brutus, legendary founder of Britain), 73, 86

Buckingham, Henry Stafford, Duke of, 10, 66, 71n, 106n, 130n, 131, 132–133, 137, 283, 285, 286, 288, 289–290